THE STRENGTH WITHIN

Fred Kerber Jr.

ACKNOWLEDGEMNTS

I would like to thank the following for their help while I wrote this story:

Amanda K., for her invaluable advice from a woman's perspective.

Dana I., for proving the concept and identifying both the small and significant issues.

The brigade at WaWa #8122, for their support, encouragement, and endless cups of coffee.

And lastly, my loving wife, Dorraine K.—without her support, this book would never have been written.

CONTENTS

Acknowledgemnts ii

Author's Note v

Prologue vii

Chapter 1 1

Chapter 2 3

Chapter 3 25

Chapter 4 39

Chapter 5 56

Chapter 6 63

Chapter 7 78

Chapter 8 107

Chapter 9 116

Chapter 10 124

Chapter 11 156

Chapter 12 161

Chapter 13 167

Chapter 14 180

Chapter 15 197

Chapter 16 219

Chapter 17 224

Chapter 18 243

Chapter 19 247

Chapter 20 256

Chapter 21 263

Chapter 22 274

Chapter 23 287

Chapter 24 299

Chapter 25 306

Chapter 26 311

Chapter 27 322

Chapter 28 340

Chapter 29 355

Chapter 30 419

Chapter 31 438

Chapter 32 444

Chapter 33 456

Chapter 34 472

Chapter 35 495

Chapter 36 510

Epilogue 523

Author's Note

Before you begin this story, I want to take a moment to address a few important points. *The Strength Within* contains sensitive themes, including trauma, abuse, mental health struggles, and the journey toward healing and self-acceptance. These elements are explored with care and are essential to the characters' journeys of healing, growth, and even love, which provides solace and a sense of belonging amidst their struggles. Love, in its many forms, becomes a beacon of hope and a reminder of the human capacity for connection and renewal. However, I encourage readers to prioritize their well-being. If these topics may be difficult for you, I encourage you to approach the story at your own pace and prioritize your well-being.

If you or someone you know is struggling, help is available. Please consider reaching out to the following resources:

- **National Suicide Prevention Lifeline**: 1-800-273-TALK (8255) (available 24/7)
- **Crisis Text Line**: Text HOME to 741741
- **RAINN** (Rape, Abuse & Incest National Network): 1-800-656-HOPE (4673) or visit rainn.org
- **Mental Health America**: Visit mhanational.org for mental health resources and support.

This work is a piece of fiction. The characters, events, and settings are products of imagination and are not based on any specific individuals or real-life events. However, any resemblance to any event might be coincidental.

You are not alone, and there is always hope, even in the darkest moments. Remember, strength can be found in reaching out, and brighter days are always ahead. Thank you for choosing to read this story, and I hope it resonates with you in meaningful ways.

Sincerely,

Fred Kerber Jr.

PROLOGUE

The sun was setting on a warm day in mid-June, painting the horizon in swirls of gold and crimson. The lake shimmered, reflecting the evening light like scattered diamonds. The two families—Umi with her twins, Stephanie and Brittney, and Gloria with her son, Brian—had spent the day enjoying playful banter and the summer warmth.

Now, as the day was winding down, a silence had fallen over the lake as other families were getting ready to leave.

Stephanie and Brian were returning from a walk along the lake's edge. They stopped at the clearing's edge, sheltered by a thin veil of trees. The golden light bathed the space between them.

Stephanie stopped and turned to face Brian, the glow of the setting sun reflecting in his steady, deep blue eyes. For a moment, they just stood there—time suspended between what was and what would be.

With quiet resolve, Stephanie tilted her face up toward him, her heart pounding. "Brian…"

Brian didn't hesitate. He leaned down, closing the space between them, and their lips met. It was soft at first, and as the moment deepened, their connection solidified—like it had always been inevitable. Brian's hands moved to Stephanie's hips, drawing her closer as the kiss grew longer.

Stephanie felt like a lifetime had passed when their lips finally parted. Her cheeks flushed, and she held him tightly, pressing her head against his shoulder. "That was worth the wait," she whispered, her voice barely audible.

Brian murmured back, "The wait?"

Stephanie smiled, her voice soft and honest. "You have no idea how long I've dreamt you'd do that."

From behind the trees, unnoticed and unseen, Brittney stood frozen.

Her breath caught in her throat, her pulse quickening as she watched the tender moment unfold — their moment. Her twin sister, Stephanie, bathed in the glow of sunset, held in Brian's arms like she belonged there as if the rest of the world didn't exist.

She wanted to turn away, to leave, to pretend she hadn't seen it. But her feet wouldn't move, and her heart twisted painfully in her chest.

"It should have been me," she thought silently to herself.

As she moved back to the rest of the family, unnoticed by Stephanie and Brian, the summer air felt heavy now, thick with something Brittney couldn't name — the slow realization that everything she had hoped and dreamed for was quickly fading away.

CHAPTER 1

The laughter from the backyard spilled into Brittney's room through the open window. She sat cross-legged on her bed, sketchpad propped on her knees, her pencil moving in short, deliberate strokes. The string lights outside framed Stephanie and Brian as they stood close, their heads bent together. His hand rested on Stephanie's shoulder, and Brittney could see the way her sister leaned into the touch — comfortable and confident.

Brittney's pencil paused. Her gaze shifted between the paper and the window, where their figures seemed to glow under the lights. The drawing didn't look right. The lines felt stiff, lifeless. She frowned, tearing the page free and crushing it into a ball. It joined several others on the floor.

From the hallway, Umi's voice broke through. "Brittney? Are you coming down? Brian just asked about you."

Her hand stilled mid-reach for a fresh page. "I'm working on something," she called, her tone tight but controlled.

There was a pause, and Brittney imagined Umi standing just outside, deciding whether to push further. The hesitation ended with the faint sound of retreating footsteps.

Brittney exhaled and leaned back against the headboard. She could still hear the voices outside, Brian's laugh mixing with Stephanie's melodic one. It was as if the two of them existed in a world that she couldn't reach, their closeness effortless and unbreakable.

Her pencil rolled off the bed, forgotten, as she reached for another crumpled page and smoothed it out against her leg.

Down below, Stephanie's voice rose. "Brian, you're so ridiculous! Get over here before you break something."

Brittney's eyes fell shut for a moment. Then, with steady hands, she began drawing again—not a new image, but the same scene from the backyard. This time, she focused on the background. The lights, the tree, the shadows. Anything but the figures in the center.

Her strokes faltered as the sounds of their laughter drifted up again, clear and bright. She didn't look up this time. Instead, she added a few more lines to the sketch, then ripped it from the pad and let it fall, joining the pile on the floor.

The pile of discarded sketches seemed to mock her, each one a reminder of her failures to capture what Stephanie had so effortlessly—Brian's love, everyone's admiration.

Brittney rose from the bed, stepping over the crumpled paper and toward the window. Her hands clenched into fists at her sides as she watched them.

She didn't know what she'd do yet, but the idea of sitting here, letting it all go unchecked, wasn't an option anymore.

CHAPTER 2

Gloria eased into her recliner, letting the day's fatigue melt into the soft cushions. The sound of the evening news played in the background while the anchor listed headlines she barely cared about. A hot cup of tea rested in her hand, its thin ribbon of steam curling into the air. Outside the big window, dusk settled over the fields in the distance, streaking the horizon with lavender and burnt orange. A sigh escaped her lips as she adjusted her feet on the ottoman.

The sudden, sharp ring of her cell phone pierced the calm. Gloria flinched, spilling a few drops of tea onto her hand.

"Ow," she muttered, fumbling for the phone. "Hello?" she answered, cradling it between her shoulder and ear.

"Hi, Gloria, it's Umi."

Gloria straightened slightly. "Hi, Umi. What's up?"

Umi's voice was steady but strained—one Gloria immediately recognized. "Did Brian tell you what happened during the second period today?"

Gloria frowned, setting her mug aside. "Only a bit. I got a call asking me to bring him a change of clothes and his crutches. When I got there, they were short on details. On the ride home, he didn't want to talk, and when we were walking into the house, I could see his good leg was bothering him. I figured I'd let him settle down before we talked. Do you know what happened?"

Umi let out a soft sigh. "I got a phone call from Superintendent Dr. Smith. Brittney and her friends pulled a prank on him. Apparently, Peter poured burning, itching powder into his shirt and pants. Then, they convinced him to shower. While he was showering, they stole his clothing and his prosthetic leg."

"That's not the worst of it," Umi continued, her voice tight. "Somehow, Brian ended up being seen by most of the senior class—nude. Dr. Smith said Brittney was one of the conspirators. Stephanie swears she didn't know about it until after it happened."

Gloria sat upright, her heart pounding as she stared out the window, watching the shadows creep across the fields. "Wow. That's much more than I got when I was there, and it explains why he was so quiet, too," she said softly, her voice steady but hollow.

"Dr. Smith wants a meeting tomorrow with all the parents and kids involved at the high school. Ten o'clock," Umi added. "I told him I'd talk and bring you."

Gloria's mind raced as she processed Umi's words. The smell of burnt tea drifted through the room, but she ignored it as she asked, "Nine-thirty then? We'll go together?"

"Works for me," Umi replied. "But there's more. Brittney is denying everything, and I'm starting to think she's not being truthful. Can we get all three kids at the table and hash this out?"

Gloria glanced at the time on the wall clock—just after 6:30. "Sure. Come over when you're ready. The tea's always on."

"Thanks, Gloria. We'll be right there."

As the call ended, Gloria let out a shaky breath, running her hands over her face. The day's quiet had shattered completely. She went into the kitchen and made sure the kettle was on.

As she stood there, she saw Umi and her twins step out of their front door. Gloria walked to the foyer, and just as she reached it, there was a light knock. The door swung open.

Umi stepped in first, her face tight with frustration. Behind her, the 17-year-old twins followed. Stephanie's expression was guarded; her lips pressed into a thin line. Brittney trailed behind, arms crossed, chin tilted upward as if daring anyone to speak first.

"Hi, Gloria," Umi greeted softly.

"Hi, Umi. Brittney." Gloria's gaze flicked to the older twin, who refused to meet her eyes.

"Hi, Mom Gloria," Stephanie said quietly, her voice carrying a hint of relief as she hugged Gloria briefly.

Gloria hugged her back. "Hi, sweetheart. Umi, kitchen?"

Umi nodded, following Gloria inside and pointing at the dining room table. "You two, sit down. And not a word from either of you," she directed, her voice strong and firm.

The girls moved to the table, the silence broken only by Brittney's exaggerated sigh as she dropped into a chair.

The kitchen was warm, the faint scent of cinnamon lingering from earlier baking. Gloria pulled a mug from the cabinet, filling it with tea as Umi leaned against the counter.

"Anything else?" Gloria asked softly, glancing over her shoulder.

Umi's shoulders slumped. "Dr. Smith thinks Brittney and her friends might have done something to Brian's leg."

Gloria froze mid-pour, tea sloshing dangerously close to the rim. Her hand trembled slightly as she set the kettle down carefully, staring at the rising steam as if it held answers. Her chest tightened, a mix of disbelief and anger swirling within her. She swallowed hard, forcing herself to breathe as the weight of Umi's words settled heavily on her shoulders.

"Oh no," she murmured, her voice barely audible.

Umi's voice lowered further. "I remember when he finally got the prosthetic and how important it is to him."

"It's everything," Gloria said quietly. "It means freedom to him."

She set both mugs on the table, her resolve hardening. "Let's start with the girls before I call Brian out."

Umi nodded. "I figured as much."

As they walked out of the kitchen, Gloria placed a hand on Umi's shoulder. "We'll get this worked out. No worries," she said softly to her best friend.

In the dining room, the tension was palpable. Gloria and Umi took their seats at either end of the table, their eyes fixed on the girls, who sat stiffly across from each other.

Stephanie sat straight-backed, her hands twisting the chains of her necklaces. Her face held a quiet guilt—caught in the middle. Brittney was slouched in her seat, her arms crossed tightly over her chest. Her gaze flickered briefly to Gloria before snapping back to the wall, her lips twitching as though holding back a retort. Her chin jutted out, and her eyes fixed on the wall behind Gloria, defiance written across her features.

Gloria folded her hands on the table, her voice calm but firm. "Brittney, Stephanie," she began, her eyes moving between the two. "I'm not mad. I'm upset because something like this happened. I need to know about Brian's prosthetic leg." Her voice softened slightly. "It's extremely expensive, and it means everything to Brian."

Brittney didn't look up. Her arms crossed tighter. "He'll get it back," she muttered, sarcasm dripping from every word.

"Do you know when that will be?" Gloria asked patiently, though her jaw tightened.

"After he does something," Brittney shot back, her tone defiant but wavering.

Stephanie snorted beside her, the sound sharp and bitter — a mix of exasperation and disbelief at her sister's defiance. "That's why I know you know more than you say. For an older sister, you're dumb."

Brittney's eyes flashed, and her lips parted, ready to fire back.

"Enough," Umi cut in, her voice cool and authoritative. "We're not here, so you two can fight. Brittney, you were asked a question, and we're still waiting for an answer. Do you know when that will be?"

Brittney's stare hardened, but she stayed silent.

The silence stretched. Gloria's gaze flickered to Umi, whose shoulders tensed as they waited for an answer that wasn't coming. Stephanie shifted in her seat, twisting her necklace tighter. The faint clink of the chain, nearing its breaking point, filled the stillness. Even the hum of the overhead light seemed louder in the void left by Brittney's refusal to speak. The weight of her silence was a wall—one none of them could break through.

Umi looked at her oldest daughter, her tone cool and deliberate. "And that proves you know more than you're telling us. Fine, Brittney. I'll let Dr. Smith deal with it all."

Brittney's defiance wavered for a moment, her eyes darting to Umi. "What do you mean? What do you think he's going to do? Make us get it and give it back?"

Umi didn't flinch. "Dr. Smith said all four of you violated the high school's ethics policy and will be expelled. If the leg doesn't show up by Thursday morning, he's calling the police to report the theft of an expensive prosthetic leg."

Brittney's expression shifted, a flicker of real worry in her eyes. "The police? He wouldn't…"

"He will," Umi said firmly. "Is your prank—your devotion to your so-called friends—worth lying to me, Gloria, and your sister? Worth being expelled? Worth repeating your senior year? Worth jail time?"

Brittney stiffened, but the color drained from her face. "That's not fair!" she exclaimed, her voice rising in frustration.

Gloria leaned forward, her voice calm but edged with disappointment. "What's unfair, Brittney? That Brian's leg is missing? That he was humiliated in front of his classmates?" Her gaze sharpened, pinning Brittney in place. "Or is it unfair that Stephanie—your sister—could lose everything she's worked for because of this?"

8

Brittney glanced at Stephanie, who sat silently, her face pale. Stephanie's hands twisted in her lap, the charms on her necklaces tapping softly as she struggled to hold back tears.

Gloria's voice softened, but her words struck with precision. "Stephanie's already been accepted to Temple. You know how hard she worked for that. But this? This could ruin it all."

Brittney's jaw tightened, her shoulders rigid. "That's not my fault," she mumbled, but her voice lacked its earlier fire.

Stephanie looked up suddenly, her voice trembling but resolute. "Yes, it is, Brittney. And you're making it worse for everyone—Mom, Brian, me, and even you."

Brittney shot her sister a glare, her fists curling in her lap. "I didn't take it, okay? I didn't!"

"But you know where it is," Umi said quietly. "And you know what you have to do to fix it."

For a moment, the room was silent, the weight of Umi's words pressing down like a storm cloud. Brittney's eyes flickered with something unreadable—guilt, frustration, or maybe fear—but she said nothing, her gaze fixed stubbornly on the table.

Gloria finally broke the silence, leaning back slightly and calling down the hall. "Brian, sweetheart, would you please come and join us?"

She reached across the table toward Umi's hand and gave it a reassuring squeeze. Umi returned the gesture, their bond unspoken but clear.

A faint creak echoed down the hallway, followed by the rhythmic thump of Brian's crutches against the hardwood floor. The sound grew louder as he approached.

9

Brian's face was pale, the strain of the day etched into his expression. He wore a loose T-shirt and sweatpants rolled up over his stump, his hands gripping the crutches tightly. His blue eyes flicked across the room—first to his mom, Gloria, then to Umi, his honorary mom—before settling on the twins. His gaze lingered on Brittney, sharp and unyielding.

Gloria's voice softened as she gestured toward the chair beside her. "Come sit, sweetheart."

Brian nodded, the slight tremble of his arms betraying his exhaustion as he lowered himself carefully into the chair. He propped the crutches against the wall and sat back, folding his hands in his lap.

He finally broke the silence, his voice low and calm but carrying a quiet intensity. "Why? What happened?"

Brittney flinched at the question, her defiance faltering for the first time. She shifted in her seat, her arms loosening slightly from their rigid cross. "I don't know," she mumbled, her voice barely above a whisper.

Brian's brow furrowed. "You don't know?" He shook his head, a bitter chuckle escaping his lips. "That's funny because Richard and Peter sure seemed to think it was your idea."

"Brian—" Stephanie's voice was soft, a note of pleading in it, but he held up a hand, stopping her.

"I'm not mad at you, Steph," he said, his gaze flicking briefly to his girlfriend before returning to Brittney. "But I want to know why. What did I do to deserve this?"

Brittney's gaze darted to the table, her fingers curling into fists. "You wouldn't understand."

"Try me," Brian replied, his voice steady.

10

"You wouldn't!" she snapped, her voice cracking as she finally looked up, her eyes red-rimmed but still blazing with anger. "You think you're so perfect that everyone loves you, but they don't. They feel sorry for you!"

A heavy silence fell over the room, her words hanging in the air like smoke.

Brian sat motionless as though absorbing the blow, but his voice remained calm. "So, you did this because you thought people felt sorry for me?"

Brittney's breathing was ragged, her shoulders rising and falling as if the weight of the confession had cost her something. "You wouldn't get it," she muttered, her gaze dropping again.

Gloria's voice broke through the tension, low and firm. "Brittney Rose Welch, look at me."

Brittney hesitated but finally lifted her head, her defiance replaced with something much smaller — almost fragile.

"You're hurting; I can see that," Gloria said, her gaze steady. "But what you did to Brian was cruel. Whatever you're feeling inside — jealousy, anger, or something else — you don't take it out on others. You don't destroy someone else to make yourself feel better."

Brittney blinked rapidly, fighting back tears. "I didn't mean —" Her voice trailed off, the words catching in her throat.

Gloria gently rubbed Brian's shoulder. "Would you tell us what happened?"

Brian looked at her. "Mom, it's really embarrassing."

Umi reached from the other side. "Skip over those parts?" she suggested.

Brian sighed deeply, glancing toward Stephanie for a brief moment before speaking. "During biology, Peter and his friends poured itching powder in my shirt and pants—it burned. Everyone there convinced me I needed to shower before it got worse. When I came out, my clothes and leg were gone.

"I grabbed a flagpole to use as a walking stick, wrapped myself in one of the towels, and started looking for my clothes and leg. While I was looking, the bell rang, and all the seniors started coming into the gym. I couldn't get back into the locker room fast enough before someone grabbed my towel and threw it into the center of the gym.

"Everyone in the gym saw me and started laughing. Mr. Dobbs and Mrs. Hutcherson walked in and started asking questions. I eventually ended up in borrowed sweatpants, sitting in Dr. Smith's office."

Umi looked at Brian, her expression both empathetic and pained. "Brian, you're right—it's very embarrassing. I'd be upset, too. Do you have any idea where your leg might be or who took it?"

Brian shook his head, his voice quiet. "No."

He let out a slow breath, his voice even softer now. "I want my leg back, Brittney. That's all. Wherever it is or however it got there doesn't matter—I just need it back."

Brittney's head snapped up, her jaw set, and her gaze locked on Brian. "What's your problem? I said you'll get it back!"

Brian's grip tightened on the edge of the table, his face flushing with anger. "That's not good enough, Brittney!" His voice rose, sharp with frustration. "You think this is funny? Do you have any idea what you did to me? What it's like to be—

how it hurt me? When I found out it was you, it felt like it did when our dads..."

He stopped talking, realizing too late he had said something wrong.

Brittney stood suddenly, her chair scraping against the floor. "I didn't take it!" she shouted, her fists clenching at her sides.

"Sit down, Brittney," Umi ordered, her tone cold and firm.

Brian pushed himself up on his crutches, balancing unsteadily. "You're a liar," he said through gritted teeth. "You know where it is, and you're just too much of a coward to admit it!"

Brittney moved toward him, jabbing a finger into his chest. "I'm not lying! You don't know everything, Brian!"

Before Brittney could get closer, Stephanie shot to her feet, shouting, "Brittney, stop it!" Her voice shook with both anger and fear. "Keep your hands off him! He's my boyfriend, not yours!"

Brittney froze, her face twisting in shock as she turned toward her sister. "Oh, I see how it is now," she said, her voice dripping with bitterness. "Perfect little Stephanie, always protecting her precious Brian."

"Stop it, both of you!" Gloria's voice snapped like a whip, cutting through the tension in the room. "This isn't helping!"

Brian shifted his weight, breathing heavily as he leaned on his crutches, his knuckles white from the pressure.

Umi pointed at Brittney. "Sit. Down. Now."

As the twins sat back down, Gloria gently tugged Brian's arm. "Please sit, sweetheart," she urged him.

"Mom, I'm done here. This is about as useful as talking to a wall," he said through clenched teeth.

He turned, his gaze locking onto Stephanie's. "Steph... I need to ask you something, and I really need you to be honest with me. Did you know about the prank—the itching powder and..." his voice faltered for a moment, "my leg—before it happened?"

Stephanie looked back at him, her eyes wide, her voice almost trembling. "Brian, what? No! I swear I didn't know anything about it. I would never go along with something like this, especially not your leg."

She paused for a moment before adding, "I don't know why Britt did that, but I promise you, I had nothing to do with it. You know me, Brian. You know I wouldn't." Her voice softened as she spoke.

Brian started, "Steph, I'm sorry. I didn't mean to hurt your feelings. It's just that..." He sighed, rubbing the back of his neck, clearly torn.

A moment later, he continued. "I know how close you and Brittney are, and people always say, 'Blood is thicker than water.' Sometimes, I can't help but wonder if there are things you'd protect her from—even if it meant me getting hurt." He paused, letting his words sink in.

When he spoke again, his voice was softer. "I shouldn't have doubted you. You're not Brittney, and I know you'd never do something like that to me. I'm sorry for even asking."

Umi leaned forward, her tone firm but gentle. "Brittney, if you know anything—and I mean anything—you need to tell us now. This stops here."

Brittney stared at the table, her fists clenched tightly in her lap. The room waited, every second stretching unbearably.

14

Finally, she exhaled shakily. "I don't have it," she whispered. "Richard took it. He said he'd hide it somewhere no one would ever find it."

Stephanie gasped softly, her hand flying to her mouth. Gloria and Umi exchanged a look of both relief and concern.

Brian's face went pale, but his voice remained steady. "Where is he hiding it, Brittney?"

Brittney shook her head, her voice cracking again. "I don't know. He wouldn't tell me."

Gloria's expression tightened, though her voice stayed calm. "We'll figure it out, Brian," she said, resting a hand on his shoulder. "I promise you — we'll get it back."

Brittney said nothing, her head lowering as tears finally began to spill silently down her cheeks.

Gloria's gaze shifted to Brian, who sat back in his chair, his hands resting on his crutches once more. She could see the exhaustion in his face, the hurt lingering just beneath the surface.

"You don't have to stay here, sweetheart," she said softly. "Go rest."

Brian looked over his shoulder as he hobbled back down the hall. "Mom, once the brick wall is gone, I'll come out and talk with everyone," he said as he worked his way to his room.

Stephanie called after him, "Brian, does that include me?" Doubt and pain were written on her face.

Brian didn't answer as he closed the door to his room.

Umi stood, her voice firm and measured. "This is far from over. Brittney, you're grounded until further notice."

The room remained silent for a moment before Stephanie whispered, her voice trembling, "Why did you let Richard get involved, Brittney?"

Brittney didn't answer. She just buried her face in her hands and sobbed.

Umi and Gloria looked at the twins, trying to understand how everything had come to this.

Umi turned to Stephanie, her face soft as she finally answered her question. "I don't think so, sweetheart. Let him calm down, okay?"

Stephanie looked at Umi, her voice tight. "When he said, 'blood is thicker than water,' he meant he doesn't believe me, doesn't he?"

Umi's gaze softened, though her answer was honest. "Yes, sweetheart. But right now, I think he's more upset than anything else."

Stephanie nodded quietly, tears brimming in her eyes. Without a word, she unclasped the delicate gold cross from her neck and held it out to Gloria.

"Mom Gloria, can you give this to Brian?"

Gloria frowned. "Why, sweetheart?"

Stephanie turned the cross over in her palm, her voice soft. "Daddy gave this to me on my fifteenth birthday, two days before the accident. I treasure it because every time I touch it, I think of him. If Brian sees how much I trust him with something this important to me, maybe he'll believe me."

Gloria reached out, her eyes warm with pride. "That's very mature of you, Steph. I'll bring it up to him later after he's had a chance to calm down."

Brittney, who had been fidgeting, suddenly scoffed, her tone sharp. "So mushy-mushy. Are we going to be here much longer?"

Umi shot her a cold look. "Not that it matters to you. You can do 'nothing' here or 'nothing' at home. Go sit on the couch with Stephanie. Gloria and I need five minutes."

The twins walked into the living room, but Brittney leaned close, her voice a whisper. "When Peter finds out your boyfriend put his hands…"

Stephanie whirled, grabbing a fistful of Brittney's long blonde hair and twisting it. "If Peter or any of your friends touches Brian because of you —"

"Let me go!" Brittney shrieked, clawing at her sister's grip.

Before anyone could intervene, Stephanie's fist swung, landing squarely on Brittney's eye. The room erupted into chaos.

Gloria rushed in, grabbing Stephanie around the waist. "Steph, let her go!"

Umi pulled Brittney back, her voice sharp and authoritative. "Enough!"

Stephanie's tears streamed freely as Gloria held her tightly from behind. "Why can't you just let us be?" Stephanie's voice cracked. "Why do you have to ruin everything for me?"

Brittney stood dumbfounded, clutching her swelling eye, unable to process her sister's fury. Stephanie broke down, her body trembling in Gloria's arms.

"I HATE YOU!" Stephanie screamed, each word striking like a blow. "HATE YOU! HATE YOU! HATE YOU!"

Brittney's hand hovered near Stephanie's shoulder, tentative. "Sis?"

Stephanie flinched as if the word stung her. "NO!" she shouted, pulling further into Gloria's embrace. "You don't get to call me that. I don't have a sister anymore! I'd rather have a cat. At least a cat's love is real."

Gloria gently guided Stephanie toward the back door. The shouting had faded into sobs, but Brittney could still hear her sister's words echoing in her head.

Brian appeared in the hallway as they passed him. He and Gloria exchanged a look—a quiet understanding on his part, sorrow on hers.

Stephanie paused at the doorway, her voice cold and raw. "No more 'I'm sorry.' No more 'I was joking.' No more of any of it, Brittney."

Brittney took a step forward. "Steph?"

Stephanie spun around, gripping the doorframe. "My name is Stephanie. Not Sis. Not Steph. Nothing else. Don't talk to me. Ever."

The door slammed shut, and silence filled the house.

Brian grabbed a bag of frozen peas from the freezer and walked over to Umi and Brittney. He handed the bag to Umi.

"Everyone okay?" he asked softly.

Umi nodded. "We'll be fine. Thank you, Brian."

Brian turned to leave, but Brittney called after him. "Brian? Brian, can we talk?"

He paused, his back still to her. "I'm nothing more than a figment of an obscure memory of your imagination," he replied, his voice low and tired. "You should ignore things like me — for my safety."

He disappeared into his room, the door clicking shut.

Umi pressed the frozen peas into Brittney's hand, her voice clipped. "Go sit down and think about all of this. And while you're at it, put this on your eye."

Brittney sank onto the couch, pressing the bag against her face. Her mind swirled with confusion, frustration, and the sting of her sister's words: *I don't have a sister anymore.*

She blinked, staring blankly at the ceiling.

How did it come to this?

*****

Gloria glanced at Stephanie as they sat on the deck swing, her voice soft. "How are you feeling, sweetheart?"

Stephanie shifted, her feet lightly brushing against the ground as they rocked.

She hesitated before answering. "Mad. Hurt. Alone."

Looking down at her hands, she twisted them in her lap. "I don't know how to stop feeling this way."

Gloria's gaze lingered on Stephanie for a moment before she reached out, gently squeezing her hand. "I know it feels heavy right now, but you don't have to carry it alone. Promise me something, okay?"

Stephanie glanced up, her brow furrowed. "What?"

"If you ever feel like you're about to do something you'll regret — anything at all — call me first. I don't care what time it is. Day or night, I'll be here to listen. Promise me, Stephanie."

Stephanie's voice was soft. "I don't know if talking will help."

Gloria's tone remained warm but firm. "Maybe not right away. But sometimes, saying things aloud makes them feel a little lighter. You don't have to figure this out on your own, sweetheart. Promise me."

Stephanie looked into Gloria's eyes, the sincerity there softening her resistance.

After a long pause, she gave a faint nod. "Okay. I promise I'll call you before I do something stupid."

"Say it like you mean it." Gloria smiled gently, brushing a strand of hair behind Stephanie's ear.

Stephanie took a deep breath. "I promise, Mom. I'll call you before I do anything dumb."

Gloria let out a small sigh of relief, pulling Stephanie into a quick hug. "Good girl. You're stronger than you think, you know."

Stephanie leaned into the embrace, resting her head on Gloria's shoulder for a moment. "I don't feel strong."

"You are. And you're not alone."

"I'm not shocked that you and Brian have feelings for each other," Gloria said.

"You're not?" Stephanie asked.

Gloria smiled. "Not at all. Here's something else—I'm not shocked about Brittney's reaction to you and Brian."

"I said she was jealous," Stephanie answered.

"I don't think that's the right word. I think the word you should be using is *envious*," Gloria explained.

"Why would Brittney envy me?" Stephanie asked.

"Because you have Brian's attention, and she doesn't," Gloria replied.

"Isn't that jealousy?"

Gloria nodded. "Her actions aren't an act of jealousy. Underneath it all, I think she's envious of you."

There was a lengthy gap in the conversation before Stephanie asked, "How do I fix that?"

Gloria looked down at the young teen. "Things of the heart are hard to just fix. Talk with her? I don't know, sweetheart."

After a moment, Stephanie straightened up, wiping at her eyes. "Thanks, Mom."

Gloria smiled softly and stood. "Come on, let's walk. It'll do us both some good."

The two walked slowly around the side of the house, their steps quiet against the grass. For the first time in hours, Stephanie felt like she could breathe.

"Thank you, Mom," she whispered again as they rounded the corner.

Gloria looked at Stephanie, her voice gentle but unwavering. "Always, sweetheart. Always."

*****

Gloria opened the front door to find Umi in the dining room and Brittney in the living room.

"Stephanie just went home," she answered Umi's unspoken question as the two friends exchanged a look.

Gloria walked into the kitchen. "Umi, I'm going for something stronger than tea. Join me?"

Brittney looked at her mom, her voice soft but deliberate. "Mom, Stephanie made me think of my cross, and I'd like to go home and get it."

Umi sat there, studying her daughter for a moment, her expression unreadable.

"Mom, I promise I'll go right to my room and not say or do anything to Stephanie," Brittney pleaded.

Umi nodded slowly. "I'm trusting you, young lady. Keep the peas on your eye so it doesn't swell too badly."

"I will. Thank you, Mom," Brittney replied.

A few moments later, the teen slipped out the door. Umi watched her go with a quiet sigh before walking into the kitchen.

"Yes, please," Umi said, finally answering Gloria.

Gloria poured two glasses of wine and handed one to her friend. She sank into a chair, shaking her head with a small smile. "What did we just live through?"

Umi took a sip, setting the glass down. "I don't know, but it's times like this I wish I had boys."

Both women giggled softly, the sound breaking the tension of the long day.

"What are we going to do about the leg?" Umi asked.

Gloria held Umi's hand. "Always worried about something, aren't you? No worries, I called Brian's shop when we got home this afternoon. They said they can get another made in two or three weeks," she replied with a small sigh.

Umi smiled, gently squeezing Gloria's hand. "Ouch. That's a long time for him to be on crutches again."

"It is. I'm glad it's insured, but the copay isn't small. Still, I'm hoping it turns up before then."

Gloria looked at Umi, her expression thoughtful. "I don't think all of this is on Brittney. We both know the twins had crushes on Brian for a long time. I don't think she'd deliberately hurt him or Stephanie. I knew she was getting distant over the summer, but this I never expected."

Umi nodded, a frown creasing her brow. "Who else could be part of this? And why?"

Gloria shrugged, swirling her wine. "I don't know."

Umi let out a small huff of air. "I have no idea how this one will work out."

After a moment, Gloria smirked, a glint of humor returning to her eyes. "Wouldn't it be funny if they shared him like they do everything else?"

Umi shot her a look but couldn't suppress a laugh. "Don't even go there! I can't imagine the problems that would bring up."

She lowered her voice with a mischievous grin. "They'd fight over things like 'He likes it better when I do it,' or 'Nope, it's when I...'"

Both women burst out laughing, the tension melting further away.

Gloria, catching her breath, added with a teasing smile, "Or the problems it would solve."

Umi whispered conspiratorially, "'Can we swap tonight? I have a headache,' or 'Not tonight for you too?'"

Laughter erupted again, loud and full, filling the quiet house. For a moment, it felt like everything was normal again.

As the laughter faded, the two women sat back, sipping their wine as the day's exhaustion caught up with them. They spoke softly about plans for tomorrow and the weekend — the kind of small comforts that held life together when everything else seemed to unravel.'

CHAPTER 3

The hallway light lit the hallway brightly, showing Stephanie standing in her doorway, hands folded, waiting as she heard Brittney coming up the stairs.

Brittney stopped outside her door, her arms folded, her gaze locked on the floor as if it might offer her some kind of escape. The sharp sounds of their argument still seemed to echo in her mind.

"What is wrong with you, Brittney?" Stephanie's voice broke the heavy silence, sharp and cutting. "Why do you always have to push until everything falls apart?"

Brittney's head snapped up, her face flushed. "You don't understand…"

"No, I don't," Stephanie interrupted, her eyes blazing. "I don't understand why you think humiliating Brian is some kind of solution to whatever you're feeling."

"It wasn't about him!" Brittney's voice rose, a tremor of frustration and desperation creeping in. She pushed off the wall, her hands gesturing wildly. "It's about you, about how you always get everything! Mom's attention, Brian, the friends, the praise, everything!"

Stephanie took a step closer, her arms still crossed tightly. Her voice trembled with a mix of anger and something softer. "Do you even hear yourself? You think I asked for any of this? You think I like watching you tear everything apart because you can't deal with your own feelings?"

Brittney flinched at her sister's words, her jaw tightening. "You think you're so perfect, don't you? Everyone does. But you're not. You're just..." Her voice cracked, and she looked away, her hands gripping the edge of her doorframe. The rest of her words seemed to wither on her lips.

Stephanie's glare softened, but her frustration remained. "Britt, I never wanted to be perfect. I just wanted to be your sister. But you don't even see me as that anymore, do you?"

Brittney turned her back, her fingers tightening on the frame of her door. Her voice was quieter now, barely audible. "I didn't mean for it to go this far."

Stephanie exhaled shakily, her shoulders relaxing slightly as the fight seemed to drain out of her. "Then stop, Brittney. Stop letting whatever's eating at you destroy everything around you."

The words hung between them, raw and unyielding. Brittney's shoulders slumped, but she didn't respond. Instead, she opened her door and stepped inside, the faint creak of the hinges breaking the silence as she shut it firmly behind her.

Stephanie stayed rooted to the spot for a long moment, staring at the closed door as if willing to open it again. When it didn't, she sighed heavily and turned toward her own room, shutting her door with more force than she intended.

They were separated now by walls, but the weight of their words pressed heavily on both sides, leaving no room for peace.

*****

Brittney slammed the door to her room, the echo of Stephanie's words still ringing in her ears. She sank onto her bed, burying her face in her hands. "You don't even see me as your sister anymore," Stephanie had said. The words cut deeper than Brittney expected, leaving a hollow ache in their wake.

She tried to tell herself it wasn't true. *Of course,* I see her as my sister. How could I not? But even as the thought surfaced, doubt crept in. Stephanie had always been there—bright, confident, perfect Stephanie—and Brittney had spent years feeling like her shadow. How long had it been since she'd looked at Stephanie without that bitterness clouding her vision?

Her chest tightened, shame clawing at the edges of her mind. She didn't want to feel like this anymore. Didn't want to be the person Stephanie saw when she looked at her. But how was she supposed to change when she didn't even know where to start?

Brittney glanced toward the corner of her room, where her sketchpad sat on the floor. Normally, the act of drawing felt like an escape, a way to make sense of the mess inside her. Tonight, it felt as distant as everything else. She reached for it anyway, flipping to a blank page, her pencil moving in hesitant strokes. The lines came together awkwardly, jagged and uneven. She frowned, tearing out the page and tossing it to the side.

"I don't know how to fix this," she whispered into the silence.

*****

Several hours later, Umi said good night to Gloria and walked home. The house was eerily quiet except for the steady tick-tock of the mantel clock. She set her purse down, her gaze shifting up the staircase as she stood in the living room, bathed in the soft glow of the nearby lamp.

"Is everyone still alive?" Umi called, her voice calm but loud enough to carry.

Two muffled voices responded from upstairs in unison, "Yes!"

Umi crossed her arms, standing near the base of the steps. "Any torn clothing?"

"No!"

"Any broken TVs, laptops, or monitors?" She added, her tone sharper.

Brittney's door creaked open, her irritated voice ringing out. "Mom, stop!"

Stephanie opened her door a moment later, leaning against the doorframe with an exaggerated sigh. "No! Okay, already!"

Umi arched an eyebrow, her voice unwavering. "Good. You're alive and breathing, and nothing expensive is broken. Now, is there anything else I need to know about?"

The twins exchanged wary glances before stepping out of their rooms and moving to the top of the stairs. Brittney slouched against the railing, arms crossed, chin tilted upward in defiance. Stephanie stood straighter, her fingers twisting the edge of her shirt.

"Mom, I'm fine," Brittney declared quickly, her voice defensive. "I'm in my room like I promised. I'm good."

Stephanie's voice followed, softer but steady. "I'm good too. If she doesn't talk to me, then all is good."

Umi took a deep breath, tilting her head slightly as she looked up at them. "Fair enough. Now can I have my say?"

Stephanie's posture stiffened, and her face paled. She remembered the last time her mother had said those words—two weeks grounded for switching places with Brittney. "Yes, ma'am," she answered softly.

Brittney shot her sister a look but stayed silent, her arms tightening around herself.

Umi moved a step closer to the stairs, her gaze sharp as it pinned both girls in place. "I just watched my twin angels fight at my best friend's house about 'who knew what.' A he-said-she-said argument over a boy."

She paused, letting her words sink in. "And don't get me started on the hitting."

Brittney and Stephanie both tensed as their mother's voice dropped an octave.

"You both are grounded for a week. Am I clear?"

"Yes, ma'am," Brittney muttered, her gaze dropping.

"Yes, ma'am," Stephanie echoed quietly.

Umi's eyes narrowed slightly. "Do either of you know why I'm mad?"

Brittney's defiance faltered. She stared at the carpet beneath her feet, her voice small. "No, ma'am."

Stephanie looked up hesitantly. "Because we were fighting?"

"That's part of it. And what else?" Umi pushed.

Stephanie's voice dropped even lower. "Because I hit Brittney?"

Umi gave a curt nod. "Almost there. Brittney, what do you have to add?"

"I didn't hit anyone," Brittney muttered, her tone stubborn.

Umi's voice snapped like a whip. "Brittney Rose Welch, really? You hit Brian twice. Just because you poked him and didn't punch him doesn't mean you're innocent."

Brittney's shoulders sagged slightly. "Yes, ma'am," she mumbled.

Umi inhaled deeply, forcing herself to soften just a touch. "I'm done with this. I will not tolerate this constant bickering over a boy. You are sisters first. If this keeps up, I will ban both of you from dating him. I'll go as far as forbidding you both from going to Gloria's house. Do you understand?"

Both girls nodded quickly, voices subdued. "Yes, ma'am."

Umi stepped back slightly, folding her arms as she looked up at her daughters. Her voice was gentler, though her words carried a weight neither twin could ignore.

"Family comes first. Always. You don't let a boy or anyone come between you. Boys come and go. Family doesn't. You two were born side by side, and you're stronger together than you'll ever be apart," Umi explained.

She paused, her gaze lingering on each of them. "Family is what keeps us standing when everything else falls apart. Do you understand what I'm telling you?"

"Yes, Mom," Stephanie whispered, her voice tinged with guilt.

"Yes, Mom," Brittney echoed, her arms loosening slightly from their rigid cross.

Umi let the silence stretch for a moment, studying their faces to ensure her words had landed.

Finally, she nodded. "Good. Lecture over. I love you both. Good night, girls."

Stephanie offered a soft "I love you, Mom, good night" as she turned and gently closed her door.

Brittney lingered for a moment longer, her gaze flicking toward Umi before she whispered, "I love you too, Mom, good night," and disappeared back into her room.

Umi stood at the bottom of the stairs for a beat, her heart heavy but resolute. The glow from the lamp cast shadows across the wall, but in her mind, she whispered softly, "Stronger together… always."

With that, she turned off the light and moved quietly to her room, leaving the house still and silent once more.

*****

Gloria glanced at the clock. It was past 9:00 p.m., three hours since Brian had walked into his room and shut the door behind him.

She knocked softly, her voice gentle. "Brian? Are you okay?"

From behind the door, his voice came, quiet but steady. "Mostly."

Gloria hesitated for a beat before opening the door. The room was dim, lit only by the soft glow of the desk lamp. Brian sat on the edge of his bed, hunched over with his elbows on his knees, his fingers idly tracing the chain of his own cross.

"Want to talk about it?" Gloria asked as she eased onto the bed beside him.

Brian nodded, his shaggy brown hair falling over his forehead.

"What's on your mind, sweetheart?"

Brian let out a long breath, his voice tinged with regret. "I feel bad about how I talked to Steph... I shouldn't have said that about 'blood is thicker than water.'"

Gloria draped her arm across his shoulders, pulling him close in a comforting side hug. "I don't think she deserved that, either," she agreed softly. "But you were hurt and angry, and sometimes words come out before we think."

Brian ran a hand through his hair, frustration etched on his face. "I don't even know why I said it, Mom. I didn't mean it. I just felt like she wasn't on my side when I needed her."

Gloria gave him a moment before replying. "She loves you, Brian. You know that, right? Umi and I both know that, too."

Brian's gaze flicked up, a shadow crossing his features. "I caught myself from bringing up Dad..."

Gloria paused, her expression softening. "But you didn't. Why not?"

"Because it would've hurt her. It would've hurt everyone."

Gloria's heart squeezed at his words. "I know it still hurts, honey, but that's not the kind of pain Brittney caused tonight. You said things you didn't mean. It happens."

They sat in silence for a moment, the only sound the faint ticking of Brian's clock. Finally, Gloria shifted slightly, watching him closely. "Brian, you have deep feelings for Stephanie, don't you?"

Brian nodded, his voice quiet but certain. "I love her, Mom."

Gloria smiled faintly, reaching into her pocket and placing something cool and familiar into his hand. "Stephanie asked me to give this to you."

Brian looked down. When he saw the delicate gold cross, his eyes widened, and his fingers curled around it instinctively. "She gave you this?"

Gloria nodded. "She said you know how much it means to her."

Brian's throat tightened as he traced the edges of the cross, memories flickering behind his eyes. "Yeah… I remember when they gave me my dad's cross, too. It's one of the few things that still feels like him." He touched the chain around his own neck, its weight familiar and grounding.

Gloria's voice softened. "Does that sound like someone who doesn't want to talk to you?"

Brian looked up, doubt flickering across his face. "How do I know I can trust her, Mom?"

Gloria took a deep breath, choosing her words carefully. "That's a tough one, son. Trust is part of love and love - well, it's a choice. You trust someone not because you have to but because you choose to. Stephanie gave you something precious tonight. That's trust in my book, Brian."

Brian's fingers closed tightly around the cross, and he let out a shaky breath. "I want to talk to her," he admitted.

Gloria smiled softly, brushing his hair back from his face like she had when he was small. "I know you do. And you should. Your dad and I had our arguments, too. Sometimes, we said things we didn't mean. But when we calmed down, we always talked it out. We chose to fix it together."

Brian swallowed hard, his voice solemn. "I messed up really bad, Mom. I shouldn't have doubted her."

"You need to tell her that," Gloria replied gently. "Send her a message and see where it goes. You've got nothing to lose but a little pride, Brian."

Brian let out a soft chuckle, shaking his head as he reached an arm around her for a short, side hug. "Thanks, Mom."

Gloria hugged him back tightly, kissing the top of his head. "You're welcome, sweetheart."

As she stood to leave, she spotted his phone sitting on the desk. With a grin, she scooped it up and tossed it to him. "No better time than the present."

Brian caught it instinctively, staring at it for a moment as if it weighed more than it should.

Gloria pulled the door shut behind her, pausing in the hallway. Passing his room a few minutes later, she heard the faint sound of his voice.

"Stephanie... I'm sorry."

Gloria smiled softly to herself, a small flicker of hope lighting in her chest. "One step closer," she whispered as she continued down the hall.

*****

Stephanie had just finished brushing her teeth and was tying her hair back when she heard muffled crying coming from Brittney's adjoining room. The sound was faint but persistent, tugging at her attention. She hesitated for a moment, gripping the edge of the sink, before walking toward the door that connected the bathroom to her sister's room.

Peeking inside, she froze. Brittney's room looked like a hurricane had blown through it. Clothes were scattered everywhere, drawers emptied and overturned, the closet doors wide open with hangers tangled and askew. A pillow lay on the floor, and Brittney sat at the edge of her bed, crying into another pillow clutched tightly in her arms.

Stephanie leaned against the doorframe, her voice soft but cautious. "Are you okay?"

Brittney lifted her head, her face streaked with tears. Her voice wavered as she choked out, "No. I can't find my Daddy's cross."

Stephanie's breath caught, her anger briefly melting under the weight of her sister's anguish. She remembered how she had felt when she lost her own cross, the ache of guilt, the fear of never seeing it again. That day, Brian had spent hours with her, sifting through her room until he spotted the delicate chain tucked over one of the bed's side beams. It had been a relief she couldn't put into words.

Her eyes softened as she glanced around Brittney's chaotic room. Stephanie remembered Brittney had hung the cross over a picture of their father. Stephanie's gaze traveled upward, and there it was: the small gold cross dangling from the edge of the frame above Brittney's bed.

"Hey, brains," Stephanie said, her voice cutting through the tense air. "Your cross is over your bed. Look up."

Brittney blinked, her teary eyes following Stephanie's gesture. A shaky breath escaped her as she spotted the cross, glinting faintly in the dim light.

Stephanie didn't wait for a response. She turned on her heel, heading back toward the bathroom. The faint sound of Brittney's relieved sigh reached her ears just as she crossed the threshold.

"Steph, can we talk, please?" Brittney's voice cracked, pleading.

Stephanie paused in the doorway, gripping the edge of the bathroom counter. For a moment, she stood perfectly still, her jaw tightening as conflicting emotions warred within her. Finally, she took a deep breath and stepped through to her side of the bathroom. The sound of the door shutting between their rooms was deliberate and final.

*****

Umi stood by the kitchen sink, staring out into the dark backyard. The sound of the refrigerator filled the quiet house as she pressed her phone to her ear. Gloria's warm, familiar voice came through on the other end.

"How's it going over there?" Gloria asked.

Umi let out a long sigh, leaning against the counter. "Brittney's antics are starting to wear everyone thin. It's like she doesn't think about the consequences, or maybe she doesn't care. First, there was the itching powder, and now, Brian's missing leg. I don't know what she's trying to prove."

"She's testing boundaries," Gloria said matter-of-factly. "It's not uncommon at her age."

"I get that," Umi replied, her voice tight. "But it's not just harmless pranks. Brian was mortified today, Gloria. And Stephanie... I've never seen her lash out at Stephanie like that."

"She's angry," Gloria said gently. "Angry at herself, at the world, at anyone who'll listen. I've seen that kind of anger before. It's easier to lash out than admit you're hurting."

Umi frowned, her grip tightening on the phone. "What *is* she hurting from? She has a loving family—a stable home. I'm not saying everything's perfect, but she's not exactly living in chaos."

Gloria chuckled softly. "I used to say the same thing about Brian. Remember when he locked himself in his room after that fight with Aaron? He had every reason to feel secure, but one small thing tipped him over the edge."

"That's different," Umi argued. "Brian felt like he'd let everyone down because of the accident. Brittney..." She trailed off, shaking her head. "Sometimes it feels like she's pushing us away on purpose."

"Maybe she is," Gloria said, her tone softening. "Sometimes kids need to know you'll stay, even when they're being impossible. It's not about fixing her behavior overnight, Umi. It's about being there, showing her you're not going anywhere, no matter how many itching powder pranks she pulls."

Umi exhaled, closing her eyes. "I just wish I knew what was going on in her head."

Gloria paused, then said, "You may not know *everything*, but you *do* know your daughter. Keep showing up, Umi. She'll come around in her own time."

The words sat heavy in Umi's chest, but they brought a measure of comfort. "Thanks, Gloria. I don't know what I'd do without you."

"You're not alone," Gloria reminded her. "And neither is Brittney. Just keep reminding her of that."

The call ended a few minutes later. Umi set her phone down on the counter and glanced toward the darkened staircase. Upstairs, the faint sound of footsteps moved across the floor, and for a moment, Umi wondered if Brittney was pacing. She sighed and turned off the kitchen light. *Tomorrow will be another day to try again.*

CHAPTER 4

The following morning, Brittney walked slowly down the main hallway of the school, her arms hugging her books tightly against her chest. Her eyes barely registered the familiar walls, lockers, and bustling students around her. She was lost in thought, replaying the events of the past two days over and over in her mind. Shame pricked her skin, but beneath it was a growing determination to set things right.

When she reached the superintendent's office, she stopped and leaned against the wall, her heart hammering in her chest. The hallway thinned as the late bell rang, the last stragglers scurrying into their classrooms. Brittney stayed rooted to the spot, taking a deep breath and clutching her books tighter.

Finally, she pushed the door open and stepped inside.

"Good morning, Miss Brittney," Mrs. Cook, the receptionist, greeted her, glancing up from her desk.

Brittney hesitated, her voice quiet but steady. "Good morning, Mrs. Cook. If Dr. Smith has a few minutes, I'd like to talk with him, please."

Mrs. Cook's expression softened as she gestured toward a chair. "He's still in the halls and should be back in a few minutes. Have a seat."

Brittney sat stiffly, her back straight and her hands gripping her books as if they might ground her. The faint hum of the copier and the distant echo of footsteps filled the silence. She didn't have to wait long before Dr. Smith strode into the office, his usual confident gait accompanied by a clipboard tucked under his arm.

"Good morning, Miss Brittney," he greeted, raising a curious eyebrow. "I wasn't expecting to see you so soon today. Is everything okay?"

Brittney stood, nerves tightening her chest. "Dr. Smith, if you have a few minutes, can we talk about yesterday, please?"

Dr. Smith studied her for a moment, his expression unreadable. "Without your mother?" he clarified.

"Yes, sir. Please," she replied earnestly.

He held the door to his inner office open, motioning her inside. "Come in."

Brittney stepped into the office, waiting as Dr. Smith settled into his chair behind the desk.

"Please, have a seat," he offered, gesturing to the chair across from him.

She sat down gingerly, her hands resting in her lap as she stared at the floor.

"What's on your mind?" Dr. Smith asked, his tone professional but kind.

Brittney took a deep breath, summoning her courage. "Yesterday was my fault, sir," she began, her voice steady but soft. "I came up with the idea and convinced Peter and Richard to go along with it. Stephanie had nothing to do with it."

Dr. Smith leaned back slightly, a hint of a smile tugging at the corner of his lips. "Why are you telling me this now?"

"Because it's the right thing to do," she answered. "I'm sorry I got her involved with my problems."

"And Brian's leg?" he asked pointedly.

"I honestly don't know where it is," Brittney admitted, guilt coloring her words. "Peter was supposed to hide it in the janitor's closet, but it's not there."

"I see," Dr. Smith replied, his tone even. "And knowing you're being expelled has nothing to do with you coming here and talking with me now?"

Brittney's gaze lifted to meet his, her expression solemn. "I'm not here for me, sir. Just for Stephanie. I don't think she should be punished for what I did."

"Just your sister?" Dr. Smith pressed.

"Yes, sir. She didn't know anything about it until someone told her during her fourth period," Brittney explained, her voice growing quieter.

Dr. Smith's sharp eyes studied her carefully. "Yesterday, you weren't fully truthful with me. How do I know you're being truthful now?"

Brittney hesitated, her hands tightening into fists in her lap. "I'm not sure, sir," she said finally.

Dr. Smith sat back, tapping his pen thoughtfully against his desk. "As of this morning, all four of you were set to be expelled for stealing Brian's leg, which is an ethics violation," he began. "But with you coming in to talk with me, accepting responsibility for your actions, and being respectful, I'm not so sure this is necessary."

Brittney's heart skipped. She sat up straighter, unsure how to respond. "Yes, sir, I understand," she said quietly, moving to stand.

"Hold on," Dr. Smith said, raising a hand. "Can you answer one more question for me?"

"Yes, sir?"

He leaned forward, his gaze piercing. "Why on earth would a student take another student's prosthetic leg?"

Brittney's cheeks flushed as she looked down, embarrassed. "I wanted Brian's attention, sir."

Dr. Smith blinked, clearly caught off guard. "And you schemed to take his leg? Where's the logic in that?"

"The plan was for Brian to come to me, and I'd help him find it. Then we'd talk, and maybe I don't know." Her voice faltered. "I forgot about the assembly yesterday, and everything went wrong."

Dr. Smith let out a low chuckle, shaking his head. "Wrong is quite the understatement, Miss Brittney. Let me get this straight. You wanted Brian's attention, so you thought stealing his prosthetic leg would win his affection?"

"Yes, sir," she replied humbly.

He shook his head again, a mix of amusement and disbelief on his face. "Sounds like something out of a sitcom."

"When you put it like that, sir, it does sound childish," Brittney admitted, her voice barely above a whisper.

Dr. Smith leaned back, rocking slightly in his chair. "Have you talked with your sister about this?"

"No, sir," Brittney confessed. "She's more upset with me than Brian is. We had a fight, and now she won't talk to me. That's why I'm here, to prove that I can do the right thing, take responsibility, and show them both that I'm sorry."

He studied her for a long moment, his expression softening. "And the mark under your eye? Proof of that argument?"

"Yes, sir," she answered, her voice tinged with guilt.

"And you're doing this to prove something to them?"

"No, sir," Brittney said softly, looking down again. "To prove it to me."

Dr. Smith sat quietly, tapping his pen against the desk as he considered her words. Finally, he spoke. "All right, Miss Brittney. If I don't see you back in this office for anything negative, I'll drop the ethics violation charges. Everyone involved will serve after-school detention for the rest of the semester."

Brittney's eyes widened. "Yes, sir. Thank you. May I ask why you're giving us a second chance?"

Dr. Smith smiled faintly. "Because you came here on your own to accept responsibility for your actions. You didn't come to save yourself; you came to save your sister. That's a sign of growth. I'm not inclined to punish progress, even if it means showing leniency. Do you understand?"

"Yes, sir," Brittney replied, her voice steady.

Dr. Smith pointed his pen at her. "But if I find out you haven't been honest with me today, all deals are off. Understood?"

"Yes, sir," she said, standing up.

Dr. Smith walked around his desk and opened the door. "Off to class with you, Miss Brittney."

Brittney paused, turning back to him. "Thank you, sir. I won't let you down."

"You're welcome," he replied warmly.

As Brittney left, Dr. Smith turned to Mrs. Cook. "Please call Brian Cole and Stephanie Welch to my office. Let them know the problem has been resolved. And no need for the parents' meeting, just inform them about the detention."

Brittney caught Mrs. Cook's gaze and offered a small smile. "Brian's in AP English with Mr. Grand, and Stephanie's in AP Math with Dr. Fisher."

"Thank you, Brittney. Have a good day."

"You too, Mrs. Cook," Brittney replied, leaving the office. For the first time in days, she felt a flicker of hope stirring within her.

*****

At lunch, Brian and Stephanie walked into the bustling cafeteria. The familiar noise of clattering trays and chatter filled the air, but Brian's attention immediately shifted to a lone figure sitting at a table near the edge of the room.

Brittney sat hunched over, her shoulders curled inward as if trying to disappear. She poked at the sandwich on her tray, her movements slow and mechanical. The usual spark in her eyes was gone, replaced by a distant, hollow expression.

44

Around her, students stole glances, whispered, and snickered, the unspoken divide between her and the rest of the room starkly visible.

Brian sighed, nudging Stephanie lightly. "We can sit close to her in case she needs some help," he said, gesturing to the empty table beside Brittney.

Stephanie hesitated, her gaze following him. Across the cafeteria, a group of teens whispered and laughed, occasionally shooting glares in Brittney's direction. She tightened her grip on her tray. "Man, they can be little shits, can't they?" Stephanie muttered, crossing her arms, her gaze hardening on Richard and Peter's group.

"Yeah," Brian replied, setting his book bag on the bench seat. "I remember being on the receiving end of that once."

Stephanie shifted her weight, still watching Brittney out of the corner of her eye. "Do you really think sitting near her is going to fix anything?" she asked, her voice quieter now but carrying a hint of frustration.

Brian glanced at her, his expression calm but firm. "No, it's not about fixing anything. She's obviously struggling. She shouldn't have to sit here alone, Steph. We're her family."

Stephanie sighed, her shoulders slumping. "I know she's struggling, but she doesn't make it easy, Brian. It's like she's trying to push us away."

"She probably is," Brian admitted, his voice low. "But that's when people need you the most. Even if they don't know how to say it."

Stephanie swallowed hard, the sharp edge of frustration dulling into something softer. "It just… it feels like everything I do makes her angrier. I don't even know how to talk to her anymore."

45

Brian nudged her gently. "You don't have to say anything. Just being there might be enough."

Stephanie hesitated for a moment longer, then nodded. "Okay. Let's sit by her."

Brian approached Brittney's table first, sliding into the seat next to her. "Hey, Britt," he said lightly, glancing at her untouched tray. "You okay?"

Brittney twitched slightly at the sound of his voice, her gaze flicking to him for a brief second before dropping back to her food. She shrugged, her shoulders tightening. "I'm fine."

Stephanie sat down across from her, setting her tray down with more force than intended. "Fine doesn't look like that," she said, trying to keep her tone neutral. Brittney's lips pressed into a thin line, but she didn't respond.

Brian gave Stephanie a small shake of his head, silently telling her to ease up. "Want anything besides your usual Coke?" he asked Stephanie, his tone light to shift the mood.

"Maybe a snack or something," she replied absently, her eyes still scanning the room.

Brian gave her a reassuring smile. "You got it. Be right back," he said, heading toward the lunch line. Off in the distance, she could hear someone talking about Brittney.

Stephanie glared in the direction of Richard's table, her hand balling into a fist. "I can't stand this," she hissed under her breath.

As she seethed, two familiar figures appeared at the cafeteria door, their eyes scanning the room. Taylor Harris and Ashley Diaz exchanged a look before heading toward Brittney. Taylor, with her confident stride and bright smile, carried an energy that seemed to deflect negativity. Ashley, more reserved but equally determined, clutched a small stack of papers and a pencil case.

"Hey, Britt," Taylor greeted brightly, sliding into the seat across from her. "Mind if we join you?"

Brittney hesitated, her eyes darting to the others in the cafeteria. "You don't have to," she muttered, her voice barely audible. "They'll just… say things about you too."

"Let them," Taylor said firmly, brushing her hair back as she unpacked her lunch. "I've been called worse things by better people."

Ashley gave a small smile, taking the seat beside Taylor. "We're not here for them. We're here for you," she added softly, her tone gentle.

Taylor leaned forward, her voice dropping slightly as she caught a few lingering glances from across the room. "Besides, they're just jealous. You've got actual friends, Britt. Not whatever Richard and Peter think they've got over there."

Brittney's lips twitched in what might have been a ghost of a smile. "Thanks, guys," she murmured, picking at the edge of her sandwich. "But it doesn't change anything. Everyone still thinks…"

"Everyone still thinks they know the truth," Taylor interrupted, her voice cutting through Brittney's self-doubt like a blade. "And guess what? They don't. They're just parroting whatever crap Richard's spewing. People like him thrive on attention, and the second they don't get it, they fall apart."

Ashley nodded, her expression sincere. "You don't have to listen to them, Britt. The people who matter? They'll see the truth. And the rest, well, they're just noise."

As Ashley spoke, Richard's voice suddenly boomed from across the cafeteria, louder and sharper than the usual chatter. "Watch out, everyone! The slut might nark you out!"

Brittney froze, her hands clenching around her tray. Taylor's eyes narrowed as she swiveled in her seat to glare at Richard and Peter's table. "Unbelievable," she muttered, her voice dripping with disdain.

Peter's voice followed shortly after, echoing through the cafeteria. "Look, the nark's got friends!"

Brittney's head dropped lower, her hair hiding her face as her cheeks burned with shame. Ashley reached over, placing a comforting hand on her arm. "Ignore them, Britt," she whispered, her voice steady. "They're not worth it."

Brian was returning to the table just as Richard's taunt rang out. His jaw clenched, his steps faltering for a moment before he forced himself to keep moving. He set the tray he was carrying down beside Stephanie and took his seat, his face tight with suppressed frustration.

"They deserve to get kicked out for this," Stephanie muttered, her voice barely above a growl.

"Yeah," Brian agreed, glancing back toward Richard and Peter's table. "But they're not worth it."

Taylor's attention shifted as she noticed a figure approaching from the far end of the cafeteria. "Heads up," she said quietly, nudging Brittney with her foot under the table. "Dr. Smith's coming."

Stephanie straightened slightly, her fists still clenched. "About time," she muttered. "Maybe he'll actually deal with them for once."

Brian leaned closer to Brittney, his voice soft. "He's got this," he assured her. "Just stay calm."

Dr. Smith strode purposefully through the room, his presence drawing the attention of students nearby. The muffled complaints and grumbles from Peter and Richard's table followed shortly after, their bravado deflating under his stern gaze.

Stopping beside Brittney's table, Dr. Smith's voice softened as he addressed her. "Miss Brittney?"

Brittney looked up hesitantly, her eyes still wet. "Yes, sir?"

"You've impressed me again today," Dr. Smith said with a small smile. "Your decision to not retaliate was the right one. I'd like to make an adjustment to your detention. Instead of serving it in Dr. Fisher's room with the others, you'll do your detention in my office."

Taylor raised an eyebrow, her curiosity evident. "Wait, that's a thing? I didn't know you could get upgraded detentions."

Dr. Smith's lips twitched with the faintest hint of amusement. "It's not a common arrangement, Miss Harris. But exceptional behavior deserves recognition."

Brittney blinked in surprise, her voice shaking slightly. "Yes, sir. Thank you. I'll be there right after the bell."

Dr. Smith nodded, his tone serious but kind. "Miss Brittney, I told you before, I reward growth. Just don't make me regret it. Understood?"

"I won't, sir," Brittney replied, her voice soft but sincere. "Thank you."

As Dr. Smith walked away, Taylor leaned back, her grin breaking the tension. "See? Even the principal's on your side. That's got to count for something."

Brittney managed a small smile, her posture relaxing slightly. "Yeah," she admitted quietly. "It does."

Ashley reached over, gently patting Brittney's arm. "We're proud of you, Britt. You're dealing with this way better than I would."

Ashley reached into her bag, pulling out a folded sheet of paper. "I thought this might cheer you up," she said softly, sliding it across the table to Brittney.

Brittney unfolded it, revealing a playful sketch of the three of them as superheroes. Her lips twitched again, this time into a faint but genuine smile, "You kept this?"

"Of course," Ashley replied, "It's our best work yet. Taylor as the fearless leader, me as the tech genius, and you are the artist who brings it all to life."

"Don't forget the one who comes up with all the great plans," Taylor added with a wink.

Brittney chuckled softly, the sound fragile but real, "Thanks, guys," she said again, her voice steadier now.

"And when you're ready," Taylor added, her voice dropping to a conspiratorial whisper, "we'll come up with a plan to make sure Richard and Peter never pull this crap again."

Brittney shook her head, a faint laugh escaping her, "No plans. Just thanks for being here."

"Always," Taylor said firmly, her tone leaving no room for doubt.

The three of them continued talking in hushed voices, their conversation a quiet but steady reminder that Brittney wasn't as alone as she felt. The flicker of hope she had earlier brightened some, small but enough to hold on to.

*****

Later that afternoon, the late bus dropped Brittney off in front of her house. She paused on the sidewalk, her gaze drifting toward Brian's front door. She knew Stephanie and Brian were inside, probably laughing or studying together. Her chest tightened, guilt and loneliness mixing in a painful knot.

Shaking her head, she turned and walked to her own front door, her steps heavy.

Brittney dropped her book bag on the dining room table. "Mom?" she called.

Umi appeared from the staircase, a warm smile on her face. "Good afternoon, Angel. How was your day?"

Brittney hesitated, fidgeting with the strap of her bag. "Okay, I guess. Did you get a call from Dr. Smith?"

"Not directly. Mrs. Cook called to say the meeting was canceled. Why?" Umi asked, stepping into the living room and sitting down.

Brittney followed, perching on the arm of the couch. "I went to Dr. Smith this morning," she began. "I explained that Stephanie had nothing to do with the prank or Brian's leg. He gave me, Peter, and Richard after-school detention for the rest of the semester instead of expelling us."

"That was very responsible of you, dear," Umi said gently. "Did he say why he changed his mind?"

Brittney's gaze dropped to her hands. "He said it was because I went to him for the right reasons. I think Stephanie

51

wasn't included because she wasn't involved. I guess he thought I deserved a chance to fix things."

"Why did you go to him?" Umi asked, her voice soft but probing.

Brittney swallowed hard. "Because it was the right thing to do. Stephanie shouldn't be punished because I did something stupid. I felt awful last night, Mom. I couldn't sleep. When I finally did, I dreamed she hated me and ran away."

"And that didn't sit well with you, did it?" Umi prompted.

Brittney shook her head, tears welling up again. "No. It made me feel worse."

Before Umi could respond, the front door opened, and Stephanie walked in.

"Hi, Mom," Stephanie said, walking over to kiss her on the cheek.

"Good afternoon, Angel. How was your day?"

Stephanie glanced briefly at Brittney, her expression neutral. "Not bad. Dr. Smith called me into his office to tell me I was excused from the meeting and the incident."

"Do you know why?" Umi asked.

Stephanie's gaze shifted toward Brittney for a fleeting moment. "I think my sister told the truth, but I'm not sure." Turning back to Umi, she added, "I'm heading upstairs to finish my homework. Mom Gloria made stuffed ziti for dinner, so I ate with her and Brian."

"That's good. Anything else?" Umi asked softly.

Stephanie glanced at Brittney, her voice tight. "Nope. That's everything." She turned on her heel and disappeared up the stairs, her door clicking softly shut moments later.

Brittney let out a long sigh, slumping slightly. "She hates me. I know it."

Umi placed a hand on Brittney's arm. "Sweetheart, I don't think she hates you. She's still angry, and that's okay. Give her time. Anger fades."

*****

After a tense dinner where Brittney wouldn't say a word, Umi decided to check in on Stephanie. She headed upstairs, her steps quiet on the carpeted hallway. Pausing outside her door, she knocked gently.

"Come in," Stephanie called, her voice tired.

Umi stepped through, closing the door softly behind her. Stephanie was sitting cross-legged on her bed, her back resting against the headboard. The light from her desk lamp painted soft, warm tones across the room, but Stephanie's slouched posture and tight grip on the pillow in her lap betrayed her mood.

"Hey," Umi said, moving to sit on the edge of the bed. "You seemed a little quiet when you came home today. You okay?"

Stephanie let out a sigh, her fingers twisting a loose thread on the pillow. "I'm fine, Mom. Just tired."

Umi tilted her head, her expression patient. "I don't think you mean the kind of tiredness that sleep can fix."

Stephanie's shoulders sagged slightly. "I'm just, uhm, I don't know. It feels like everything's harder lately. Brittney, the pranks, the way she acts like everything I do is wrong. I try to help, but it's like she doesn't want me around."

"She doesn't know how to let you in," Umi said gently. "When people are hurting, sometimes they push away the ones they need the most. That doesn't mean she doesn't care."

Stephanie frowned, hugging the pillow tighter. "It doesn't feel like she cares. Not about me, not about us. Sometimes, it feels like she just wants to make everyone as miserable as she is."

From the bathroom, Brittney froze, her hand hovering above the sink. She'd only come in to grab a tissue but stopped when she heard her name. Stephanie's words cut deep, even though a small part of her thought was that *she was not wrong.*

"She's not doing it to hurt you, Steph," Umi said softly, her tone steady but firm. "Brittney doesn't have the words for what she's feeling. She doesn't know how to say she's scared or sad or frustrated, so she lashes out instead. It's not fair to you, and it's not okay, but it's not because she doesn't care."

Stephanie blinked rapidly, biting her lip. "Then how am I supposed to deal with her? Because I'm running out of ideas, Mom. Every time I try to help her, she acts like I'm the enemy."

"You're not her enemy," Umi said, reaching out to smooth a strand of hair from Stephanie's face. "You're her sister. And no matter how much she fights you, she knows that. Deep down, she knows you're there for her, even if she doesn't show it right now."

Brittney's chest tightened, Umi's words twisting in her gut. She clutched the edge of the sink, her knuckles whitening. *Why does she keep defending me?* she thought, anger and shame swirling together. *Why can't I just be better?*

"Do you really think she feels that?" Stephanie asked, her voice barely above a whisper.

"I do," Umi said firmly. "I think Brittney is carrying more than she knows how to handle. But you can't carry it for her, Steph. All you can do is remind her that she's not alone. And trust that she'll figure out the rest when she's ready."

Stephanie exhaled slowly, nodding. "I'll try. I just… I miss when things were easier between us."

"They will be again," Umi said, offering a small smile. "It won't happen overnight, but it will happen."

Brittney's hand trembled as she quietly crept back toward her side of the bathroom. Her heart pounded as the weight of their words settled over her. She hated the truth in Stephanie's frustration, and Umi's unwavering belief in her only made the guilt heavier. As she slipped back into her room, she pressed her back against the door and slid to the floor. She didn't deserve their patience, but a small part of her desperately wished she did.

In Stephanie's room, Umi leaned forward to hug her tightly. "We'll get through this," she said softly.

Stephanie rested her head against her mom's shoulder, her voice muffled. "I hope so."

"We will," Umi said, the certainty in her tone steady and sure.

CHAPTER 5

Thursday morning, the hallway buzzed with the usual pre-lunch energy, students milling around lockers and exchanging hurried conversations before the next class. Brian adjusted the strap on his book bag, his focus on the end of the corridor where Stephanie waited with a few of her friends—Ashley, Taylor, and Amber. As he made his way toward her, Richard and Peter appeared from around the corner, their laughter cutting through the din like nails on a chalkboard.

"Well, if it isn't the hobbling hero," Richard sneered, stepping into Brian's path with an exaggerated grin. "What's the matter, Brian? Missing something? Couldn't keep up with the rest of us without your fancy leg?"

Brian froze, his jaw tightening as he adjusted his balance on the crutches. "Move, Richard," he said evenly, his voice low but firm.

Peter smirked, stepping up beside Richard. "Aw, come on, Brian," he taunted. "He's just trying to have a little fun."

Stephanie, who had been chatting with her friends a few lockers away, noticed the confrontation and hurried over. "Brian, let's just go," she urged, placing a hand on his arm. Her voice wavered, but her eyes were steady. "He's not worth it."

"Oh, look who's here," Richard said with a cruel grin, his gaze shifting to Stephanie. "Are you like your sister and come to save your crippled boyfriend? How sweet."

Brian's fists clenched at his sides, but he kept his gaze locked on Richard. "Say whatever you want about me," he said through gritted teeth. "Leave them out of it."

Richard's grin widened. "Why? Does it hurt your little feelings, Brian? What are you gonna do, swing at me with your sticks?" He stepped closer, his tone dripping with malice. "Or maybe you'll just fall on your face?"

Without warning, Richard kicked one of Brian's crutches. The sudden motion caused Brian to stumble, his balance teetering precariously. He managed to recover before falling, but his bag slipped from his shoulder, hitting the ground with a dull thud, followed by the sound of a crutch hitting the floor right next to it. The hallway fell silent, all eyes now locked on the brewing confrontation. Stephanie gasped, her hand flying to her mouth, while her friends looked on in stunned disbelief.

Brian's patience snapped. Dropping his remaining crutch, he lurched forward, grabbing Richard by the front of his shirt and slamming him against the row of lockers with a loud metallic clang. "You want to try that again?" Brian growled, his voice a dangerous whisper.

"Brian, stop!" Stephanie cried, tugging at his arm. "He's not worth it!"

Peter stepped forward, puffing out his chest. "Let him go, Brian!" he barked, though his voice lacked conviction.

Before anyone else could intervene, a commanding voice cut through the tension. "Enough!"

Dr. Smith strode into the scene, his sharp gaze taking in the scene with practiced authority. "Mr. Cole, release him. Now," his voice was strong and firm.

Reluctantly, Brian let go, someone pushing his crutches into each hand as he stepped back. He ran a hand through his hair, trying to calm himself. Richard straightened his shirt, his smirk quickly returning. "He started it," Richard said smoothly, rubbing the spot where Brian had grabbed him.

"He's just mad because he can't keep up with the rest of us," Peter added.

"That's a lie!" Stephanie shot back, her voice trembling with anger. "You know he was teasing Brian!"

Dr. Smith raised a hand to silence the growing murmurs from the crowd of students. "Enough. Both of you," he said, his sharp gaze flicking between Brian and Richard. Turning to Peter, he asked, "Mr. Lemon, what happened here?"

Peter shifted uncomfortably but quickly adopted a defensive tone. "Brian just went after him. We didn't do anything."

"That's not true!" one of Brian's friends interjected. "Richard was making fun of Brian's leg, and he kicked his crutch!"

"Yeah," another friend chimed in. "We all saw it."

Stephanie nodded emphatically. "He's lying, Dr. Smith. Brian didn't do anything until Richard kicked him."

Dr. Smith looked at each student in turn, his expression unreadable. He glanced at Brian's crutch, noticing a faint scuff mark. Finally, he straightened, his tone brooking no argument. "Mr. Perez, Mr. Lemon, my office. Now. The rest of you, move along," his voice just as firm and commanding as before.

As Dr. Smith escorted Richard and Peter down the hallway, the murmurs started up again, students exchanging theories about what had just happened. Brian stood frozen for a moment, the adrenaline still coursing through him, until Stephanie placed a hand on his arm. "Are you okay?" she asked softly.

Brian nodded, though his jaw was still tight. "Yeah," he said, his voice quieter now. "I'm fine."

*****

Whispers rippled through the cafeteria when students didn't see Richard or Peter at their table and speculated about what had happened. Most assumed it had to do with the confrontation in the hallway, though no one seemed to know the full story. For Brittney, their absence was a small but meaningful reprieve, a break in the unrelenting storm she had been weathering.

Still, she couldn't help but hover near the doorway for a moment longer than necessary, her tray balanced awkwardly in her hands. The buzz of speculation filled the room, and she felt every glance that flicked her way, every whispered word that carried her name. *They don't know everything. Not yet,* she told herself, but it did little to ease the knot tightening in her chest.

Her gaze flickered to the far corner of the room, where Brian usually sat, his absence a glaring void. She had no idea where he had gone after the fight, but the tension in his face earlier was burned into her mind. He wasn't the only one missing, though. Richard's table was empty, too, and the absence of both boys left a strange void in the cafeteria's usual rhythm. She hated how that void made her feel like a weight was lifted but threatening to drop again at any second.

Taylor and Ashley joined her, their chatter pulling her from her thoughts. She forced herself to smile as she followed them to their usual table, letting their easy conversation drown out the noise around her.

"Hey, Britt," Taylor greeted, sliding into the seat across from her. Ashley followed quietly, offering a small wave before pulling out her sketchbook. Their presence didn't erase the whispers she'd noticed earlier or the occasional sideways glances from others, but for the first time in days, she didn't feel entirely alone.

Brittney sat still, her tray untouched in front of her. The whispers were quieter now, but they hadn't disappeared completely, still rippling at the edges of her consciousness. She caught snippets of conversations from nearby tables — speculations about Brian, about Richard, about what might have happened. Each word felt like a pinprick, sharp and impossible to ignore.

Her fingers tightened around the edge of her tray, and the plastic cooled against her skin. Part of her wanted to scream at everyone to shut up, to remind them that they didn't know anything, but her voice stayed locked in her throat. Instead, she kept her head down, letting the weight in her chest grow heavier. A small, traitorous part of her felt relief, though, relief that, for once, she wasn't the center of the storm.

It didn't make her feel any better. If anything, it made her stomach churn worse.

*****

That night, Umi and Gloria went shopping, leaving the three at Umi's house. The house was quiet except for the dishwasher in the kitchen and the faint sounds of a TV show in the living room. Brittney stood at the edge of the living room, twisting the hem of her sweater in her hands. The glow of the TV flickered across the walls, highlighting Brian and Stephanie on the couch. They were sitting together, but not close, a distance that Brittney couldn't tell was intentional or not.

"Hey," she said softly.

Brian glanced up, his expression unreadable. "Hey."

Stephanie turned, giving her a small nod. "Hi, Britt."

Brittney hesitated. The words she'd rehearsed in her mind felt like they'd scattered. "Can I talk to you? Just for a minute?"

Stephanie exchanged a glance with Brian before sitting up straighter. "What's up?"

Brittney stepped into the room but stayed standing, unsure if she should sit. "I know I've been... difficult. And I wanted to say I'm sorry. For everything."

Brian raised an eyebrow, his tone cautious. "Everything?"

Brittney nodded, her fingers tightening around the fabric of her sweater. "I've been awful to you both. I didn't mean to hurt anyone, but I did. And I know saying sorry doesn't fix it."

"Why now?" Stephanie asked, her voice quieter but still firm. "You've said stuff like this before, Britt. And then..."

Brittney flinched. "I know. I don't blame you for not believing me. I just..." Her throat tightened, and she took a steadying breath. "I just wanted you to know I'm trying. That's all."

Brian leaned forward slightly, resting his elbows on his knees. "What are you trying to do, Brittney?"

"To be better. To stop messing everything up. I don't know how yet, but..." Her voice cracked, and she shook her head. "I don't want you to hate me."

There was a long pause. Stephanie's face softened just a little, though her hands were clenched tightly in her lap. "I don't hate you, Britt. I never have. But I don't understand why you do the things you do."

Brittney blinked rapidly, the weight of the words hitting her hard. "I don't understand it either. Not all of it."

Brian sighed, sitting back. "Well, that's a start."

The faint hope in his words stung more than any anger might have. Brittney looked at both of them, her voice barely above a whisper. "I know I don't deserve it, but I hope... someday, you'll trust me again."

Stephanie hesitated before nodding slowly. "We'll see."

It wasn't forgiveness, but it was enough for now. Brittney exhaled, the tension in her chest loosening just slightly. She didn't try to stay. Instead, she stepped back toward the doorway, glancing over her shoulder. "Thanks. For listening."

Brian gave a small nod, his expression still guarded. "Good night, Britt."

"Good night," she echoed, her voice soft.

As she climbed the stairs, her emotions swirled—shame, relief, and fear all tangled together. It wasn't a resolution, not really, but it was a step. Maybe that was all she could ask for.

CHAPTER 6

At home that evening, Brittney sat in the dining room, quietly working through her homework. The sound of the TV in the living room and the occasional clatter from the kitchen filled the otherwise still house.

After finishing her last problem, she gathered her books and stood, stretching her sore shoulders. Walking into the kitchen, she found Umi stirring a pot on the stove.

"Do you need any help, Mom?" Brittney asked hesitantly.

Umi glanced over, a smile softening her features. "You're done early today. Not as much to do?"

"It wasn't as hard today," Brittney replied, setting her books down on the counter.

"Good," Umi said, nodding toward the cabinet. "If you don't mind, can you set the table for five? Gloria and Brian are coming over for dinner tonight."

"Sure, Mom. What's for dinner?"

"Salmon, baked potatoes, and salad," Umi answered.

Brittney moved mechanically as she set the table, placing each plate and fork with meticulous care. Her hands operated on autopilot, but her mind churned with thoughts she couldn't silence. The idea of Brian sitting at the table tonight made her chest tighten, her grip on the silverware bordering on too firm.

It wasn't his fault; she knew that somewhere deep down. But every time she saw him, it was like a mirror reflecting everything she didn't want to see. Brian, with his calm demeanor and easy way of handling things, only made her feel more out of control. And yet, part of her wished she could be angry with him. It would be easier if she could blame him for everything—for the shame that twisted her stomach, for the nights she couldn't close her eyes without seeing things she wanted to forget, and for the way the truth sat like a rock in her throat, too heavy to spit out but too bitter to swallow.

She pressed a plate onto the table a little harder than necessary, her jaw tightening. *If I could just push it onto him.* The thought came unbidden, sharp, and unwelcome. But maybe it would make the ache inside her stop, if only for a little while.

She closed her eyes for a moment, breathing through the pressure building in her chest. She knew it wasn't fair. She knew it wouldn't fix anything. But the storm inside her wouldn't stop, no matter how hard she tried to hold it back. She knew what was going to happen, knew there was no way around it, and had little choice in the matter.

A few minutes later, Brittney had the table set, each place neatly arranged with silverware and napkins. She carried her book bag upstairs and paused at her door, glancing toward Stephanie's closed door across the hall. She hesitated for a moment, wishing Stephanie was inside, then stepped inside her room, closing the door quietly behind her.

A short while later, the front door opened, and Gloria, Brian, and Stephanie stepped inside. The warm smell of baked salmon greeted them, mingling with the sound of Umi moving about in the kitchen.

"Hi, Mom Umi," Brian said, his voice cheerful despite the tension lingering in the house. "Dinner smells great."

Stephanie leaned over, placing a quick kiss on Brian's cheek. "I'll be right back," she said before heading toward the stairs.

Umi called from the kitchen, "Stephanie, Angel, please tell your sister dinner is ready."

As she passed her sister's room, she pounded a fist on Brittney's door. "DINNER," she called curtly, not waiting for a response before retreating to her own room.

Within minutes, everyone had gathered at the table. The clink of utensils against plates was the only sound as the meal progressed, the silence thick and unyielding.

Finally, Brittney cleared her throat, her voice soft, breaking the quiet. "I have some news I need to share with everyone."

Gloria set down her fork, her expression curious but kind. "What's on your mind, sweetheart?"

Brittney took a deep breath, her hands trembling slightly. "I'm expecting."

The room froze. All eyes turned toward her, and the air seemed to grow heavier.

Umi was the first to speak. "Expecting?" she repeated, her tone careful as she tried to keep her voice calm.

Brittney nodded, managing a small, hesitant smile. "Yes. You're going to be *Obaasan*, Mom."

Stephanie's gaze snapped toward her sister, her expression sharp. "Who's the happy dad?" she asked, sarcasm dripping from her words.

Brittney hesitated, her eyes darting to Brian. "I haven't told him yet," she said softly.

Brian's face drained of color. "Me?" he exclaimed, nearly choking on his soda.

Brittney nodded slightly, her gaze dropping to the table. "Yes."

Brian stood abruptly, his chair scraping loudly against the floor. "No fracking way," he said, his voice rising in disbelief.

At the same time, Stephanie shot up, slamming her napkin onto the table. "Bitch! I knew you were planning something!"

"Easy!" Umi said sharply, reaching a hand toward Stephanie, her voice commanding.

Gloria's initial shock gave way to a more measured response. "Brittney, are you sure?" she asked gently.

Brittney reached into her back pocket, pulling out a pregnancy test strip. She handed it to Umi. "Yes."

Gloria turned her gaze to Brian. "Brian, dear, we all make mistakes. Are you sure you can't be the father?"

Brian's frustration was palpable. "No, Mom," he said, his voice firm. "There isn't a chance in hell I could be the father."

Brittney's voice was soft but insistent. "Yes, about five weeks ago."

Brian erupted, his frustration boiling over. "That's a lie, and you know it, Brittney Rose!"

"Mom, Brian's already proven he wasn't with her then. Aaron Fitzgerald told us both Brian was with him at the math club meeting," Stephanie added, her voice rising as she glared at her sister.

Umi stood, her voice cutting through the chaos. "Everyone, calm down! Let's take this one step at a time."

Brian took a deep breath, visibly struggling to control his temper. "Mom Umi, I've never lied to you. I'm not a father to anyone's kid. Not Brittney's, not anyone's."

Gloria turned to her son, her tone gentle but firm. "Brian, are you absolutely sure?"

Brian's voice was almost a growl. "Mom, I've never been with her. There's no way."

The argument spiraled out of control from there, voices overlapping as everyone tried to make their case. For over an hour, they went back and forth, presenting their points and frustrations.

Finally, Stephanie stood abruptly, her face pale with anger. "Mom, believe whatever you want, but I know in my heart Brian isn't the father," she said firmly before turning toward the stairs.

Umi's voice followed her. "Stephanie, I don't want you interfering between Brittney and Brian."

Stephanie turned back, her eyes blazing. "Meaning you want me to break up with Brian?"

Umi nodded slowly. "Yes, honey."

"No!" Stephanie shouted, her voice breaking. "Mom, she's lying!" Spinning on her heel, she ran up the stairs, slamming her door behind her.

Gloria looked at Brian, her expression pained. "Brian, dear, I think Umi is right. You should stop seeing Stephanie for now."

Brian's eyes flashed with hurt and frustration. "Mom, she's got you both snowed. And now you want me to..." He couldn't finish the sentence, shaking his head in disbelief.

He stood there for a moment before speaking softly. "Good night, Moms."

Turning toward the door, he started to leave.

"Brian, maybe you can stay so we can talk?" Brittney's voice was barely above a whisper, but it stopped him in his tracks.

Brian spun around, leaning heavily on his crutches. His voice was cold. "You have my leg stolen, humiliate me in front of the entire senior class, you claim I'm the father of your baby, you're forcing me to break up with Stephanie, and now you want to talk?" He scoffed, shaking his head. "If I were you, I wouldn't plan a wedding anytime soon. I don't think I'll ever talk to you again."

Gloria looked at her son, her voice soft but reproachful. "Brian, was that necessary?"

Brian's jaw tightened. "Yes, it is, Mom." Without another word, he turned and walked out. The door closed with a solid thud.

*****

It was nearing ten o'clock when Umi finally decided Stephanie might have had enough time to cool down. The house was quiet except for the sound of the central air, and Umi stood at the bottom of the staircase, hesitating before making her way up. The weight of the evening's tension settled heavily on her shoulders, but she knew she couldn't leave things unresolved.

At Stephanie's door, she knocked softly, her voice gentle but steady. "Stephanie? Angel, can we talk?"

From the other side of the door, Stephanie's muffled voice came sharp and tinged with frustration. "Why, Mom? So you can ignore what I say? Or do you just want me to scream my frustration out?"

Umi's jaw tightened, and her voice firmed. "Stephanie Ann Welch, watch how you talk to me, young lady."

A tense silence hung between them for a moment. Then Umi heard the faint sound of Stephanie crying. Her sobs were muffled but unmistakable.

"I'll watch how I talk to you," Stephanie finally replied, her voice cracking, "when you start listening to what I'm telling you."

Umi closed her eyes briefly, her heart aching at her daughter's words. She exhaled slowly, softening her tone. "We'll talk about this tomorrow, Angel. I love you. Good night."

There was no response from the other side of the door.

Umi stood there for a beat, her hand hovering near the doorknob as if she might try again. But she let it drop, deciding to leave the potential argument for another time. As she stepped back, the sound of Stephanie's quiet sobs lingered in her ears.

Crossing the hall, Umi paused in front of Brittney's door. The soft sound of stifled sobbing reached her, tugging at her maternal instincts. She knocked gently.

"Are you okay, Angel?" she asked softly.

A beat passed before Brittney's voice came through, muffled but steady. "Yeah, I'm fine, Mom. Good night."

Umi hesitated, her fingers brushing the doorframe. "Good night, Angel," she said, her voice filled with quiet warmth before turning away.

Umi descended the stairs, her thoughts heavy as she moved through the dimly lit house. The kitchen caught her eye, and she peeked inside. The dinner dishes had been washed and neatly put away, a small but meaningful gesture that softened the ache in her chest.

She wandered through the quiet rooms, shutting off lights as she went. The house felt emptier than usual, the weight of unspoken emotions pressing down on it. When she returned to the staircase, she paused, glancing up toward her daughters' rooms.

From her vantage point, she could faintly hear them both. Stephanie's muffled cries drifted from one side of the hall, raw and full of frustration. From the other, Brittney's softer sobs carried a different weight, one of guilt and regret.

Umi sighed deeply, her heart aching for both of them. *Two daughters crying for the same cause but for entirely different reasons,* she thought. *One mourns what she's lost, and the other mourns what she wants but doesn't know how to fix.*

Turning off the final light, Umi made her way upstairs to her bedroom. She lingered briefly outside her daughters' doors, closing her eyes as if willing their pain to lessen.

"Good night, my Angels," she whispered softly, her voice barely audible as she walked into her room and shut the door behind her.

*****

Gloria knocked softly on Brian's bedroom door. The quiet of the house felt heavier than usual, pressing against her as she stood in the hallway. "Brian? Are you okay?"

"I'm fine," came his curt reply.

"Do you want to talk?" she asked.

There was a pause before Brian responded, his voice edged with frustration. "Are you going to listen to me or just blow me off?"

Gloria's jaw tightened, her voice firm but calm. "Brian, that's a very disrespectful question for a son to ask his mother."

She waited a moment, but no reply came. "Brian?" she pressed again.

"Mom, I'm not in the mood to talk," he said flatly.

With a deep breath, Gloria opened the door. "Seeing as I'm the mom, I make the rules, and I say we're talking. Your options are that we either talk now or talk later, but it's happening one way or another."

Brian was lying on his bed, his history book open in front of him. He glanced at her briefly, then went back to reading. Gloria walked in and sat at the edge of the bed, waiting patiently.

Finally, Brian closed the book and sat up, his expression guarded. "What do you want, Mom?"

Fred Kerber Jr.

"To talk about what's going on. But first, you need to understand that the way you spoke to me earlier was disrespectful, and I won't tolerate it," Gloria said firmly.

Brian sighed, standing and grabbing his crutches. He began pacing the small space of his room, the thud of the crutches punctuating his words. "I don't get it, Mom. Stephanie and I have told you the truth. We've shown you the facts. Why don't you believe us?"

Gloria followed him with her eyes, her tone even. "I think you're embarrassed because you got caught doing something you shouldn't have done. Maybe by accident?"

Brian stopped mid-step and turned to face her, his frustration spilling over. "Mom, I'm not lying. I can't be a father."

Gloria leaned forward slightly, her gaze steady. "Okay, I'm listening. Tell me why you can't be the father."

Brian hesitated, his face flushing red. "Because I'm a virgin," he admitted, his voice quieter but resolute.

Gloria raised an eyebrow. "So, you and Kelly didn't have sex?"

Brian's temper flared, his voice rising. "No, Mom! We didn't. If Dad were here, he'd have shut this bull crap down the second it started. And for the record, I still have the full box of condoms I bought!"

"Brian Richard Cole!" Gloria snapped, her tone sharp. "You're one wrong sentence away from serious trouble. Watch your language. Your dad isn't here; I am. And I'm doing the best I can with what I know, hear, and see."

Brian's shoulders slumped, the anger draining from him. "Mom, I'm sorry. But I swear I've never touched Brittney."

Gloria's voice softened as she took in her son's frustration and sincerity. "Okay, Brian. Let's start over. Why do you think Brittney is lying?"

Brian shook his head, his voice catching slightly. "I don't know. I don't understand any of this. But this isn't just about her lying; it's about what you're asking me to do."

Gloria tilted her head. "And what's that?"

Brian went to his desk and opened a drawer, pulling out a small ring box. He walked over and handed it to her.

Gloria opened the box, her eyes widening at the matching engagement and wedding bands inside. "Brian... are you saying you proposed to Stephanie?"

He shook his head. "Not yet. I'm planning to do it on Christmas Eve. I asked for her ring size weeks ago, so she probably suspects."

Gloria stared at the rings, then back at her son. "Brian, that's beautiful, but if you are the father of Brittney's baby, this changes everything. Couples break up all the time before they get married."

Brian's eyes met hers, steady and unflinching. "Mom, I'm not the father. And I'll say this as politely as I can: if you insist that I break up with Stephanie, I'll move out. On February 12, when she turns eighteen, it'll be her choice whether to move in with me or not. And when Brittney's baby is born, I'll demand a paternity test. When it proves I'm not the father, I'll never have to hear about any of this again."

Gloria's mouth fell open slightly, her voice tinged with disbelief. "Are you threatening me, young man?"

"No, Mom," Brian said softly. "It's not a threat. It's the truth. If you can't believe your own son when he's telling you the truth, then something's wrong here, with us."

Gloria stood, her hands trembling slightly as she pointed at his nightstand. "Brian, I will not accept the way you're talking to me right now. Hand me your driver's license."

Confusion flickered across Brian's face, but he complied, retrieving his wallet and handing her the card.

While holding it up, Gloria's tone was firm but measured. "One week. You're grounded from driving. If you need to go somewhere, I'll take you. Talk to me like this again, and the consequences will be more severe. Am I clear?"

Brian blinked, the tension easing from his posture. "That's it?"

"This time, yes," Gloria said. "But don't think I'm letting you off easy. You need to learn to communicate better when you're upset. Am I clear?"

"Yes, ma'am," Brian said, his voice subdued.

Gloria stood and wrapped her arms around him in a tight hug. "Brian, I'm sorry for putting you through this. I really am. I have my reasons for everything I've said, but you need to know it's because I love you. All of you."

Brian's voice wavered as he returned the embrace. "I love you too, Mom. I'm sorry for what I said."

Gloria pulled back, her expression softening. "Thank you. Now, go finish studying for your test before I change my mind."

She gave him a playful swat as he stepped away, earning a faint smile.

*****

Later that night, Gloria sat in her recliner, her thoughts heavy as she stared at her phone. She scrolled through her contacts and tapped Umi's name.

After a few rings, Umi answered. "Hi, Gloria. What's on your mind?"

Gloria sighed. "Hi, Umi. We need to talk about this whole mess with Brittney. Are you free for a bit?"

"Of course," Umi replied cautiously. "What's going on?"

Gloria hesitated. "I've been thinking about everything—what Brian's been saying, what Brittney's been claiming—and I'm starting to believe him."

"What changed your mind?" Umi asked.

Gloria took a deep breath. "It's a combination of things. Brian was adamant, Umi. He was emotional, sincere, and… well, he showed me something tonight that caught me completely off guard."

"What was it?"

"He showed me a ring box," Gloria said. "Matching engagement and wedding bands. He's planning to propose to Stephanie on Christmas Eve."

Umi gasped. "I didn't realize they were that serious."

"They are," Gloria said. "And Brian's convinced me he's telling the truth."

Umi paused. "I'm not saying I don't believe Stephanie or Brian, but Brittney's claims don't make sense otherwise. Why would she lie about something like this?"

"I've been asking myself the same question," Gloria said. "Something feels off, but I can't put my finger on it."

Umi sighed. "Do you think letting them keep seeing each other is the right choice?"

"Yes," Gloria said firmly. "After everything Brian said tonight, I'm confident they're not lying. And if I keep standing in his way, I'm afraid I'll lose him. He is ready to move out over this, Umi. That's how serious he is."

Umi exhaled audibly. "I had no idea things were that serious."

"Neither did I," Gloria admitted. "But Umi, we need to figure out why Brittney's doing this. If she's lying, there's a reason, and I don't think it's just about Brian."

"I agree," Umi said. "Something's going on, and we need to get to the bottom of it. But for now, I think you're right about Brian and Stephanie. If she wants to keep seeing him, I won't stand in their way."

"Thank you," Gloria said, relief evident in her tone.

"Just one thing," Umi added. "If Brittney's baby *is* Brian's, I'll expect him to take full responsibility."

"I agree. We both know he will, but I don't think that's going to happen. But Umi... he's not the father. I feel it in my bones," Gloria reassured her.

Umi's voice softened. "I hope you're right. For all their sakes."

"Me too," Gloria replied. "If you notice anything that might explain what's going on with Brittney, let me know."

"Of course," Umi said. "And Gloria? Thank you for calling. This... this helps."

"Same here," Gloria said, a small smile tugging at her lips. "Good night, Umi."

"Good night," Umi replied before the call disconnected.

CHAPTER 7

S tephanie had her backpack and a light jacket on as she walked down the sidewalk. She glanced at her phone; it was three-thirty in the morning. When she reached the top of a long uphill walk, the town of Mifflet lay below, its lights twinkling peacefully in the distance. She smiled. She made her way to a covered bus stop, her mother's voice echoing in her mind, "I don't want you interfering between Brittney and Brian."

Behind the bus stop, an unmarked police unit sat parked with its lights off. Inside, Deputy Grace observed Stephanie walking down the hill and sitting on the bench. Over the next thirty minutes, he watched as two buses passed without her boarding either of them.

"Unit 23, Central," Deputy Grace called on his radio.

"Unit 23," the radio replied.

"Investigating a suspicious female at the bus stop in Mifflet," he said as he exited his car.

78

"Unit 23, 10-4," the radio confirmed.

Deputy Grace approached quietly, his flashlight off. "Hello?" he called out.

Stephanie jumped, startled. "Oh!" she exclaimed, standing abruptly.

"Please, stay seated. I didn't mean to startle you, ma'am. Is everything okay?"

Stephanie slowly sat back down, looking up at him with red, puffy eyes. She clutched her bag tightly to her chest, her fingers trembling. "I'm okay."

"I'm Deputy Grace of the Beaverdam Police Department. Are you sure, ma'am?" he asked, his tone softening as he noted her disheveled state.

Stephanie's voice cracked. "I... I'm fine," she said softly, though her tears betrayed her words.

Grace glanced at her thin jacket and shivering frame. "You're cold. Let me grab something for you." He returned moments later with a heavy jacket from his car and draped it over her shoulders. "Here, this should help."

Stephanie managed a faint smile through her tears. "Thank you, sir."

"I just need to make sure you're not a mad bomber, drug dealer, or something like that," he said lightly, trying to ease her tension.

Stephanie let out a soft, watery chuckle. "No, sir. No bombs or drugs."

Grace smiled. "Good to know. What's your name?"

"Stephanie Welch," she answered softly.

"Do you have your ID, Miss Welch?"

"Yes, sir," she said, fishing it out of her bag with trembling hands. "Please call me Steph."

"You hiked from Oak Lane to here? That's a hike for this early in the morning. You sure you're okay?"

Stephanie hesitated before shaking her head, tears spilling anew. "No, sir," she whispered. "I... I'm not okay."

Grace's expression softened. "Can you tell me what's going on?"

Stephanie hesitated, her voice cracking. "It's my sister, Brittney. She said if I broke up with Brian, she'd give him back his leg."

"His leg?" Grace asked, his tone sharpening slightly. "What do you mean?"

Stephanie clutched her bag tighter. "Tuesday, she and her friends put itching powder in his clothes and stole his prosthetic leg while he was in the locker room. She's been using it to get back at me, to get him."

"She's holding his leg hostage?" Grace's brows furrowed. "That's serious, Miss Steph."

Stephanie nodded miserably. "I tried to tell my mom, but she thinks I'm just lying to stay with Brian. Brittney's lying to everyone, and no one believes Brian or me."

Moments later, another police unit pulled up. Master Deputy White stepped out, her demeanor calm and confident. She approached Grace, speaking quietly.

"What's the situation?" White asked.

Grace filled her in quickly, his tone low. "Miss Stephanie Welch, seventeen. The sister's got a prosthetic leg she stole from

80

a guy, her boyfriend Brian. Sounds like there's more going on here than just teenage drama."

White frowned, glancing at Stephanie. "She's seventeen, out here alone, and this late? Let's tread carefully. I'll talk with her."

Grace nodded. "I'll stay close. Let me know if you need anything."

Deputy White approached with a nod to Grace before taking a seat beside Stephanie.

"Hi, Miss Steph. I'm Master Deputy White, shift commander for Beaverdam PD. Can you tell me more about this prosthetic leg?"

Stephanie's shoulders tensed as she bit her lip. "It's not just the leg, ma'am." She paused, fighting to steady her voice. "Brittney said she's pregnant... and she's telling everyone Brian is the father."

Deputy White nodded slightly, encouraging her to continue. "It's not true," Stephanie added quickly, her voice breaking. "Brian swears it didn't happen, and I believe him. But Brittney keeps lying, and now everyone thinks I'm just trying to hang onto him."

White's gaze softened. "Has Brian reported his missing prosthetic?"

Stephanie shook her head. "No. I don't think so. He's been using his crutches. My mom... she doesn't believe me. She thinks Brittney's telling the truth about everything."

White exchanged a glance with Grace, who stepped back toward his unit. "I'll check if the school filed anything related to this," he said quietly before opening his laptop inside the patrol car. As Stephanie continued speaking, Grace typed quickly, pulling up records tied to the incident.

"Found something," Grace called out softly after a few minutes. White glanced over her shoulder as Grace continued. "The school reported an incident involving itching powder and a missing prosthetic. They flagged it as a prank, but it lists Brittney Welch, Peter Lemon, and Richard Perez as involved. The prosthetic hasn't been recovered."

White exchanged a glance with Grace before focusing back on Stephanie. "Miss Steph, this is a serious matter. Stealing a prosthetic isn't just a prank; it's a crime. I think we need to look into this further."

Stephanie hesitated, then nodded. "Yes, ma'am. Please."

White placed a reassuring hand on her shoulder. "Good. First, let's get you somewhere safe and warm. Do you have someone you trust we can call?"

Stephanie wiped her eyes. "My honorary mom, Gloria. She made me promise to call her if I ever... did something stupid or dumb. I guess this counts as one of them."

White's smile returned. "Maybe not that bad, just a bit drastic. That sounds perfect. Let's give her a call."

Stephanie dialed the number with trembling fingers. When Gloria answered, Stephanie's voice broke. "Mom, I'm so sorry..."

Gloria's voice immediately shifted to maternal concern. "Steph, where are you?"

"The bus stop in Mifflet," Stephanie managed.

"I'm coming to get you. Stay put," Gloria said firmly.

White took the phone. "Good morning, ma'am. This is Deputy White. Miss Stephanie is safe, and we'll bring her to you shortly."

"Thank you, Deputy. I'll be waiting," Gloria replied.

White handed the phone back to Stephanie. "See? It's going to be okay. Talk with your mom for a minute," she suggested.

White motioned for Grace aside. "What do you think of what we heard?" Deputy White asked Grace.

"I believe her. I think we've got enough for probable cause about the prosthetic," Deputy Grace answered.

"Same here. Take your unit and go sit at the house as a backup. I'll follow in a minute," Deputy White instructed.

Moments later, Deputy Grace's unit was on the road. A minute later, Deputy White and Stephanie were on their way.

*****

In the other room, Brian stirred awake, hearing his mother's voice during the call. Though he couldn't catch all the words, the urgency in Gloria's tone was enough to move him into action. He got up and quickly dressed, his mind racing with concern for Stephanie. As Gloria hung up the phone, Brian was already pulling on his jacket, ready to meet the deputies when they arrived.

*****

As soon as the call with Deputy White ended, Gloria called Umi.

Sleepily, Umi answered the phone. "Hello?"

"Umi, it's Gloria. Stephanie ran away, she is with the police in Mifflet. She's safe, fine, and not in trouble. They're bringing her here," Gloria said.

Umi sat up, instantly awake. "What do I need to do?"

"Nothing right now, but I think we should talk before they get here," Gloria replied.

"Right. I'll be right over," Umi said, hanging up the phone.

Gloria finished dressing and opened her door to find Brian standing there, dressed.

"Is Steph all right?" he asked.

"She's very upset. Other than that, she's fine," Gloria answered.

A minute later, mother and son were sitting on the front porch, waiting for Deputy White to bring Stephanie home.

A few minutes later, Umi gently closed the door to her house and walked across the lawn to Gloria and Brian's porch.

"Did you talk with her?" Umi asked.

"Only for a minute. She's really upset," Gloria answered.

Umi glanced at Brian, shaking her head. "I don't know what else I can do. I've talked with them, begged them, threatened them, but nothing's worked," she confided in Gloria.

Gloria looked at Umi. "I'm thinking about having Stephanie stay here for a few days. You know, until things cool down between her and Brittney," Gloria suggested.

"It'll be nice to have a day or two without them fighting," Umi answered.

"Good. I thought you'd agree," Gloria answered with a smile.

"We all know Brittney will be here every day once she knows what's going on," Brian told them.

"I know. I'm not sure how to stop that without making things worse," Gloria replied.

"I don't know either," Umi added.

"You both are always telling us to own up to what we do. I think, right now, for Brittney's best interests, you tell her the truth," Brian suggested.

Umi looked at Brian. "I'm not sure I understand what you mean, Brian," Umi said.

"I think you should simply tell her that until you can know for sure, you're going to let Stephanie stay here for a while, and she's not to come over," Brian explained.

"Oh no. If we do that, then she'll just nag and argue about coming over or switching with Steph," Umi replied.

Brian thought about this for a few seconds and looked at his mom. "I'll go to the hotel in Mifflet for a few days."

Umi shook her head. "No, Brian. Sweet offer, and thank you, but I can't put you out of your own home."

"Mom, family helps family. This helps you, Stephanie, at the same time, and it could help Brittney, too," Brian tried to convince her.

Umi looked at Gloria. "I can't let you do this. Explain it to him, Gloria."

Gloria looked at her best friend. "Umi, you and I know once Brian's made up his mind, there's no changing it, and I agree with him."

While they were talking, no one noticed a car pull up and park across the street from them.

Umi thought about Brian's offer for a full minute before asking, "Are you sure you want to do this?"

Across the lawn, Umi's front door opened, and Brittney stepped out in her pajamas and looked around. Once she noticed Gloria and her mother, she walked over.

Before Brittney got close, Brian answered softly, "Yes."

Everyone was standing up when Brittney came over.

"Hi, Moms," she said, then turned to her mother. "Mom, did you know Stephanie snuck out of the house?"

Umi looked at her daughter. "Yes, sweetheart, I did."

Brittney added, "Something woke me up. I went to check on you, and you were gone. So, I looked in her room, and the bed is still made."

Umi sighed. "Brittney, dear, Stephanie's run away."

Brittney looked at Brian, then down to the ground. "Maybe she couldn't handle Brian, who is going to be a father," she suggested.

Brian looked at her. "Not a chance in hell, Brittney."

Umi put her hand on Brittney's shoulder when Brittney commented, trying to sound confident, "Which is it? She can't deal with the truth, or you're my baby's daddy?"

Brian's temper started to ramp up. "I'm not your whelpling's daddy."

Brittney forced herself to calmly say, "You most certainly are."

Brian's temper grew as he took a step closer to Brittney, leaning on his crutches. "I've never had sex with you, and I'll never have sex with you because I don't have sex with sluts."

Brittney's mouth dropped. "You bastard," she exclaimed and slapped him hard across his face.

86

Umi pulled Brittney away from Brian, and Gloria pulled Brian away from Brittney.

"Calm down, you two. Now's not the time for this discussion again," Umi said.

No one heard the car door close or saw Deputy Grace walking over.

Gloria watched as Brian leaned against his crutches, sticking his hands into his pockets. "You hit like a girl," he said, backing up from everyone.

Gloria saw the deputy walking up behind Brittney at the same time Brittney lunged at Brian. Brittney's breathing quickened, her fists clenching at her sides as her frustration boiled over.

"You...," was all she got out when a strong hand grabbed her hand.

The faint sound of boots on pavement went unnoticed until Deputy Grace's voice cut through the tension.

Brittney turned and only saw her mother's arm. "Let me go!" she screamed at her mother.

Umi backed up several steps away from Brittney, noticing the deputy's arm on her daughter's hand.

"Calm down," Deputy Grace said with a firm and commanding voice.

Brittney turned further, grabbing at the hand on hers. "Let me go!"

"Good morning, everyone. I'm Deputy Grace of the Beaverdam Police Department," he introduced himself. He grabbed Brittney's hand, spun it around behind her back, and held it in a pressure hold. "Calm down and stop struggling," he repeated.

Brittney struggled to get loose. "Let me GO!" she screamed.

"Okay, young lady, last chance. Calm down, now," Deputy Grace said in a much louder and firmer voice.

"LET ME GO!" Brittney screamed, still struggling to get away from Deputy Grace's hold.

Deputy Grace grabbed her other hand and brought them both behind her lower back. "I'm going to detain you while we figure out what is going on," he said firmly.

After a brief struggle, Deputy Grace closed the first of the handcuffs on Brittney's wrist.

"Please, no, no, no, you can't do this to me. I haven't done anything wrong!"

Deputy Grace calmly replied, "Hitting the young man in front of you, resisting a deputy, and not listening to a lawful order is doing nothing? Calm down and talk with me. I can take these off just as fast as I put them on," as the other cuff closed.

Brittney looked at Umi. "Mom, tell him no, please? I can't do this anymore," she pleaded.

"Remember, Umi, the truth," Gloria said.

Umi was watching her daughter struggle. "Brittney, do what the deputy tells you to do. And I think you should do it now before you get into deeper trouble." Behind her back, she slipped her hand into Gloria's hand, holding on as if she were struggling to stand.

Deputy Grace released Brittney. "If you calm down, this will be much easier for everyone."

Brittney struggled against the cuffs. "They're hurting me," as panic rushed over her.

"Relax and stop moving, and I'll see if I can loosen them some. But you've got to calm down and bring your voice down; people are sleeping," Deputy Grace offered.

Brittney continued to struggle against the cuffs. "They hurt my wrists!"

Deputy Grace keyed his radio. "Unit 23, Central. One detained."

While this was going on, Master Deputy White's unit pulled into Gloria's driveway.

The radio replied, "Unit 23, one detained. 10-4."

Before she got out, she looked at Stephanie in the front seat. "Miss Stephanie, it looks like something is going on out there. Could you sit here until someone comes for you?"

Stephanie looked at her hands and spoke softly, "Yes, ma'am. See, everywhere I go, it's causing problems."

Deputy White looked at the young lady. "It only *looks* like that. Sit tight, and I'll be back in a few minutes."

Deputy White keyed her radio. "Unit 22, Central."

As Deputy White approached the group, Brian stepped back, still with his hands in his pockets, leaning on his crutches, leaving plenty of room for everyone.

"Unit 22," the radio replied.

Deputy White looked around at everyone, then stepped to Brittney.

"On scene with unit 23," she replied into the radio.

"Young lady, I need you to calm down, relax, and talk softer, or I'm going to arrest you for disorderly conduct," she instructed Brittney.

Brittney stopped moving but continued to struggle against the cuffs. "But these are hurting me!"

"22 on the scene with 23, 10-4," the radio answered.

Deputy Grace spoke firmly. "Miss, this is your absolute last chance to listen. Calm down and lower your voice."

"You can't do this to me! I've done nothing wrong!" Her voice was still loud.

Deputy Grace placed a hand on her shoulder, guiding her toward his unit. "That's enough. Let's take a moment to cool off."

"NO! I'm not some child you can put into timeout!" she screamed at him.

Deputy Grace's voice remained steady but firm. "Right now, you're not helping yourself by behaving this way. Let's calm down and handle this the right way."

Moments later, they were at the door to his cruiser. When Deputy Grace opened the door, Brittney tried to move away. "No!"

"Yes, young lady, get into the car now," he said firmly and calmly.

Brittney struggled harder, trying to push away from the back door to the cruiser. "No! No! You can't!"

"Stop resisting me and get into the car," he said firmly and louder.

From Deputy White's unit, Stephanie could make out that Brittney was giving the deputy a tough time. She silently prayed that she'd calm down as tears started flowing again.

Deputy White walked over, and they both pressed Brittney against the back of the unit.

While Deputy White searched her, Deputy Grace started, "You have the right to remain silent…"

While he spoke, Brittney cried, "No! NO! NOOO!"

With some effort, both deputies placed Brittney in the back of the patrol car, shutting the door with a deliberate thud. Her muffled sobs were barely audible through the thick glass.

White turned to face the group gathered on Gloria's driveway, her expression calm but firm. "Good morning, everyone. I'm Master Deputy White from the Beaverdam Police Department," she said, her voice steady as she scanned the group.

Deputy Grace stepped back, keying his radio. "Unit 23, Central."

The group exchanged introductions quietly, their voices tinged with the weight of the situation.

"Because of what we all just witnessed, I'll need everyone's IDs," Deputy Grace said, his tone professional but edged with empathy.

Brian took a small step forward, his crutches creaking under his weight. "I'll grab ours, Mom. Mom Umi, do you want me to get yours and Brittney's purses?" he asked, his voice quiet but steady.

Gloria and Umi nodded.

Inside his house, Brian paused by the familiar table where keys and purses rested, taking a deep breath before collecting the items. His fingers brushed lightly over his father's old keychain, a small, worn memento that had lived there since the accident. He swallowed hard before grabbing Gloria's purse. He walked behind his mom, handing her the purse. He crutched his way around the group and into Umi's house, their purses hanging on the wall where their jackets were kept.

Returning, he passed Umi her and Brittney's purses. As he turned to Deputy White, his expression was strained. "How much trouble is Brittney in?"

Deputy White exchanged a glance with Deputy Grace. "At the moment, quite a bit. What I've seen here and heard from Miss Stephanie's account suggests she's acting out emotionally. But arranging for Mr. Brian's prosthetic to be taken, that's serious."

Brian's jaw clenched as he glanced at the patrol car. "I wish this wasn't happening. I love her like a little sister," he said softly.

Deputy White looked at Brian. "I take it you're Brian, the boyfriend?"

Brian nodded. "Yes, ma'am."

Deputy smiled. "Miss Stephanie thinks very highly of you. Why don't you go and bring her over?"

Brian didn't need to be told twice and set off to get Stephanie. The moment he opened the door, she jumped out and hugged him tightly. "Brian, I love you," her voice just a whisper.

Brian balanced his crutches as he hugged her back. "And I love you, Steph," he replied softly and tenderly.

The couple walked back to the group of adults, Stephanie hugging Gloria, then crossed over and held her mother tightly, tears running down her cheeks. "I'm so sorry, Mom," she managed to get out.

Umi returned the hug. "It's all good, my angel."

Deputy Grace shifted his stance, studying Brian. "One big family, huh?"

Brian nodded, his voice quieter now. "We all lost our dads in the same accident, sir. Two years ago. My dad, Mom Umi's husband, and my leg... all because someone tried to beat a train. Since then, we've been family."

Deputy White's face softened as she studied Brian. "Was that in Lakewood? February 18th, 2020? A DUI driver racing the train?" she asked.

Brian nodded, his throat tightening. "Yes, ma'am. You remember?"

"I was on scene," Deputy White replied. Her tone shifted, a mix of sadness and admiration. "I'm sorry for your loss; it was a horrible accident. Seeing you all here today, doing as well as you are, it's remarkable."

Brian looked at her, a flicker of pain crossing his face. "We wouldn't have gotten through it without each other. Stephanie, Brittney, my moms, they kept me going."

Stephanie moved back to Brian, wrapping her arms around him protectively. He pulled her into a side hug, his crutches wobbling slightly as he leaned on her for support. "They're my world," he said simply.

Deputy White observed the interaction before turning her attention to Umi. "Mrs. Welch, does Miss Brittney's recent behavior feel unusual to you?"

Umi's brow furrowed. "Yes. She's been distant since the middle of the summer, more withdrawn. It's hard to pinpoint why."

Brian shifted uncomfortably. "Five weeks," he said suddenly. "That's when she started flirting with me. Saying things like, 'I'll do the things she won't,' and… other things."

Deputy Grace's expression darkened. "Has she done anything else?"

Brian hesitated, glancing at Stephanie for reassurance before replying. "She told me if I dumped Stephanie, I'd get my leg back."

Deputy White exchanged a look with Deputy Grace before turning back to Umi. "Do you think there's any chance Brittney isn't being truthful about her pregnancy or the father?"

Umi's lips pressed into a thin line as she considered. "We're sure she's lying about the father, just not why."

Deputy White nodded and excused herself, walking toward the patrol car. She opened the door and crouched slightly to meet Brittney's tear-streaked gaze.

"Miss Brittney, I need you to answer a question honestly," Deputy White said gently but firmly. "Did you have anything to do with Brian's missing prosthetic leg?"

Brittney's hands gripped the hem of her pajama shirt, her knuckles white. For a moment, the only sound was the faint rustle of leaves in the breeze. Finally, her voice cracked. "Yes, ma'am. I'm the one who arranged it. I'm sorry. I didn't mean for everything to go this far."

Deputy White nodded slowly. "I appreciate your honesty. But, Miss Brittney, this has serious consequences. You're in trouble, more than you might realize."

Tears streamed down Brittney's face. "Am I going to jail?" she whispered, her voice trembling.

"Yes, ma'am, you are," Deputy White replied, her tone firm.

Brittney looked down at her lap, her breath hitching. "I didn't think... I just... I wanted him to notice me," she admitted, her voice barely audible.

Moments later, she added, "Ma'am, I'm, umm, not dressed under my pajamas," she said just as softly.

Deputy White observed her for a moment before speaking. "I'll talk with your mom about letting you get dressed. Sit tight and stay calm."

When Deputy White returned, she shared Brittney's confession. Umi's face fell as she processed the information. Gloria placed a hand on her arm in silent support.

Brian looked down at the ground, shaking his head. "I don't understand how or why," he said, his voice thick with emotion. "But this... this isn't okay."

Deputy Grace turned to him. "Do you want to press charges for the theft or for the assault?"

Brian's shoulders slumped. "Against my sister? No way. That doesn't help anyone. No sir."

Deputy White stepped closer to Umi. "Miss Brittney mentioned she isn't dressed under her pajamas. Would it be okay for her to go inside and change?"

Umi nodded, her voice subdued. "Of course. Do you need me to come with you?"

"Yes, ma'am," Deputy White replied. Together, they walked toward the patrol car, leaving the others to discuss the missing prosthetic.

Deputy White opened the door, and Brittney looked up at her, tears still falling.

"Miss Brittney, you know I don't have to do anything for you, right? I can simply get into the driver's seat and take you off to jail. That's not how I'm wired, so I'll make you an offer. If you give me your word, you will obey my commands, keep calm, and keep your voice down, and I'll let you finish getting dressed and loosen the cuffs. If you start up at any point, I'm going to put every charge I can think of against you. Deal?"

Softly, Brittney replied, "Yes, ma'am, I promise."

Deputy White reached in to help her. "Okay, come out of the car."

Brittney was quiet while they walked across the lawn.

When Umi reached the door, her eyes connected with Brittney's.

"Mom, I can't do this anymore. I'm so sorry about this; I mean all of this," Brittney said softly.

"Brittney, honey, I love you. No matter what you do, I will always love you. I need to know something," Umi commented.

Brittney shook her head. "Brian's not the father. Oh, how I wish he was, but I know he's not."

Umi was shocked by her answer as she stood by the door and let the other two walk in. Her face paled again, trying to process why she would lie about something like this, why she wouldn't say who the real father was.

"Why not tell us who?" Umi asked.

"Because the father is someone you'd never let in the house. He's bad and said he'd do terrible things to me—us—if anyone found out," Brittney explained softly.

Brittney's words hung in the air, cutting through the faint rustle of the wind outside. Umi's heart clenched, a wave of emotions crashing over her: anger at the unnamed man, sorrow for Brittney's pain, and guilt for not seeing the signs earlier. She swallowed hard, keeping her voice steady even as her chest tightened.

"Brittney, honey, I love you," Umi said, her voice softer now but edged with desperation. "No matter what you do, I will always love you. But… I need to understand. Why didn't you tell anyone? Why carry this alone?"

Brittney hesitated, her gaze falling to the floor. "Because you'd hate him, Mom. I hate him. I'm ashamed and embarrassed of everything. He said he'd make us all pay if I told anyone; he'd hurt you, Stephanie, Brian, and Mom Gloria. I believe him." A moment later, her voice just a whisper, she added, "I still do."

The words struck Umi like a blow, her composure faltering for a brief moment. She fought the urge to pull Brittney into her arms, knowing her daughter needed more than comfort; she needed solutions. Umi's mind raced, piecing together the lies, the distance, and the tension that had been building for months. How had she missed this?

"I should have seen this coming," Umi thought, guilt gnawing at her resolve. "How did I let it get this far?"

She exhaled shakily, brushing Brittney's hair from her face. "No one should make you feel this way, Brittney. No one. Whatever happens next, we'll figure it out together. I promise."

Brittney led the way to her bedroom. Once in the room, the deputy let her shoulder go. "One second, Miss Brittney," and uncuffed her. Once the cuffs were off, Brittney rubbed her wrists, noticing red welts going around each.

Brittney quickly opened a drawer and pulled out fresh undergarments. Deputy White looked them over quickly and tossed them onto the bed. Quickly, she undressed and then redressed while Deputy White and Umi watched.

Deputy White noticed Brittney's *daddy* cross around her neck, pointing at it. "If that is special to you, I suggest you leave it here, just to be safe," she suggested.

Carefully, Brittney removed the small necklace from her neck and reached toward Umi. "Mom, can you keep this for me, please?"

Umi took the necklace and put it on. "I'll keep it on until you get home, my angel."

Brittney's voice was low. "I don't feel like an angel, Mom."

Brittney turned around and placed her hands behind her back. "Thank you, Deputy White."

Deputy White commented while she cuffed her, "You're welcome. I'm going to offer you some free advice. You see how you're acting right now?"

"Yes, ma'am."

"Act like this when we get you to booking and the entire time you are there. They won't put up with an emotional outburst like you had earlier," Deputy White warned her.

"Yes, ma'am."

"How do the cuffs feel, Miss Brittney?" Deputy White asked.

"Much easier, ma'am. Thank you."

As the trio were walking out, Umi asked Brittney, "Does anyone else know about what you've been through?"

Brittney's response came hesitantly, her voice trembling. "Peter. Peter Lemon. He saw almost everything each time it happened. Each time, I let it happen."

Umi stopped mid-step, her chest tightening at Brittney's words. She reached out instinctively, resting a hand on her daughter's arm. "Brittney, honey, this isn't your fault. He made you feel trapped, and no one should have that kind of power over you. You're stronger than you think, even if you don't see it yet."

Deputy White slowly turned Brittney until she was looking into her eyes. "Did he say he would hurt anyone if you didn't do what he wanted?"

Brittney shook her head. "Yes, ma'am."

As they walked across the lawn to Deputy White's cruiser, Deputy White commented, "Miss Brittney, listen to this, please. If someone threatened you or your family to get you to do something, that's illegal. If this is what happened, you should go to the police and file a report."

"But if I did these things, how would that help?" Brittney asked.

"Well, we'd do an investigation, and if we discover what you are claiming is true, the state will prosecute the person. And because he or they forced you to make several bad decisions, the judge will take this into consideration during sentencing," Deputy White answered.

Brittney nodded. "Yes, ma'am. Thank you."

Moments later, Brittney was in the back seat.

"Mrs. Welch," Deputy White started, "I think you should follow up on what Brittney just told us. I also highly recommend you get a lawyer. Brittney will be in front of the magistrate on Monday morning. Arraignments start at 10 a.m., and she can be called any time after that."

Umi nodded. "She'll be in for the weekend?"

"Yes, ma'am. There's not much we can do about that. Once she's processed and booked, she'll have access to a phone. It's an outgoing, collect calls-only phone," Deputy White explained.

Stephanie looked at her mom. "Mom, I overheard Britt talking on the phone a few nights ago, and it sounded like she was telling someone she didn't want to do something. She said something like, 'I can't do that,' and the last thing I remember hearing her say was, 'Okay, I'll do it,' but it didn't sound right. I couldn't hear anymore because I closed the bathroom door."

Deputy White looked at her. "What do you mean by 'it didn't sound right?'"

"I don't know. It just didn't sound like her, like she was giving in on something," Stephanie answered.

"Mrs. Welch, that's another reason why you should follow up on this. It could be important," Deputy White said.

Deputy White looked at Grace, noticing his small nod. "I'm only charging Miss Brittney with disorderly conduct and grand larceny in the third degree. I'm not going to file any resisting charges," Deputy White explained.

"Thank you, Deputy. Why?" Umi asked.

Deputy White smiled. "I've got two teens at home, and I've watched them fight over the same boy a few times. I have an idea of what you might be going through. And, honestly, I think there's a lot more behind what we've learned this evening."

"Good night and good luck, everyone," Deputy Grace said.

"Good night. We'll be in contact if we need any more information," Deputy White added.

After everyone said their goodbyes to the deputies, they got into their police units and left.

Umi looked at Brian, her eyes wet. "Brian, I want you to know Brittney admitted that you're not the father. I can't tell you how sorry I am about this."

Brian pulled Umi into a hug. "Mom, it's all good. No worries. Does this mean I can date and kiss Stephanie?"

Umi and Stephanie both smiled big as Umi nodded. "Yes."

Moments later, Stephanie and Brian shared a very enthusiastic but short kiss. As the kiss broke, he reached around his neck and took off her *daddy* cross, putting it around her neck.

As he clasped it, he said softly, "I'm sorry I doubted you. I love you, Stephanie. With all my heart, soul, and being, I love you," Brian told her, not aware that everyone else heard him.

"Brian Richard Cole, you are my world, my love, and my rock. I love you," Stephanie replied.

They followed up their declaration of love with a soft, tender kiss while everyone looked on.

Gloria led everyone into the house. "Come inside, lovebirds. I know it's early, but I'm going for some tea. Umi?"

"I'm right behind you," Umi replied, watching Stephanie and Brian sit on the couch and cuddle together.

Standing just inside the kitchen door, they watched Brian and Stephanie get comfortable and cuddle under a thick blanket. With a gentle kiss, they both cuddled deeper into the blanket and closed their eyes.

Once the tea was ready, they moved to the table. The house was still, the kind of quiet that felt heavier than silence. Umi sat at the dining room table, her hands clasped tightly around a steaming mug of tea. Across from her, Gloria leaned back in her chair, arms crossed, her expression a mix of exhaustion and worry.

"She used to be my sunshine," Umi said softly, staring into the dark liquid. "Brittney was the one who could light up a room with a smile. Now? It's like I don't even recognize her."

Gloria reached across the table, resting a steady hand on Umi's. "She's still in there, Umi. You know that. This... this version of Brittney, it's her pain and fear speaking. It's not who she is."

Umi's shoulders slumped. "But I let it happen, Gloria. I should have seen it — the lies, the distance, the way she pulled away from us. What kind of mother doesn't notice when her child is crying out for help?"

Gloria shook her head, her grip firm. "Don't do that. Don't turn this into your failure. We both missed the signs. But Brittney's not lost, Umi. She's hurting, but she's still here. And as long as she's here, there's hope."

For a moment, the only sound was the ticking of the mantle clock in the living room. Umi sighed deeply, running her fingers through her hair. "She admitted Brian isn't the father tonight. She said the real father... he's someone dangerous. Someone who threatened all of us."

Gloria's face darkened, her jaw tightening. "Richard?"

Umi nodded slowly. "I think so. But she's too afraid to say it outright. What scares me most is how much control he still has over her. She's willing to tear this family apart just to keep this a secret."

Gloria sat forward, her voice low and resolute. "Then we fight for her. We don't let this man, or anyone else, hold that kind of power over her. If Brittney can't fight for herself, then we'll do it for her."

Tears welled in Umi's eyes, but she blinked them away, her voice trembling. "What if it's too late, Gloria? What if we've already lost her?"

Gloria reached out, squeezing Umi's hand tightly. "It's not too late, not for Brittney. Tonight, she started talking. That's the first step. We have to stay strong for her, Stephanie, Brian, and for ourselves. We can't let this break us."

A faint knock at the kitchen door broke the moment. Umi stood slowly, her legs heavy, and looked up to find Stephanie, her eyes red-rimmed and puffy, at the door.

"Mom Gloria," Stephanie said softly, looking past Umi. "Can I talk to you?"

Gloria glanced at Umi, who nodded. "Of course, sweetheart," Gloria said as Umi guided her younger daughter to Gloria's lap and then sat back down. Umi watched as her younger daughter curled into Gloria's embrace, tears falling freely.

Stephanie's muffled voice broke the silence. "Why did she do this, Mom? Why does she hate me so much?"

Gloria stroked Stephanie's hair, her voice calm and firm. "She doesn't hate you, Steph. She hates herself. She's hurting, and she doesn't know how to deal with it. This isn't your fault."

Umi stayed rooted in her chair, her heart aching for both of her daughters. For a brief moment, she allowed herself to hope that somehow, through the pain and chaos, they could find their way back to each other. Stephanie hugged Gloria, got up and hugged her mom, and went back to the couch, cuddling into Brian's embrace.

The two friends talked quietly in the kitchen. When they walked out, they could see both teens, their eyes closed while they held each other.

"They make such a cute couple. I feel so bad about trying to make her break up with him for Brittney's sake," Umi said softly.

"Same here. Everything she said sounded so true; she had us all convinced it was Stephanie who was lying," Gloria reminded her as they sat in the dining room.

"What do you think about this thing with someone threatening Brittney?" Gloria asked.

"I'm not sure. I know what she's been doing is out of character for her, but with the lies she's told me, I can't tell," Umi answered.

"And then there's the seductive behavior and the outright bribing to consider," Umi added.

"Considering how thin she is, it won't be long until she's showing. Could these be signs of desperation?" Gloria asked.

As they talked about the possibilities, Gloria suggested they look at Brittney's cell.

"That's not a bad idea. If we find anything there, it's more for when I go to the police," Umi stated.

Gloria smiled. "It might provide a better insight into Brittney's actions and thoughts."

Umi looked at herself. "I'm going to shower and get dressed. When I come back, I'll bring the cell phone and some stuff for Stephanie."

"Sounds good. I think I'll do the same. We can let the lovebirds sleep while we go out for breakfast. How does that sound?" Gloria asked.

"Like a plan. Give me half an hour, and I'll be back," Umi replied.

Both got up as Gloria commented, "See you then."

Sometime later, Umi returned with two bags. She placed them on the coffee table in front of Brian and Stephanie, knowing Stephanie would recognize the bags as hers.

Gloria came from the back of the house and said softly, "Ready?"

"Yup, and I have Brittney's cell. I had to figure out her passcode. Wasn't hard at all. Care to guess what it is?" Umi asked.

Gloria grabbed her purse and headed toward the door. "Brian's birthdate?"

Umi was right behind her. "It's the time Stephanie was born."

Gloria answered once they were in the car, "Isn't that interesting."

"Isn't it? I did some quick searching and found a lot of text messages from Richard, and guessing by what I'm reading, I think she is secretly dating him or something like that," Umi answered.

"Wow," Gloria said while they drove to their favorite restaurant.

"There are a few messages that scare me. One from Brittney reads, 'I can't do that to my sister,' and another reads, 'He's not buying it. I've done everything you told me to do. Call,'" Umi said.

"Umi, I think we should go to the police now. If what Brittney said is true, all of us could be in trouble if we think about it. Steph and Brian are so close, and with us being close, it worries me," Gloria commented.

"Do you think it's that bad?"

"I don't know, but I don't think we should wait and risk anything," Gloria replied.

"You're right," Umi answered.

"It's early, and I don't know how long we're going to be there. Let's grab some food first," Gloria suggested.

CHAPTER 8

An hour later, Umi and Gloria sat in the stark waiting area of the police department, the sounds of low murmurs and conversations filling the air. Umi clutched Brittney's phone, the screen still lit with the troubling messages she had discovered. Deputy White spotted them from across the room and approached, her expression unreadable.

"Mrs. Welch, Mrs. Cole," Deputy White greeted, nodding to each of them.

"Deputy, you need to see this," Umi said, handing over the phone. The messages were clear evidence that Brittney's actions were tied to something far more troubling.

Minutes later, they were ushered into an office where SVU Detective Harvy Barns waited. Deputy White briefed him on the events of the morning: Brittney's admission about the prosthetic leg, her claim of being threatened, and her uncharacteristic behavior.

After a long conversation between the three, Barnes' brow furrowed as he scrolled through the text messages. "Mrs. Welch, do you think these texts and Brittney's actions are part of a larger story like Deputy White believes?"

Umi nodded firmly. "Yes, Detective Barns. She's been completely out of character for weeks. She's doing things she wouldn't normally do, picking fights with her twin sister, for one. Afterward, she looked shocked, like she didn't expect what happened."

Gloria added, her voice steady but laced with concern. "We've both seen Brittney aggressively try to get Brian's attention in ways that don't feel right. After reading these texts, I think she's protecting someone. Not by choice."

Harvy leaned back in his chair, drumming his fingers on the desk as he processed their words. "We'll open an investigation and follow it to the end. I understand Brittney is in custody and will be charged on Monday. We'll work as quickly as possible. Do either of you feel unsafe or worried right now?"

Gloria glanced at Umi before answering. "A bit," she admitted.

Umi nodded. "Some, but not enough to ask for extra help yet."

"Understood. If you remember anything else, feel threatened, or notice anything unusual, call me immediately," Barns said, sliding two business cards across the desk.

"Can I hold onto the phone?" Barns asked. "I'd like our tech unit to go through it for more evidence or information."

Umi stood, her resolve steady. "Of course. The passcode is 0818."

Barns scribbled the code down. "Got it. We'll be in touch if we find anything."

"Please don't hesitate to call if you have questions," Gloria added, shaking his hand.

Minutes later, they were back in Gloria's car, heading home.

"Wow," Gloria murmured, glancing at the clock. "It's already noon. I'm glad we ate before we came here."

Umi was about to respond when her phone buzzed. The screen flashed "Restricted." She answered, her voice cautious. "Hello?"

A computerized voice responded, "You have a collect call from Brittney Cole. Do you accept the charges?"

Umi's heart sank. "Yes." In the background, she heard Brittney's shaky voice. "Please, Mom."

Umi placed the phone on speaker, her voice steady despite her worry. "Hi, sweetheart. Gloria and I are here. How are you making out?"

Brittney's voice trembled. "I'm so sorry, Mom. I never want to come here again."

Gloria's tone softened. "You sound exhausted, sweetheart. Did you get any rest?"

"Not much. I'm scared something might happen if I close my eyes. Mom, I watched them strap a woman to a chair today because she lost control. They put a mask on her and wheeled her into a corner… I don't want that to be me."

Umi's heart ached at the fear in her daughter's voice. "Honey, we've been working hard today to get answers. The police are investigating what you told Deputy White and me. But I need you to keep being responsible and calm, okay?"

"I will, Mom. Please… if you see Deputy Grace, tell him I'm sorry for how I acted. And thank Deputy White for being fair with the charges."

"That's my girl," Umi said, her voice filled with pride. "Now listen to me. Gloria and I are finding a lawyer, and when you talk to them, Brittney, you have to tell the whole truth. No holding back, no hiding anything."

Brittney hesitated. "Even if it means you'll be in danger?"

"Yes, honey. Especially then. Do you understand why it's so important?" Gloria added gently.

Before Brittney could reply, an automated message cut in. "You have 10 seconds remaining on your call."

"I think so," Brittney said hurriedly. "One of the deputies told me one of the charges could mean seven years in prison. I'll do whatever you say, Mom."

The line went dead before Umi could respond.

*****

When they arrived home, Brian and Stephanie were curled up on the couch, their expressions softer than the tension-filled morning. Plates on the coffee table hinted they had eaten recently.

"Hello, lovebirds," Gloria teased as she walked in.

"Hello, Moms," they replied in unison.

Umi and Gloria took turns explaining the morning's activities and their call with Brittney. The rest of the day passed quietly. Brian and Stephanie stayed cuddled on the couch, watching TV, while Umi and Gloria spoke softly in the dining room. For the first time in weeks, the house felt calm.

*****

Early Saturday afternoon, there was a knock at Brian's front door. When Brian opened it, he was greeted by two students and Dr. Fisher, one of Brian's professors. Dr. Fisher held a large duffel bag in his hands.

"We believe this is yours," he said, handing the bag to Brian with a big smile.

Brian opened it eagerly, his face breaking into a relieved smile as he pulled out his prosthetic leg. "Where was it?"

"The drama prop room," Dr. Fisher replied. "It was hidden under a blanket. We think that whoever took it hadn't figured out how to get it past the metal detectors."

Brian inspected the leg carefully. "It looks good. I'll try it on later. Thank you for organizing the search party, Dr. Fisher. What was the prize?"

Dr. Fisher smiled warmly. "We're happy to help. The team that found it won a Subway lunch and gift cards to Dairy Queen."

After everyone said their goodbyes, Brian tried on the leg, finding it in perfect working order. The relief in his expression was unmistakable.

Not long after, Brittney called, and the family gathered around the cell phone, listening and giving her words of encouragement. After the call, Gloria and Umi talked softly about Brittney's state of mind, both agreeing she was more depressed than the day before.

*****

Umi placed her phone down on the dining room table with a soft sigh, her fingers lingering on its edge. The faint aroma of freshly brewed tea filled the room, but she didn't reach for her cup. Across from her, Gloria sat with her hands wrapped around a mug, her expression a mix of worry and quiet determination.

"She sounded terrified," Umi said, her voice low. "I've never heard her like this before. I think she still believes Richard will retaliate, with or without the police being involved."

Gloria nodded slowly, her brow furrowing. "She's right to be afraid. Richard's dangerous, but the police have the evidence now. That has to count for something."

Umi pressed her palms flat against the table, exhaling sharply. "I keep thinking about what we missed. How did it get this far without any of us realizing what was going on?"

"You can't blame yourself for this, Umi," Gloria said firmly. "Brittney's been hiding things for a long time. She didn't want you to see it."

Umi's gaze dropped to her hands. "And now she's sitting in a jail cell because of him. She keeps saying she's protecting us, but from what? What's he holding over her that's so bad she'd let herself be arrested instead of telling us?"

"She's ashamed? Or embarrassed?" Gloria asked gently. "I think she thinks if you knew everything, you'd see her differently," she added a moment after asking.

The sound of soft footsteps in the hallway drew their attention. Stephanie appeared in the doorway, her arms crossed tightly over her chest. She hesitated, glancing between the two women. "Is this about Brittney?"

"Come in, Steph," Gloria said, gesturing to the chair beside her. "Sit with us."

Stephanie walked over, pulled out a chair, and sank into it. "What's going on? Did she call?"

"She did," Umi said. "She's scared. She doesn't trust anyone, and we think she's worried about what Richard might do if she says too much."

Stephanie frowned, her hands twisting in her lap. "I don't get it. Why would she even get involved with someone like him? She's not stupid. She had to know he was bad news."

"You're right, she's not stupid," Gloria said gently. "But sometimes people like Richard are good at hiding who they really are until it's too late."

Stephanie scoffed. "Still doesn't explain why she didn't come to us. We're her family. Doesn't she trust us?"

"She doesn't think we'd understand," Umi said softly. "Or worse, she thinks she's protecting us by keeping quiet."

Stephanie leaned back in her chair, her jaw tightening. "Protecting us from what, though? What could he possibly do to us?"

"I think that's what she's afraid of," Gloria said. "And until she tells us the whole truth, we're working in the dark."

Umi's phone buzzed softly on the table, and she glanced at it before turning her attention to Gloria. "Do you think Brian should come over? I think we need to talk this through as a family."

Gloria hesitated, then nodded. "Yeah, he should be here."

Fifteen minutes later, Brian sat at the table, his expression tense. He leaned forward, resting his elbows on the wooden surface, his hands clasped together. Stephanie sat beside him, her gaze bouncing between Umi and Gloria.

"We went to the police yesterday," Umi said, breaking the silence. Her voice was steady, but there was a weight behind her words. "We took Brittney's phone and showed them the messages Richard sent her and her replies."

Stephanie's head shot up. "You did? What did they say?"

Gloria placed her mug down carefully. "They're taking it seriously. There's enough evidence to suggest Richard's been threatening her, but they need Brittney to fill in the gaps and details. Without her story, it's hard to act decisively."

"But she's not going to talk, is she?" Stephanie said, her tone sharp. "Not if she's scared he'll come after us."

Umi admitted, "She's convinced that if she says anything, Richard will retaliate, and not just against her. Against all of us."

Brian frowned, his fingers tightening into a clasp. "What exactly did the police say they could do?"

"They promised to open a full investigation and told us to call if we felt we were in danger," Gloria said. "But it's complicated without her story. They need more than what we gave them to really go after him."

Stephanie let out a frustrated sigh, leaning back in her chair. "So we're stuck. She's too scared to talk, and the police can't do anything until she does."

"That's why we're here," Umi said, her voice calm but resolute. "We need to figure out how to help her feel safe enough to tell the truth."

Brian leaned forward, his jaw tightening as he met Umi's eyes. "She doesn't have to be scared for us. We can handle this. The police are involved now. Richard isn't untouchable. He can't just do whatever he wants."

"But what about her?" Stephanie asked, her voice softer now. "She's in there by herself, probably thinking we hate her about everything Richard's done, everything he could still do. How are we supposed to convince her to trust the police when she barely trusts us?"

Gloria reached across the table, resting her hand gently on Stephanie's. "It's not about convincing her. It's about showing her she's not alone. She needs to know we're here, no matter how scared she is."

Stephanie exhaled shakily, her frustration giving way to something softer. "I just... I hate seeing her like this. It's like she's a completely different person."

"She's still Brittney," Umi said gently. "She's just... lost right now. But we'll help her find her way back."

Brian nodded, his gaze unwavering. "We need to make sure she knows we're not going anywhere. If she's scared of Richard, then we make her feel safe enough to fight back."

Umi's shoulders eased slightly, a faint smile softening her features. "Brian, dear, if she's afraid to fight back, then we fight *for* her. That's exactly what we are doing."

Gloria smiled at Umi's comment, realizing she had used the same words she said to her best friend not long ago. She glanced at Umi, seeing her eyes flick up to hers and the small smile as the two spoke volumes without a word.

CHAPTER 9

B oth families were seated in the courtroom gallery, waiting for Brittney's case to be called. The proceedings had begun promptly at 10:00 a.m., and they had watched as defendant after defendant was brought in through a side door, dressed in bright orange jumpsuits, handcuffs connected to chains at their waists. Each was escorted to the defense table by a deputy to meet their attorneys.

As the last defendant exited, the judge addressed the bailiff, "Do we have any more guilty pleas we can address before lunch?"

The bailiff handed the judge a folder. "Yes, Your Honor. There is a case with a plea deal in place. The ADA and defense counsel are ready to proceed."

The judge accepted the folder with a nod and a faint smile. "Call the case."

The bailiff's voice rang out. "Case 3443, *State* versus Welch, Brittney Rose. All concerned parties, please come forward."

Umi sat up straighter, her heart pounding as she heard Brittney's name. Next to her, Gloria exchanged a worried glance with Brian and Stephanie. At the defense table, Brittney's attorney, Rosa Williams, stood, readying herself as the judge reviewed the file.

A moment later, the door near the back of the room opened, and Brittney entered, escorted by a deputy. Her movements were stiff, her head bowed. Her hair hung limp and mostly brushed, a stark departure from her usual polished appearance. Her face was pale, etched with exhaustion and the weight of sleepless nights. As she stepped forward, she glanced briefly at the gallery, her eyes meeting Umi's for the briefest moment before darting away. She looked as though she were on the brink of a breakdown, but the subtle nod from Umi gave her the strength to keep moving.

The judge glanced at the ADA. "Mr. Miller, going for a hat trick today?"

ADA Scott Miller offered a faint smile. "Just the luck of the draw, Your Honor. Permission to approach?"

"Granted. Both counselors approach the bench," the judge instructed.

Rosa Williams introduced herself as she approached. "Good morning, Your Honor. Rosa Williams, representing the defendant, Brittney Rose Welch."

The judge nodded. "Good morning, Mrs. Williams." He turned to Miller. "This file lists Larceny in the Third. What's changed?"

"Your Honor," Miller began, his tone professional but firm, "new evidence indicates the defendant was coerced into committing the alleged larceny. In light of these circumstances, the state moves to dismiss the larceny charge. We have negotiated a guilty plea to Disorderly Conduct in exchange for a lenient sentence."

The judge turned to Rosa. "Mrs. Williams, what leniency are you seeking?"

"Your Honor, we request a nominal fine and time served, given my client's clean record and her cooperation with the state," Rosa replied.

The judge's expression was thoughtful as he reviewed the file. "First offense, clean record, no issues with the arresting deputies?"

"All true," Miller confirmed. "However, we have not yet spoken with Deputies Grace or White regarding their interactions with the defendant."

The judge leaned toward the bailiff. "Please summon Deputies Grace and White to the courtroom."

"Yes, Your Honor," the bailiff replied, departing quickly.

"Let's proceed in the meantime," the judge instructed, motioning for the attorneys to return to their tables.

Once seated, Miller rose and addressed the court. "For the record, Your Honor, the state moves to dismiss the charge of Larceny in the Third. We recommend a guilty plea to Disorderly Conduct, with leniency in sentencing, based on extenuating circumstances."

"Mrs. Williams, does the defense concur?" the judge asked.

"Yes, Your Honor," Rosa confirmed.

The judge turned his gaze to Brittney. "Miss Welch, please stand."

Brittney rose shakily to her feet. "Yes, sir," she said softly.

The judge's tone was measured as he addressed her. "Do you understand that pleading guilty to Disorderly Conduct can result in up to 90 days in jail, fines of up to $5,000, and court costs? Additionally, this conviction will remain on your record for up to five years."

Brittney nodded. "Yes, sir," she whispered.

"As part of my courtroom policy," the judge continued, "I require allocution from any defendant entering a guilty plea. Are you prepared to explain your actions and accept the court's judgment?"

Brittney swallowed hard. "Yes, Your Honor."

"Very well. I accept your plea," the judge said.

The courtroom fell silent until the door opened, and Deputies Grace and White entered. They stood near the front as the judge reviewed his notes.

Turning to Deputy White, the judge asked, "Deputy, can you provide an account of your interactions with the defendant?"

Deputy White stepped forward. "Yes, Your Honor. When I arrived on the scene, the defendant was already in cuffs, detained by Deputy Grace for striking the victim. Initially, she was emotional and non-compliant, but after a brief struggle, she calmed down. She later cooperated fully, providing information relevant to the case. This cooperation continued during booking, where she remained quiet and compliant throughout the weekend."

The judge nodded, then addressed Brittney. "Miss Welch, can you explain why you were arrested?"

Brittney's voice trembled. "Because I acted out, Your Honor. I was screaming and not listening to Deputy Grace. I was behaving like a child."

The judge's tone softened slightly. "Do you believe Deputy Grace was wrong to arrest you?"

"No, sir," Brittney said, tears welling in her eyes. "I deserved it."

The judge studied her for a moment. "Miss Welch, do you have anything you wish to say to the victim?"

Turning to the gallery, Brittney's voice broke. "Brian, Stephanie... I'm so sorry. I can't express how ashamed I am. I know I hurt you, and I would do anything to take it back," tears streamed down her face as she spoke.

The judge tapped his desk gently. "Take a moment to collect yourself, Miss Welch. Was that Brian Cole and Stephanie Welch you were addressing?"

"Yes, sir," Brittney replied.

"Mr. Cole and Miss Welch, please stand," the judge instructed.

Brian and Stephanie rose, their hands clasped tightly.

"Mr. Cole, how would you describe your relationship with the defendant?"

"She's like a little sister to me, Your Honor," Brian said firmly.

"And has your prosthetic leg been returned?"

"Yes, Your Honor. It was found in the school's prop room, undamaged."

"Miss Welch," the judge turned to Stephanie, "are you satisfied with your sister's apology?"

"Yes, Your Honor," Stephanie said softly.

"Thank you both. Please be seated," the judge said before turning his attention back to Brittney.

"Miss Welch, this court prioritizes justice and rehabilitation. I sentence you to six counseling sessions, to be completed within three months, and time served. Upon completion, this case will be dismissed. No fines or court costs will be imposed."

Brittney's eyes widened. "Thank you, Your Honor," she whispered.

The judge's expression softened. "Miss Welch, use this opportunity to learn and grow. Remember, family comes first."

"Yes, sir. I will," Brittney said, tears spilling freely now.

As she looked at her family, she saw Umi's tear-filled eyes and Gloria's encouraging smile. For the first time in what felt like an eternity, a small flicker of hope ignited within her.

"Good luck, young lady," the judge concluded, bringing down his gavel. "Case adjourned."

As the bailiff removed Brittney's restraints, Rosa Williams placed a comforting hand on her shoulder. "You'll be with your family soon; they're waiting for you."

Brittney hesitated. "I'm too embarrassed," she whispered.

"They love you, Brittney," Rosa said gently.

A short time later, Brittney exited from a door marked "Defendants Exit" and, in large letters above it, "Authorized Personnel Only."

Stepping into the grand hallway, Brittney's resolve broke as Umi and Gloria opened their arms. "I'm so sorry, Moms," she sobbed, clinging to them.

"We're here for you, Angel," Umi whispered, her voice steady despite the tears in her eyes. "Always."

Brittney paused, her eyes darting to the side where Brian and Stephanie stood, their faces soft. Her voice wavered as she whispered, "Mom, can it just be us in the car?"

Umi frowned, concern flickering across her face. "Why, honey?"

"I... I don't think I can look Brian or Stephanie in the eyes. I'm too embarrassed about what I've done," Brittney admitted, her voice trembling.

Before Umi could respond, Stephanie stepped forward, her movements hesitant but deliberate. Without a word, she wrapped her arms around Brittney, pulling her into a tight embrace.

"All I want is my big sister back," Stephanie said softly, her voice breaking as tears filled her eyes.

Brittney's shoulders shook as she returned the embrace. "Me too," she choked out, her tears falling freely.

Brian joined them a moment later, pulling both sisters into a hug. His voice was steady though thick with emotion. "And I want my little sister and best friend back."

Brittney glanced up at him, her face streaked with tears. "Even after all the pain I caused you?" she asked, her voice barely audible.

Brian tightened the hug. "Yes."

Behind them, Umi and Gloria exchanged a look, their expressions a mix of relief and quiet pride. Umi whispered, "And I have my angels back."

Brittney's voice broke as she admitted, "Richard said all of you would hate me if you found out what I did. And I believed him."

Gloria's voice was firm as she stepped closer. "Richard was wrong. That's not how family works. Family comes first. Always."

No one noticed a figure behind a pillar, watching them as they walked out. "Watch out, bitch."

CHAPTER 10

When they started to walk down the stairs to the courthouse, Umi's phone rang. As she answered, everyone stopped and watched her. Umi waved them on as she spoke on the phone. A minute later, she was walking to catch up with everyone.

As everyone got into the car, "Brittney, that was Captain Bishop and Sergeant King, detectives from the police department. They called because they need to interview you about what happened with Richard," Umi explained.

Stephanie could feel Brittney tense up the moment Umi finished speaking.

Brittney's voice was low. "Right now?"

"Yes, dear, while everything is fresh in your mind. They will be waiting for us at the house," Umi explained.

"Mom, I can't. Not now," Brittney said softly.

Stephanie looked up at Umi. "Interview her for what, Mom?"

Umi looked back at Brittney's face, clearly understanding her daughter's feelings. "Not now, Stephanie. Maybe later, okay?"

"Is she in trouble?" Stephanie asked.

"Oh no, dear. Not at all. Please, Angel, let it drop for now, okay?" Umi almost pleaded with her.

Stephanie squeezed Brittney's hand. "Okay, Mom. Brittney, just know I'm here whenever you want to talk."

Brian looked at Brittney. "I'll share something with you, Brittney, if you want to hear it."

Brittney nodded gently.

Brian looked at her, his face solemn. "I used to feel guilty about the accident. For months, I thought it was my fault. My therapist said I needed to stop punishing myself because of it."

Everyone looked at Brian as he continued.

"My thinking was, if I didn't have the archery contest, we wouldn't have been there, and the accident would have never happened. There are times I still feel like I caused it," Brian confessed.

Stephanie nodded. "Is that why you stopped shooting?"

Brian nodded.

Brittney asked, "How did you get over it?"

"Every Monday after school, I went to therapy and did a lot of talking. One day, while we were talking, I began to realize and believe it wasn't my fault, and I started feeling better that afternoon. I remember the day clearly because you and Steph were waiting for me to come home, and you both gave me my daddy's cross," Brian's voice caught in his throat.

"Brittney, I love you as much as I love Stephanie. I'd move mountains for either of you if asked. I will always be here for you, no matter what," Brian explained.

Brittney was still looking at Brian when she asked, "Talking about it? Telling the whole story? Is that how you worked past it?"

From upfront, Umi answered, "Yes, Angel. If anything, it helps you understand why it happened. It's not just telling what happened; it's more about how you felt about what you were doing and why."

Brittney nodded. "Is that why I was ordered to go to counseling?" Brittney asked.

"Yes, it is, Angel," Umi answered.

Umi reached a hand between the seats and placed it on the pile of hands already on Brittney's lap. "Brittney, Angel, just be brave and talk with the detectives. That's all you have to do."

Brittney looked up at her mom. "Even if," her voice fell off, thinking of Richard's threats.

Umi squeezed her hand. "Yes, dear."

After several seconds, Gloria added, "Brittney, remember, we love you unconditionally. Brian, when we get home, you and Stephanie go in and watch TV or something while Brittney, Umi, and I go to Umi's place. If we need you, we'll call. Okay?"

Brian nodded. "Yes, Mom."

Minutes later, while Brian and Stephanie were walking into his house, Brittney said softly to Umi, "Mom, I'm nervous. What if they don't believe me?"

Gloria opened the door and let Umi and Brittney walk in. "Brittney, just tell them everything as you remember it. Be truthful, and don't try to hide anything. You do that, then there's nothing to worry or be nervous about."

Brittney sat on the couch, looking around as if in a daze. Umi sat next to her, holding her hand. "You're going to be fine."

Gloria brought in several bottles of water from the kitchen. "Brittney, do you want me to go home? I don't want to make anything harder for you."

Brittney looked at her mom, then Gloria, before she answered. "No, Mom, I need you both here. I need you both to hear this... all of this from me."

Just as Gloria was about to sit down, the doorbell rang.

"Hello, I'm Gloria Cole," Gloria said as she opened the door.

"Good afternoon, Mrs. Cole. I'm Captain Ashley Bishop, and this is my partner, Sergeant Mary King. We're from the SV unit with the Beaverdam Police Department. Is Brittney Welch here?" Captain Bishop asked.

"Come in, please," Gloria said, opening the door all the way. "Brittney and her mom, Umi Welch, are on the couch."

As the two detectives walked in, Sergeant King asked Gloria, "And you are?"

"I'm an honorary mother. I've known Brittney and her twin, Stephanie, their entire lives," Gloria answered.

Umi stood up. "Thank you for coming. This is my daughter, Brittney. Please come in and have a seat," she said, pointing to Brittney.

Captain Bishop sat in the recliner next to Brittney, while Sergeant King sat next to Gloria on the love seat.

"Hi, Brittney, how are you?"

Brittney nodded. "Okay, I guess, ma'am," she said softly.

Captain Bishop leaned closer to Brittney, her voice calm. "Relax, okay? We know this is going to be hard. We're not here to blame or judge you for anything. We just need to hear what happened."

Brittney nodded. "Yes, ma'am."

Sergeant King looked at Umi and Gloria, then to Brittney. "We know things can be easier if the parents aren't in the room. Would you like to go someplace more private?" she asked.

Brittney looked at Sergeant King. "No. I need them here. I want them to hear this from me," she said softly but firmly.

Captain Bishop looked at Brittney. "How about we start at the beginning with how you met Richard?" she suggested.

Brittney shook her head. "It kind of starts before then, way before then. See, Stephanie and I have been crushing on Brian for a long time. We'd daydream together about him, our fantastic lives, adventures, and romance; Brian was always the hero, the champion, and, as we grew up, lovers. When I noticed Brian had eyes for Stephanie, I so wished it was me. I could see her starry eyes when we talked about him. Then, she described her first kiss with him, and, God, I wished it were me.

"I wanted it to be me so bad, for him to pay that kind of attention to me. After Stephanie and Brian started going steady, I felt like a third thumb. One day, sometime after July 4th, I was walking to Mifflet, and I saw some teens playing basketball, so I walked over, sat down, and watched. A couple of the guys were watching me when Richard came over and introduced himself. He flirted with me for a while until his friend Peter called him back into the game.

128

"They played every day, and I was there watching. I'd bring water or Gatorade for them. They liked it; they liked me. Richard was always saying nice, sweet things to me. He was a gentleman, just like Brian is. Then, one afternoon when it was hot, he invited me into his car to cool off in the air conditioning."

Brittney paused, her cheeks turning a soft rose color.

Captain Bishop leaned in and warmly asked, "Brittney, take your time and continue. What happened next?"

Brittney looked at Umi and whispered, "I'm sorry, Mom," before she continued.

"We kissed. I let him touch me, on my breasts. Then, it started getting overwhelming, and I asked him to stop, and he did. He said that I was a tease and that I owed him one. I explained that it was just too much, too fast, and that was all. He was still nice when we got out of his car.

"For the rest of the week, I watched him playing, thinking how hot he looked. After they were done playing, we'd all go to Dixies for soda and some munchies. He told me he had made deliveries for a company, and he asked about me. I told him about what happened with my dad and Brian. He and Peter started making jokes that I should be paying when we're at Dixie's."

"That Saturday, Peter was driving, and Richard and I were in the back seat. We were kissing, and he kept slipping his hand up my shirt. I told him to stop, especially with Peter right there, but he said Peter couldn't see a thing and told me to be quiet. I told him no, but he continued. He told Peter to go to a shop.

"Once we got there, he told Peter to get lost, that he was going to be there for a while. As soon as Peter was out of sight, Richard started kissing me hard, touching me all over, and being rough. I asked him to be sweet and gentle and slow down. He did, for a while, but he kept pressing me to," she paused, her eyes getting wet.

Sergeant King said softly, "Take your time, Brittney. What happened next?"

Captain Bishop reached a handover and gently squeezed Brittney's. "You're not at fault here. I know it's tough, Brittney. Just like Mary said, take your time," in a calm but firm voice.

Brittney nodded and took a deep breath while looking down. "He wanted me to do oral, but I couldn't. He, um, was ready and was pulling my head, and I said no, that we're done."

Brittney stopped as tears ran down her face. Umi had a hand on her shoulders, holding her tight. Gloria moved to sit on Brittney's other side, holding her other hand.

Brittney looked at her mom, her tears falling onto the carpet.

Captain Bishop squeezed gently. "What happened next?" she asked softly.

Brittney started sobbing. "He said I was a tease, that I owed him, and now he was going to get his payback. He flipped me over and pulled down my pants and panties, then he, um, well," Brittney looked at her mom, "I'm so embarrassed, Mom," while she sobbed.

Umi hugged her closer and went to say something, but Sergeant King interrupted her. "Brittney, there's nothing to be embarrassed about. Richard did this, not you," she reassured the teen.

Captain Bishop added, "Mary is right. This isn't your fault. You are being so brave right now. You are helping us make sure Richard doesn't do it again. Brittney, take your time and go on," in a calming but firm voice.

Brittney took a deep breath. "He forced me to have sex. It was horrible! It hurt; he grabbed, smacked, and pinched me hard. He bit me several times, and when I told him to go easier, he only got rougher. He left marks all over me. When it was finally over, as he was dressing, he told me to get dressed and added, 'Now that we're going steady, you should be coming here every afternoon. And if you think you're breaking up with me, I'll make sure everyone in the school knows you're a slut.'"

Brittney broke down completely. Gloria handed her some tissues, holding her tight. "It's okay, Angel, we're here, and he's never going to do it again."

Captain Bishop watched the teen. "Brittney, look at me," and waited for her to look up.

It took a while before Brittney could look at Captain Bishop. "Yes, ma'am," she said softly.

"Please, call me Ashley, okay? You just did the bravest thing you could do; you told someone about what happened. I know it's the first step of many, but this is always the hardest step."

Brittney nodded. "Yes, Captain Ashley."

"What you are doing now is going to make sure Richard can't do it again," Captain Bishop continued.

A few minutes later, Brittney added, "There's more. A lot more. I'm so embarrassed about it, all of it."

Sergeant King spoke up. "Remember, Ashley said it's none of your fault. Richard did this to you. There's nothing to be embarrassed about. When you're ready, tell us what happened next."

After a few more minutes of silence, Brittney continued. "As he got out of the car, he hollered that I needed to get dressed faster or else. I followed him into this shop. In the back corner, there was a makeshift living room with couches, chairs, and a big TV. Peter was sitting there as Richard walked over. 'I told you she was a slut. You should try her,' pointing at me. I hurried into the bathroom and overheard Peter answer, 'No thanks, I'm not into sloppy seconds.' I wasn't in the bathroom long when Richard started pounding on the door. 'Come on out, we're waiting on you.'"

"When I walked out, Peter was still on one of the couches; Richard was sitting on the other with an evil smirk on his face. He said to me, 'Show us that sexy body of yours.' I said no, and I could see the anger in his eyes. Peter said softly, 'Let it go, Richard,' but I guess Richard ignored him because he said, 'Strip now,' his voice was mean, sounding like if I didn't, I'd regret it."

Brittney's tears were still falling freely down her cheeks. "This is so hard to say."

Sergeant King replied softly, "We know."

Brittney looked at Umi, her eyes big and puffy, and went to say something, but words failed her.

"It's okay, Angel. It doesn't matter what you did; we will always love you unconditionally," Umi said softly while squeezing her hand, tears welling in her eyes.

At the same time, Gloria hugged her from the other side. "We all do, Brit, unconditionally."

Brittney took a deep breath and continued.

"Both of them watched as I took off my clothes. I tried to cover myself, but Richard kept telling me to put my hands down. I could see the marks on my arms from earlier. Then he told me to lie down on the couch. I told him that I was hurting, but he demanded that I do it. He told me that if I didn't do what he wanted, he would hurt my family."

132

Captain Bishop spoke softly. "Do you remember what he said?"

Brittney looked up. "It was something like, 'Your pretty little sister and mother won't be as pretty if you keep arguing with me. Now shut up and get on the couch.' He said this quite a few times while this was going on."

"Now or later on, over the course of time?" Sergeant King asked quietly.

"Almost every time I was there. It scared the crap out of me. I didn't want anything to happen to them," Brittney answered.

While the conversation was going on, both detectives could see the shock, horror, and tear streaks on Umi's and Gloria's faces.

Captain Bishop gently pushed. "What happened next?"

Brittney looked down at her lap. "He assaulted me in front of Peter. He bit, pinched, and slapped me a lot. One time, he bit my, um, breasts so hard I screamed and cried. He only laughed," Brittney answered shakily.

"What was Peter doing while all of this was going on?" Sergeant King asked.

"Every now and again, he'd look over. He looked scared, frightened, I don't know, but all he did was sit there."

Captain Ashley looked at Sergeant King while asking Brittney, "He didn't do anything?"

"No, ma'am, I mean Captain Ashley," she replied.

Captain Bishop gently pushed again. "What happened next?"

Brittney looked up. "When he was finished, he told me to get up, go home, and wash up. He added that I had best be there tomorrow afternoon, and I had better keep my mouth shut about all of it."

"What did you do?" Sergeant King asked.

"I got dressed as fast as I could and left. Then, on the walk home, I cried. When I got home, I took a long shower, changed, and washed my clothes. I felt so filthy and dirty that I didn't even want to go downstairs for dinner. When I went down for some water, I saw Mom and Stephanie watching the news. Mom asked if I was okay; I said I wasn't feeling well and went back upstairs. I was sure if I told them anything, Richard would keep his promise," Brittney explained.

Captain Bishop leaned in slightly, her voice soft yet steady. "Brittney, you're doing so well. Take your time. Can you tell us more about what happened after that?"

Brittney nodded, her hands twisting nervously in her lap. She glanced at her mother, then Gloria, before looking down at her lap. "It... it didn't stop after that. He started demanding things from me. Once classes started, he'd text me after school, telling me to meet him. If I didn't reply fast enough, he'd call, yelling that I was wasting his time."

Gloria gasped softly, clutching Brittney's hand. "Oh, sweetheart," she whispered.

Brittney continued, her voice trembling. "When I'd meet him, he'd always start out nice, asking about my day or complimenting me. But then it would change. If I didn't do what he wanted right away, he'd get angry. He forced me to perform oral sex on him," Brittney looked down. "I always gagged and threw up, then he'd laugh and say I'll get used to it. Once, he grabbed my arm so hard it left bruises for days. He said it was my fault for making him mad."

Umi's grip tightened on Brittney's shoulder, her face pale. "He hurt you like that?" she murmured, her voice shaking.

"Yes, Mom." Tears welled in Brittney's eyes, but she pressed on. "He'd pinch me, slap me if I didn't move fast enough, or if I tried to say no. And the biting... he bit me so hard sometimes I'd scream, and he'd laugh at me."

Captain Bishop's expression remained composed, but her eyes softened. "You're being incredibly brave, Brittney. Can you tell us more about what he said to you during these times?"

Brittney hesitated, taking a deep breath. "He'd call me names. Almost always, he called me *bitch*. He'd say I was worthless, a tease, or... a slut. He'd tell me I was lucky he even wanted me. If I cried, he'd say I was being dramatic, that I should just deal with it because I 'owed' him, or that he owned me."

Sergeant King glanced at Captain Bishop, her jaw tightening briefly before she turned back to Brittney. "And Peter, he was there?"

"Yes," Brittney whispered, her voice cracking. "Peter... he was usually there. Sometimes, he'd look like he wanted to stop it, but he never did. Richard would joke about it, saying Peter was too scared to 'join in.' He'd make me... do nasty, gross, and disgusting things... in front of Peter while he watched."

Sergeant King asked softly, "Things like?"

Between sobs, she managed to say, "Many times... it... was... putting things inside of me... in both... both... places."

Gloria's gasp turned into a soft sob, and she pulled Brittney into a side hug. "Oh, my angel," she whispered. "I'm so sorry."

Brittney clung to Gloria for a long minute, then pulled back, wiping her face. "He always made it clear I had no choice. Once, he told me that if I ever tried to stop seeing him, he'd make sure Stephanie paid for it. He said he'd hurt her so badly she wouldn't even look like herself anymore."

Umi's breath caught audibly, and her tears spilled over. "Oh, Brittney," she murmured, pulling her daughter close. "You should have told me."

"I'm scared, Mom," Brittney sobbed. "I didn't want anything to happen to you or Stephanie, Brian, or Mom Gloria. He said... he said he'd make me regret it if I ever talked."

Captain Bishop leaned forward, her tone gentle but firm. "Brittney, what you're telling us is important. You're helping us understand what happened, and you're giving us what we need to stop him. Take your time. What else did he do?"

Brittney hesitated, her body trembling as she took a deep breath. "Sometimes he'd tie me up," she said softly. "He said it was 'so I wouldn't try to get away.' He'd laugh when I cried or begged him to stop. And if I said it hurt, he'd do it harder, like he wanted to punish me for saying anything."

Captain Bishop nodded solemnly, her voice steady. "You're doing so well, Brittney. Did he ever threaten you directly while this was happening?"

Brittney nodded, her voice barely a whisper. "He'd tell me I was his property, that I didn't have a right to say no. He said I should be grateful he even bothered with me. A few times, he'd take his belt and beat my bottom because I was... too slow to do something."

Sergeant King's voice was calm but resolute. "Is there more you can tell us? Like marks?"

Brittney's voice cracked as she answered. "Yes. Bruises, scratches, bites... sometimes he'd slap me so hard my face would sting for hours. Once, he pushed me against a wall so

136

hard my head hit it, and I saw stars. The bites were hard. I screamed one time, and he hit me so hard I was groggy. The bites are so bad they bled for several days. Some still are."

Gloria's hand flew to her mouth as she stifled a sob, her other arm wrapping protectively around Brittney. Umi looked visibly shaken, her hands trembling as she held her daughter.

"Brittney, did anyone other than Peter ever see anything?" Sergeant King asked softly.

Brittney looked down at the carpet, nodding. "On Halloween, he made me dress in this, um, really revealing costume that showed all of the bite marks on my chest and breasts. It had a collar with a dog chain on it. He made me go into the Stop and Go with him, and the girl inside asked me if I was okay. He pulled the chain so hard that I fell on the floor as he screamed at the girl to mind her own, um, f-ing business."

Captain Bishop glanced at Sergeant King, nodding as she pressed softly, "Anyone else?"

There was a long pause before she spoke, her voice soft as tears ran down her cheeks again. "One more time. On the day it snowed, before Thanksgiving, he made me go into his car and get a backpack while I was naked. He forced me out to get it, and when I came running back in, the door was locked.

"I remember pounding on the door, begging, screaming. It felt like I was outside for a long time; I was so cold, and I was shivering. The guy from the store next to the shop came out; he saw me, and as he was walking over, Richard opened the door, yanked me inside, and slammed the door shut.

"I was so embarrassed. Richard took his belt and smacked my butt so hard it left welts; he said it was because I was overreacting," she continued as the tears continued to fall.

Sergeant King looked at Umi. "That was what, two weeks ago?"

Umi nodded. "Yes, about a week before the prank with the itching powder," she answered softly.

Captain Bishop looked at her. "Anyone else?"

Brittney started sobbing softly, her shoulders shaking as she shook her head no.

Umi pulled her tight, holding her in her arms while Gloria started gently stroking her hair, whispering into her ear, "It's all right, Angel. It's going to be all right."

Sergeant King looked at Captain Bishop, shaking her head slightly.

Captain Bishop nodded before speaking again. "Brittney, you've shown incredible strength by telling us all of this. I know it's been difficult, but you're helping us make sure he can't hurt anyone else. One important question, Brittney. Did you ever tell him to stop?"

Brittney nodded, wiping her tears. "Many times. I begged him to stop; I pleaded with him; I promised I'd do things for him or to him if he stopped, but it only made him do whatever harder," Brittney paused for a moment, trying to catch her breath when another wave of uncontrollable sobbing overtook her.

Umi hugged her daughter tightly, her own tears streaming down her face. "It's okay, Angel. No more today, okay, my love? You've been so brave, and I'm so proud of you."

"Captain Ashley, one thing I really need to tell you. It's about the itching powder and missing leg. When I told Richard I was pregnant, he was really mad. He told me that I had to get Brian to be the dad or else. He had an idea about getting me to

138

force Brian to be the dad. This is why the itching powder and missing leg things happened," Brittney softly admitted.

Captain Bishop stood and gently placed a hand on Brittney's shoulder. "Brittney, that explains a lot of other questions. But, like your mom said, you've done more than enough for today, Brittney. If you remember anything else, you can always tell us later. You're not alone in this."

There was a long pause where no one spoke; all that you could hear was Brittney's soft sobbing. Slowly, the sobbing slowed down, and the tears ended.

A few minutes after that, Captain Bishop asked, "How long has this been going on, Brittney?"

Brittney thought for a moment. "From about mid-July, almost every day in the afternoon, and after classes started, after school, and some weekends too. The last time something happened was last Monday," she answered.

Sergeant King asked warmly, "Is that the Monday the week when Brian's leg went missing, and you told your moms you were expecting?"

Brittney nodded. "Yes, ma'am."

"Did Peter ever do anything to you?" Sergeant King asked.

"No, ma'am, but he was there almost all of the time," she answered.

Sergeant King looked Brittney in the eyes, watching her eye movement when she asked, "Are you sure Richard is the father of your baby?"

Brittney's face was solemn as she nodded. "Yes, ma'am."

There was a long silence while Captain Bishop looked at Sergeant King and then said, "Brittney, what you just did, telling us all what happened to you, was very brave of you. It must have taken a lot of courage. Thank you for telling us."

Sergeant King looked at Gloria. "Mrs. Cole, how about you, Brittney, and Captain Ashley go and get some fresh air while your mom and I talk for a few minutes?" she suggested.

Understanding, Gloria stood up. "Sure. Come on, Brittney, let's get some fresh air."

Captain Bishop stood up, handing her a business card. "Mrs. Welch, if anything else comes up, or if Brittney remembers anything more, please call me. Doesn't matter when, okay?"

Umi stood up, taking the card. "What are our next steps?"

Captain Bishop looked at her. "Have you seen any of these injuries she's talking about?"

Umi shook her head. "You know as much as I do, Captain. This is the first time I've heard any of this. Gloria and I noticed a change in her over the summer, and a bigger one was the incident with Brian's leg, which brought us to your department. The night she changed in front of me, it was too dark in her room for me to really see anything."

Captain Bishop thought for a moment and replied softly so Brittney didn't hear, "I'm going to recommend you either take pictures of these injuries or go to the hospital and have them do a rape kit. It's very valuable evidence. I'll let King tell you all the details. For now, just hang tight and let us work on the case."

Umi nodded. "Okay. Thank you for everything."

Moments later, Sergeant King and Umi were sitting alone in the living room.

"Mrs. Welch, does it seem to you that Brittney is a bit overly emotional about all of this?" Sergeant King asked softly.

Umi shook her head. "No. She's always been like this. Both my girls have been diagnosed with bipolar disorder. Brittney's worse off than Stephanie; she gets depressed and emotional when things are really bad, but we manage."

"That's not in their file. Why's that?"

"When my husband was alive, we both decided not to have them labeled as special needs. We both believed it would make things worse for them, and for the most part, we were right. I have the documentation from their doctor if you need it. As it is now, their last visits were at the beginning of the summer, June, I believe, before any of this started," Umi replied.

A moment later, "Is this important?" Umi added.

"Well, without the documentation, the defense will do exactly what I just did and try to exploit it. If it's out in the open, then it won't be as bad. I take it you never saw these injuries, have you?" Sergeant King asked.

"No, like I just told Captain Bishop, you know as much as I do. This was the first time she'd said anything to anyone. This is beginning to sound like you don't believe her," Umi commented with an overly firm voice.

"No, Umi, it's not that. We have to vet all victims, and her emotions are almost off the scales. Right now, all we have is a 'she-said, he-said' story. That doesn't work too well. The more information and evidence we get, the better it is. I will say this: I believe her, without a doubt," Sergeant King replied.

Umi looked at her. "I'll go get their folders. Just as a reminder, the 'she-said' part of this is only 17 years old, hence your involvement here, and I'm sure he's older," her tone just as firm as she walked to the hutch and pulled two thick folders from one of its drawers. "Look, I'm sorry about how I said that. Really. And thank you for believing her," she said as she handed the folders over.

"It's okay, Mrs. Welch. I get it all the time; I know this is upsetting. No worries. Now, Mrs. Welch, we'll check into everything. It's obvious to me that something bad happened, to what extent, and the details that we need to figure out," Sergeant King reassured her.

"What are our next steps?" Umi asked.

"For right now, sit tight, let us get more details, and get pictures of these injuries if you can," she answered.

"Can we do them, or do you recommend someone or someplace else?" Umi asked.

"Well, the perfect place would be the hospital to do a rape kit, but that's a bit invasive and may cause Brittney to shut down and stop talking with anyone. Do you have a family doctor that Brittney trusts that you can take her to?" Sergeant King asked.

"Yes, we do. Will she know what to do?" Umi asked.

"If you give me her name, I'll call and give them a heads up. Okay?"

"Perfect. I have one of the office cards on the fridge," Umi said as she walked into the kitchen and back.

"Mrs. Welch, if you see, hear, or notice anything out of the ordinary, or Brittney remembers anything else, please don't hesitate to call either the captain or myself, okay?" The sergeant said as she walked to the door.

"Will do, Sergeant King. Thank you for everything," Umi replied as Sergeant King walked out the door.

Moments later, Gloria and Stephanie came back in, and Umi directed everyone to the living room. "Okay, we've got some homework to do."

Brittney looked up. "Homework?"

Umi smiled. "Yes. Both the captain and the sergeant suggested we do some things to help you and the investigation."

Brittney looked up. "Like what?"

Umi looked at Brittney, her face and voice soft. "Brittney, I need you to show Gloria and me the wounds Richard gave you."

Brittney's face turned a soft shade of red. "All of them?"

"Are the ones that hurt the most on your breasts?" Umi asked.

Brittney nodded, her blush deepening.

"Where he bit you, did it bleed?"

Brittney nodded, softly saying, "Yes."

Umi sighed. "Can you show me some of the ones that bled?"

Brittney pulled down the collar of her shirt and her bra top to show two rows of scabbing bite wounds across the top of her breast. "The bottom is worse," she said softly.

Umi's voice was still soft. "Are any closer to the nipples?"

Brittney's face was a bright red as she nodded her head. "Yes. They are the worst ones; they're still bleeding," she answered softly.

"Angel, are both breasts about the same?" Umi asked.

Brittney nodded.

Gloria looked. "Brittney, I think you should see a doctor about them. You know how dirty a mouth is, and if any of them get infected, it could cause problems with your breasts."

Brittney looked at Umi. "Really? Is it really that bad?"

Umi asked, "When were the last ones made?"

Brittney blushed fully. "Monday, after school. They're the ones closest to the, um, nipples," she said softly.

"The week of the whole leg thing?" Gloria asked.

Brittney nodded. "They still hurt. A lot. I've been taking Aleve; it helps some, but that's all," she added softly.

Umi. "Yes, Angel, really. Do you have any other bite marks like those?"

Brittney nodded. "Yes, on my butt cheeks and on the back of my shoulders. And one on my ribs."

Umi looked at her daughter. "I love you, and I know this sounds mean, but you need to have a doctor look at all the bites and the other marks Richard did to you. For two reasons: the most important being your health, and the other for evidence."

"But Mom, it's embarrassing," Brittney said softly.

"How about I call Dr. Heather and see if you can do a quick video call and let her decide?" Umi suggested.

"I guess I can do that," she replied quietly.

"But, Brittney, you've got to promise, if she says you should go in, we go, no complaints. I'll go as far as to try and make sure it's only Dr. Heather, you see, promise me," Umi offered.

Brittney sighed, nodding in agreement. "I promise, Mom."

"Good, I'll get that scheduled as soon as I can. Now, there may be other doctors you will need to see, specialists, and things like that. It's necessary. I know you've been through a lot, but your health comes first, and we need to make sure we are helping the detectives, okay?" Umi explained.

Brittney nodded. "Okay."

"Two more little things. You know, Stephanie and Brian love you and are more than likely to be very upset with everything today, especially the probability of other appointments. We need to tell them something, not all the details, but enough so they stop worrying about you and help if they can. You understand that?"

Brittney nodded.

Gloria spoke up. "I'll tell them only enough so that they understand how serious it is, nothing like what you explained to the detectives. Okay?"

Brittney looked down at the floor. "Are you sure, Mom? I don't want Brian or Stephanie to..."

Gloria cut her off. "Brittney, I've never lied to you. Never. They will understand, and they will still love you unconditionally. You've got to trust me on this, please, Angel. We can't leave them in the dark; they'll start feeling like you did when they started dating," Gloria explained.

Just as Gloria finished explaining, Umi gasped, like she had just figured out something horrible.

Both Brittney and Gloria looked at her, waiting to hear what she had to say.

"Angel, tell me truthfully, have you been taking your medication every morning?" Umi asked gently.

Brittney shook her head. "No. When I ran out, I thought you and Dr. Jenny were changing or stopping them."

Umi's face paled. "No, honey, I think I forgot about it."

Gloria looked at Umi, heavy, firm, and confident. "Oh no, Umi, don't you go there. Things happen; we fix them and go on," as she walked over and took Umi into a hug, whispering into her ear, "It's not your fault. It's Richard's. Period. You hear me? I love you as much as I did, Tom, and you did Kaito. We both know what I just saw on your face, and what I told you is true. Please? You've got to believe me, if not for your sake, then for Brittney's."

Umi hugged her back, whispering back, "I feel like it."

Gloria held her tight. "I know you do. I can feel it, and I can feel your fear."

Gloria looked down at Brittney, her mind already made up. "Brittney, come here, please."

Umi wondered at what Gloria had in mind as Brittney came over.

"Brittney, join us in the hug and tell your mom what Captain Ashley and Sergeant Mary told you several times," Umi directed.

Brittney looked at her mom. "It's not your fault, Mom," her voice full of conviction.

"Brittney, do you believe what you just said?" Gloria asked.

Brittney's eyes never came off her mother's eyes. "I believe it."

Gloria looked at Umi. "And do you?" she asked softly.

All three hugged tighter as she replied, "I believe it. Thank you, both of you," she said quietly.

Gloria's mind moved forward into mom mode. "One second, folks," and stepped away from the other two.

146

"Alexia. What's the status of Brittney's prescription?"

A moment later, the device replied, "Good afternoon, Gloria. Brittney has one prescription ready for pickup."

Gloria looked at her best friend. "Sorry, folks, 'Mom-Mode' is in effect. I'm going to get Stephanie and Brian; we're going to go and get that script. While we're in the car, I'm going to tell them Brittney was sexually assaulted by Richard a number of times and that he also physically and mentally abused her. I may need to add some minor details if they ask, but that's all. Brittney, if you want to tell them more, that's on you. Everyone got it?"

Umi smiled. "Thank you. I love you, Gloria."

Brittney hugged Gloria tightly. "Thank you for being here, Mom."

Gloria smiled as she walked towards the door. "You two might want to see if Dr. Heather can get on that video call sooner rather than later," and walked out.

Brittney looked at her mom. "Is she always this bossy with you, Mom?"

Umi smiled, holding her daughter tightly. "Only for the ones she loves the most. Let's get some phone calls made, okay?"

Brittney hugged her mother tightly. "Thank you, Mom. For everything."

*****

Gloria walked into her house to find both Stephanie and Brian cuddled on the couch, watching a movie.

The moment the door opened, Stephanie looked up, her face riddled with concern. "Mom, please, what's going on?"

Gloria grabbed her keys and purse. "Shoes on, we have an errand to run, and you both are going. Chop, chop, let's go," her tone was firm and persistent, as if she was trying to get 'slow kids' to move faster.

Gloria only had to wait a minute in the car before the two teens got into the back seat.

"Okay, serious family talk. That means it doesn't leave the family, got it?"

Brian answered as Stephanie nodded her head.

Gloria took a deep breath and started. "Okay, this is right to the point. Brittney was sexually assaulted, mentally and physically abused by Richard, several times, over a long period of time."

Gloria watched Stephanie's face in the rearview mirror as she heard her gasp.

"What happened..." Stephanie started.

Gloria cut her off. "Let me finish. Sometime in mid-July, Brittney ran into a couple of teens playing basketball at the courts outside of Mifflet. This Richard guy started flirting with her, and the two started talking, and, well, it eventually ended up with the first assault. He used her love for all of us to force her not to talk about it and to keep it going. This is how she ended up pregnant, and the sexual advances, accusing Brian of being the father and trying to get Brian's attention," she explained.

Brian's face dropped, and Stephanie's eyes got wet.

"This is the first Umi and I heard any of this, and Brittney's very upset over it all."

Brian swallowed hard. "I had no idea, Mom. What can we do?"

"Stephanie, I want you to know that you and Umi were directly threatened by Richard if she didn't do what he told her to do or if she spoke out. Because all of us are very close, the threat kind of involves us, too. For the last four hours, Brittney has been in crisis, and it took both detectives, Umi and I, to get her through it," Gloria continued.

Stephanie nodded. "Okay," she said as tears ran down her cheeks. Brian held her close while Gloria continued.

"She has some serious injuries that will probably require medical attention. In particular in private places, which makes it even harder for her to talk about it. Understand what that means?" Gloria asked.

Both teens nodded as Stephanie spoke softly, "We don't bring it up?"

Gloria smiled. "Spot on. There are a lot of details that should, and for now, unless Brittney brings them out, will remain private. Clear?"

Brian squeezed Stephanie harder. "Yes, ma'am."

Gloria pulled into their CVS, turned, and looked at Stephanie, her voice soft, firm, and commanding. "Sweetie, truthfully, have you been taking your medications like you should be?"

Stephanie nodded. "Yes, ma'am, every morning at seven a.m.," she replied softly.

"Good. Lastly, but the most important thing is that nothing changes between the three of you. I promised Brittney this, and I know how the three of you are, but I want this to be clear. Please, don't prove me wrong. No one is in trouble. The two of you need to be like Umi and I, be there to support and help her," Gloria explained.

Stephanie's wet eyes looked up at Gloria's. "How do we do that?"

Gloria thought for a moment. "Don't bring it up unless she talks with you about it. If she gets upset, comfort her. Let her talk about it and listen to her. The biggest thing you both have got to do, without a doubt, is to believe and reassure her it's not her fault, she didn't do anything wrong, and, just like you said at the courthouse, you love her unconditionally."

Brian looked up. "Mom, we'd both do that now, so what's the difference?"

Gloria smiled. "I knew you both would get it. The only difference now is you can't blame her or get angry with her about things because now it's really important. Brittney's going to be going through a lot of things, and we need to be there for her."

Stephanie nodded. "Okay, we can do that," she said as she looked at Brian.

"Stephanie, one more thing, and it's important. Brittney confessed about a number of your 'twins' talks, and, now more than ever, if she leans on Brian, don't get jealous, angry, mad, or anything. Got it?" Gloria asked.

Stephanie opened her mouth to say something, but Gloria cut her off. "It won't be like that. I know you and Brian both are still somewhat, um, raw about everything over the past few weeks, which is why I brought it up. If anything, the three of you should get closer during this time. Believe me, both of you, there's a lot at stake for Brittney right now. You both may not know it, but she still thinks you both hate her or will hate her after this conversation. Please, do your best to prove that feeling wrong."

Brian first looked at Stephanie, then his mom. "We can do that, Mom. Don't worry about it."

"I knew you both would understand; now, all we have to do is get Brittney to understand and believe," Gloria said with a forced smile.

"While I'm inside, the two of you should think about this conversation. If you have any questions about what I've told you, or what Umi and Brittney need, and my expectations of you both, ask them when I get back. Please don't wait until we get home; I may not be able to answer them. Okay?" Gloria asked.

Brian nodded. "Yes, Mom."

Gloria was in the CVS for a short time while the teens talked about what Gloria had just said. As they discussed things, Stephanie had an idea and explained it to Brian.

Brian was saying while Gloria was getting into the minivan, "Sounds like a plan to me. But you get to tell them."

Gloria turned to look at the teens. "Tell who what?"

"Mom, can we run to Walmart really quick? I have an idea, and I want to make it happen," Stephanie asked.

Gloria smiled. "Idea first, before I agree to anything."

Stephanie looked Gloria in the eyes. "Brittney and I have been sharing everything for our whole lives, and now I want to get three little necklaces, one for each of us, and I'm going to tell Brittney that I'm willing to share Brian with her."

Gloria's face dropped. "Share Brian? I don't think that's such a great idea. What if she gets the wrong idea?"

Stephanie smiled. "I'll talk with her in a 'twins' meeting and give her some rules: no secrets, honesty, and we've got to be open about everything. If she agrees, I will give her the necklace, and when Brian comes over, we will both give him his."

Gloria smiled. "That's really sweet of you, Stephanie, but it's a lot. Are you sure?"

Stephanie smiled, nodding. "Very sure. Remember our talk on the porch after our fight? This is going to fix all of that."

Gloria reached a hand to her. "Stephanie, you are simply awesome. Brian, how do you feel about this?"

Brian smiled. "After Stephanie explained it to me, I don't see any other way. Besides, I like the idea," he answered, his smile turning into a smirk.

Gloria made it as if she was going to smack him. "Don't be a pervert, young man!"

Brian made a sly face. "Well, I don't know. That's a hard thing not to do."

Before either could reply, he added, "Mom, Stephanie's rules cover all of that. Besides, the way you described what happened, I don't think she's going to be in the mood for anything like that."

*****

Hours later, at Brian's house, Gloria was in her recliner; Brian and Stephanie were cuddled under a blanket on the couch, having just finished watching Stephanie's favorite movie, "50 First Dates."

When the local news came on, Stephanie looked over to Gloria. "Mom, have you heard from Mom or Brittney?"

Gloria looked at the clock, realizing it was ten when she answered. "No, dear, I haven't."

Brian pulled Stephanie closer when he said, "I'm getting worried. It must be bad."

Gloria looked at her son. "Brian, remember, 'No news is good news.' Don't jump to conclusions, okay?" she reassured her son.

Stephanie pressed tighter to Brian. "Me too. It's hard not to get worried. They've been gone a long time," she said softly.

Gloria said confidentially, "Well, we know Dr. Heather said to come in right away. That's all we know. It seems like it could be foreboding, but before you get worried, wait for something to be worried about, okay, dear?"

Gloria hoped her confidence covered her own worries while she spoke.

Gloria thought through everything she'd witnessed, her mind not paying attention when her cell started ringing. As if coming out of a daze, she answered, "Hi, Umi."

"Hi, Gloria. Sorry it took so long to get back to you. Dr. Heather had us go into Lakewood because the wounds were so bad."

"Oh my God. What'd they do?" Gloria asked.

"Lots of pictures, a mammogram, lots of cleaning, impressions. Brittney lost control twice; the second time, they had to give her a mild sedative so they could finish. She has to go and see a mastologist in Pittsburgh. Gloria, it's bad," Umi said, almost in tears.

"Umi, hang in there; I'll be right over. Why don't you get a bag ready for Stephanie so she can sleep here? We can sit and chat all night if you want, okay?" Gloria offered.

"Thank you. See you in a few," Umi replied with measured control as she ended the call.

Gloria looked at the teens. "Okay, we know it's serious. You both heard me, so I'm going to say this because I'm the mom, not because of anything else. Let's assume, for the time being, Stephanie, you'll be in our guest room. Both of you, your word, no games, and no shenanigans," Gloria began.

Brian glanced at Stephanie, then looked at his mom. "My word, Mom, nothing you or Mom Umi wouldn't approve of," he said sincerely.

Stephanie looked up as well. "I promise, Mom," her voice was just as sincere.

"Good. If I'm not home, make sure you get up in time for the bus. Brian, watch your phone for any messages. Are we good?"

"We got it, Mom. Please let us know if there's anything we can do," Brian answered.

"Come with me to get Stephanie's bag. Jackets, it's cold outside," Gloria finished as she disappeared into her bedroom.

Stephanie turned to Brian, hugging him. "I'm worried, Brian."

Brian held her tightly. "So am I, sweets. So am I. Want me to walk with you?"

"I thought your stump was hurting?" she asked with a small smile.

"That doesn't matter. Let's get going," Brian answered his own question.

A minute later, Gloria was opening the door to Umi's house.

Umi gave the teens a quick rundown, explaining what was going on and that Brittney was in bed. After Brian and Stephanie gave Umi tight hugs and reassurances, as soon as the door closed behind them, Umi turned and held Gloria, laying her head on her shoulders, and let her emotions flow; her tears rolled down her cheeks as her sobs took control and rocked her body.

Gloria held her best friend tightly, a hand gently on Umi's head, rocking her gently, softly whispering, "It's going to be okay."

CHAPTER 11

O ver the course of the following week, Brittney could hear students whispering and pointing at her. Taylor and Ashly tried to convince her it was only talk, but they could tell Brittney was getting more and more anxious each day about it.

On Friday, Brittney received a note to report to Dr. Smith's office after lunch. The sound of the late bell echoed through the hallways as Brittney sat in the uncomfortable chair outside Dr. Smith's office, her stomach twisting in knots. The receptionist, Mrs. Cook, offered her a small, reassuring smile before returning to her paperwork. Brittney's thoughts raced. *Why was she here? What now?*

The door to the office opened, and Dr. Smith stepped out, his expression as composed and unreadable as ever. "Miss Brittney, please come in."

Brittney stood, clutching her books to her chest, and followed him inside. His office was meticulously tidy, with framed certificates and photos of family adorning the walls. The blinds were drawn, casting a muted light over the room.

"Have a seat," Dr. Smith said, motioning to the chair opposite his desk.

Brittney lowered herself into the chair, her fingers gripping her books tightly. "Did I do something wrong, sir?"

Dr. Smith leaned back in his chair, folding his hands neatly on the desk. "Not exactly. But I thought it was time we had a conversation."

Her heart sank. That kind of phrasing never meant good news.

"Brittney," he began, his tone measured and calm, "I've been hearing some troubling things. Rumors, to be specific."

Her face flushed with heat, and she dropped her gaze to her lap. "They're not true," she mumbled. "Whatever people are saying, it's just... lies."

Dr. Smith tilted his head slightly, studying her. "I'm not here to accuse you of anything. I understand that rumors can spiral out of control, and I've seen firsthand how cruel students can be. But I've also been made aware of other situations, things that might explain why these rumors have taken hold."

Brittney looked up sharply, her eyes wide with fear. "Like what?"

Dr. Smith's voice softened. "The prank involving Brian, for one. The accusations surrounding your... personal life. And, of course, the incident in the cafeteria earlier." He paused, allowing the words to sink in before continuing, "Brittney, this is not about punishment. This is about ensuring that you feel safe and supported here."

Her throat tightened as tears pricked her eyes. "I don't feel safe," she admitted, her voice trembling. "I feel like everyone's watching me, whispering about me, like I can't even breathe without someone judging me."

Dr. Smith nodded slowly. "That's exactly what I was afraid of."

Brittney hesitated, her voice breaking as she continued. "I didn't mean for any of this to happen. The prank, the lies, it's all gotten so out of control. And now... now it feels like I'm drowning."

Dr. Smith leaned forward, his tone firm but compassionate. "I won't pretend to fully understand what you're going through, Brittney. But I can tell you this: you're not alone. There are people who care about you and want to help. Your teachers, your family... even me."

Brittney sniffled, wiping at her eyes. "But what can I do? How do I make it stop?"

Dr. Smith let out a measured breath. "That's something only time and effort can resolve. But I do have a suggestion, something that might make things a bit easier in the meantime."

She looked up, her expression wary but curious.

"I'd like to offer you the option to switch to remote learning," he said gently. "You'd still be a full-time student, but you wouldn't have to be physically present at school. It would give you a chance to focus on your studies without the added pressure of navigating the social environment here. There will be a few days when you will have to come in, but other than that; it will be all at home or where you can log in from."

Brittney's mouth fell open slightly, the offer catching her off guard. "You'd... do that for me?"

Dr. Smith smiled faintly. "Brittney, my job isn't just about enforcing rules. It's about ensuring that every student has a chance to succeed. If this is what you need to feel safe and supported, then yes, I'd absolutely do that for you."

For a long moment, Brittney sat in stunned silence, the weight of the offer settling over her. It felt like a lifeline, a chance to step back from the chaos and regain some semblance of control.

Finally, she nodded. "I think... I think I'd like that. At least for a while."

Dr. Smith leaned back, his expression turning serious but kind. "That's good to hear. But, Brittney, I need to make one thing clear. If we make these arrangements, you have to promise me that you'll keep up with your studies. Remote learning requires discipline, and I need to know you're committed. This isn't about taking an easy way out; it's about finding a way forward."

Brittney straightened in her seat, her eyes filled with determination despite the tears threatening to spill over. "I promise, Dr. Smith. I'll do my best. I won't let you down, sir. You won't regret giving me this chance."

Dr. Smith studied her for a moment, then nodded. "That's all I needed to hear. We'll get started on the arrangements. And remember, Brittney, this doesn't mean you're giving up. It just means you're taking a different path for now."

"Thank you," she said softly, her voice thick with emotion. "Thank you so much."

Dr. Smith stood, extending a hand to her. "You're welcome. And if you ever need to talk, my door is always open."

Brittney shook his hand, a small but genuine smile breaking through her tears. For the first time in what felt like forever, she felt a glimmer of hope. It wasn't a solution to everything, but it was a start, and that was enough.

As she left the office, the hallway seemed a little less suffocating, the whispers a little less loud. She had a long way to go, but for the first time, she believed she could get there.

CHAPTER 12

T hat night, the faint glow of the bedside lamp cast soft shadows across Brittney's room, wrapping the space in muted warmth. Outside the window, the streetlights flickered, their halos shimmering faintly through the cold night air. Brittney sat cross-legged on her bed, her hands resting on a blank sketchpad that had been open for hours. The pencil she usually held with practiced ease now felt heavy, motionless in her grasp.

The house was unusually quiet. Umi's voice, steady but muffled, carried faintly from the living room. Brittney guessed she was on the phone again, probably with Gloria. Talking about her. Everyone seemed to be talking about her lately.

Her door creaked open softly, and Umi peeked in. "Brittney? Can I come in?"

Brittney didn't look up. "Sure."

Umi stepped inside, closing the door gently behind her. She had that look again, the one she'd been wearing all day. Kind, patient, but cautious. Like she was walking on eggshells, it made Brittney's stomach twist.

"I've been talking to Dr. Heather and the court liaison," Umi began, easing down onto the edge of the bed. "We've arranged for you to start counseling. They suggested we begin with a video session tonight."

Brittney's fingers curled around the edges of her sketchpad. "Tonight?" she echoed, her voice sharper than she intended. She immediately regretted it when she saw Umi flinch.

"Yes," Umi said, her voice calm. "Just one session to get started. You don't have to share anything you're not ready to. But Brittney... this is important."

Brittney's gaze dropped to the crumpled tissues on her nightstand. "And if I say no?"

Umi's hand rested lightly on Brittney's knee. "I don't think you will."

That made Brittney glance up. Umi's eyes weren't hard or demanding; they were filled with something else. Hope. Brittney hated it. Hope made her feel like she was already letting people down before she even tried.

"Fine," she muttered. "But don't expect it to fix anything."

Umi gave her a soft smile, leaning over to kiss her forehead. "I don't expect it to fix anything tonight. But it's a start."

Fifteen minutes later, Brittney sat cross-legged on her bed, her phone propped up on a stack of books. The room felt smaller somehow, the walls pressing closer as the sound of the call connecting filled the space.

On the screen, a kind-looking woman with silver-streaked hair adjusted her glasses. Her voice was warm and calming. "Hi, Brittney. I'm Dr. Meyers. It's nice to meet you."

Brittney shifted uncomfortably, her hands twisting in her lap. "Hi," she said, barely above a whisper.

Dr. Meyers offered an encouraging smile. "Before we start, I want you to know there's no pressure. You can share as much or as little as you want tonight. How does that sound?"

Brittney nodded slightly. "Okay, I guess."

The counselor tilted her head. "What's on your mind right now?"

Brittney hesitated, her gaze darting toward the blank sketchpad beside her. The weight of the past few days, the SVU interview, and the way Stephanie had looked at her pressed down like a heavy fog. She wanted to say something, anything, but everything felt too big to put into words.

"I don't know," she said finally. "Everything, I guess."

Dr. Meyers' expression didn't change, and her calm presence was steady. "That's okay. Let's take it one piece at a time. How about this: what feels the heaviest right now?"

The question lingered, and Brittney's throat tightened. She took a shaky breath, her voice breaking as she said, "That I ruined everything."

"What does 'everything' mean to you?" Dr. Meyers asked gently.

"Brian. Stephanie. My family." Brittney's hands curled into fists on her lap. "I hurt all of them, and I don't even know why I did it."

The counselor leaned forward slightly. "It sounds like you've been carrying a lot of guilt. But you're here, and that tells me you want things to be different."

Brittney's gaze flicked to the screen, her fingers loosening. "I don't know how to make it different."

"That's what we'll work on together," Dr. Meyers said. "You don't have to have all the answers right now. Taking this step, talking to me, it's already a big step forward."

The conversation shifted as Brittney slowly began to speak about her frustrations. She avoided eye contact, her words halting and uneven, but once she started, it became easier to keep going. Dr. Meyers guided her with gentle questions, letting Brittney lead the way.

They talked about the prank on Brian, how it had seemed harmless in her mind but spiraled into something she couldn't control. Brittney admitted to feeling invisible, how jealousy toward Stephanie had clouded her judgment, and how she never intended for anyone to get hurt.

"I don't know why I thought it would make me feel better," Brittney said at one point, her voice trembling. "It didn't. It just made everything worse."

Dr. Meyers nodded, her voice calm. "It's hard to think clearly when we're overwhelmed. But the fact that you're reflecting on it now shows growth, Brittney. You're learning from what happened, and that's a step forward."

For the first time that night, Brittney allowed herself to believe that might be true.

When the session ended, Brittney sat motionless on the bed. Her phone screen had gone dark, but the counselor's words lingered in her mind: *Hurt can heal.* She wasn't sure if she believed it, but a small part of her wanted to.

She reached for her sketchpad, flipping it open to the blank page she'd abandoned earlier. Her pencil hovered over the surface before touching down. The lines were slow and tentative, but they came. For the first time in weeks, she felt like she was drawing something worth finishing.

Downstairs, she heard Umi's voice again, murmured but steady. Brittney didn't need to hear the words to know her mom was still talking about her. But for once, it didn't feel suffocating. Instead, it felt... safe.

The pencil moved faster now, the lines taking shape. She wasn't sure what she was drawing, but it didn't matter. For the first time in a long time, it felt like she was doing something right.

Umi sighed, cradling a mug of tea as she sank into the armchair across from Gloria. The soft ticking of the clock on the mantel was the only other sound in the quiet living room. Gloria, seated on the couch, watched Umi with a knowing look, her hands folded around her own cup.

"How is she?" Gloria asked gently.

"She's... holding on," Umi replied after a pause, her gaze lingering on the faint glow of the kitchen light spilling into the room. "Some days, it feels like she's making progress. Other days, I feel like I'm losing her all over again."

Gloria nodded, her expression thoughtful. "It's not easy watching them struggle. You want to step in and take the pain away, but that's not how it works."

Umi leaned back, her fingers tightening around the mug. "I know. I keep telling myself I can't fix this for her, but it's hard to let go. She's my daughter, Gloria. I don't want her to feel like she's alone."

"She's not," Gloria said firmly. "You're here, aren't you? She knows that even if she doesn't say it. Kids like Brittney... they push the hardest when they're hurting the most."

Umi let out a quiet breath, her lips curving into a faint smile. "You always know what to say."

Gloria chuckled softly. "Not always. But I've had my share of sleepless nights worrying about Brian. You remember when Brian refused to leave his room after the accident?"

Umi nodded, her brow furrowing. "He was so angry with himself."

"And with everyone else," Gloria added. "But the only thing that brought him back was knowing he had us. Even when he didn't want to admit it."

Umi tilted her head, considering the words. "You think Brittney feels that?"

Gloria smiled gently. "I think she's starting to. But it's a process. She'll stumble, she'll push, and she'll fight it every step of the way. But as long as we're here when she's ready, she'll find her way."

The clock chimed softly in the corner, marking the late hour. Umi glanced at it and sighed. "I just hope she knows how much I love her. Even when I'm pushing her to do the hard things."

"She knows," Gloria assured her. "Kids always know. Even if it takes them a while to show it."

They sat in silence for a while, the warmth of their tea and the quiet companionship easing the weight of their worries. Upstairs, the faint scratching of Brittney's pencil against paper continued a soft rhythm in the night.

CHAPTER 13

Three days later, the late afternoon sun bathed the Welch living room in soft, golden light, casting long shadows on the floor. Stephanie sat cross-legged on the couch, her literature textbook open on her lap, a pencil poised in her hand but unmoving. The sound of the dishwasher in the kitchen added a soothing backdrop to the otherwise quiet house.

From the dining doorway, Umi appeared with a steaming mug of tea, her gaze falling on her daughter. "That essay must be tough. You've been staring at the same page for ten minutes," she teased gently.

Stephanie looked up, managing a faint smile. "It's *Othello*. Betrayal and backstabbing. Great family-friendly material."

Umi chuckled, sitting on the arm of the couch. "Sounds like fun. What angle are you taking?"

Stephanie shrugged, twirling the pencil between her fingers. "I'm writing about how perspective changes how betrayal is viewed, but... it feels wrong somehow. Like I'm missing something."

"Maybe it's not the essay that's bothering you," Umi said, her tone light but pointed.

Stephanie froze for a moment, then shook her head. "It's fine, Mom. Just school."

"Uh-huh," Umi replied, her knowing look softening into a small smile. "And I'm just an innocent bystander."

Before Stephanie could respond, the front door swung open, and Gloria's voice rang out, "Knock, knock! Hope you don't mind us barging in!"

Gloria stepped inside, carrying a container of cake in one hand and her purse in the other. Brian followed behind, hands shoved in his jacket pockets, his gaze immediately landing on Stephanie.

"Let me guess," he said, leaning casually against the doorway. "Homework meltdown?"

Stephanie scowled. "It's not a meltdown. And it's not just homework."

"Sure it's not," Brian teased, his grin widening. "You look like you're gearing up for battle."

Gloria placed the container on the counter, turning to Umi. "We thought we'd check-in. And I brought dessert treats. One less thing for you to worry about tonight."

"Thank you," Umi said warmly. "But if you're staying for dessert, you're doing dishes."

Gloria laughed. "Fair deal."

Brian took a seat on the edge of the couch. "So, what's *really* going on, Steph? Because you're giving off serious dragon-slaying vibes."

Stephanie shot him a sharp look. "Nothing's going on. It's just... a lot, okay?"

Gloria's gaze flicked between Umi and Stephanie, a glimmer of understanding in her eyes. "Brian, sweetheart," she said gently, "why don't you let us have some girl talk? Go entertain yourself for a bit; watch one of your monster movies. You know, the ones with the rubber suits and creatures that look faker than a bad wax museum?"

Brian raised an eyebrow, mock offense spreading across his face. "Hey, those are classics! But fine, I'll leave you to it."

Brian stood, giving Stephanie a reassuring nudge on the shoulder as he passed. "Good luck. Don't let them gang up on you too much."

Stephanie rolled her eyes but smiled faintly. "I'll be fine. Go."

Once the door clicked shut behind him, Gloria settled into a chair, and Umi leaned forward, resting her elbows on her knees. The room felt quieter now, the earlier lightness fading into a more introspective calm.

"Steph," Umi began, her voice soft but firm, "have you thought about talking to Brittney? About the fight?"

Stephanie hesitated, her gaze dropping to the textbook in her lap. "I have... but not exactly."

Gloria raised an eyebrow, leaning forward slightly. "What do you mean by 'not exactly'?"

"I mean," Stephanie said, fidgeting with her pencil, "I know I need to apologize. I don't want Brittney to think I don't care

169

about what happened. And I've been thinking about my idea, about sharing Brian, and how to bring it up. It's not just about the fight; it's about fixing things between us. I just... I don't want to mess it up."

Gloria tilted her head, her lips curving into a thoughtful smile. "That's a lot to put in one conversation, Steph. But it sounds like you've been thinking this through."

Umi nodded slowly. "It's a good place to start, Angel. Apologizing is the first step, and bringing up Brian shows you're serious about making this work. The timing feels right, but it's not just about the words; you need to show her that this is about *her*, about your relationship."

Gloria leaned forward, her tone gentle but serious. "If you bring this up, it has to come from a place of love, Steph. Brittney needs to feel like this isn't just a solution; it's about her belonging and being important to you."

Stephanie nodded, her voice trembling slightly. "That's the whole point. I don't want her to feel like she's being left out or like I'm pushing her away."

"She might not accept everything right away," Umi said. "But this is about opening the door. Show her you care, and she'll see it."

Gloria added softly, "It's a big step, sweetheart. But I think it's the right one."

Stephanie nodded again, her resolve strengthening. "Okay," she said finally. "I'll talk to her tonight."

Umi reached out, squeezing Stephanie's hand. "Good. Take your time. One step at a time."

Gloria smiled warmly. "You're doing the right thing, Steph. Brittney needs to see that you're ready to make this work."

Stephanie stood, clutching her textbook tightly. She hesitated for a moment, then glanced toward the stairs. "Thanks," she murmured before heading toward Brittney's room.

As the sound of her footsteps faded, Umi leaned back with a soft sigh. "One step at a time," she repeated.

*****

Stephanie gently knocked on Brittney's door. "Britt?"

She waited a few moments and knocked again, gently opening the door. Brittney's room was dimly lit, the soft amber glow of her desk lamp casting long shadows on the walls. The space, unusually tidy, felt too neat to be comfortable. Brittney sat cross-legged on her bed, clutching a pillow tightly against her chest, her eyes darting to the door as Stephanie quietly stepped inside and closed it behind her.

Stephanie hesitated, her hands clutching a small gift bag, before crossing to the bed. She perched on the edge, her expression unusually soft.

Brittney's eyes narrowed slightly, her voice sharp with weariness. "What do you want, Steph? Haven't I been through enough this week?"

"I know, Britt," Stephanie said softly, crossing the room and sitting at the edge of the bed. "This week was... a lot. And I'm not here to lecture you. I promise. I just... I need to talk to you."

Brittney frowned, suspicion lacing her voice. "About what?"

"About us. About everything that's happened," Stephanie replied, her hands clasped nervously in her lap. "I've been thinking a lot about the fight we had... about what I said and what I did. I was so angry, Britt. I'm sorry."

Brittney blinked, her voice trembling with a mix of anger and sadness. "You mean when you punched me? And when you told me you hated me?"

Stephanie winced, guilt flashing across her face. "Both. All of it. I was wrong, Brittney. I was hurt and frustrated, but that doesn't excuse what I did. I shouldn't have hit you, and I shouldn't have said those things. You're my sister. My twin. I love you, and I hate that I let my anger get in the way of that."

"You really hurt me, Steph," Brittney said quietly, her grip on the pillow loosening just slightly. "Not just with the punch. I thought I lost you."

"You didn't lose me," Stephanie said quickly, her voice full of quiet conviction. "I was mad, sure. But I never stopped loving you, Britt. I never will."

Brittney's shoulders sagged, the tension in her body easing just a fraction. Her voice came out small, vulnerable. "Then why did it feel like you hated me?"

Stephanie hesitated before answering, her gaze falling to her lap. "Because I didn't know how to handle it. I was so hurt by everything that happened—the lies, the arguments, the fight—and I felt like you didn't care about me anymore. But I see now... I was wrong. And I think I understand why you did some of the things you did."

Stephanie took a deep breath. "I know you tried to fix things. I was called into Dr. Smith's office, and he explained to me what you did. When I came home, I should have said something to you, but I couldn't. I'm so sorry."

Brittney flinched, pulling the pillow tighter. "I didn't want to hurt you, Steph. I just... I don't know. I felt so lost. So jealous."

Stephanie's lips quivered into a small, sad smile. "Not jealous, Britt. Envious. There's a difference."

Brittney frowned, confused. "What difference?"

"Jealousy is being afraid someone will take what's yours," Stephanie explained gently. "Envy is wanting something someone else has. And that's what this is, right? You saw me with Brian, and you want what we have."

Brittney hesitated, her voice barely audible. "Yeah. I wanted what you had. I wanted to feel loved. The way he loves you."

Stephanie hesitated. "The truth?"

Brittney nodded softly, looking Stephanie in the eye. "And I still do," her voice soft, just over a whisper.

Stephanie smiled softly. "You deserve that, Britt. And I think I know a way to make things better."

Brittney's eyes narrowed slightly, suspicion creeping in. "What do you mean?"

Stephanie reached for the gift bag she had brought and handed it to Brittney. "Open it," she said, her voice calm but a little nervous.

Brittney frowned but obeyed, pulling out a delicate necklace. The charm was simple but meaningful, a small heart split into two halves, with the words "Together Always" etched along the edges. Her breath caught as she held it up, her eyes flicking to Stephanie.

"It's beautiful," Brittney murmured. "But... why?"

Stephanie straightened, meeting her twin's gaze with quiet determination. "Because I've decided something. Britt, we've shared everything our whole lives—clothes, toys, birthdays...

Mom and Dad's attention. And now, I want us to share something else."

Brittney's grip on the necklace tightened, her brow furrowing. "What are you talking about?"

Stephanie took a deep breath. "I'm talking about sharing Brian."

The room fell silent, Brittney staring at her sister in disbelief. "You're kidding, right?"

"No," Stephanie said, her voice steady. "I'm serious, Britt. I love Brian, and I know you love him too. I don't want to fight anymore. I don't want to lose you."

Brittney's jaw dropped, her voice trembling. "You're serious? You're saying... we'd both..."

Stephanie nodded, a small, reassuring smile playing on her lips. "Yes. We'd share him. No secrets, no lies. Just honesty and trust. I've already talked to Brian about it. He loves you, and he's open to the idea if we both agree."

Brittney stared at her sister, searching her face for any sign this was a cruel joke. But Stephanie's sincerity was unmistakable. Slowly, a small, incredulous smile began to form on Brittney's lips.

"He loves me? This is insane," she whispered. "You're actually serious about this?"

"Dead serious," Stephanie replied. "We'd set rules, of course. No sneaking around. If one of us spends time with Brian, the other knows about it. And we have to respect each other's boundaries. If something feels off or uncomfortable, we talk about it. No secrets, that's the big rule. I'm not talking about birthday presents or things like that; I'm talking about feelings, desires, and the things we do."

Brittney's grip on the necklace loosened, a quiet laugh bubbling up from her chest. "This is so weird. I can't believe we're actually talking about this."

Stephanie chuckled, her expression softening. "We've always done things our own way, Britt. Why stop now?"

Brittney let out another laugh, and the sound was lighter this time. "Okay," she said softly. "Let's try it."

Stephanie's smile widened, and she reached into her lap, pulling out another gift bag. "This one's for Brian. When he comes over, we'll give it to him together. Deal?"

Brittney nodded, her eyes shining with a mix of excitement and nervousness. "Deal."

As the initial wave of nervous giggles subsided, Brittney leaned back against the wall, her pillow now discarded beside her. Her expression turned thoughtful, a flicker of something wistful crossing her face.

"You know," Brittney began, her voice soft, "this… sharing thing… it feels a little like something out of one of our old stories."

Stephanie tilted her head, intrigued. "Old stories?"

"Yeah." Brittney smiled faintly, her gaze distant. "Remember when we used to play pretend? We'd make up all those ridiculous fairy tales like we were princesses waiting for our prince. Except we always decided we'd share the same prince so we could stay together."

Stephanie's lips curved into a grin. "Oh, yeah. The prince who always wore a cape and rode a white horse, even if we only had the old mop and blanket to use as props."

Brittney giggled, and the sound light was genuine. "And how we made him promise to love us both equally, or else we'd lock him in the tower with a dragon."

Stephanie laughed along with her, the warmth of the memory filling the room. "I guess some things don't change, huh?"

Brittney's expression grew more serious, though a small smile lingered on her lips. "Maybe we should do something like that now."

Stephanie blinked, caught off guard. "Like what?"

"A ceremony," Brittney said, her voice gaining confidence. "Something to make it official. You know, so it's not just words. Something... romantic, like we always dreamed about when we were kids."

Stephanie considered this for a moment, her brow furrowing. "You mean, like... vows or something?"

"Not vows, I'm thinking promises, and not too formal," Brittney clarified. "Just something special. For us. And Brian."

Stephanie nodded slowly, her own excitement beginning to build. "Okay. I like this. But what kind of ceremony? What would it look like?"

Brittney's eyes sparkled with a mix of nostalgia and determination. "It has to be beautiful, like one of our stories. Candles, flowers, maybe even some music. And it needs to be meaningful. Like... we each say something to Brian, and he says something back to us."

Stephanie's grin widened, and she leaned forward eagerly. "Okay, I'm in. But what kind of things would we say? And what would Brian have to do?"

Brittney tapped her chin thoughtfully. "Well, we'd have to tell him why we love him. What makes him special to us? And he'd need to do the same. But…" She hesitated, her cheeks flushing slightly. "It shouldn't just be about love. It should also be about trust and being honest with each other."

Stephanie nodded, her eyes lighting up. "Ooh, and we could each give him something, like a token or a keepsake. Something that symbolizes… I don't know, our bond or whatever."

Brittney clapped her hands together, her excitement bubbling over. "Yes! And he could give us something too. Maybe matching bracelets or rings or something."

Stephanie tilted her head, a teasing grin on her face. "Rings? Going all out, aren't you?"

Brittney shrugged, giggling. "What can I say? I've always been dramatic."

A moment later, Stephanie added, "Got it! We have Brian give you and me matching necklaces, and then we both put one on him!"

The two dissolved into laughter again, the tension of the day melting away as they began brainstorming in earnest.

"What about the setting?" Stephanie asked. "Where would we do this?"

Brittney's expression turned pensive. "Somewhere quiet and private. Maybe in the backyard, with fairy lights and candles. Or… oh! What if we did it in that little clearing by the lake?"

Stephanie's eyes widened. "The one where we used to play as kids? That would be perfect."

Brittney nodded, her smile widening. "Exactly. And we could decorate it with flowers and ribbons. Make it look magical, like a prince and his princesses."

Stephanie leaned back, letting the image form in her mind. "Okay, so we've got the place. And the decorations. What else?"

"Umm," Stephanie hesitated, her voice softening, "it's cold outside. We need someplace inside, like the family room downstairs," Stephanie suggested.

Brittney hesitated. "Perfect. And we can keep Brian out of there until then. But there should be a moment where we... I don't know, we promised to support each other. Like, not just to Brian, but to each other too. This whole thing only works if we're all on the same page, right?"

Stephanie reached out, squeezing her sister's hand. "Right. I like that. Maybe we each say something to each other before we talk to Brian."

The two looked at each other, warmth in her eyes. When Brittney said, "Stephanie Ann Welch, I promise to always love you, be honest, truthful, and brave when we need to talk," her eyes glistened in the warm light of the room.

Stephanie's eyes immediately wetted. "Brittney Rose Welch, I promise to always love you, to be honest, truthful, and brave when we talk," she repeated.

As the words left her mouth, Brittney leaned close, her hands going around her sister. "Thanks, Steph. For... all of this. I don't know if I deserve it, but... thank you."

Stephanie's voice was gentle but firm. "You do, Britt. We both do."

The two sat in silence for a moment, the weight of their shared understanding filling the room. Then Stephanie broke the quiet with a mischievous grin.

"So... what are we making Brian wear for this?"

Brittney burst into laughter, wiping at her eyes. "I don't know! Something nice, I guess. But nothing too fancy. He'd look ridiculous in a tux."

"True," Stephanie agreed, giggling. "Maybe just a button-up shirt. Oh! And we should make him bring something. Like flowers. For both of us. We still have our junior prom dresses, right? We can use them."

Brittney clapped her hands together. "Yes! And he has to bow. Like a proper prince."

Stephanie shook her head, still laughing. "Poor Brian. He has no idea what he's in for."

As their laughter subsided, Brittney sighed contentedly, her expression softening. "This is going to be perfect, Steph. I can feel it."

Stephanie nodded, her own excitement mirrored in her twin's eyes. "Yeah. It really is."

Brittney sat back. "Do the moms know?"

Stephanie smiled. "I had to tell Gloria in order to get to Walmart."

Brittney smiled. "Do you think we can get them to be our 'witnesses' to this, um, ceremony?"

Stephanie smiled and wiped her face dry. "I think they'd be honored."

CHAPTER 14

That Wednesday night, dinner was unusually lively. The tensions from the previous weeks were gone, and the dining room was alive with the soft clatter of forks and plates and the warm hum of conversation. Gloria passed a basket of bread across the table, her eyes sparkling as she caught Brian fidgeting with his napkin.

"You're going to wear a hole in that napkin if you're not careful," she teased, her grin widening. "What's on your mind, Brian?"

Brian froze mid-fidget, his cheeks reddening. "I was just… thinking about all of this. Making sure I don't mess anything up."

"You can't mess it up," Stephanie chimed in, leaning forward with a playful smile. "Unless you trip over your own feet. Then all bets are off."

Brian groaned though a small smile tugged at the corner of his mouth. "You're so helpful."

"Yeah, I can see it now," Brian added, his tone dry but laced with humor. "I trip, panic, grab for something, and it just happens to be your dress. Then you fall, grab Britt's arm, and she ends up going down, too. The whole thing turns into a comedy routine."

Stephanie burst out laughing, nearly choking on her drink. "Oh my God, Brian! You'd be a one-man disaster."

Brian shrugged, a grin breaking through his mock seriousness. "Hey, at least I'd make it memorable."

Even Brittney couldn't help but giggle softly, her lips twitching into a small smile. "Memorable... sure," she murmured, her voice hesitant but amused.

Gloria chuckled, handing Brian the butter dish. "You'll be fine. Just don't forget what I told you—no *pervert* jokes."

Brian tilted his head thoughtfully, his grin turning slightly mischievous. "Well, they wouldn't be *pervert* jokes. But can we just end the whole *pervert* thing, please? I'm sorry I even joked about it!"

Gloria raised an eyebrow, clearly holding back a laugh. "Noted. We'll retire it. For now."

Umi chuckled, her voice warm. "Relax, Brian. This isn't a test. It's about being present and being honest. You've already passed the hardest part—earning their trust."

Brian nodded, though his fingers tightened slightly around the napkin in his lap. "Thanks, Mom Umi."

As the conversation shifted, Brian took another bite of the meal in front of him. He paused, glancing toward the table with a thoughtful look. "This is really good. Who made dinner tonight?"

Stephanie's grin widened as she gestured toward Brittney with her fork. "That'd be Brittney. She's the cook tonight."

Brittney blinked, startled by the unexpected praise. Her cheeks flushed as she glanced up at Brian. "I just… followed the recipe," she said quietly, her voice soft.

Brian's smile deepened, genuine and warm. "Well, you nailed it. Seriously, Britt. This is really good."

Brittney's lips twitched into a small, hesitant smile, though her gaze quickly fell back to her plate. "Thanks," she murmured, her voice barely audible.

Stephanie reached over, nudging her sister lightly. "See? You don't give yourself enough credit."

Brittney shrugged slightly, but the faint smile remained on her face. Stephanie caught the moment, slipping her hand under the table to give Brittney's hand a gentle squeeze. Brittney glanced at her, and Stephanie offered her a quiet, reassuring smile.

"You'll see," Stephanie said, her tone low and just for Brittney. "It's going to be perfect. We'll make it perfect."

Brittney swallowed hard, her voice coming out in a whisper. "Okay."

Gloria and Umi exchanged a quick glance, their expressions softening but leaving space for the twins' moment.

"Speaking of perfect," Gloria said, leaning back in her chair. "Brian, any final thoughts about Saturday? Or are you ready to win the trust and affection of two headstrong girls for life?"

Brian let out a nervous laugh. "I mean when you put it like that..."

Stephanie grinned, her hand still resting on Brittney's under the table. "No pressure, Brian. Just remember who's who. I'm Stephanie, and I'll be in lavender, and she's Brittney, dressed in blue," she said jokingly.

Brittney looked up at Brian then, her expression soft and unsure. "I'm sure... you'll do great," she said hesitantly, her voice quiet.

Brian smiled, a warmth in his eyes that seemed to settle Brittney's nerves. "Thanks, Britt."

Gloria chuckled as she began collecting plates. "Okay, enough seriousness. Who's doing the dishes tonight?"

Brian sighed, standing up and reaching for a stack of plates. "Guess I've got my first job as the guy dating two headstrong girls."

Laughter rippled through the table as the family moved toward the kitchen, the atmosphere warm and light as the conversation drifted toward the weekend's plans.

*****

By Saturday evening, the girls transformed the family room into a scene straight from a childhood fairy tale. Soft, golden string lights crisscrossed the ceiling, casting a warm glow over the space. A line of electric candles flickered along the perimeter, their light dancing over carefully arranged flowers and ribbons draped across the furniture. It was magical, serene, and perfect.

Brian stood near the door, nervously adjusting the ribbon tied around the small bouquets of wildflowers in his hands. The room, glowing with soft light, seemed to shimmer with a warmth that only heightened the weight of the moment. His crisp button-up shirt felt tighter than usual, and he shifted on his feet, glancing toward Gloria and Umi, who were standing together near the edge of the room.

"You look like you're about to walk into a job interview," Gloria said softly, her lips curving into a small, reassuring smile. "Relax, sweetheart."

Brian chuckled nervously, the sound more like an exhale. "I'd probably be less nervous if it were a job interview. This feels... big. Like everything changes after tonight."

"It *is* big," Umi said, stepping forward, her expression kind but steady. "And things will change. But big doesn't have to mean bad. It means growth. And if anyone can handle that, Brian, it's you."

He nodded slightly, looking down at the bouquets as his fingers fidgeted with the ribbon. "I want to believe that. I really do. I love them, both of them, but what if I can't make it work?"

Gloria moved closer, placing a firm but gentle hand on his shoulder. "Every relationship takes work, Brian. It's not about being perfect; it's about being there. About being honest, learning from your mistakes, and sticking with them even when times are hard. You've already shown you can do that."

"Exactly," Umi added, her voice filled with quiet conviction. "Relationships aren't a straight path, especially not this one. There will be challenges, yes, but the three of you have something rare. You've learned what it means to share, to forgive, to grow together. That's a foundation most people don't even dream of starting with."

Brian glanced up at them, his expression uncertain but hopeful. "What if I'm not enough? For both of them?"

Gloria squeezed his shoulder, her tone unwavering. "You already are. You wouldn't be here if you weren't."

Umi stepped closer, her eyes warm with reassurance. "Brian, I've raised two headstrong, beautiful, and sometimes frustrating girls. I've watched them laugh, cry, and fight over everything, from toys to boys, and who has the bigger slice of the pie. But they always come back to each other. They've chosen you, and that says a lot about who you are."

Brian's lips twitched into a faint smile. "Thanks, Mom Umi. I just... I don't want to let them down."

Gloria's grin turned playful, her voice lightening the mood. "Then don't. And if you do, just make sure you grovel. We moms love a good grovel."

That earned a real laugh from Brian, the tension in his shoulders easing. "Noted. Groveling. Got it."

"And," Umi chimed in, her eyes sparkling with mischief, "maybe don't leave the toilet seat up. That's a battle you'll never win."

Brian grinned, the humor easing his nerves even further. "Groveling and toilet seats. I'm learning a lot tonight."

Gloria stepped back slightly, her gaze softening as she took in the glowing room. "Brian," she said, her tone more serious now, "you've always been a part of the girls' lives; tonight just confirms how all of you feel about each other. But remember, it's not the ceremony that matters most; it's what you do afterward. Keep showing up for them, both of them, every single day."

Umi nodded, her voice quiet but firm. "And don't forget, relationships don't just take work; they take support. You're not alone in this. Lean on us if you need to. We're here for you, just like you've been there for our girls."

Brian's throat tightened with emotion, and he nodded, looking between the two women who had shaped so much of his life. "Thank you," he said softly. "Both of you. I wouldn't have made it this far without you."

Gloria glanced at her watch, her smile widening. "Well, you're about to make it a little further. They'll be here any minute. Are you ready?"

Brian took a deep breath, straightened his posture, and for the first time that evening, his voice was steady. "Yeah. I'm ready."

At that moment, the sound of soft footsteps approached the room, and Gloria and Umi exchanged a knowing glance before stepping to the side. The twins entered together, both wearing flowing dresses that complemented each other. Stephanie's was a pale lavender, while Brittney's was soft blue. Around their necks, they each wore the matching necklaces from their earlier conversation, the charms glinting in the light.

Stephanie gave Brian an encouraging smile as they approached him while Brittney's gaze flicked nervously to the floor. When they reached him, Stephanie took the bouquets from his hand and handed one to Brittney. Then, with a small nod, she stepped forward.

Stephanie's voice was steady, though her cheeks were flushed with emotion. "Brian, you've been a part of our lives for as long as I can remember. You've been my best friend, my partner, and the person I trust most in the world. And now, we're standing here, ready to take this step together, not just you and me, but for all three of us."

She turned to Brittney, taking her sister's free hand in hers. "Brittney and I have always been a team, and tonight, we're making a promise — to each other and to you. To be honest, to be supportive, and to make this work."

Brittney's eyes glistened with unshed tears as she squeezed Stephanie's hand. "Brian, I know I haven't always been fair. I know I've made mistakes, mistakes I'm still trying to fix. But I love you, and I care about you, and I want this to be something real. For all of us."

Brian's gaze softened, his nervousness melting away as he looked at the two of them. "I love both of you," he said, his voice low but firm. "Stephanie, you've been my anchor, my constant. And Brittney, you've challenged me and pushed me to see things differently. You're both so important to me, and I want this to work as much as you do."

Stephanie handed Brian a small box, her fingers trembling slightly. "We got these for you," she said with a smile. Inside, two necklaces rested side by side, each with a charm shaped like a key. "They're for us to wear, to remind us that trust is the key to making this work."

Brian took the necklaces, his expression softening as he held them up. "Thank you," he said, his voice soft. Carefully, he placed one around Stephanie's neck, then turned to Brittney. She tilted her head slightly, her hair falling back as he clasped the necklace around her neck. When he was done, she looked down at the charm, her fingers brushing it lightly.

"Now it's my turn," Brian said, reaching into his pocket. He pulled out a small silver chain with a heart-shaped charm. "This is for both of you. The heart represents us together. No matter what, we'll always be connected."

Stephanie and Brittney each took an end of the chain, their hands meeting in the middle. Together, they clasped the necklace around Brian's neck, their fingers brushing briefly against his skin.

The twins turned to face each other, their expressions mirroring the depth of their bond. Stephanie spoke first, her

187

voice trembling with emotion. "Brittney Rose Welch, I promise to always love you. To be honest, truthful, and brave when we need to talk. You'll always be my sister, my twin, and my best friend."

Tears spilled over Brittney's cheeks as she replied, "Stephanie Ann Welch, I promise to always love you. To be honest, truthful, and brave when we need to talk. You're my other half, and I'll never let anything come between us again."

They hugged tightly, their necklaces clinking softly as they held each other.

Brian stepped forward, his voice steady and sincere. "Stephanie Ann Welch, Brittney Rose Welch, I love you both with all my heart. I promise to always be honest, respect, and support you. I will never take for granted what we have together. You're both incredible, and I'm lucky to have you in my life."

The three of them stood together in the glow of the lights, their hands joining in the center. For a moment, the room was silent, save for the faint crackle of the candles. Gloria and Umi exchanged a glance, their eyes wet with emotion.

Gloria cleared her throat, stepping forward. "Well, that was... beautiful," she said, her voice trembling slightly. She smiled at Brian and then at the twins. "You three have something very special here. I hope you all realize how rare and precious this is."

Umi nodded, her voice softer but no less heartfelt. "Brittney, Stephanie, you've shown so much courage tonight. It's not easy to open your heart like this to each other and to Brian. I'm proud of you both."

Brittney wiped at her eyes, a small, nervous laugh escaping her. "Thanks, Mom. I… I didn't think I'd ever feel this good again."

Stephanie smiled, her arm slipping around Brittney's shoulders. "We're stronger together. All of us."

Brian looked at Gloria and Umi, his voice filled with gratitude. "Thank you both. For everything. For raising two amazing women and for trusting me to be a part of their lives like this."

Gloria's lips twitched into a playful smile. "Don't make us regret it, Brian."

The room filled with soft laughter, the tension melting away as the five of them settled into a more relaxed atmosphere. The candles flickered, their light casting warm shadows over faces filled with hope and love.

Stephanie nudged Brittney softly, leaning close to her ear and whispering with a playful grin, "Go kiss your boyfriend."

Brittney's breath hitched, her eyes darting to Brian, who stood nearby, watching the twins with a soft smile. "I… I can't," Brittney murmured, her voice trembling. "Should I? Can I?"

Stephanie tilted her head, her expression warm and encouraging. "Trust me, Britt, yes. I know you've been dreaming about this for as long as I have." Her words carried a quiet conviction that cut through Brittney's doubt.

Brittney hesitated, glancing at Brian again. His gaze met hers, steady and kind, as though he already understood the storm of emotions running through her. She turned back to Stephanie, her voice barely above a whisper. "Are you sure?"

Stephanie nodded, her own tears glinting in the candlelight as she gently squeezed Brittney's hand. "Positive. He loves you just as much as he loves me. This is what we talked about, Britt. Go ahead."

Taking a shaky breath, Brittney stepped forward, her heart pounding in her chest. Each step felt heavy with meaning, as though the entire room held its breath along with her. When she finally reached Brian, she hesitated, her fingers clutching the charm of her necklace for reassurance.

Brian tilted his head slightly, his voice soft and steady. "Hey," he said, his hands falling to his sides, a small smile tugging at his lips. "You okay?"

Brittney let out a nervous laugh, her cheeks flushing. "I don't know," she admitted. "But I'm trying."

He took a small step closer, closing the gap between them, his voice lowering to a gentle murmur. "You don't have to try, Britt. Just be here. With us. With me."

Her breath caught, and for a moment, she simply stared at him, the warmth in his eyes melting away the last of her fear. Slowly, hesitantly, she reached up and placed her hands lightly on his shoulders.

"I've wanted this," she whispered, her voice trembling with both vulnerability and anticipation, "for so long."

Brian's smile softened, his hands coming up to rest lightly on her waist. "Me too," he said, his words carrying the weight of a promise. "For so long."

Time seemed to stretch as Brittney leaned in, her movements tentative at first, giving herself space to pull back if she needed to. But when Brian didn't move away, when his arms gently steadied her, she let herself close the distance. Their lips met in a kiss that was soft and searching as if testing the waters of this new dynamic.

The kiss deepened slightly, the hesitance fading as Brittney's confidence grew. When they finally pulled apart, Brian's forehead rested lightly against hers, his voice a quiet whisper. "You're not alone, Britt. Not anymore. Not ever."

Brittney blinked back tears, her heart swelling with a mix of relief and joy she hadn't felt in months. "Thank you," she said, her voice barely audible. "For… everything."

From the corner of the room, Stephanie sniffled quietly, tears streaming freely down her face as she pressed a hand to her mouth. Her joy radiated through her trembling smile, her heart full as she watched her sister take this step.

Umi and Gloria stood together, watching the scene unfold with soft smiles. Umi's hand brushed against Gloria's briefly, and they exchanged a quiet glance, their unspoken understanding of the moment clear.

"They're growing up," Umi murmured, her voice thick with emotion.

Gloria nodded, her eyes glistening as she watched the trio stand together. "And they're learning what it takes: love, trust, and a lot of patience."

Umi chuckled softly, her voice carrying a warmth that matched her expression. "Sounds familiar, doesn't it?"

Gloria smiled knowingly, squeezing Umi's arm gently before turning back to the teens. "It does."

As the three stood together, hands joined, and Stephanie's giggles broke the silence. "Okay, okay, this is beautiful and all, but Brian…" She arched a teasing eyebrow at him, her tone mock-serious. "You know this doesn't mean you get to be a *pervert*, right?"

Brian's face flushed a deep red as his head snapped toward Gloria, who smirked knowingly.

"She did warn me about that," Brian mumbled, rubbing the back of his neck sheepishly. "I swear I'm not. I mean, I wasn't planning to..." He stopped, realizing he was digging himself deeper, and let out a defeated laugh. "Yeah, I'm just going to stop talking now."

Brittney burst into laughter, her earlier nervousness dissolving as she covered her face with one hand. "Good call, Brian."

Stephanie laughed so hard she had to grip Brittney's arm for support. "I love how you just walked right into that one."

Gloria's laughter rang out as she clapped her hands together. "Oh, he's going to fit right in. Poor kid doesn't stand a chance."

As the laughter faded, Umi glanced around the room, her gaze softening. As they began to walk out of the room, she leaned toward Gloria and said with a touch of mischief, "Wow, after this, I can't imagine how their wedding will be."

The comment caught everyone's attention, and for a split second, the room was silent. Then, the five of them dissolved into laughter, the sound ringing out as they stepped into the hallway.

Brittney glanced at Brian, her face still flushed from laughter. "You know," she said, her tone teasing but warm, "you're stuck with us now."

Brian smiled, slipping an arm around both twins' shoulders. "I wouldn't have it any other way. But maybe it's you two who are stuck with me now," causing both girls to giggle softly.

Gloria and Umi followed a few steps behind, their expressions warm as they watched the trio walk ahead. Umi glanced at Gloria, her voice low but thoughtful. "Do you think they know how much they've grown tonight?"

Gloria's lips curved into a knowing smile. "Maybe not yet. But they'll feel it. And they'll keep growing."

Umi nodded, her gaze lingering on her daughters before turning to Gloria. "We did okay, didn't we?"

Gloria squeezed her arm gently, her voice carrying quiet certainty. "We did more than okay."

As the five of them made their way into the living room, the glow of the candles faded behind them, leaving the family room bathed in a soft, lingering warmth. It was a moment they'd all carry forward, a reminder of the love and trust that bound them together.

*****

Two weeks later, Umi, Gloria, and Brittney were back in the courtroom, sitting quietly in the gallery as the morning proceedings unfolded. Unlike the first time, Brittney's nerves felt slightly more manageable. Her counseling sessions had begun, and the structured support had started to ease some of the weight she carried. However, the familiar surroundings of the courtroom still made her stomach churn.

The judge called for a brief recess before returning to the bench. Moments later, the bailiff's voice echoed. "Case 3443, *State versus Welch, Brittney Rose*. All concerned parties, please come forward."

Brittney took a deep breath as she stood, clutching her hands tightly together. Umi placed a comforting hand on her shoulder, whispering, "You've done well. Be proud of yourself." Gloria offered a reassuring smile as Brittney walked to the defense table with Rosa Williams, who had agreed to assist in presenting her progress to the court.

The judge's familiar presence was as imposing as ever, though his expression was softer this time. "Good morning, Miss Welch. It's good to see you again."

"Good morning, Your Honor," Brittney replied, her voice steadier than she expected.

"ADA Miller, or should I say District Attorney Miller," the judge addressed the DA. "I understand you requested this hearing. Please proceed."

Scott Miller rose from his seat, a folder in hand. "Thank you, Your Honor. I requested this hearing to bring to the court's attention Miss Welch's compliance with the court order. Over the past two weeks, she has attended her counseling sessions without issue and has demonstrated full cooperation with her counselor, who provided a written report for the court."

He handed the folder to the bailiff, who passed it to the judge. "The report highlights her willingness to engage with the process and her active participation in sessions. Given her progress, the state believes it is important to acknowledge her effort and commitment to the terms of her sentence."

The judge reviewed the document, nodding as he skimmed its contents. "This is an excellent report, Miss Welch. Your counselor has noted significant progress in a short amount of time. It appears you are taking full advantage of the opportunity this court has provided you. That's exactly what I hoped for when I issued my ruling."

Brittney's cheeks flushed as the judge's words sunk in. She looked down, fiddling with her fingers. "Thank you, Your Honor," she murmured.

The judge's tone grew even warmer. "Miss Welch, it's not easy to face the consequences of one's actions and commit to change. I'm proud of the steps you've taken so far. Continue this path, and you'll find the strength to rebuild and move forward."

Though the judge's words were kind, Brittney couldn't help but cast a wary glance at Scott Miller, who sat back at his table. She still associated him with the prosecution, the one who, in her mind, wanted her behind bars. The sting of that belief lingered, even as the positive outcome unfolded around her.

The judge continued, "As this report reflects, Miss Welch has exceeded all requirements set forth by the court, completing more sessions than were mandated and surpassing all expectations. This level of dedication reflects her commitment to growth and rehabilitation. I encourage her to maintain this momentum and continue building trust with her family and community. Good luck, Miss Welch. With that, the case is dismissed, and this hearing is adjourned."

As the gavel struck, Brittney exhaled a deep breath she hadn't realized she was holding. Rosa placed a hand on her arm, leaning in. "You did great today," she said softly.

Brittney nodded but couldn't shake the unease that settled in her chest when her eyes landed on Miller. She muttered under her breath, "He wanted me in jail."

Rosa frowned slightly but didn't press. "Let's focus on the progress you've made. That's what matters now."

As Brittney rejoined her family in the gallery, Umi hugged her tightly. "You're doing so well," she whispered. Gloria smiled, adding, "We're so proud of you, Brittney."

Despite their encouragement, Brittney's thoughts lingered on Scott Miller. She couldn't shake the conviction that he'd been against her from the start. That belief would remain like a small thorn, unnoticed by others but sharp to her.

CHAPTER 15

Sergeant King knocked on Captain Bishop's door. "Got a minute, Cap?"

Captain Bishop looked up. "Sure, King. What's up?"

Sergeant King sat down. "I just got off the phone with Umi Welsh, giving her an update."

"How's she doing?" Captain Bishop asked.

"It's been five weeks since she realized the medication slip up; she's still upset but working through it. She's still blaming herself, thinking because she forgot to get Brittney's meds is what caused everything," Sergeant King replied.

"And Brittney?"

"She's attending counseling and some sessions with her mom. She's working on it and making progress. She's scared about the trial, and I think she needs some encouragement from someone other than us," Sergeant King answered.

"Who are you thinking of?"

Sergeant King smiled. "ADA Miller. It's the only logical choice. We portray him as if he's defending her, sort of like a hero, so she can trust him and the process. I think it will also help a lot with the trial prep."

"That could backfire on us, real fast, knowing she was off her meds when all of this was going on, and her emotional reactions," Captain Bishop answered.

"I could see that, but I can see the two having a good rapport before she takes the stand. If she trusts him and the process, I think she's less likely to have an emotional break," Sergeant King explained.

"Good points. I think it's a good idea. I'll reach out to Miller and get his take on it. Any other information on the *perps*?"

"Well, most everyone at the school that we spoke with sees Peter and Richard as these super cool guys—kind and can get anything someone wants. We know Perezs' has ties into the drugs at the school, so either he's that good, or he's a pawn in a bigger game," Sergeant King reported.

"A bigger game?"

"Yeah, but we can't tell until I get a chance to interview him. All we have right now is a quick talk about both Welch teens. He was a bit evasive while we talked. His body language was off; he only made eye contact a few times. That sort of thing," Sergeant King explained.

"Figures. That's the tattle-tail sign of someone hiding something."

"Yeah, and get this: he was hitting on me during the whole conversation. I think if Barnes weren't there, Perez would have pressed me harder. I guess Barnes's 'big man' presence intimidated him," Sergeant King commented.

"And how did Lemon react?"

"Oh, he's definitely hiding something. Behind his jock role, he's dealing with something serious. The body language, and more importantly, his choice of words, is telling a different story than he is. My question is, do we have enough to bring either in?" Sergeant King asked.

"Not sure. We have Dr. Heather Jamison's report and the mastologist's report. Jamison did a good job in documenting everything, including impressions of all the bite marks," Captain Bishop said, handing a folder to Sergeant King.

"We interviewed Lemon's parents. Both are adamant that Peter didn't do anything. He's always with them at church, goes to Bible study every Wednesday, and gets good grades. All three portray the 'perfect family.' We did a quick follow-up at the church; nothing out of the ordinary there. Both parents say he's been a bit distant the past few weeks, but they both said they think it's got to do with some girl he was dating," Sergeant King continued reporting.

"And Perez's parents?"

"The father's in year three, serving a seven-year stint in upstate New York for drug charges. The mother kicked him out when he turned eighteen and moved to Mississippi. She hasn't talked to him since. He's got an older brother, but we can't find him. Nothing is coming back when we look for him. If he's off-grid, he's good at it," Sergeant King continued.

"Interesting. Anything about drugs?"

"Nothing. If there's anything going on like that, we can't find it. With everything else, is it enough to get a warrant?" Sergeant King asked.

"We know Miller always wants the 'i's' dotted and the 't's' crossed before he goes for a warrant. I think we do. I'm still worried about Stephanie and how she's going to handle the trial," Captain Bishop replied.

"Yeah, I get that too; part of the reason why I think we should introduce Stephanie and Miller now," Sergeant King explained.

"You've convinced me, King. When I talk with Miller, I'll press for it. What about the other teens?"

"Both are super supportive of Brittany and Umi. Stephanie told me that she is 'sharing' Brian with her."

"Sharing?" Captain Bishop asked.

"Yeah, that's what she said. While we were interviewing her, she told me that her idea is for Brittney to have a more intimate relationship with Brian. There are very clear rules, but Brittney practically jumped at the chance," Sergeant King explained.

"What are the rules?" Ashley asked.

"No secrets between any of them, total honesty and communication. That's about the extent of it. In exchange, Brittney has a boyfriend. She was adamant that Brittney and Brian already have feelings for each other, and they've shared everything else before this happened," Sergeant King explained.

"Is it working for them?"

"Yeah, both said as much. Stephanie said they had this romantic, ceremony-like event and exchanged promises and necklaces. Umi and Gloria both thought it was a great idea. When we interviewed Gloria, she was very clear that Stephanie had come up with the idea. And the way they did it was a big turning point for Brittney; 'very romantic' was the term she used," Sergeant King continued.

"Great. It might be a bit of an issue during the trial, but it definitely works. Any information on the shop Brittney was talking about?"

"We had eyes on it for nearly two weeks, and nothing out of the ordinary. Both boys would go there in the afternoons and work on a car or two. If they are doing anything else, we can't see any signs of it. Looking at the money trail, he's living off a trust fund he just got access to. He's got money; the financials are showing a steady weekly dividend payout of five thousand. The trust fund is huge, just over two hundred and fifty million dollars."

"Well, that stinks. Either they are very good, or something is hiding elsewhere. Let's scrub social media, banks, cells for both. We're missing something, but I don't want to get buried in the weeds of that. We'll get the Narcotics squad on it, and we'll focus on the Welchs. Anything else from Brian or Stephanie's interviews?" Captain Bishop asked.

"Not really. They both confirmed the timeline Brittney laid out and her change in attitude, demeanor, and actions. Most of what they know is more centered around the itching powder prank and the missing prosthetic leg," Sergeant King concluded.

"Okay, then. Umm, have we heard back from Brittney's counselor?"

"No. She's sticking to her guns about patient-doctor confidentiality," Sergeant King replied.

"Okay, have Umi ask her to talk with you and Burns, and when I talk with Miller, I'll ask about a warrant for the records. Anything else?"

Sergeant King shook her head. "Not right now. I'll get back with you as soon as we have made some progress."

Captain picked up the phone as Sergeant King was walking to the door. "Okay. Thanks for the update."

A moment later, on the phone, she greeted ADA Miller: "Hi, Miller. It's Bishop. How are you doing?"

Moments later, "I heard something like that; congratulations, DA," she answered.

She continued, "We need warrants for the Welsh case. The counselor, Dr. Jennifer Meyers, is on a high horse about releasing the victim's records. Also, King and I both think you and the victim, Brittney Welch, should meet sooner than at trial prep. The idea behind this is so she's comfortable with you and the process. We both believe it will go a long way in helping her keep control."

There was a long pause while she listened to his reply.

"Yeah, I know that. It's part of the reason why we want to have you two meet beforehand," she explained.

"Okay, that works. I'll get it set up. Next, did you see the update I sent over this afternoon?" Captain Bishop asked.

"Yeah, I know, the i's are dotted and the t's are crossed. We're working on it. Right now, we only have her word and the physical evidence on her body. We do have them together; several teens who were playing basketball all place them together, and both Perez and Lemon driving away in a car with her quite a few times.

"That places them both at the first assault and a number of others. We also have the store owner of Dixie's Pop Stop, and two of his employees place them together nearly every day of the week until school starts. Is that enough to bring them in for questioning?" Captain Bishop asked.

She smiled as he spoke. "I'll get King and Barnes on it as soon as we hang up. How about a warrant for bite impressions from Perez?"

"Both?" she asked.

"I get it. Anything else?" she asked.

"Okay, I'll see you early next week when I bring Brittney in to meet you."

"Yes, I think that's a better idea. It will take some of the tension out of the meeting," Captain Bishop answered.

"Okay, I'll get with Umi Welsh and get it set up for Monday afternoon."

"That works. Thanks. And, again, congratulations on the promotion, Miller," Captain Bishop said as she hung up the phone.

Moments later, she was in her squad room. "King and Barnes, Miller said pick up Perez and Lemon. Also, ADA Miller is now officially DA Miller."

After everyone said their comments, Sergeant King looked up from her desk. "Barnes, if they're doing like we've seen, they are either at or on their way to their shop. Cap, we'll grab some uniforms and pick them up there. Warrants?"

"Miller said he'll meet you there with them."

*****

Sergeant King strode into the squad room, gripping Richard Perez firmly by the arm. His cuffed wrists strained against her hold, and he jerked back with every step.

"Hey, Cap," King said as she approached Captain Bishop, her tone even but firm. "We found them right where we expected. This one," she shook Richard slightly, "couldn't keep his mouth shut the entire way here. CSI was starting their sweep when we left."

Captain Bishop raised an eyebrow, her expression neutral but edged with authority. "Put him in interview room one. Lemon goes in the cage. Let him stew a bit."

Moments later, Peter sat hunched in the small holding cell, his face pale, his hands fidgeting nervously. Across the hall, Richard shuffled into the interview room, his defiance apparent in his sneering grin.

"Stop yanking me, bitch," he snarled at King, his voice low and venomous. "I'll file charges on you for this."

King's grip tightened briefly, her voice calm but sharp. "Keep calling me that, and you'll find out just how tough I can be."

She shoved him into a chair and stepped back. Richard leaned back, smirking. "You're all the same. Loud until someone fights back."

King ignored the jab, glancing over her shoulder as Detective Barnes entered the room. He walked to Richard's side, placing a steady hand on his shoulder as he uncuffed him. "You're not the first loudmouth we've dealt with, and you definitely won't be the last," Barnes said, his voice casual but carrying weight. "Word of advice: watch your tone. Both the captain and sergeant can be very unpleasant when pushed."

As Barnes walked out, Captain Bishop stepped into the room, her presence calm yet commanding. She took a seat across from Richard while King leaned casually against the wall, arms crossed.

"Well, Richard," Bishop began, her tone measured, "since we're on a first-name basis, let's get something straight. You call me or my sergeant a 'bitch' again, and you'll spend the night caged like the dog you're acting like. Clear?"

Richard's sneer faltered, but only for a moment. "Crystal," he muttered, leaning back in his chair.

"Good," Bishop said, opening a thick folder and spreading its contents on the table. On one side lay a series of photos — close-ups of bruises, bite marks, and other injuries. On the other, a stack of documents detailing witness statements and reports.

King stepped forward, her eyes sharp. "You know why you're here, don't you?"

Richard's grin returned. "Let me guess. That little bi... tease didn't like the way I handled her. Sounds like her problem, not mine."

Bishop didn't look up from the file. "Careful, Richard. You're already in over your head. Keep digging, and we'll help you bury yourself."

King slid a photo across the table. It showed deep bruises on Brittney's arms and legs. "She asked for this?" King asked, her voice cool.

Richard glanced at the image and shrugged. "Yeah. She liked it rough. These church girls, they put on a show, but they're wild underneath. She begged for it."

"You're saying Brittney begged you to hurt her like this?" Bishop's tone was calm, but her gaze was unrelenting.

"She's a tease," Richard said, leaning forward. "She's all about getting a guy worked up, and when it gets too hot for her, she backs off. But not with me. I gave her what she really wanted."

King slid another photo forward, this one showing a severe bite mark on Brittney's shoulder. "She asked you to bite her like this, too?"

"She said, 'Bite me,' so I did. What's the problem?" Richard's voice was filled with misplaced confidence.

Bishop finally looked up, her expression unreadable. "She says you forced yourself on her, that she screamed and begged you to stop."

Richard snorted. "She's lying. The little slut got herself pregnant, freaked out, and now she's making stuff up."

King didn't blink, her voice sharp. "Watch your language, Richard. Let's talk about timelines. When did you start dating Brittney?"

"After school started. She told me she was eighteen," Richard replied, his tone defensive.

"Wrong," Bishop said, sliding another document toward him. "Witnesses at Dixie's Pop Stop place you two together in July. Brittney was seventeen. She still is."

Richard's smirk faltered. "Doesn't matter. Romeo and Juliet laws cover that."

King leaned closer. "Not in this state. Both parties have to be at least seventeen when the relationship starts. Brittney was underage. You weren't. That's statutory rape."

Richard shifted in his seat, his confidence cracking. "You don't know what you're talking about."

Bishop didn't respond. Instead, she slid another photo across the table, this one heavily redacted but showing clear evidence of severe injuries to Brittney's breasts. "You're saying she asked for this too?"

Richard looked at the photo, his bravado draining. "She liked it rough," he muttered, less certain now.

Before Bishop could press further, Barnes knocked lightly on the door and stepped in. "Sorry to interrupt, Captain. CSI found security cameras at the shop. They're pulling footage now."

Bishop's lips curled into a faint smile. "Thanks, Barnes," noticing Barnes was motioning for her to come over. As she stood up, King continued talking with Richard.

As Bishop came back to the table, sitting down, she nodded at King.

King turned back to Richard, her tone casual. "Well, that'll clear up any confusion, won't it? The footage will show us what happened and when. Or do you have something you'd like to share before we see it?"

Richard's jaw tightened. "I'm done talking with you, bi..." he stopped himself before continuing. "Get me, my lawyer."

King gathered the photos, sliding them back into the folder. "Your call. But when that footage comes in, it's going to tell us a lot. Might want to think about helping yourself now."

Richard stood abruptly, his chair scraping the floor. "Yeah, yeah. Call me when you've got something real."

Barnes stepped in to escort Richard to the holding cell. As he passed Peter, who was sitting in the cage, Richard snarled, "Keep your mouth shut and ask for your lawyer."

Peter just looked at him as Barnes pulled him out of the cell, locked it, and escorted Peter to the interrogation room. While he was removing the cuffs, Barnes spoke softly.

"Young man, I'm going to give you some cheap but valuable advice. I trust both Captain Bishop and Sergeant King with my life. If I were you, I'd ignore your little buddy out there and listen to them. There's no harm in listening, you know? And, who knows, you might hear something that helps you," Barnes advised Peter.

Through the one-way mirror, Captain Bishop and Sergeant King watched him.

King commented, "See how his eyes are down, and his head is slumped? He's got a story he's dying to tell. He called his mom, and we're expecting them at any time now. I think we have Barnes bring them in here and let them listen while we highlight his complicities in Richard's actions."

Bishop smiled. "Good plan. He might need some urging, but I'm sure he'll come clean."

Barnes walked in, standing next to King. "Are we waiting on something?"

Bishop turned to Barnes. "Nice touch, Barnes. I think he was listening to you. His parents are due at any time. Can you pop your head in there and tell Peter something came up, and it's going to be a few minutes? And when they get here, bring them in here, and we're going to let them hear the interview. I'll want you to watch and pick up on any comments while we're interviewing him."

Barnes said, "Got it, Cap," as he turned and walked out. A few seconds later, Bishop and King watched as Barnes opened the other door to the room and stepped in.

"Peter, the Captain, and Sergeant are going to be a few minutes; something urgent came up. They'll be in as soon as they can," he said to the teen.

King smiled. "Nice touch."

While they waited, they discussed facts they had already gathered from their investigation.

"Oh, and Miller got us the warrants for bite impressions for both Perez and Lemon. As soon as he's done at arraignment, he'll be brought in for those. And get this: it's a mandatory warrant; the medical examiner has the authority to put either of them out if they don't comply. I'd pay to watch that," Bishop explained.

"Wow, Miller's not playing, is he?" King asked.

Bishop shook her head. "Not at all. I can't wait to hear his reaction after this afternoon's interview with Perez."

King nodded. "Right now, all we have is the physical abuse, felony assault with a deadly weapon. I just wish Brittney had come forward earlier."

Bishop looked at her. "We both know some victims take years before they can come forward. I wish there weren't such a stigma against victims of sexual assault. It would make our investigations that much easier."

King looked at her. "I know. It took me years before I could even admit something was going on and more time before I could change it. When you came out to Mississippi for that joint case, something you said to the victim resonated with me, and I made things change."

Bishop, "Did you ever see a therapist about it?" Her voice filled with concern.

"Yeah, I did. Sort of had to before I could come up here. I've got to tell you, Ashley, moving up here and working with this department, even though it's much smaller, has been the best move I've ever made. Thank you for inviting me up," King admitted.

"And I don't regret a moment of that decision. I can't tell you how happy I was when you accepted the invitation. Barnes even liked the idea, and he's one of those 'hard to please' guys," Captain Bishop admitted.

There was a light knock on the door, and Barnes popped his head in. "Cap, the Lemons are here."

"Great, Barnes, please show them in," Bishop said.

"Ready?" Bishop asked.

"Yup, let's make it happen, Captain," King said with a small grin.

"Good afternoon, Mr. and Mrs. Lemon. I'm Captain Ashley Bishop, and this is my partner, Sergeant Mary King."

Mrs. Lemon spoke first. "Good afternoon. I'm Margaret, and this is my husband, Peter," she greeted them.

A moment later, she added, "How much trouble is Peter in?"

King looked at the woman, assessing her at once. "He's in quite a bit. He's seen repeated sexual and physical abuse of a minor and never did anything about it."

Margaret looked at King. "And how does that get him in trouble?"

Bishop spoke up. "It makes him a co-conspirator in the crimes committed. In the eyes of the law, because he didn't do anything, he's as guilty as the person who committed the crimes," Bishop explained, her voice gentle but firm.

Peter spoke up. "And you're sure he witnessed these horrific acts?"

King pointed at the one-way mirror. "Look at him. I can see it, and I've only spoken with him for about five minutes. You know him better than either of us; what do you see?"

Margaret's face paled. "I can see it," she said softly, then added, "How can we help?"

Bishop gave King a slight nod before King spoke.

"Right now, we are inviting you to listen. Because of his age, we really didn't need to meet. I thought, after our brief discussion the other week, you'd both appreciate the gesture. Our goal is to get Peter to tell us what happened. That's the primary focus. If he helps himself and comes clean, I know our DA will give him a good plea bargain. But that offer is only a last-ditch effort to get him to talk with us," King explained.

Margaret looked at Peter through the mirror, then at her husband. "Do you want me to talk with him?" she offered.

King replied, "In most cases, we know young adults tend to speak freer when their parents aren't around. But, if it comes to that, we may ask you."

Peter looked at Bishop. "Should we get a lawyer now, before you start?"

Bishop looked him in the eye. "That's your choice, but because Peter is over eighteen, he has to ask for one. However, getting him a lawyer is something that needs to happen, regardless of how this interview happens. I know our DA tends to be much more generous when defendants cooperate with us earlier than later during the process."

Peter thought about things for a moment. "If things get too much for him, could you give us a chance to talk with him? And, if needed, ask him to ask you for a lawyer?" he asked.

Bishop thought about it for a second. "I think we can make something like that work. Honestly, we don't think it's going to be that rough for him. Once he starts talking, it's going to move fast. It's getting him to talk, which will be the hard part. If it looks like he won't do it on his own, we can pause and give you a chance to intervene, so to say, and recommend that he get a lawyer. This will give you, him, and us a chance to get him to help himself without infringing on his rights," she said, her tone and voice firm.

Margaret nodded, softly answering, "Okay. Thank you, Captain."

Through the one-way mirror, King studied Peter, commenting aloud as she followed Bishop to the door, "He's nervous, fidgeting, and you can see his face; he wants to talk about something."

Bishop opened the door to the interrogation room and walked in, King right behind her. "Hello, Peter. I'm Captain Bishop, and this is my partner, Sergeant King. You remember Sergeant King, right?"

Peter nodded. "Yes, ma'am," recognizing her immediately. "We spoke at school a few weeks ago."

Bishop sat down opposite Peter and opened the thick folder she was holding. "We've got some things we need to clear up, okay? Depending on how you answer, this shouldn't take too long."

"What kind of questions?" he asked.

"Before we do anything, do you remember your rights when you were arrested?" Bishop asked.

Peter nodded.

"Good. Do you want to talk with us or wait for an attorney to get here for you?" she asked.

Peter faced Bishop. "Can I ask for a lawyer later?"

King nodded. "That's your right, at any time. We'd prefer it if you talked with us first."

Peter nodded. "I'll talk with you," he said softly.

King looked at him. "Good. Now, to answer your question, we are going to talk about Brittney Welch and what Richard Perez did to her."

Peter's face paled as he looked down, understanding King's statement.

Bishop leaned forward slightly. "Peter, this is your chance to make things right. We know you saw what Richard was doing; all you need to do now is help yourself and Brittney by telling us what happened."

"I didn't do anything wrong," Peter said softly as if he was trying to convince himself more than anyone else. "I just... I just didn't want to get involved."

King pressed the point. "Peter, in the eyes of the law, you *are* involved. You watched as Richard made Brittney do things she didn't want to do. You listened to her cry, scream, beg, and plead for him to stop, and you didn't do anything. Not just once, either, but quite a few times. That makes you part of the problem as if you did the things to her yourself."

Peter flinched at her words, his head popping up. "I didn't hurt her!" he snapped, his voice rising. "I didn't do anything; I didn't touch her; I didn't..."

Bishop cut him off, her voice firm, her tone more patient than King's. "And that's the problem. You didn't have to touch Brittney to hurt her. You were complicit. You watched Richard sexually, physically, and mentally abuse Brittney, and you didn't stop him. You didn't tell anyone; you did nothing. That makes you just as guilty as Richard and just as responsible as he is," Bishop explained.

Peter's hands trembled; his head lowered as he stared at his hands. "I didn't want any of this to happen. Richard said it was a fantasy of Brittney's and that everything would be fine. Later, he said that if she told anyone, they wouldn't believe her."

King pushed. "And that didn't sound strange to you? If it really was a fantasy of Brittney's, then why would Richard tell you no one would believe her?"

There was a long silence before Bishop spoke, her tone soft but firm. "Peter, you want to help Brittney, right? Well, now is the time to help her and yourself. Don't try to protect Richard or hide behind him. Be the young man your mom and dad know you are, and tell us what you know."

King gently coached. "We can see you want to tell us. Do the right thing and help Brittney now before it's too late."

Peter's eyes darted between the detectives. "I... I saw what Richard... I watched what he did to her. And I didn't stop him. I was scared of him, what he'd do if I tried. I didn't want to make things worse for myself."

Peter's admission hung in the air like a heavy weight. His eyes welled with tears, and he looked up at the detectives. "I didn't want to be involved. But I am. I should've said something. I should've stopped him. And I didn't."

Bishop nodded slowly, her face softening slightly. "Thank you for telling us, Peter. I know it's not easy to admit something like this. But you're doing the right thing now. You're helping to make sure he doesn't do this again and to help get Brittney justice. And this is the first step."

Peter wiped his face with the back of his hand, his shoulders trembling. "I... I never thought it would be like this. I never thought he'd hurt her like this."

King sat back, folding her arms. "Peter, Richard is the one who's guilty of everything. You keeping his secrets makes it worse. But you're making it right by telling us the truth now. That's all we can ask for."

Peter nodded slowly, still visibly shaken but no longer hiding the truth. "I'll do whatever I can to help. I just want to make things right for Brittney..."

Bishop leaned back in her chair, her eyes cold but understanding. "Okay, let's start from the day you met Brittney and go forward. And Peter, don't leave anything out. That's important for everyone."

Peter started his narration of the events he saw, going into detail and answering questions Captain Bishop or Sergeant King brought up while he spoke.

About two hours later, King looked up at him, studying his face for a moment. "Peter, you're doing very well. How about a quick break? Give yourself a chance to recompose, use the gentlemen's room, and get a drink. We have got a few more details to cover, and then we're done. How does that sound?"

Peter looked up, his eyes puffy. "I could use a break, thank you," he answered softly.

Bishop nodded slightly as King stood up. "I'll get Barnes to take you. We'll see you in a few minutes."

Both detectives got up and walked into Bishop's office, where Margaret and Peter Sr. were sitting, Barnes sitting behind them.

Margaret got up. "Captain Bishop, thank you for how you did that. I don't think I could have done better."

Peter stood up. "I agree. Do you think we can see him before you continue?"

Bishop looked at Barnes. "Please take him to the men's room and get him a drink."

"I'm on it, Cap," he answered as he walked out of the room.

Bishop shook her head. "I'd prefer you'd wait until we're done; we've only a few more details to cover, and he's doing great. That is, unless you want to tell him to stop talking and wait for a lawyer," she explained, being very generous in her offer.

Margaret shook her head and looked at her husband. "No, we want him to finish the interview, but I want to give him some words of encouragement."

King shook her head. "Knowing you are here and heard everything might cause him to stop talking," she warned.

Peter looked at King. "I get it. Okay, let's finish this interview. I've already called my lawyer for him and explained exactly what we are doing. She said she'll be right over."

Margaret asked, "Why are you treating him like this? What I mean is, why are you being so gentle? It's nothing like other things I've seen or heard about."

Bishop looked at her. "He's been tormented and bullied. We do care about the defendants as much as we care about the victims. Being treated like he's a victim is actually helping him open up and tell us what he knows."

Margaret smiled. "All I can say is, God bless you and thank you."

King looked at Margaret with a soft face. "I do recommend you get him in to see a therapist. It will go a long way in getting him back to being himself."

Margaret nodded. "I'll see to it. Again, thank you for everything."

*****

Sometime later, Barnes knocked on Captain Bishop's door. "Hey, Cap, Lemon's lawyer wants to have a word with you."

Captain Bishop looked up. "Sure, bring him in."

Bishop stood up as she recognized the attorney who walked in. "Hi, Kathy, I haven't seen you in a long time," she said as she extended her hand.

"Hi, Ashley, yeah, it's been a minute. Some quick questions for you about my client, Peter Lemon."

Bishop pointed at a chair. "Have a seat, and we'll go over it."

Kathy sat down. "You realize my client told you everything, right?"

Bishop nodded. "He did. And when DA Miller and I get caught up, I'm going to recommend he take his actions into serious consideration."

"So, you are still going to charge him?" she asked, somewhat in disbelief.

"Kathy, you know we can't send a message that promotes complicity. This went on for several months, and at any time, he could have come forward," Bishop explained.

"And you don't think him being forced to keep Perez's secrets is worth anything? I mean, he's been cooperative

217

throughout everything; that really deserves something," Kathy argued her point.

"Kathy, I'll tell you what. How about I let you and DA Miller talk it out? I'll report the cooperation from start to finish, filling in the details we weren't aware of and fully corroborating the victim's statement and story. I'll add that his parents were helpful, too," Bishop offered.

"Well, I can't argue with that, now, can I?" Kathy replied with a small grin.

Sometime later, after the two caught up and Kathy left, Captain Bishop called Scott Miller to give him an update.

CHAPTER 16

Later that week, Brittney was bringing in the mail, leafing through it, and found a letter addressed to her. She sat in the living room while she read it.

Umi came in from the kitchen. "What's that, Angel?"

"It's an invitation to classes at an art studio in Mifflet. Doctor Jenny suggested that I try something like this. I guess she asked them; I don't know," Brittney answered, handing the letter to Umi.

Umi quickly read the letter. "Well, Angel, if Doctor Jenny suggested it and went as far as to have them invite you, it might be worth it for you to try. Think you might be interested in trying?" Umi asked softly.

"Mom, what if someone there recognizes me from school or the news?" Brittney's worry was written across her face, her anxiety ramping up quickly.

Umi sat next to her oldest daughter. "Angel, I love you, and this might sound harsh, but you can't live your life in a box, being afraid of the world. At some time or point, you are going to have to face this fear. I get it, and I honestly understand, but I think you might be worried about nothing or overthinking it," Umi explained softly.

"Mom, I don't know," Brittney answered softly.

Umi gently rubbed her shoulders, careful of where her bite marks were. "I know it won't be anything like school," Umi gently coached her.

"How can you be so sure, Mom?" Brittney asked, her anxiety calming down some.

Umi smiled. "Well, first of all, the people there are going to mostly be adults. Yes, there may be some of your classmates there, but they are there because they want to be there, not like the school where they have to be. This isn't a reason to skip on the offer. Next, I bet it never comes up, and if it does, it will probably be in your support. Remember, dear, they only know what they've seen in the news or, at worst, what Richard may have told them before he was arrested," Umi reassured her.

Brittney reached out and held her mom's hand. "Do you think I should go?"

"Angel, I think you should try. That's all I can ask of you. That's all anyone can ask of you. You might like it; you never know," Umi answered gently.

"And if you find out you don't like it, you can always stop," Umi added.

"You won't get mad?" Brittney asked softly.

"I'd be more upset if you didn't try than if you tried and decided you didn't like it. Some things in life you have to try before you say no. Like sushi. You didn't even want to try it until Stephanie dared you to. And now, you order it whenever you can," Umi answered.

Brittney reached for Umi's cell. "Okay, Mom. I'll try."

A few seconds later, Brittney was talking to someone at the art studio.

*****

The credits of a movie started rolling on the screen, its music filling the cozy living room. Brittney, Stephanie, and Brian sat on the couch; Stephanie was sandwiched between them. The glow of the TV screen cast a soft light across their faces as they lingered in the warmth of each other's company. Stephanie stretched, stifling a yawn, before her eyes fell on Brittney beside her.

"Britt," Stephanie said softly, leaning closer, "your hair...it's a bit greasy."

Brittney's hand flew self-consciously to her head, her cheeks flushing. "Yeah, I haven't had the energy to wash it. The stitches...it's hard to reach everything without opening the wounds."

Stephanie's expression softened with concern. "Would you let me help you wash it? I can be gentle."

Brittney blinked, caught off guard by the offer. Her face turned a deeper shade of pink as she stammered, "I...um...are you sure?"

Stephanie smirked, nudging her sister lightly. "Of course, silly. We're twins, remember? I've seen every part of you...literally."

Brittney's blush deepened, and she let out a nervous laugh. "Okay, but...the wounds..."

Stephanie's smirk softened into a warm smile. "I'll be careful. Come on."

Tears glistened in Brittney's eyes, and she nodded. "Thank you, Steph."

Stephanie stood and extended her hand, helping Brittney to her feet. "Let's get you fixed up."

As they headed to the bathroom, Brian glanced after them. "Need me for anything?" he asked, his voice light but supportive.

Stephanie looked back over her shoulder, a playful smile tugging at her lips. "Not yet. We've got this."

In the bathroom, the warm steam curled around them as Stephanie carefully adjusted the shower's spray. Brittney stood beside her, hugging a towel tightly around herself.

"So," Stephanie started casually, handing her sister a shower cap for the stitches, "are you going to tell me how your hair got this way?"

Brittney's gaze dropped, her voice low. "I just...I didn't feel like I could do it. Every time I tried, I...it hurt too much, and I got scared."

Stephanie placed a comforting hand on Brittney's shoulder. "That's why I'm here. You don't have to do it alone."

Brittney hesitated, then nodded. "Thanks, Steph. Really."

As Stephanie gently massaged shampoo into Brittney's hair, Brittney's cheeks turned pink again. "This is kind of embarrassing," she admitted softly.

Stephanie chuckled, her tone teasing but kind. "You're adorable when you're flustered. Relax, Britt. I've got you."

When they finished, Brittney emerged from the shower with a clean towel wrapped around her and her damp hair falling over her shoulders. She glanced shyly at Stephanie. "Hey…would it be okay if Brian braided my hair? He's good at it."

Stephanie's smile was gentle. "Britt, you don't need my permission to ask Brian for something. He's your boyfriend, too. And I know he'd be happy to."

Brittney's lips curled into a small smile. "Thanks, Steph."

Later, Stephanie came downstairs to find Brittney sitting cross-legged on the floor, Brian kneeling behind her, fingers deftly weaving her hair into a neat braid. The sight brought a soft smile to Stephanie's face as she leaned against the doorframe.

"Don't forget, it's my turn next," Stephanie teased, drawing both their gazes.

Brian grinned, holding up the nearly finished braid. "I'll fit you in after this masterpiece."

Brittney looked up at her sister, her eyes brighter than they had been in weeks. "Thanks, Steph…for everything."

Stephanie crossed the room, kneeling beside them and placing a hand on Brittney's shoulder. "Anytime. We're in this together."

The three of them stayed there for a moment, the bond between them stronger than ever.

CHAPTER 17

The following day, late in the afternoon, Umi and Gloria sat in the living room, their conversation interspersed with quiet moments of reflection as they waited for Captain Bishop and Scott Miller.

"How was Brittney's first art class?" Gloria asked, her voice soft and encouraging.

Umi hesitated, her expression thoughtful. "She seemed happy. They gave her a drawing pad and supplies, and she worked on something for a while. She was quiet and really focused, but... I thought I saw tears in her eyes. By the time I went to check, she was already cleaning up, so I didn't ask."

Gloria offered a reassuring smile. "Sounds like a positive start, though. Art can be a great outlet for her."

Umi nodded, though her expression remained pensive. "I know I need to step back and let her find her way, but it's hard.

I feel like I'm watching my confident, strong little girl turn into someone unsure and afraid. It's like she's lost herself."

Gloria reached over, taking Umi's hand in hers. "Kids stumble and fall. It's part of growing up. What matters is that we're here to help her stand, brush off the dirt, and move forward. Brittney will get through this, Umi. She's got you, me, her sister, and Brian to guide her."

Umi's grip tightened. "How do you think she'll handle meeting Scott like this?"

Gloria exhaled thoughtfully. "That's tricky. She might distrust him or even associate him with her time in lockup. It's hard to say, but we'll help her see that he's here to support her now."

"I hope so," Umi replied, her tone laced with worry. "She's been through so much."

Gloria glanced toward the window and spotted a car pulling up. "They're here."

Umi stood, smoothing her hands over her skirt as she walked to the door. She opened it just as Captain Bishop and Scott Miller approached, their expressions professional but kind.

"Hello," Umi greeted warmly.

"Good afternoon, Mrs. Welch," Scott said, extending his hand.

Umi shook it firmly. "Please, call me Umi. It's nice to officially meet you. You remember Gloria Cole?"

"Of course. It's good to see you again, Gloria. And please, call me Scott."

They exchanged polite smiles as Umi led them to the living room. Once seated, Scott addressed the elephant in the room. "I'm sure you understand why we're here."

Umi nodded, her expression serious. "To help Brittney trust you and the process. But we're concerned about how she'll react."

Scott leaned forward slightly. "What concerns you most?"

"She'll think you're not here for her," Umi admitted. "I'm afraid she'll resent you, distrust, or even be afraid of you because of her prior case."

Gloria added, "She's never fully recovered from that ordeal. The arrest, the court case—it all took a toll. She's not the same girl she was before."

Captain Bishop, seated beside Scott, spoke with calm authority. "It's important that Brittney trusts Scott. We're committed to building that trust, even if it means regular visits."

Gloria nodded. "That kind of commitment is reassuring. We'll do our part to reinforce it, but I think Brian and Stephanie will be key. Brittney trusts Brian more each day."

Scott smiled. "Good to hear. Building trust is a process, and it helps that she has strong support."

Just then, Umi's phone buzzed. She glanced at the screen. "The teens are on their way."

Moments later, their voices drifted down the hall. As they entered the room, Brittney froze mid-step, her eyes locking on Scott. Her face paled, and she took a shaky breath.

Brian immediately stepped behind her, his arms wrapping around her protectively. "What's wrong, love?" he whispered.

Her voice was barely audible. "It's him. The prosecutor from my court case."

Brian tightened his hold. "Brittney, remember what we talked about? He's here for you, not against you."

Stephanie moved to Brittney's side, taking her hand. "It's okay, Britt. Really."

Brittney shook her head, her voice rising with panic. "But I didn't do anything this time!"

Brian gently turned her to face him, his eyes steady. "You didn't, sweetheart. He's here to help."

Her voice cracked as she pleaded, "Promise me, Brian. Please."

Brian cupped her face, his tone unwavering. "I promise. All you have to do is listen."

Captain Bishop approached, her voice calm and steady. "Brittney, Scott is here to help you. Nothing more."

Brittney's gaze shifted to the captain, then back to Brian. Slowly, she nodded, though her tension was palpable. "Okay. I'll listen."

As they settled into the living room, Scott began to speak. His tone was gentle but firm, and he carefully explained his role and the steps ahead. Gradually, Brittney's posture softened her questions reflecting a growing engagement with the conversation. By the end, she nodded, her trust tentatively extended.

"I'll stop by next week to give you an update," Scott said as they stood to leave. "If you have questions, don't hesitate to ask Captain Bishop or me."

Brittney's voice was soft but steady. "Thank you."

*****

Later that night, a bending snowstorm swirled through the evening air, the wind carrying flakes that danced and shimmered like tiny crystals under the glow of Christmas lights. The thin veil of snow painted the small town of Bryan Athan in a quiet, pristine blanket of white. Through the bow window, the colorful glow of the lights outside illuminated the cozy interior, where warmth and a sense of fragile peace lingered.

Stephanie and Brian sat together on the plush couch, their fingers intertwined under a soft, fleece blanket draped across their laps. Across the room, Brittney sat curled in the recliner, a blanket covering her legs, her sketchbook resting on top. The muffled howling of the wind added to the sense of intimacy inside.

At the edge of the kitchen, Gloria and Umi stood, half-hidden in the shadow of the entryway, their gazes fixed on the trio in the living room. Gloria leaned against the wall, her arms crossed loosely over her chest, while Umi stood beside her, one hand covering her mouth to stifle any sound.

For a few moments, only the faint scratching of Brittney's pencil filled the room. Stephanie glanced at Brian, her gaze soft but steady. She cleared her throat, breaking the silence.

"Britt," Stephanie began, her voice gentle, "do you remember what Mom always told us when we were younger? Especially when we fought?"

Brittney paused her sketching, looking up with a hint of wariness. "You mean about being twins and how we're stronger together?"

Stephanie nodded, a small smile tugging at her lips. "Exactly. 'Stronger together.' I think about that a lot, especially now."

Brittney's gaze dropped back to her sketchbook, her hands tightening around the edges. The pencil rolled off onto the floor as her voice wavered. "It's hard to feel strong when you've done things that hurt the people you love," she admitted softly.

Umi let a small gasp escape her mouth as she heard Brittney's confession. Brittney's fingers tensed slightly around the edges of her sketchbook, her gaze flickering briefly toward the kitchen. She hesitated, her voice faltering, before Brian leaned forward.

Brian leaned forward, resting his elbows on his knees. His voice was calm, steady, and warm. "Britt, we all make mistakes. What matters is what we do to make things right. Stephanie and I are here for you, just like you'll be here for us when we need you. That's how this works, always."

In the kitchen, Gloria reached out and gently squeezed Umi's arm, her expression softening as Brian spoke. Umi's eyes glistened, and she nodded silently, her gaze fixed on her daughters.

Stephanie leaned closer. "And now that we're three, we're even stronger."

Brian tilted his head slightly, his gaze steady on Brittney. "When are you going to start believing us? I mean, seriously, Britt, do I have to pick you up, smother your face in kisses, and sit you down here to prove it?"

Brittney's eyes widened, a flicker of anxiety crossing her face as she waved a hand in protest. "No! You're not doing that. I mean it, Brian, don't you dare."

Brian grinned, his expression soft but mischievous. "Oh, I dare," he teased as he stood, his prosthetic clicking softly against the wooden floor. "Come on, Britt. You need to stop hiding over there and let us show you how much you matter."

Before Brittney could protest further, Brian gently leaned down, scooped her up into his arms with surprising ease, and pressed a series of light, playful kisses to her cheek. She squirmed, her laughter mingling with her protests. "Brian, stop! This is ridiculous!" she exclaimed, though her voice lacked any real resistance.

Stephanie giggled, scooting to make room under the blanket as Brian settled Brittney down between them. He tucked the fleece around all three of them, his arm draped across Brittney's shoulders.

"There," he said with a satisfied grin. "Now you're stuck with us. No more hiding, no more excuses. You're part of this, Britt. Got it?"

In the hallway, Umi clutched Gloria's arm again, her lips curving into a smile that shone with relief. Gloria, her eyes moist, nodded slightly, her gaze flicking back to the trio.

Brittney blinked, her eyes welling with tears as she looked between Brian and Stephanie. Her voice trembled. "You really mean that?"

Stephanie reached over, taking Brittney's hand and squeezing it tightly. "Of course, we mean it, Britt. You're part of us and always will be. That's why we did the whole promise ceremony, so we all could feel it, know it, and believe it."

Brian's expression softened as he studied Brittney's face. Slowly, he leaned in, his movements deliberate and tender. Stephanie watched, her smile deepening as Brian's lips met Brittney's. The kiss was slow and gentle, lingering as Brittney's initial tension melted away. Her shoulders relaxed, her breathing steadied, and she leaned into the kiss, letting herself feel the full weight of Brian's affection.

When their lips finally parted, Brittney looked up at him, her cheeks flushed, her voice barely above a whisper. "That was... nice. I guess I am a part of this, aren't I?"

Brian chuckled softly, pressing a light kiss to Brittney's forehead. "You've always been a part of this. I'm glad you're finally starting to believe it."

Stephanie squeezed Brittney's hand again, her voice filled with warmth. "Welcome to the team, Britt. You're stuck with us now."

Gloria and Umi exchanged a look, their silent understanding carrying a quiet joy.

The atmosphere shifted when Brittney hesitated, her voice breaking the peace. "Can I... can I ask you something? It's personal, really personal, but I have to know," her voice soft.

Stephanie nodded immediately. "Of course."

Brittney fidgeted with the edge of the blanket, her cheeks flushing. When she finally spoke, her voice was quiet, almost fragile. "Do you think... Do you think making love should hurt?"

The question hung in the air, heavy with unspoken meaning. Brian's gaze softened, and he exchanged a quick glance with Stephanie before taking Brittney's hand in his. In the hallway, Umi's breath caught, and she reached for Gloria's hand, squeezing it tightly.

"Brittney," Brian began, his voice gentle but resolute, "making love... it's nothing like what you've experienced. It's the exact opposite. It's not about taking or hurting; it's about giving. It's about taking all those little moments—the handholding, the kisses, the gestures that make your heart race—and rolling them into something even more meaningful."

He gently lifted her hand to his lips, brushing a kiss over the back of it. His eyes never left hers. "It's the chance to share that excitement, that connection, with your whole body. To make your partner feel with their body the love you have for them."

He turned her hand slightly, placing a soft nibble on the curve of her thumb before kissing the same spot. "Like this," he murmured, his lips moving to another spot on her hand for a gentle nibble followed by a kiss. "Every kiss, every touch, is meant for you to know you're loved, treasured and that everything about you matters to me. I just kissed you, and during that kiss, all that mattered to me was you understanding how I felt and that everything about you was important to me."

As he spoke, Brian continued the pattern, nibbling softly at her wrist, then kissing the spot where his teeth had grazed her skin. His lips moved up her arm, each kiss deliberate and tender. "It's about sharing the joy of a kiss, not just on the lips, but anywhere. Making love isn't about fulfilling an urge; it's about expressing everything you feel for someone, gently and lovingly, with tenderness."

When he reached her shoulder, he paused, his voice barely above a whisper. "It's about taking what's in your heart and letting it flow through your touch, so your partner knows exactly how much they mean to you."

He leaned back slightly, his warm eyes meeting Brittney's. "How does that feel, Britt?" he asked softly. "Be honest with me. How did those little nibble kisses make you feel?"

Brittney blinked, her cheeks flushed as she processed Brian's words and the gentle kisses that lingered on her skin. Her fingers curled slightly in his hand, and for a moment, she couldn't find the words. Before she could answer, Stephanie's voice, filled with a mix of wonder and excitement, broke the silence.

"That's…" Stephanie paused, her cheeks glowing pink, her eyes shining with emotion. "That's incredible." Her breath hitched slightly as she leaned toward Brian, her hand finding his free one. "I've never… I've never thought about it like that before. I mean, I know making love is supposed to be special, but the way you explained it…" She trailed off, her voice softening as her gaze flicked to Brittney.

"It's about love. Pure, real love. It's not just about the touch; it's about what's behind it. The emotion. The connection." Stephanie's cheeks deepened in color as she added, almost shyly, "And the way you kissed her, Brian, the way you explained it, I feel that whenever we kiss. I'm… a little flustered, hearing you say how it made me feel," she laughed softly, her voice light and warm. "But in the best way."

She took a deep breath, her gaze moving between Brian and Brittney. "It's… it's overwhelming, in a good way. Because you realize that every touch, every kiss, is about saying, 'You matter.' And knowing someone feels that way about you, it's… it's unlike anything else."

Gloria placed a hand on Umi's shoulder, gently guiding her toward the kitchen. They stepped away silently, their retreat ensuring the triad would remain undisturbed.

Brittney's fingers opened and squeezed Brian's hand, her voice soft and gentle. "Brian, I loved it. It was the most incredible thing I've ever felt. Thank you," and her voice went softer, "I love you."

The three sat there, embracing the quiet emotions that raced through their bodies.

Brittney's lips parted, but before she could say anything else, Stephanie grinned and broke the moment with a playful tone, bumping into Brittney softly. "Okay, before we start crying, I have an idea. Let's watch something fun."

Brian chuckled, leaning back onto the couch. "Oh no. What are you thinking, Steph?"

Stephanie's grin widened. "*Elf*. Will Ferrell is a ridiculous Christmas elf and is exactly what we need right now."

Brittney let out a soft laugh, the weight of the conversation lifting as warmth spread through her chest. "That actually sounds... perfect."

Brian stood with a mock groan, stretching. "I'll get the popcorn."

*****

Gloria placed her mug of tea on the counter and leaned against it, her arms folded as she let out a soft sigh. "Umi... did you see that? I mean, really see it?"

Umi nodded, her hands wrapped around her own mug, her expression thoughtful but warm. "I did. It was... beautiful. I didn't know they had come this far, Gloria. The way they communicate, the love they're building—it's incredible."

Gloria smiled faintly, shaking her head. "I was worried at first, you know? When all of this started, this idea of the three of them being... together. I thought it would fall apart, that someone would end up hurt. But seeing this? It's... it's different. It works."

Umi's eyes glistened as she set her mug down. "It's not just that it works. They're healing each other. Brittney... she's finally letting herself feel something real. And Brian..." Her voice softened. "He has so much love to give, and the way he's sharing it with both of them without leaving either one out, it's remarkable."

Gloria chuckled lightly, glancing toward the living room doorway. "Stephanie looked so flustered when Brian explained what making love really is. And Brittney... did you see how she relaxed against his body? That's not just love, Umi. That's trust. He's helping her believe in something good again."

Umi nodded, her voice quiet but steady. "He's teaching her how to feel safe, how to believe she deserves to be loved. And Stephanie..." Umi smiled. "She's glowing, Gloria. She's watching her sister and her boyfriend find this connection, and instead of jealousy, there's joy. Pure joy."

Gloria let out a slow breath, her expression growing thoughtful. "You know, Umi, I've always told Brian to follow his heart, to do what feels right for him. But seeing this, seeing how he's brought your girls together... I think he's teaching us something, too."

Umi raised an eyebrow. "Oh? And what's that?"

"That love doesn't have to fit into a box," Gloria said with a small laugh. "It doesn't have to look the way people expect it to. It just has to feel right for the people in it. And those three?" She gestured toward the living room. "They're making it work in a way I never imagined."

Umi leaned back against the counter, her gaze distant but peaceful. "Do you think they'll last? That this will... endure?"

Gloria smiled, her eyes softening. "I don't know. But after what we just saw, I think they've got a better chance than most. Because what they have isn't just love; it's honesty, trust, patience, and a whole lot of heart. And that's something worth believing in."

Umi nodded slowly, her voice quiet but firm. "I believe in them, Gloria. I really do."

Gloria smiled at her best friend, taking her hand. "I guess they learned from us, too, huh?"

Umi smiled right back, squeezing her hand. "When Kaito passed, I worried I wouldn't be enough for them, that I couldn't give them what they needed. But seeing this... seeing how they've grown together? I know we didn't do so bad, Gloria."

The two women shared a quiet smile before turning their attention back to their tea, their hearts a little lighter after witnessing the depth of the trio's bond.

A moment later, Umi looked up. "Gloria, where do you think Brian learned what he just said? I mean, it's not... well, it's like he was thirty-something when he was talking. Like he's..."

Brian cleared his throat quietly, a rose color on his cheeks as he finished Umi's sentence. "It's because that's how I feel when I kiss either of them, Mom," he answered softly, being careful the girls didn't hear him.

Gloria and Umi jumped at his voice. Gloria stood there, staring at him. "How much of that did you just hear?" she asked softly, a soft red glow on her cheeks.

Brian smiled softly. "Enough to know not to repeat any of it, Mom."

Umi reached over and hugged him. "You are such a gentleman, Brian."

Brian smiled, grabbing the tin of flavored popcorn. "Dad and I talked about more than just cars and computers," he replied softly, turned, and left to join the girls.

Gloria spoke softly. "It's times like this when I think he knows a lot more than he lets on."

Umi nodded. "And you taught him to be a gentleman about it," squeezing her hand.

*****

Late that night, only the sound of the heater could be heard. Stephanie lay in her bed, tossing and turning, her thoughts going over Brian's description of love. Over and over, she replayed the conversation in her head. Finally, she got up and walked into the bathroom that joined hers and Brittney's rooms. She peeked in, and the soft glow of moonlight spilled through the window, casting long shadows across Brittney's room.

Brittney sat cross-legged on the bed, absently twirling the charm of her necklace between her fingers, her own thoughts keeping her awake. Her hair fell in loose waves over her shoulders, and the necklace, Brian's gift from the promise ceremony four weeks ago, felt heavier tonight, weighted with thoughts she hadn't yet found the courage to share.

Stephanie knocked quietly on the door. Before Brittney could answer, Stephanie pushed it open and stepped inside. Stephanie's expression was calm but searching.

"Britt," she said softly, "I couldn't sleep. Can we talk?"

Brittney glanced up, startled. "Yeah… sure."

Stephanie crossed the room and sat next to her sister on the bed. For a moment, neither of them spoke. The stillness was broken only by the faint rustle of the sheets as Stephanie shifted.

"I've been thinking about what Brian said earlier," Stephanie began, her voice careful, "when he talked about what it means to make love."

Brittney's hand stilled on the charm. "Oh."

Stephanie hesitated, then met her sister's eyes. "When he kissed you and nibbled on your arm like that, what was it like?"

Brittney's eyes widened, and she pulled back slightly, shaking her head. "I... I don't know. It's not..."

"Britt," Stephanie interrupted, her tone gentle but insistent, "I need to know. Please."

Brittney hesitated, her hands twisting nervously in her lap. "It's... hard to explain."

"Try, please?" Stephanie's voice was almost a plea. She reached out, running her fingers lightly through Brittney's hair, an old comforting gesture that always seemed to soothe them both. "I really need to know," she added softly.

Brittney took a shaky breath, her gaze dropping to her lap. Slowly, her hands stilled, and when she looked up, her expression was far away, her voice soft and dreamy. "It was... like time stopped. Everything else faded away. It was just him and me, so close I could feel his heartbeat. When he leaned in, I could see every little detail—how his eyes softened, how his lips curved—like he wasn't just kissing me, but giving me a part of himself."

Her voice trembled slightly as she pressed on. "When his lips touched mine, it was like the whole world went quiet. Nothing else mattered. I felt... safe. Like I belonged, even if it was just for that moment."

Stephanie listened quietly, her fingers still stroking Brittney's hair as she spoke. When Brittney's words trailed off,

Stephanie smiled faintly, her eyes glistening with emotion. "I know exactly what you mean."

Brittney blinked, startled by her sister's response. "You do?"

Stephanie nodded, her voice soft and thoughtful as she began to speak. "The day at the lake, when Brian kissed me for the first time... it felt the same way. Everything else disappeared. It was like the world stood still just for us. He looked at me like I was the only person in the world that mattered. And when he kissed me, it wasn't just about the kiss. It was... everything. Like he was telling me I was safe, that I belonged. That he wanted me to be part of something bigger than myself."

Her voice faltered slightly as she met Brittney's gaze. "I didn't want it to end. I wanted to stay in that moment forever."

Brittney tensed, guilt flashing across her face. She dropped her gaze to her lap again, her fingers fidgeting with the hem of her shirt. When she finally spoke, her voice was steadied with determination to be brave. "I... I saw it, Steph."

Stephanie blinked in confusion. "What do you mean?"

"That day at the lake," Brittney said, her voice trembling. "I saw you kissing him. I saw everything."

Stephanie froze, her breath catching. "You... you saw us?"

Brittney nodded, tears welling up in her eyes. "I didn't mean to. I was coming back from the cooler, and I heard voices. I thought I'd just slip by, but then... I saw you."

Her voice cracked, and she wiped at her cheeks. "You looked so happy, Steph. The way he held you, the way you looked at him — it was like nothing else in the world mattered. And all I could think was... that should've been me."

Stephanie held her breath and said nothing, giving Brittney the space to continue.

"It hurt so much," Brittney whispered, her voice breaking. "I'd dreamed about that moment for so long. Every fantasy I'd ever had about Brian... it was all gone. Ripped away. It wasn't just losing him. It felt like I was losing you, too."

Her tears spilled over, and her voice dropped to a whisper. "I felt invisible, Steph. Like a third thumb. Like I didn't belong anymore."

Stephanie's heart ached at the raw pain in her sister's voice. She reached out, pulling Brittney into a tight hug. "Oh, Britt. I'm so sorry you felt that way. You'll always belong. Always."

Brittney clung to her, her tears soaking into Stephanie's top. "I don't know how to fix it," she sobbed. "I feel like I've ruined everything."

Stephanie pulled back, cupping Brittney's face in her hands. "You haven't ruined anything," she said firmly. "You're here, and we're talking. That's what matters. You'll always be my sister, my twin, my other half. Nothing will ever change that. Remember our promises to each other during our ceremony? I believe in that promise I made to you."

Stephanie leaned forward, resting her forehead against Brittney's.

After a few moments, Brittney added, her voice quiet but thoughtful. "You know... what Brian said earlier, about making love... it's exactly like what I felt. Every word."

Stephanie nodded slowly, her fingers still brushing gently through Brittney's hair. "Me too. When he talked about sharing a part of himself, about making you feel safe and wanted... that's exactly what I feel with him, too."

Brittney tilted her head, her brows furrowing slightly. "Do you think that's just... who he is? That he can make people feel that way?"

Stephanie paused, considering her sister's question carefully. "Maybe. But I think it's more than that. I think it's how he feels about us. About you. About me. He doesn't just kiss or hold someone because it's easy or expected. When Brian gives you something, it's real. And it means something."

Brittney's lips curved into a small smile, though her voice was tinged with awe. "It felt like he was speaking a whole other language like everything he couldn't say out loud was in that kiss."

Stephanie smiled back, a warmth spreading through her chest. "Yeah. That's exactly it. Like the kiss said all the things words couldn't."

They fell quiet again, the weight of their realization settling over them like a shared secret. Finally, Brittney broke the silence, her voice trembling slightly but steady. "Steph... I think we both saw different sides of him, but they're the same. He made us both feel safe like we belong. Like we're enough."

Stephanie reached out, taking Brittney's hand in hers and squeezing gently. "Because we are, Britt. To him. To each other. To everyone who loves us."

Brittney's smile grew, and she squeezed her sister's hand in return. "You're right. I think that's what he was trying to tell us all along."

Stephanie leaned in, resting her forehead against Brittney's once more. "And I think he's going to keep telling us in all the ways that matter."

The quietness of the house returned, and the weight of the night gave way to something softer, something lighter.

Stephanie shifted, lying back against the pillows and gently tugging Brittney down beside her. Without a word, Brittney followed, curling close like they had so many times as children. Stephanie's arm draped over her sister's shoulder, her fingers brushing soothing patterns across Brittney's back.

For the first time in a long while, there was no tension between them, no unspoken hurt. They were just two sisters together, safe in the warmth of their bond. Slowly, their breaths evened out, and their hands relaxed where they had clasped together. The quiet of the room wrapped around them, and like in their younger years, they drifted off to sleep, both content in the comfort of knowing they had found their way back to each other and to a place where they truly belonged.

CHAPTER 18

Brittney had spent the past week reflecting on her conversation about love, the question lingering in her mind. Now, as she sat quietly in the art studio with her sketchpad in hand, she wondered if the images she created could untangle the emotions swirling within her. The room was warm, filled with gentle chatter and the soft scratch of pencils on paper. Students of various ages were seated at easels or clustered around tables, each absorbed in their work. The faint smell of graphite and paint held Brittney in the present moment.

For the first time in weeks, her hands didn't tremble. She had spent the past hour sketching an idea for the day's assignment: a scene that evoked hope. Her pencil moved almost instinctively, creating a soft rendering of sunlight breaking through trees.

"How's it coming?" a calm, encouraging voice interrupted her focus. Brittney glanced up to see Mr. Hargrove, the art teacher, standing beside her. He was a man in his fifties with kind eyes and a gentle demeanor that put everyone at ease.

"It's coming along," Brittney replied softly, tilting the sketch toward him.

Mr. Hargrove studied it for a moment, his face lighting up with a smile. "You've got such a wonderful eye for light and atmosphere, Brittney. I'm really glad you decided to join the class. That natural talent of yours just keeps getting better."

Brittney's cheeks warmed at the praise. She'd always assumed he'd invited her because of a conversation with her therapist, but the encouragement felt genuine. "Thank you," she murmured.

"Actually, I've got an idea for a project I think you'd enjoy," Mr. Hargrove continued. "It's a collaborative piece, and I think it'll be a fun challenge for you."

Brittney tilted her head, curious but hesitant. "A project?"

Mr. Hargrove's smile widened. "Yes. A new student just joined the class, and I think the two of you would work well together. You'll be creating a comic book. Does that sound like something you'd like to try?"

Brittney's stomach tightened. She wasn't sure she was ready to work with anyone, especially after everything that had happened. "Who's the partner?" she asked cautiously.

"Ashley Diaz," Mr. Hargrove said, nodding toward the opposite corner of the room.

Brittney's heart skipped a beat. Ashley Diaz was sitting at an easel, her head tilted slightly as she worked on a vibrant painting of a city skyline at sunset. Her long, dark hair was pulled into a loose braid, and her focused expression softened as she leaned back to evaluate her work. Brittney hadn't spoken to Ashley in nearly two months, not since she started remote learning.

"Ashley?" Brittney asked quietly.

"She likes the idea," Mr. Hargrove said. "And I think the two of you could create something truly special. She mentioned that you two used to work on comics together in middle school."

Brittney hesitated, her fingers gripping the edge of her sketchpad. "Does she…"

Mr. Hargrove's expression softened. "She knows some of what's happened, Brittney. But I think you'll find that she's more understanding than you expect."

Brittney's throat tightened, but she nodded. "Okay. I'll try."

"Good," Mr. Hargrove said warmly. "How about you go over and talk and see what you come up with."

With a deep breath, Brittney stood and gathered her sketchpad. Her legs felt unsteady as she crossed the room. When she reached Ashley's table, she hesitated, her voice catching in her throat.

"Hey," she finally managed.

Ashley looked up, her dark eyes widening in surprise. For a moment, Brittney braced herself for the worst—for judgment, for rejection. But instead, Ashley smiled.

"Brittney! Hey, we missed you so much," Ashley said warmly, setting down her brush. "Mr. Hargrove said we might be working together. I'm glad."

"You are?" Brittney's voice was small, uncertain.

"Of course," Ashley said, her smile unwavering. "We used to have so much fun making comics in middle school. I've missed that."

Brittney stared at her, struggling to process Ashley's easy acceptance. "I thought... I thought you might hate me. Because of the rumors and how they started talking about you."

Ashley's expression softened, and she shook her head. "Brittney, I don't believe everything I hear. Richard and Peter were always full of it. And after what happened to them, it's pretty clear they were the real problem. You should know there are others, many others, who feel the same way I do. You've got more people on your side than you think."

Brittney's eyes stung as she fought back tears. "You don't know how much that means to me."

Ashley reached out, resting a hand on Brittney's arm. "You're not alone, okay? I'm here. And if you're up for it, I think we could make an amazing comic together."

For the first time in what felt like forever, Brittney felt comfortable with someone outside her home. "I'd like that."

They spent the rest of the class talking in hushed tones, and their heads bent over a blank sheet of paper as they sketched out ideas. The comic book, they decided, would be about two sisters overcoming obstacles and fighting for each other. It felt personal, but in a way that gave Brittney hope — hope that she could heal, create, and reconnect with the world around her.

As the class ended, Ashley nudged her playfully. "You know, I'm going to make you do the hardest parts of this, right?"

Brittney laughed softly, the sound surprising even herself. "Bring it on."

CHAPTER 19

L ater in the week, Gloria and Umi sat across from each other at the table, their hands full of cards, a mix of concentration and laughter filling the room. A half-empty carafe of tea sat nearby, the rich aroma mingling with the faint scent of a recent meal.

"You're bluffing," Umi said, narrowing her eyes as she studied Gloria.

Gloria grinned, tapping her cards on the table. "Am I? Only one way to find out."

Before Umi could make her move, Brian appeared in the doorway, his expression hesitant. He glanced back toward the living room, where the twins were curled up on the couch, softly chatting and laughing.

"Moms?" Brian's voice broke the rhythm of the game. "Can I talk to you? Privately?"

Gloria and Umi exchanged a glance, their amusement giving way to curiosity and a touch of concern. Gloria set her cards down and leaned back in her chair. "Of course, sweetheart. What's on your mind?"

Brian shifted his weight, his hands stuffed in his pockets. "Can we go to my room? It's... kind of important."

Gloria's brow furrowed slightly, but she nodded, standing and gesturing for Umi to follow. "Lead the way, Brian."

The three of them made their way down the hall to Brian's room. Inside, the space was neat, a testament to his careful nature. A well-worn desk sat in one corner, a bookshelf lined with novels and trinkets in another. Brian hesitated by the bed before sitting on its edge, motioning for his moms to take the chairs near the desk.

Gloria and Umi settled in, their expressions patient but expectant.

Brian took a deep breath, pulling a small ring box from his pocket. "You've already seen this, Mom," he said, opening the box to reveal a delicate engagement and wedding band set. The bands gleamed under the soft light, their intricate design understated but elegant. "Mom Gloria, this is for Stephanie. I... I've been planning to propose to her on Christmas Eve."

Gloria's eyes softened, a proud smile spreading across her face. "It's beautiful, Brian. She's going to love it."

Umi nodded, her hands clasped tightly in her lap. "You've thought this through. It's a lovely choice."

Brian exhaled, his shoulders relaxing slightly. Then, hesitating for just a moment, he reached into his other pocket and pulled out a second ring box. This one he opened more slowly, revealing another set of engagement and wedding

248

bands. The design was similar to Stephanie's but subtly different, simpler, with a touch of uniqueness.

Gloria's smile faltered, replaced by a look of confusion. "Brian? What...?"

Brian's voice was steady, but his hands trembled slightly as he held the box. "This one is for Brittney."

Umi's eyes widened, her lips parting as if to speak, but no words came.

Brian pressed on, his gaze shifting between his two mothers. "I know this is... unconventional. But I love them both. I've thought about this a lot, and I can't imagine my life without either of them. They've always shared everything, and... I want to share my life with both of them."

He hesitated, then added, "Christmas is in two weeks, and when we go to Rockefeller Center this year, I want to propose with the New York skyline in the background. Maybe you could take pictures for us? I want it to be super special for them both. Please agree with me. I know all of your arguments... I've been thinking this over since we had our promise ceremony and the talk that I, umm, didn't hear between you both."

The room fell into a heavy silence. Gloria leaned forward, her voice measured. "Brian, marriage isn't just about love. It's a legal and emotional commitment. Are you sure you understand what you're asking for?"

Brian nodded, his expression earnest. "I do. I know it'll be complicated. But they've been through so much, and they're stronger together. I want to be part of their strength, to support them both equally."

Umi's voice was soft, almost hesitant. "Have you talked to them about this? Do they even want this?"

Brian shook his head. "Not yet. I wanted to talk to you first. I need your support, your blessing before I even bring this up with them."

"Before you answer, please think of this. We know Stephanie will marry me, and when we do, things will change. I don't want that. I want what we have right now, and if you were to ask them, they'd say they want what we have forever. I don't think Brittney would handle that change well. Heck, I know I wouldn't, and I don't think Steph will either. I know in my heart this is what I want and that both of them do too," Brian explained, his voice soft and gentle but with a firmness Gloria recognized.

Gloria exchanged a long look with Umi, unspoken thoughts passing between them. Finally, Gloria turned back to Brian, her expression a mix of love and concern.

"Sweetheart, this is… a lot to process," she said gently. "But we know how much you care about them. We need to think about this, to talk about it. And you need to be sure this is what you truly want, for all of you."

Brian nodded, his jaw tightening with determination. "I've never been as sure of anything else as I am of this. I know that we can't be legally married. I get that, and I'm planning on talking about this with either Monsignor Glenn or Father Mike at St. Barnabas about it. Right now, before I go any further, I want you both to know how I feel, and what I want to do."

Umi reached out, placing a hand over his. "We'll think about it, Brian. But whatever happens, we're here for you. Always."

Gloria smiled softly, her hand joining Umi's. "No matter what, we'll figure this out together. You're not alone in this."

Brian exhaled, a small, relieved smile breaking through his tension. "Thank you. That's all I needed to hear."

When everyone walked back into the living room, as Brian settled between the twins, Brittney asked, "What was that all about? Is everything okay?"

Brian leaned over, kissing her forehead. "Couldn't be better. Just something about my stump that I needed to show them," he fibbed.

Stephanie whispered, "You do know I can tell when you're fibbing, right?"

Brian's face blushed slightly. "If you can, then you need to keep it quiet. I promise, both of you, it's nothing bad, okay?"

Stephanie and Brittney, at the same time, kissed him on opposite sides. "Love you," they said in unison.

Brittney leaned forward so she could see Stephanie. "You have to teach me how to read him like that," she said with a soft giggle.

Stephanie smiled. "It's easy. Just look for dimples when he tries to hide behind his smile," she said with a playful look at Brian.

*****

Three days later, Brian sat nervously in the waiting area of St. Barnabas's Church office, rehearsing in his mind what he wanted to say. His hands fidgeted with the hem of his jacket as he tried to settle the words into a logical order. Despite his best efforts, his thoughts kept jumbling together, the weight of the conversation ahead pressing heavily on his chest.

The soft, golden light spilling from Father Mike's office was warm and inviting, spilling into the hallway and casting gentle shadows. From his seat, Brian could see shelves lined with books and religious artifacts, a testament to the depth of Father Mike's faith and studies. A well-loved crucifix hung prominently on the wall, surrounded by icons and framed scripture verses. On the desk sat a handful of family photos, worn around the edges from years of handling, evidence of a priest deeply connected to both his faith and his loved ones. The faint scent of candles added a calming serenity to the room, though it did little to calm Brian's nerves.

The door to the office opened, and Father Mike stepped out, his expression lighting up as he spotted Brian. His warm, cheerful tone cut through the tension like a ray of sunlight. "Brian, my boy, you look like a man carrying the weight of the world. Come on in before you hurt yourself."

Brian managed a nervous chuckle, standing and shaking the priest's offered hand. "Thanks, Father. I appreciate you making time for me."

"Always, Brian. You've got that 'serious business' look about you, so let's hear it. Coffee? Tea? Holy water?" Father Mike quipped as he took a seat behind his desk, gesturing for Brian to sit.

Brian laughed softly, the tension easing a little. "No, I'm good. Thanks."

Father Mike leaned back in his chair, studying the young man before him. "So, what's on your mind? Girl troubles? Or should I say… girls?"

Brian hesitated, rubbing the back of his neck. "Yeah, it's about Stephanie and Brittney. Father, I love them both. Deeply. I know it's unconventional, but my feelings for them are real, and I don't know how to deal with this."

Father Mike's smile faded slightly as he leaned forward, resting his arms on the desk. "Unconventional doesn't mean wrong, Brian. It just means rare. Tell me more about what's on your heart."

Brian nodded, his voice steady but tinged with vulnerability. "Love isn't a box. It doesn't come in just one shape or size. What works for one couple might not work for another. My love for Stephanie and Brittney isn't something you see every day, but neither is love itself."

Father Mike tilted his head, nodding slowly. "Most people don't think like you do, Brian. For a lot of folks, love has rules, limits, and boundaries. But you're seeing it as something expansive, something infinite."

Brian leaned forward, his hands clasped tightly. "That's just it. I don't believe love is a finite thing, like money in a wallet. The more you share it, the more it grows. My love for Stephanie doesn't take away from my love for Brittney. They're both unique, and I cherish them both differently, but no less deeply."

Father Mike's eyes glimmered with a mix of admiration and thoughtfulness. "That's a profound way to look at it. It's rare, and it's beautiful. And I bet it's why you're here, isn't it?"

Brian nodded. "Yes. I want to make this commitment to them. To both of them. I know it's not legal to marry more than one person, but I need to find a way to honor what I feel for Brittney without taking away from Stephanie."

Father Mike exhaled slowly, steepling his fingers. "Brian, I can't legally or canonically marry you to both women. The church and the law are clear on that. But I hear what you're saying. This isn't about legality; it's about love, and that's a far more complicated thing."

Brian's shoulders sagged slightly. "I thought as much. But… is there anything you can do? Some way to acknowledge both relationships?"

Father Mike's expression softened as a thought came to him. "Do you know about handfasting?"

Brian's brow furrowed. "I've heard of it, but I don't know much."

"In the 1600s, before marriage certificates were common, couples would perform handfasting ceremonies. It was a binding agreement between them, based on vows, love, and mutual respect. It wasn't about the law; it was about the promise." Father Mike leaned back, a small smile playing at his lips. "If you don't need a certificate and are comfortable with your vows, perhaps this could be a way to honor Brittney."

Brian's eyes lit up. "That sounds perfect. Can you perform the handfasting?"

Father Mike's smile turned rueful. "Ah, that's where we run into another snag. As a priest, I can't officiate a handfasting. It's outside the church's purview. But I can offer my blessings — to you and both women, as couples, not as a married trio, but as individuals who deeply care for one another."

Brian sat back, letting the words settle over him. "Your blessing means everything, Father Mike. I'm not asking for the impossible, just for this love to be acknowledged for what it is."

Father Mike reached across the desk, placing a hand on Brian's shoulder. "Then you have it. Your love, unconventional as it may be, is sincere and rooted in goodness. And that's worth celebrating."

Brian's tension melted away, replaced by a grateful smile. "Thank you. Truly."

Father Mike grinned, leaning back in his chair. "Now, about this love of yours... you'd better have some strong coffee ready. You'll need it to keep up with two strong-willed Welch women."

Brian laughed, the sound lighter than before. "I think you're right about that."

They spent a few more moments discussing practicalities, sharing a laugh here and there, before Brian rose to leave. As he stepped out of the office, he felt a sense of peace settle over him. Father Mike's words echoed in his heart: Love, unconventional as it may be, is sincere and rooted in goodness.

CHAPTER 20

A week later, that Friday, Umi sat on the couch, her phone pressed to her ear as she listened to Captain Bishop's steady voice. The warm afternoon sunlight filtered through the curtains, casting soft patterns on the living room floor. A mug of tea rested on the table in front of her, untouched.

"I'm sorry, Umi," Captain Bishop said. "We won't be able to make it over today. Something urgent has come up."

Umi nodded, even though Bishop couldn't see her. "I understand. I'm sure things come up at your office all the time, and things can be unpredictable."

"Thank you for being so understanding," Bishop said, her tone genuinely apologetic. "We'll reschedule as soon as we can. Please let Brittney know we're still here for her, and that she's doing great."

"I will," Umi promised. "Take care, Captain."

"You too, Umi."

The call ended, and Umi set the phone down with a soft sigh. She leaned back, her eyes drifting to the mug of tea before her thoughts turned to Gloria. Picking up the phone again, she dialed.

Gloria answered after the second ring. "Hey, Umi. Everything okay?"

"Yes, just giving you an update," Umi replied. "Captain Bishop and Scott can't make it today. She said something urgent came up."

"That's too bad," Gloria said, her voice thoughtful. "How's Brittney holding up?"

"She's doing well, I think. The art classes have been a good outlet for her. And Ashley... Ashley's been a real blessing."

"I'm glad to hear that," Gloria said, a smile evident in her tone. After a pause, she added, "Have you thought any more about Brian's plans?"

Umi hesitated. "I have. It's... a lot to consider. You?"

"Same," Gloria admitted. "It's unconventional, but... you know Brian. He's always been so thoughtful, so deliberate about the people he loves. And the twins... they've been through so much. Maybe this is exactly what they want, you know? I also thought about his logic about how they would handle things, and quite frankly, I agree with him."

Umi's voice softened. "Do you think they're ready for something like this?"

"They're stronger than we sometimes give them credit for," Gloria said. "And Brian... he's been thinking about this for a long time. I told you about Stephanie's ring back when all of this started. He's not rushing into it. He knows what he's asking."

"Has Brian talked with anyone at the church yet?" Umi asked.

Gloria thought for a few seconds. "I know he went there, but I haven't spoken with him about it yet. However, I'll say this about it—he hasn't been gloomy or upset, so maybe he's got something good to share."

Umi nodded, her resolve firming. "Well, if it's good, and if we say yes, we need to support them fully. No half-measures," she paused, "and it has to be after graduation."

Gloria's smile was audible again. "We'll talk with him before dinner tonight and hear him out. And I'm with you about it."

*****

Umi and Gloria sat at the dining table, the soft clink of teacups filling the space. Afternoon sunlight streamed through the curtains, bathing the room in a warm glow. Both women were deep in thought, the quiet occasionally broken by the faint creak of a chair or the sound of a spoon against ceramic.

"I keep thinking about what Brian said," Umi began, stirring her tea absentmindedly. "The way he talks about Stephanie and Brittney... it's not just love. It's devotion. He truly sees them as equals."

Gloria nodded, her expression contemplative. "I've always known Brian had a big heart, but this... it's more than I expected. He's not just thinking about himself; he's considering both girls, their feelings, and what this means for the family."

Umi sighed, her gaze drifting to the teacup in her hands. "It's a lot to take in. The idea of honoring both relationships without upsetting the balance... It's bold."

"It's Brian," Gloria said with a small smile. "And let's be honest, Umi. If anyone can pull this off, it's him."

The sound of a cupboard opening in the nearby kitchen drew their attention. Brian had wandered in, rummaging for something. Gloria took the opportunity to call out, her tone light but curious. "Brian, you seem awfully chipper today. Care to tell us why?"

Brian paused, turning back toward the dining room with a sheepish smile. "I guess you could say I had a good talk with Father Mike."

Gloria exchanged a quick look with Umi, then gestured toward an empty chair at the table. "Well, don't keep us in suspense. Come sit and tell us about it."

Brian grabbed a can of soda and joined them, the spring in his step unmistakable. He set the can down and leaned back, his expression calm but clearly pleased.

"Father Mike was amazing," he began. "He helped me see things clearly. We talked about love, how it's not something that fits into neat little boxes. It's infinite. The more you give, the more it grows."

Umi tilted her head, intrigued. "And he agreed with that?"

Brian nodded. "He did. He said most people see love as limited, but the way I feel for Stephanie and Brittney... he called it rare but beautiful."

Gloria leaned forward slightly, her brow furrowing. "Did he have any advice on how to navigate this?"

"He did," Brian said, his smile widening. "He talked about handfasting, a tradition from the 1600s. It's not about legality. It's about promises and commitment. He said it could be a way to honor my bond with Brittney without undermining my marriage to Stephanie. So, to keep it equal, I'd do a handfasting with both of them."

Umi's eyes widened slightly. "Handfasting? That's... interesting. What did he suggest?"

Brian leaned his elbows on the table, his voice steady. "He said he couldn't perform a handfasting himself because it's not part of the church's sacraments. But he offered his blessing. To all of us as individuals and as couples. He said it's about acknowledging the love and care we have for one another."

Both women sat in thoughtful silence for a moment, processing his words. Finally, Gloria broke the silence. "And how do you plan to present this to the twins?"

Brian's confidence didn't waver. "I'll tell them exactly what Father Mike told me. This isn't about paperwork or societal norms. It's about promises, love, and respect. I'll make sure they both know how much they mean to me."

Umi smiled softly, her worry easing. "You've really thought this through, haven't you?"

"I have," Brian said firmly. "This isn't just about me. It's about them, about us, and making sure we all feel seen, valued, and loved."

Gloria gave a small chuckle, shaking her head. "Well, Brian, it sounds like you've got a plan. But are you ready for the challenge of presenting this to two strong-willed Welch women?"

Brian grinned. "I think I'm up for it. And if I'm not, there's always coffee or tea."

The three of them shared a laugh, the atmosphere light but filled with understanding.

"Thanks for listening," Brian said, standing and pushing in his chair. "I'll leave you to your tea."

"Brian," Gloria called after him, her tone warm. "No matter what, you have us in your corner."

Brian gave a grateful nod, his smile unwavering as he left the room.

As the door clicked softly behind him, Umi leaned back in her chair, letting out a long breath. "He really is remarkable, isn't he?"

Gloria smiled knowingly. "He is. And I think... I think we can trust him to handle this."

Umi glanced toward the door, her expression softening. "I think you're right."

They sat in companionable silence for a few moments before Gloria chuckled. "He's going to need all the coffee in the world, though."

Umi laughed, raising her teacup in agreement. "Here's to Brian, and his unshakable optimism."

*****

That evening, the family gathered around the dining table for dinner. Plates clinked softly as everyone helped themselves to the spread of food, the room filled with the comforting murmur of conversation.

As the meal wound down, Gloria set her fork down and glanced at Brian, her expression calm but purposeful.

"Brian," she said, drawing his attention. "The answer to your question is yes."

Brian froze mid-reach for his glass of water, his brow furrowing slightly as he tried to process her words. Then, as realization dawned, a wide, relieved smile spread across his face.

"Really?" he asked, his voice quiet but filled with emotion.

Gloria nodded. "Really."

Umi's small smile mirrored Gloria's as she added, "We're with you, Brian. All the way."

The twins, seated on either side of Brian, exchanged confused glances. Stephanie leaned closer, her curiosity evident.

"What are you talking about?" she asked.

Brittney joined in, her tone just as curious. "Yeah, what's going on?"

Brian leaned back in his chair, his grin turning playful but sincere. "You'll find out soon enough."

"Brian," Stephanie pressed, her eyes narrowing in mock suspicion. "What are you up to?"

"Nothing bad," he said cryptically, his smile unwavering. "I promise. Just wait."

The twins exchanged skeptical looks, but their curiosity only deepened. Gloria and Umi, seated across the table, shared a knowing glance, their poker faces firmly in place. Each wore a faint, satisfied smile, content to let the moment linger as they watched the family they'd nurtured grow closer still.

CHAPTER 21

A week later, Christmas Eve day arrived, and in Brian's mind, it took forever. As he walked up the driveway to the girls' home, a light dusting of snow crunched under his boots. His breath puffed in the chilly air. He knocked once before stepping inside, greeted immediately by warmth, laughter, and the faint smell of cinnamon.

"Brian!" Brittney called from the living room, standing on the couch to adjust the string lights. "You're just in time! Grab a pillow; we're setting up."

Brian set his bag by the door and stepped into the cozy disarray, teasing, "I love the attitude! It's great to see you smiling and getting into the Christmas spirit, Britt."

Brittney turned to face him, her grin wide as she pointed at Stephanie. "Ask her! It's all her fault."

Stephanie laughed, shaking her head. "Just making sure you're in peak holiday spirit."

Brian shook his head. "Love it. I simply love it."

"Don't mind the chaos," Stephanie added, untangling a strand of lights on the floor. "We're in full holiday prep mode."

Brian walked into the living room, grabbing a handful of popcorn from the bowl on the table. "Christmas chaos looks good on you guys. What's the movie lineup?"

"That's the question," Stephanie replied, standing up with her now-functional lights. "We're trying to decide, and it's already turning into an argument."

"It's not an argument," Brittney said, hopping down from the couch. "It's a passionate discussion. Obviously, we're starting with *Home Alone*. It's a classic."

Stephanie groaned. "No way. We've started with *Home Alone* every year. Let's shake it up. *Elf* is way funnier."

"Fun doesn't mean better," Brian interjected, grabbing another handful of popcorn. "How about *It's a Wonderful Life*? Perfect start for a day like this."

Stephanie snorted. "And cry before noon? Hard pass."

"Yeah, Brian," Brittney teased, sitting cross-legged on the couch. "We need something with action. Or at least traps."

Brian shrugged, unfazed. "Fine. But if we're watching *Elf*, I get to pick next."

Stephanie pointed a finger at him. "You're not sneaking in a sob fest before the second round, either."

As the debate escalated, the sound of keys jingling at the door pulled their attention. Gloria and Umi stepped in, each carrying reusable bags filled with Christmas treats from the church bake sale. Gloria raised an eyebrow at the scene, her gaze flicking to the popcorn and fairy lights.

"Looks like movie prep is in full swing," Gloria said, setting her bags on the counter.

"Full swing," Stephanie confirmed. "And we're stuck on what to start with."

"Brian wants us crying by lunch," Brittney added.

"I said *It's a Wonderful Life*! That's called holiday spirit, not crying."

"Of course, Brian does," Umi said, smiling softly as she set her bag down. "He's our resident romantic. Speaking of which," she added, sliding into an armchair, "what about starting with *The Holiday*? It's funny, sweet, and festive."

Gloria nodded. "Or *Love Actually*. Classic Christmas romance."

Stephanie groaned dramatically, dropping onto the couch. "Not you two! We can't start with romance. It's Christmas, not Valentine's Day!"

"But it *is* about love," Brian said, grinning. "And isn't Christmas all about love?"

Brittney rolled her eyes but smiled. "We love your hopeless romantic streak, Brian. It's sweet… but maybe not all the time."

"Fine," Brian relented, laughing. "But I get the final say on the second movie."

As the debate circled back to *Home Alone*, Gloria's eyes landed on Brittney, who was humming cheerfully while fiddling with a string of lights. "Why are you so bubbly today?" she asked with a playful smirk. "You're practically glowing."

Brittney grinned and pointed at Stephanie. "Because she promised to tickle me until I cried and then fill me up with cookies until I'm on a sugar high."

Umi chuckled, shaking her head. "Sounds like bribery to me."

"Effective bribery," Brittney shot back, grabbing a cookie.

Brian threw a pillow at Stephanie, grinning. "You're such a softie."

Stephanie caught the pillow mid-air. "Hey, whatever it takes to keep the holiday spirit alive."

"All right, all right," Gloria said, sitting down beside Umi. "Let's settle this. One vote each. Brittney?"

"*Home Alone*," she said firmly.

"Stephanie?" Umi asked.

"*Elf*. Way funnier."

Brian leaned forward. "*It's a Wonderful Life*. I'm standing my ground."

"Mom?" Stephanie asked, glancing between Umi and Gloria.

Umi exchanged a conspiratorial look with Gloria before they both said, "*The Holiday*."

The room erupted into groans, laughs, and playful protests, the perfect start to their holiday tradition.

*****

That night, the cold air sparkled with the promise of snow as the family's well-loved tradition of visiting New York City was in full swing. Gloria maneuvered the minivan through light traffic while Umi sat beside her in the passenger seat, her hand resting casually on the armrest. The twins were nestled in the middle row, bundled in scarves and hats. Brian occupied

266

the back row, leaning against the window with a thoughtful smile.

The conversation was light, filled with excitement about the tree, the lights, and the festive atmosphere they all looked forward to each year.

"I hope they've added something new to the light show this time," Stephanie said, leaning toward Brittney.

"I just want to see it all lit up," Brittney replied, her face bright with anticipation. "Pictures don't do it justice."

In the back, Brian discreetly pulled out his phone. He typed a quick text to Umi detailing the exact location he wanted for the proposal. A soft ding filled the car, drawing Stephanie's attention.

"What was that?" she asked.

Umi glanced at her phone and smiled, tucking it away. "Just a reminder about dinner reservations," she replied lightly. Stephanie and Brittney nodded, their curiosity fading as the conversation shifted back to holiday cheer.

*****

The family arrived at Rockefeller Center, the towering tree glittering against the backdrop of the New York skyline. The sound of the crowd's excitement filled the air as they watched the light show and marveled at the festive decorations. Gloria and Umi stayed a few steps behind, quietly discussing Brian's text.

"It's a beautiful spot," Umi said. "I can see why he chose it."

Gloria nodded. "He's put so much thought into this. Let's make sure it's perfect."

After the festivities, the family began the journey home, still chattering about the sights and sounds of the evening. As they drove through the city, Brittney looked up from the window, her brow furrowing.

"This isn't the way we usually go," she said.

"I'm trying a different route," Gloria replied with a casual shrug. "Thought we'd see if it's faster."

When they reached their destination, the minivan came to a stop. Gloria let out a soft laugh. "Well, that didn't work like I thought. Anyone want to see the skyline like we've never seen it before?"

Curious murmurs rose, and everyone climbed out of the van. The family followed a winding path that opened to a breathtaking view of the New York skyline, the city lights shimmering against the night sky. Brian paused, his heart pounding as he spotted the place. He guided the twins to stand side by side, with the skyline stretching out behind them, the city lights twinkling like stars. His voice was steady but filled with emotion as he spoke.

"Wait here a second," he said, positioning them carefully so the shimmering skyline formed the perfect backdrop.

Gloria and Umi exchanged a knowing glance, stepping back quietly and pulling out their phones.

Brian knelt on one knee, his voice soft and steady. "Stephanie," he began, drawing her attention. Her eyes widened as she turned to him, disbelief and wonder mingling on her face.

"You have been my light, my best friend, and my anchor for as long as I can remember. You see the best in everyone, even when they don't see it in themselves. I want to spend the rest of my life loving you the way you deserve. Will you marry me?"

Stephanie's hands flew to her mouth as tears filled her eyes. "Yes," she whispered, her voice trembling. "A thousand times, yes."

Brian smiled as he slipped the ring onto her finger, his heart soaring.

Then he turned to Brittney, still kneeling. Her expression was a mix of surprise and disbelief.

"Brittney," he said, his voice soft but resolute, "You've always had a fire inside you, a strength that inspires everyone around you. I love you for your courage, your softness, and the way you make everything in my life brighter just by being you. I want to stand by your side through everything for the rest of our lives. Will you marry me?"

Tears spilled down Brittney's cheeks as she shook her head in disbelief. "You can't be serious…"

"I've never been more serious about anything," Brian replied earnestly.

Stephanie's excitement was contagious as she nudged Brittney, laughing through her own tears. "Say yes, Britt. Come on, say yes! We know you want to; just do it!"

Brittney's lips trembled before breaking into a wide, emotional smile. "Yes," she whispered. "Yes, I'll marry you," soft tears rolling down her cheeks.

Brian slipped the second ring onto Brittney's finger, his own eyes misting over. He stood, pulling both girls into a tight embrace as the city lights sparkled behind them.

"You both just made me the happiest man in the world," he commented into their ears.

Gloria and Umi, standing a few steps away, clapped softly, their smiles radiant. Gloria snapped pictures of the three of them against the skyline, capturing the moment they all became one family.

The walk back to the van was filled with excited chatter, the twins' laughter and questions cutting through the cool night air. As they climbed back inside, Stephanie turned in her seat to look at Brian in the back row, her eyes gleaming.

"Brian, how long have you been planning this?" she asked, her voice eager.

Brian leaned forward slightly, addressing her and Brittney in the middle row. "Long enough to make it perfect," he said cryptically.

Brittney frowned playfully, though her hand lingered on the ring. "Perfect? You didn't tell us anything! What about dinner reservations? The 'faster' way home? Was that even real?"

Umi chuckled softly from the front seat. "Sometimes little fibs are necessary," she said, her voice teasing.

Stephanie leaned closer to Brittney, her expression thoughtful, "So... have you ever thought about a wedding? I mean, we always talked about princes, knights, castles, and dragons when we were kids..."

Brittney's eyes lit up as she joined in, "And a prince in shining armor! Don't forget the prince."

Brian grinned, shifting his attention back and forth between them, "I don't think a knight can top a prince proposing to two princesses. But if you both want castles, princes and knights, we'll figure it out."

The twins giggled, caught up in the fairytale energy of the moment. Brian chuckled with them, but as the laughter ebbed, his expression softened. The lightheartedness of the moment faded into something deeper.

"You know," he began, his voice calm but earnest, "there's something Father Mike and I talked about that I want to share with you both."

Stephanie tilted her head, curiosity flickering in her eyes. Brittney's playful smile lingered, though her gaze sharpened as she leaned in slightly, sensing the shift in his tone.

Brian took a breath, steadying himself, "When I spoke to Father Mike, I told him how much I love both of you. How unconventional it is, but also how real it is. He understood, and he said something that stuck with me: love isn't about fitting into a box or following someone else's rules. It's about promises and the way we honor those promises."

Stephanie nodded slowly, her curiosity growing, "That makes sense. But what are you getting at?"

Brian smiled, glancing at her and then at Brittney, "He told me about something called a handfasting. It's an old tradition from before the 1600s, before marriage certificates. Back then, couples would bind themselves to each other through vows. It wasn't about the law. It was about love and mutual respect."

Brittney's eyes lit up again, this time with a different kind of excitement, "That sounds like something out of a storybook! A promise sealed with love? I love it already."

Stephanie's brow furrowed slightly, though her tone was gentle, "But how would it work? I mean, what would it mean for us?"

Brian leaned forward, his hands resting on his knees, "It would be a way to honor the bond we share without making it illegal in the traditional sense. Father Mike can't perform a handfasting; it's outside the church's purview, but he offered to bless us, as couples, to acknowledge what we mean to each other. And, in the eyes of the law, we'd only be three roommates."

The van grew quiet for a moment, the weight of his words settling over them. Stephanie broke the silence, her voice thoughtful. "It sounds beautiful, but... what will people think? It's not exactly normal."

Brittney hesitated, glancing down at her hands. "Yeah. What if they don't understand? What if they think it's... weird?"

Brian's smile was calm, his confidence unshaken. "They might. But what matters is how *we* feel about each other, not what anyone else thinks. This isn't about proving anything to anyone else. It's about us, about being true to who we are and what we mean to each other. As far as anyone is concerned, we will have our rings. We are married. If they doubt or question it, well, it's on them. Only the ones who really matter to us, the ones we trust, will know the truth."

Stephanie met his gaze, her expression softening. "You're right. It's about us, not them."

Brittney looked up, her hesitation melting into a wide smile. "I love it. It's perfect."

Brian reached for their hands, taking one of Stephanie's and one of Brittney's in his. "No matter what, I'll always stand by you both. This is just one way to show it."

They sat in a shared moment of quiet unity, the bond between them stronger than ever. Then, as if on cue, Brittney's romantic imagination sparked again.

"We could use ribbons in our favorite colors!" she exclaimed, her enthusiasm bubbling over.

"And write our own vows," Stephanie added, her smile growing. "Something only we'd understand."

Brian laughed, the joy and love in his voice unmistakable. "If that's what you want, I'll find the ribbons and write a hundred vows if I have to."

The mood lightened once more, and the playful energy returned as the twins started planning how to incorporate handfasting into their dreams of a fairytale wedding. Their excitement was infectious, spilling over into the rest of the van.

The conversation flowed easily, filled with dreams of a fairytale wedding and playful teasing. Gloria and Umi exchanged small smiles. Their poker faces slipped just enough to show their pride and love.

As the van rolled toward home, the family's unity was palpable, a bond that would carry them through whatever came next.

CHAPTER 22

Scott sat at the small desk in his office, papers scattered in neat chaos before him. The trial date was set — March 1st. He picked up his phone, his fingers lingering over the screen before dialing. The call connected after two rings.

"Hello, Scott," Umi's warm, steady voice greeted him.

"Hey, Umi," Scott replied, leaning back in his chair. "Got a minute to talk? It's about the trial date."

"Of course," Umi said, a slight edge of anticipation in her tone.

"It's officially set to start on March 1st," Scott began. "We've got everything prepared, but I wanted to touch base with you and make sure you're comfortable with everything. This is going to be intense, but I'm confident we're ready."

"March 1st," Umi repeated, her voice measured. "That's a long time from now. I suppose there's no time that's truly ideal, though." She paused, her tone softening. "Scott, how long do you think the trial will take?"

"That depends on a few factors," Scott admitted. "With Judge Harlow presiding, she keeps things on schedule. If the defense doesn't waste time with unnecessary delays, we could wrap it up in about a week. But if they drag their feet or file motions to stall, we might be looking at closer to two weeks."

Umi sighed softly, a mix of relief and determination in the sound. "I'll make sure everyone understands it might not be over quickly. Brittney will need extra reassurance."

"She will," Scott agreed. "And Stephanie, too. Sometimes, the ones trying to hold everything together need support the most. Let her know it's okay to feel overwhelmed."

"I will," Umi promised. She hesitated, then added, "Scott, I'm worried about the defense. Do you think they'll go after Brittney too harshly?"

"They'll test boundaries," Scott acknowledged his voice firm. "But we've prepared for that, and we'll keep up with reminding her about things. Judge Harlow won't tolerate bullying, and Brittney won't face this alone. We've got strong evidence, a solid case, and a team committed to seeing this through."

Umi exhaled, some tension easing from her tone. "I trust you, Scott. But I can't help worrying about the emotional toll on everyone. Brittney's already struggling, and Stephanie, I can see…" She trailed off.

"Stephanie's strong," Scott said gently. "And she has people who love her. You, Gloria, and Brian are her anchors. Just remind her she doesn't need to be Brittney's shield. Being there is enough."

"You're right," Umi said. Then, after a moment, she added, "Scott, how do you stay so steady? It's like you always know the right thing to say."

Scott chuckled softly. "It's not about always knowing, Umi. It's about focusing on what we *can* control. We've prepared for this. The rest is about showing up, sticking to the facts, and doing the work."

"You're good at this," Umi said with a faint laugh. "It's comforting to know we have someone like you in our corner."

Scott's tone softened. "It's what I'm here for, Umi. We'll get through this. And when it's over, I want you to remember that this is the beginning of healing, not the end of the story."

"I'll hold on to that," Umi said. "Thank you, Scott. Really."

"Anytime," he replied. "And if anything comes up—questions, concerns, anything at all—you call me. Day or night."

"I will. Thank you," Umi said again before they hung up.

Scott leaned back in his chair, letting the calm of the moment settle over him. He was ready to fight for them, and he knew they were ready, too.

*****

As soon as Umi ended her call with Scott, she stared at the phone in her hand for a moment before dialing Gloria's number. The familiar sound of ringing filled the silence, and soon, Gloria's voice answered warm and familiar.

"Hey, Umi," Gloria said, her tone carrying its usual calm confidence. "What's up?"

"It's about the trial," Umi began, leaning against the kitchen counter. "Scott just called. The trial date is set—March 1st."

"Almost three months," Gloria said, her voice steady but thoughtful. "That's a wait. How are you feeling about it?"

"Scott says we're ready," Umi replied, her voice measured. "He estimates it could take a week, maybe two, depending on how cooperative the defense is. And Judge Harlow will keep things on track. But Gloria, I can't help worrying about Brittney and Stephanie. They've been through so much already."

"They have," Gloria agreed, her voice softening. "But we know they're strong. And they've got us. We just need to be careful about how we tell them. Brittney's anxiety will spike if we don't handle this right."

"I was thinking the same," Umi said. "And Stephanie... She's been trying so hard to be Brittney's rock. I don't want her to feel like she has to carry all of this."

Gloria chuckled softly. "That girl's more like her mother than she realizes. Always taking on too much because she loves too deeply."

Umi smiled faintly, the warmth in Gloria's words easing some of her tension. "That's why I thought we should plan this carefully. Maybe a family meeting after dinner? Something calm and straightforward, where everyone can ask questions and feel supported. It's not like it's tomorrow, but if we give them long enough to relax about knowing it's coming, it should ease things a bit. What do you think?"

"I like that idea," Gloria said. "We can set the tone, reassure them that we're prepared and that we'll get through this together. Brittney needs to know she's not alone, and Stephanie needs to know she doesn't have to solve everything herself."

"Exactly," Umi replied. "But how do we keep their anxiety in check when we bring it up? Brittney's been doing great, and

I don't want to see her backslide, and Stephanie can't help but absorb it."

There was a thoughtful pause before Gloria spoke again, her tone deliberate. "Umi, I think we should talk about Brian, too. He's already been such a stabilizing presence for Stephanie, and Brittney trusts him, even if she struggles to show it. His love and that proposal… that's going to be a huge help for both of them."

"His proposal," Umi repeated, her voice soft with a mix of emotions. "I know how much he loves her. And I trust him with Stephanie's heart. But do you really think we should bring *that* up now? Think she might misassociate things?"

"I think we should," Gloria said firmly. "When we tell them about the trial, it's not just about what's ahead. It's about reminding them what they *have*—each other, their family, a lifetime of tomorrows, and someone like Brian who's going to be there for them both, no matter what. That kind of love and trust, Umi… it's a powerful thing."

Umi was quiet for a moment, the weight of Gloria's words settling over her. "You're right," she said finally. "Brian's been a rock for all of us. Maybe hearing that will help them see there's hope in all of this, me included."

"And we'll remind them that we're in this together," Gloria added. "If anything, it'll give Stephanie strength and show Brittney she's not as isolated as she feels."

"Okay," Umi said, her resolve strengthening. "Let's aim for dinner tonight. We need a good meal, have our conversation, and then move on to something fun, like karaoke or something. Keep the conversation casual but focused, and move on."

"Perfect," Gloria agreed. "We'll make a cake for after dinner—something sweet always helps soften the edges."

Umi smiled. "You know what, Gloria? I don't know how I'd do this without you."

"You'd manage," Gloria replied warmly. "But you don't have to. That's what family's for."

*****

Dinner was quiet but warm, the kind of meal that gave everyone a momentary reprieve from the tension looming ahead. Gloria had prepared a comforting spread of roast chicken, mashed potatoes, and green beans while Umi's homemade chocolate cake sat waiting on the counter, tempting everyone to linger just a little longer. The small talk around the table felt natural, even if there was an undercurrent of anticipation.

As the last plates were cleared and dessert was served, Umi took a deep breath. She glanced at Gloria, who gave her a small, reassuring nod. It was time.

"Everyone," Umi began, her voice calm but firm, "there's something important we need to talk about."

Brittney looked up from her half-eaten slice of cake, her expression wary. Stephanie's brow furrowed slightly, her hand instinctively reaching out to touch Brian's arm for reassurance. Brian sat straighter, his steady presence anchoring the moment.

Umi continued her tone even. "Mr. Scott called earlier today. The trial date has been set. It's starting on March 1st."

The room fell silent, the weight of her words sinking in. Brittney's fork clattered against her plate as her hand trembled slightly, vivid memories of why all of this happened racing through her mind. Stephanie tightened her grip on Brian's arm, her lips pressing into a thin line.

"I'm not ready. Do I have to see him?" Brittney spoke up, her voice barely above a whisper, her eyes filling with worry.

Umi reached out, taking Brittney's trembling hand in hers. "You *are* ready, Brittney," she said firmly, her voice filled with quiet strength. "You've come so far, and you're braver than you realize."

Brittney's lip quivered, but she nodded faintly as Umi continued. "Mr. Scott will make sure you're as prepared as possible," she said gently. "And yes, you have to see him, but you won't be alone. We'll all be there for you."

Brian leaned forward, his voice calm and reassuring. "Brittney, you're not alone. Remember, you've got all of us. We're in this together."

Stephanie nodded, her voice soft but firm. "Brian's right. We've got your back, Brittney. No matter what."

Gloria smiled, her gaze sweeping over the teens. "And it's not just about getting through the trial. It's about remembering what you have—each other, your family, and the love that's stronger than all of this."

Umi glanced at Brian, meeting his steady gaze. "Brian's love for both of you is one of those things," she said softly. "His proposal… it's not just a symbol of your future. It's a reminder of how much strength love can give all of you, all of us."

Brian's face flushed slightly, but his voice was steady as he spoke. "We are going to build a future together, all three of us, but it's more than that. We're all family. We'll face this trial as a family, and we'll come out stronger."

Tears welled in Brittney's eyes, her voice trembling. "I'm scared."

Umi squeezed her hand gently. "It's okay to be scared, Angel. But you're not facing this fear alone. You've got to remember this. We're here. All of us."

Stephanie squeezed Brittney's other hand, her own tears threatening to spill. "You've always been my sister, Brittney. No matter what's happened, that hasn't changed, and it never will."

Gloria sat back slightly, letting the moment settle before speaking. "Umi and I thought it would be helpful to have a family meeting like this whenever we need to check in during the trial. Maybe after dinner, like tonight. That way, we can keep each other grounded and work through any questions or worries together."

"I like that," Brian said. "A time to talk things out, no judgment. Just family."

Brittney nodded slowly, wiping her eyes. "That sounds… good. I think I'd like that."

"Then it's settled," Umi said, her voice steady with quiet determination. "We'll face this trial together. And we'll come out stronger."

As the family lingered around the table, the air felt lighter, their bond unshaken despite the challenges ahead. In the warmth of the room, surrounded by love and support, the path forward didn't seem quite so daunting.

Gloria nodded toward Brian. "Brian, how about you go set up the karaoke machine?"

Brian smiled back. "Great idea," as he stood up.

Sometime later, the living room buzzed with post-dinner energy, the remnants of their meal replaced with bowls of popcorn, glasses of soda, and the glowing menu of the karaoke machine on the TV. The teens started a showdown, with performances ranging from passionate to wildly off-key.

"You've gotta admit," Stephanie said, tossing a pillow at Brian, "we're killing it."

"Killing my eardrums," Brian replied, dodging the pillow and grabbing the mic. "Let me show you how it's done."

"You mean 'how to cry onstage'?" Brittney teased, earning a round of laughter.

Brian ignored them, scrolling dramatically through the song list. "When you have soul, you don't cry; you inspire."

His ballad was heartfelt and hilariously over-the-top, complete with arm gestures, dramatic kneeling, and an invisible audience. Everyone was in hysterics by the time he finished.

"Brian," Stephanie said, wiping tears of laughter from her eyes, "not everything has to be romantic!"

"Everything important does," Brian countered, tossing her the mic. "You'll thank me when you're older."

Stephanie groaned but grabbed the mic anyway. "Whatever, Romeo. At least I know how to have fun while singing."

As she queued up a pop anthem, Brittney jumped up to act as her backup dancer. Together, they gave an energetic performance filled with wild gestures and exaggerated harmonies, leaving Brian shaking his head.

"You two are ridiculous," Brian said, laughing as he clapped.

At that moment, Gloria entered the room, balancing a tray of cookies. She paused, raising an eyebrow at the scene in front of her. "What exactly is going on in here?"

"Karaoke showdown," Brittney explained, grabbing a cookie as she hopped back onto the couch. "Brian's trying to turn it into a rom-com."

"It's not a rom-com," Brian argued, straightening his shirt. "It's art."

Umi followed Gloria into the room, her teacup in hand. She surveyed the room, scattered pillows with a soft smile. "And nobody thought to invite us?"

"You sing?" Stephanie asked, wide-eyed.

"Of course," Gloria replied, setting the tray down. "But unlike you three, we don't need theatrics."

Brian grabbed the mic, holding it out to Gloria. "Prove it, Mom. Let's see what you've got."

Gloria raised an eyebrow, then glanced at Umi. "What do you think? Should we give them a real show?"

Umi's smile widened. "I think they're overdue for one."

The teens exchanged wary glances as Umi took the remote and scrolled through the song list. After a brief whispered conversation with Gloria, they settled on "Shallow" from *A Star Is Born*.

"No way!" Stephanie gasped. "You two are gonna duet?"

"Watch and learn," Gloria said, taking one mic while Umi picked up the other.

As the opening notes filled the room, Umi began with the soft, heartfelt intro, her voice smooth and rich. The teens exchanged wide-eyed glances, clearly impressed. When Gloria joined in with the powerful chorus, their harmonies blended effortlessly. Gloria's passionate delivery paired perfectly with Umi's calm, steady tones, creating a performance that left the teens completely stunned.

By the time they finished, the teens erupted in cheers.

"Mom Gloria!" Brittney exclaimed. "You've been holding out on us!"

"And Mom!" Stephanie added, clapping wildly. "That was, like, professional level. Why aren't you two in a band?"

Gloria handed the mic back with a satisfied smirk. "Sometimes, it's fun to keep a few surprises up our sleeves."

Umi sat down, sipping her tea. "And it's a good reminder: teamwork always wins."

Brian shook his head, still clapping. "Okay, new rule: You two are officially required to duet at every karaoke night."

"Required?" Gloria teased, raising an eyebrow. "Are you sure you can keep up with us?"

"They'll need a lot of practice," Umi said, her eyes twinkling with amusement.

Stephanie grabbed the mic, her grin wide. "All right, Britt, we've gotta up our game. Duet?"

"Let's do it," Brittney replied, jumping up.

Their chaotic but heartfelt rendition of a pop hit had its own charm, though it couldn't match the polish of Gloria and Umi's performance. The mothers exchanged a knowing glance, their laughter mingling with the music.

Before Brian could grab the mic again, Gloria leaned forward. "You know, one duet might not be enough. What do you say, Umi?"

Umi's serene smile widened. "I say they need another lesson."

The teens froze mid-laugh as the mothers took their mics again. Gloria scrolled through the options and selected "Invincible" by Pat Benatar.

Stephanie gasped. "You're teaming up *again*? This is rigged!"

"Not rigged," Gloria said as the opening chords played. "Strategic."

When Umi began singing, her calm, controlled delivery carried a subtle power that drew everyone in. Gloria followed with the fiery intensity of the chorus, the two mothers blending their styles perfectly. By the time they hit the final chorus, "We will be invincible!" the teens were on their feet, clapping and cheering along.

As the song ended, Gloria struck a triumphant pose while Umi bowed slightly, earning another round of thunderous applause.

"That was amazing!" Brittney shouted, clapping furiously. "How are you two this good?"

"Seriously," Stephanie added, shaking her head. "It's like you've been practicing in secret."

Gloria set the mic down, her smirk playful. "Maybe we have. Or maybe we just know how to work together."

Umi sat back down, her serene smile still in place. "Teamwork, girls. It's how we win. Combine your strengths, you're unstoppable, invincible."

Brian raised an eyebrow, grabbing the remote. "So you're saying the only way we can beat you is if we team up?"

"Exactly," Gloria replied, reaching for her tea. "You're good on your own, but together, you're a force to be reckoned with."

Stephanie folded her arms, looking skeptical. "Team up with Brian's singing? That's a big ask."

"Hey!" Brian said, feigning offense. "I'm right here."

"You'd better learn fast," Umi said lightly, "Because if you can't work together, we'll just keep winning."

Brittney leaned forward, her grin wide. "All right, you're on. Steph, Brian, truce?"

Stephanie hesitated, then sighed. "Fine. But if he tries to take over, the deal's off."

"Agreed," Brian said, grabbing the mic. "But I get to pick the song."

"No!" Brittney shouted, snatching the remote. "We'll pick *together*."

As the teens began their surprisingly well-coordinated rendition of a classic pop anthem, Gloria and Umi exchanged a smile. Their laughter mingled with the music, wrapping the night in the perfect blend of joy, chaos, and teamwork.

CHAPTER 23

The hallway at Bryan Athan Senior High bustled with students heading to class, the chatter and clang of lockers filling the air as the lunch break wound down. Stephanie walked briskly, her books clutched to her chest, her mind racing with frustration. She had heard the whispers earlier in the week and again today—cruel, cutting rumors about Brittney. The words were vile, branding her a "slut" and speculating that her pregnancy was the result of sleeping around.

Stephanie's heart pounded as she spotted the source of the rumors, Heather, leaning casually against a row of lockers. Her patience snapped. She marched straight toward the girl, her voice sharp and unyielding.

"Why don't you shut your mouth for once?" Stephanie said, her words slicing through the hallway noise. Heads turned, the usual lunchtime energy dropping to a tense hush.

Heather smirked, unaffected. "Oh, look who's playing the protective sister. Guess Brittney can't fight her own battles."

Stephanie's grip on her books tightened, her knuckles whitening. "You don't know anything about Brittney. Keep her name out of your filthy mouth."

Heather stepped closer, her voice dripping with mockery. "Filthy? Funny coming from someone whose sister's knocked up. And we all know why. She's been with half the guys in this school."

Stephanie's books hit the floor with a loud thud. Her voice cracked with fury. "She's pregnant because she was raped, you disgusting liar!" Gasps rippled through the crowd gathering around them.

For a split second, Heather's expression faltered, but she recovered quickly, her smirk widening. "Oh, please. That's rich, coming from someone whose sister couldn't keep her legs closed. You wanna talk about lies? At least I owned up to my abortion."

Stephanie's vision blurred with rage. "You're the real slut here!" she shouted before swinging her fist and connecting with Heather's jaw.

The crowd erupted in chaos as Heather stumbled back, clutching her face. A teacher appeared, his voice booming. "Enough! Both of you, stop it now!"

Stephanie barely registered the firm grip on her arm as the teacher pulled her back. Heather, still clutching her jaw, glared daggers at Stephanie.

"You're both coming with me to Dr. Smith's office," the teacher barked, steering them down the hallway.

Stephanie sat stiffly in a chair outside Dr. Smith's office, her hands trembling with lingering anger. Across from her, Heather fumed silently, a faint bruise forming on her cheek. The tension between them was palpable.

The door opened, and Dr. Smith emerged, his expression a mix of disappointment and curiosity. "Miss Stephanie," he began, his tone even but firm, "I have to admit, you're one of the last students I'd expect to see in here."

Stephanie said nothing, her gaze fixed on the floor.

"Both of you, inside," Dr. Smith instructed, holding the door open.

Once seated, he folded his hands on his desk and surveyed the two girls. "Now, one at a time. What happened?"

Heather jumped in first, her voice laced with venom. "She attacked me completely unprovoked!"

Stephanie's head snapped up, her voice trembling with rage. "Unprovoked? You've been spreading disgusting lies about my sister!"

Dr. Smith raised a hand, his calm demeanor commanding silence. "Let's slow down. Miss Heather, start from the beginning."

Heather shifted in her chair, her tone defensive. "I was talking with some friends when she came storming over, yelling at me for no reason. I only said what everyone else was thinking. Brittney's pregnant, and people are talking about it."

Dr. Smith's gaze sharpened. "Heather, did you call her sister a... 'slut' or make other derogatory comments?"

Heather hesitated, her face flushing slightly. "I might've said something like that, but it's not like I'm the only one. Everyone knows she's been around."

Stephanie let out an incredulous laugh. "You didn't just say it. You've been spreading those lies all week!"

Dr. Smith turned to Stephanie, his tone measured. "Stephanie, did you throw the first punch?"

Stephanie hesitated before nodding. "Yes, sir. But only after she insulted my sister and called her a slut."

Dr. Smith leaned back in his chair, taking a deep breath. "Heather, spreading rumors like this, especially ones that demean or harm another student, is not only cruel but a violation of school policy. And Stephanie, I understand your anger, but resorting to violence is never acceptable."

Heather's jaw tightened. "I wasn't the one who hit someone."

Dr. Smith nodded firmly. "And you, Heather, weren't the one who stopped when you should have. This could have been avoided if you'd shown some restraint."

The room fell silent for a moment before Dr. Smith continued. "For now, both of you will serve one week of after-school detention in Mr. Dubbs's classroom. Additionally, Heather, you will write an apology letter to Brittney and turn it into this office by the end of your detention today. And, Miss Heather, it will be at least one full page. Stephanie, you will write a reflection explaining why violence isn't the solution, even in difficult situations, also due by the end of detention today, also at least one full page. Am I understood?"

"Yes, sir," Stephanie muttered, her voice subdued.

Heather crossed her arms but eventually grumbled, "Yes, sir."

"Good. I expect this to be the last time either of you is in my office for something like this. You're dismissed. Go to class."

Stephanie stood quickly, her face still flushed with anger. As they exited the office, Heather muttered under her breath, "This isn't over."

Stephanie shot her a glare but kept walking, her hands trembling as she made her way to her next class.

*****

Umi Welch sat at the dining room table, sorting through bills, when her phone buzzed. She glanced at the screen and saw the school's number. Her heart skipped a beat as she quickly answered.

"Hello, this is Umi Welch."

"Good afternoon, Mrs. Welch," Dr. Smith's familiar voice greeted her. "I hope I'm not interrupting."

"Not at all," Umi replied, sitting up straighter. "Is everything all right?"

Dr. Smith hesitated for a moment, his tone softening. "I wanted to discuss something sensitive regarding Stephanie. There was an incident at school today."

Umi's chest tightened. "What happened? Is she all right?"

"Yes, she's fine," Dr. Smith assured her quickly. "But there was a heated argument with another student, Miss Heather Fernandez. It escalated, and unfortunately, Stephanie threw the first punch."

Umi closed her eyes, exhaling slowly. "That doesn't sound like her. What was the fight about?"

Dr. Smith's voice grew more serious. "Miss Heather was spreading rumors about Brittney, which were very harmful ones. Stephanie told me that the rumors were false, and she revealed something... sensitive about Brittney's pregnancy."

Umi's throat tightened. "She told you, didn't she?"

Dr. Smith paused before answering. "Yes. She said Brittney's pregnancy was the result of a sexual assault. I wanted to confirm if that's true before I proceed with any follow-up at school."

Umi's voice trembled as she replied, "It's true. We've been handling it quietly as a family, and both teens have been through so much already."

Dr. Smith's tone softened further. "I'm deeply sorry to hear that. Please know that anything shared with me stays confidential. I only asked to ensure I responded appropriately to what happened today."

"Thank you, Dr. Smith," Umi said, her voice steadier now.

"I've already addressed their behavior, and both will have after-school detention for a week because of their actions, though I made it clear I understand why she reacted," Dr. Smith paused for a moment. "And, Mrs. Welch, before we end the call, I wanted to share some good news."

"Good news?" Umi repeated, curiosity replacing her worry.

"Yes," Dr. Smith said warmly. "Brittney's grades have improved significantly since she's been on remote learning. Her teachers have been particularly impressed with her focus and participation. She's excelling in all of her subjects."

A smile spread across Umi's face. "That's wonderful to hear. Brittney's been working hard."

"She has, and I think it's worth noting. I've told her before that I highly value growth, and this is significant growth," Dr. Smith added.

Umi's eyes lit up with an idea. "Dr. Smith, would you mind telling her that yourself? Hearing it from you might mean even more to her."

Dr. Smith chuckled lightly. "I'd be happy to. Is she home now?"

"She is," Umi said, already standing and heading toward Brittney's room.

*****

Umi gently pushed open Brittney's door, careful not to startle her. Brittney sat at her desk, her laptop open, headphones on. On the screen, a teacher gestured animatedly, explaining a concept.

Umi smiled at the sight of her daughter so focused. She knocked lightly on the doorframe.

Brittney glanced up, holding a finger up as the teacher finished the lesson. Moments later, she pulled her headphones off. "Hey, Mom. What's up?"

"Dr. Smith is on the phone," Umi said, stepping into the room.

Brittney's brow furrowed. "Am I in trouble?"

"Not at all," Umi assured her. "Actually, he has something good to share. I'll put him on speaker."

Brittney hesitated but nodded, closing her laptop as the screen went black.

Umi tapped the speaker button. "Dr. Smith, she's here."

"Good afternoon, Miss Brittney," Dr. Smith's warm voice filled the room.

"Hi, Dr. Smith," Brittney replied cautiously.

"I won't keep you long," he began. "I just wanted to tell you how impressed I am with your recent progress. Your grades have improved significantly, and your teachers have noticed how engaged and focused you've been. You're doing an excellent job."

Brittney's eyes widened, a small smile tugging at her lips. "Really?"

"Really," Dr. Smith affirmed. "Your participation in class has been exemplary, and the effort you're putting in hasn't gone unnoticed. Keep it up, Brittney. You're on a great path."

Brittney glanced at her mother, her cheeks flushing slightly. "Thank you, Dr. Smith. That means a lot. I promised you I'd do my best."

"You did, and I'm very impressed. You've earned it," he replied. "And don't hesitate to reach out if you need any help. We're all rooting for you."

As the call ended, Brittney looked up at Umi. "I didn't think anyone noticed."

Umi sat on the edge of her bed, her smile gentle. "People notice more than you think, Angel. You've been working so hard, and I'm so proud of you."

Brittney's voice was soft. "Thanks, Mom. I just... I want to do better. For myself, for you, for everyone, the baby."

"And you are," Umi said, reaching out to squeeze her hand. "Step by step, you're doing it."

For the first time in a while, Brittney allowed herself to believe it.

*****

Dr. Smith ended his call with Umi Welch, his fingers drumming thoughtfully on his desk. He reached for the intercom and pressed the button for the school office.

"Mrs. Cook, could you ask Ms. Daniels to join me for a phone call? It's important."

"Yes, Dr. Smith," the secretary replied.

A few moments later, Dr. Smith's phone rang. He picked up immediately.

"Dr. Smith, this is Michelle Daniels. You needed to speak with me?"

"Yes, Michelle. I have a sensitive matter to discuss." His tone was deliberate, careful. "I've just had a conversation with Umi Welch regarding a situation involving her daughters, Brittney and Stephanie. It's about something very personal and difficult in Brittney's life that surfaced during a confrontation between Stephanie and another student, Heather Fernandez."

There was a pause on the line before Ms. Daniels responded, her voice soft but firm. "I've had a few conversations with Taylor Harris about Brittney over the last month or so. Taylor hinted that something serious happened to her, though she didn't provide many details. I suspected it might be something like this. Is Brittney okay?"

Dr. Smith exhaled. "She's making progress, according to her mother. Her grades have improved, and she's been focused in class, which is remarkable under the circumstances. But Heather has been spreading harmful rumors about her, and during a heated exchange, Stephanie disclosed that Brittney's pregnancy is the result of a sexual assault."

Ms. Daniels' tone tightened with concern. "That's incredibly painful for their family. Do you think Heather knows the truth, or was she just repeating rumors?"

Dr. Smith shook his head, though she couldn't see him. "I don't believe Heather knows. From what I've gathered, she's parroting baseless gossip. But this puts me in a difficult position. Should I talk to Heather and correct the narrative? Or would doing so risk violating Brittney's privacy and make things worse for her?"

Ms. Daniels paused thoughtfully before responding. "That's a delicate situation, and I'm glad you're being cautious. If Heather truly doesn't know the truth, telling her could create a whole new set of problems, especially if she doesn't handle it maturely. However, if we leave her unchecked, she might continue to spread these rumors, further damaging Brittney's reputation and mental health."

"So, what would you recommend?" Dr. Smith asked.

"I think our focus should remain on protecting Brittney," Ms. Daniels said firmly. "If Heather's behavior continues, we can address it without revealing the truth. Framing it as bullying and harassment is enough for the school to act. But we can't control what happens once she leaves this building."

Dr. Smith nodded, making a mental note. "That's wise, Michelle. I'll keep the truth confidential. For now, I'll have another conversation with Heather and make it clear that this behavior must stop without addressing the specifics of Brittney's situation."

"Good," Ms. Daniels agreed. "And I'll reach out to Taylor to check-in. It sounds like she's been a solid support for Brittney, but I want to make sure she's not shouldering too much on her own. This kind of burden can be overwhelming for a teenager."

"Agreed," Dr. Smith said. "Thank you for your input, Michelle. If you feel Brittney might benefit from additional support, let me know how we can assist her."

"I'll keep you updated," Ms. Daniels promised. "Thank you for handling this so carefully, Dr. Smith."

*****

Dr. Smith decided not to wait. With a few firm taps on his keyboard, he sent a note to Heather's teacher requesting she report to his office. Ten minutes later, Heather sat across from him, arms crossed, her posture defensive.

"Heather," Dr. Smith began, his tone measured, "I called you here because of the incident earlier with Stephanie Welch. I've already spoken to her about her actions, and now I need to address yours."

Heather's expression hardened. "I already said I didn't start anything. She attacked me!"

"I understand that you feel wronged," Dr. Smith said calmly. "But the conflict didn't happen in isolation. It began because of rumors you've been spreading about Brittney Welch."

Heather's eyes darted to the side, her face flushing. "I wasn't spreading rumors. I just said what people were already saying."

Dr. Smith's voice sharpened slightly. "That doesn't make it acceptable. Words can be deeply harmful, Miss Heather, and perpetuating gossip, whether you believe it or not, can destroy someone's reputation and sense of safety."

Heather shifted uncomfortably. "I didn't mean to hurt her. I was just... talking."

"Talking has consequences," Dr. Smith said firmly. "You will stop participating in any discussion about her personal life, effective immediately. Am I clear?"

Heather hesitated, then nodded reluctantly. "Yes, sir."

Dr. Smith softened his tone slightly. "Miss Heather, you're better than this. I don't believe you fully understand the harm you've caused, but I'm giving you an opportunity to make amends. Use it wisely."

Heather nodded again, looking down. "When I write my letter, I'll apologize and mean it, sir."

"Good," Dr. Smith said. "You're dismissed."

As Heather left the office, Dr. Smith felt a pang of hope. The situation wasn't resolved, but it was a step forward.

CHAPTER 24

The warm, cheerful laughter from the living room dimmed slightly as a knock echoed from the front door. Umi rose from her chair, brushing her hands on her jeans as she walked to answer it. The living room was bustling with activity; Amber was joking about the mess someone had made of the icing on the cake, and Stephanie was in the middle of teasing Taylor about her recent haircut.

When Umi opened the door, she was momentarily taken aback. Standing on the front step, looking a bit nervous but determined, was Heather Fernandez. Her hands clutched a small envelope, and she glanced up at Umi with an awkward smile.

"Hi, Mrs. Welch," Heather said hesitantly. "I'm... uh... here to see Brittney. I wanted to apologize."

Umi studied her for a moment, then nodded, her voice calm but firm. "Come in."

As Heather stepped inside, the chatter in the living room stopped. The girls exchanged glances, and Stephanie's expression turned icy the moment her eyes landed on Heather.

"Well, this should be good," Stephanie muttered under her breath, her tone cutting.

Taylor raised an eyebrow, crossing her arms. "What are you doing here, Heather? Trying to ruin another day?"

Heather winced but held her ground. She glanced at Umi, who gave her a reassuring nod, then squared her shoulders.

"I'm here to apologize," Heather said, her voice steady. She looked directly at Brittney, whose face showed a mix of surprise and unease. "Brittney, I owe you a big apology. Can I... explain?"

Brittney hesitated but nodded slowly. Umi gestured for everyone to settle down. "Let's give Heather a chance."

Heather took a deep breath, stepping closer to Brittney. "After what happened at school, my mom sat me down. She was so disappointed in me for what I said and did. She asked me to think about how I'd feel if someone spread those kinds of rumors about me. At first, I brushed her off... but she wouldn't let it go. She told me to imagine being in your shoes, pregnant, dealing with everything, and then having people tear me down for it. Then I thought about what I did with Tom, my abortion," she explained, her voice soft and sincere.

Heather's voice softened, her eyes glistening with emotion. "It really hit me, Brittney. I wouldn't have been able to handle it. I was wrong, so wrong. And I've been thinking about this for days. I overheard Amber talking with Stephanie about your birthday and figured this was my chance to say sorry."

Brittney's eyes brimmed with tears, her voice shaky. "Heather, I... I don't know what to say."

Heather stepped closer, her voice breaking. "I'm so sorry, Brittney. For all of it. For the rumors, the names, everything. I wouldn't blame you if you hated me forever, but I need you to know that I'm truly sorry."

Brittney let out a soft sob, wiping her eyes. "I don't hate you, Heather. I just… it really hurt when Steph told me. But I accept your apology."

Heather smiled through her own tears, relief flooding her face. "Thank you. That means a lot."

The two girls hesitated for a moment before leaning in for a brief but heartfelt hug. The room was silent, the tension dissipating.

Stephanie got up, walked over, and tapped Heather on the shoulder. "Heather?"

She stood up, looking at Stephanie. "I'm sorry, Stephanie. For picking the fight; everything."

Stephanie opened her hands, gesturing for a hug. "And I'm sorry for punching you. I shouldn't have done that either."

The two hugged. "You do have a mean hook," Heather giggled softly. "I had a black eye for a week."

Brittney spoke up. "Yeah, I know that, don't I, Steph?" with a giggle.

Umi broke the quiet with a warm smile. "Heather, would you like some cake?"

Heather nodded, her smile turning shy. "Yes, please, ma'am. Thank you."

As the mood lightened, Brittney opened the small envelope Heather had brought. Inside was a simple card with "Happy

Birthday" written in neat handwriting, and tucked inside was a $50 gift card.

Brittney gasped, holding up the card. "Heather, this is way too much! A gift card for..." She paused, reading the store name aloud. "Mama's Nest?"

Heather flushed slightly. "Yeah... my mom suggested it. She said it would mean more to me and you if I used my own money for it. Seeing and talking with you, I understand why. I hope it helps with... you know, clothes and stuff."

Brittney's lip quivered, and she pulled Heather into another hug. "Thank you. That's so thoughtful."

Amber broke the moment with a cheeky grin. "Wow, Heather, trying to outdo all of us with that gift? I think I brought her a scented candle."

The room erupted into laughter, and the tension fully dissolved. Heather sat down on one end of the couch, and the celebration resumed with renewed energy. The cake was served, jokes flew, and for the first time in days, Brittney felt a little lighter. Heather's apology wasn't just a turning point; it was the start of healing, and Brittney couldn't be more grateful.

*****

The cozy living room was alive with the warm glow of lamps and soft laughter. The remnants of the earlier birthday cake sat on the dining table, a mix of mismatched plates and forks surrounding it, as another untouched cake waited patiently for round two of celebrations. Gathered in the living room, Umi, Gloria, Brian, and the twins shared an easy camaraderie, the sense of closeness palpable.

Umi stood and retrieved two gift bags from the corner, one lavender, and the other blue, and handed them to her daughters with a smile. "Open mine first," she said, settling back into her seat.

Brittney grabbed the blue bag eagerly, her curiosity piqued. Pulling out the tissue paper, she revealed the first item: a T-shirt with a loading bar and the words "Baby Loading... Please Wait" printed underneath. Laughter erupted around the room.

"Oh, my gosh, Mom!" Brittney laughed, holding it up.

Stephanie leaned closer to read it, grinning. "That's perfect."

Brittney reached in and pulled out another T-shirt. This one had a pair of small feet beneath the text: "You're Kickin' Me, Smalls." The room roared with laughter again.

Gloria wiped at her eyes, chuckling. "That's adorable!"

The third T-shirt was a deep purple with bold white text: "I'm the kind of woman that when my feet hit the floor, the devil says, 'Oh crap, she's up.'"

Brittney held it up, shaking her head in amusement. "Okay, this one's my favorite. It's like you read my mind, Mom."

"You're welcome," Umi said with a sly smile.

Brittney reached into the bag again and pulled out a soft, baggy cashmere sweater. Her smile turned tender as she hugged it to her chest. "Oh, this is so comfy." Without hesitation, she slipped it on, sighing with contentment as she adjusted it.

Stephanie waited patiently as Brittney admired the sweater before diving into her lavender bag. Her face lit up as she pulled out a matching cashmere sweater, properly sized for her.

"Of course, we're twins," Stephanie teased, slipping the sweater over her head.

She reached back into the bag and pulled out a T-shirt, freezing when she read the words: "I'm the kind of woman that when my feet hit the floor, the devil says, 'Oh crap, she's up.'" She burst into laughter.

"Seriously, Mom?" Stephanie said, holding it up for everyone to see.

Brittney smirked. "You're welcome to join the club, Sis."

Brian cleared his throat, handing each twin an envelope. "These are from me," he said, his voice casual but his expression mischievous.

Brittney opened hers first, reading the card. A romantic message was scrawled in Brian's handwriting, but her brow arched as she reached the end, where a single question waited: "Who's first?"

She glanced up at him with a smirk. "Me! Because I'm the oldest!"

Stephanie groaned dramatically, already knowing what her card would say. "Oh, that again?"

Brian shrugged, grinning. "It's not my fault you were late to the party."

"You've been milking that for seventeen years, Britt," Stephanie said, laughing.

Gloria handed each twin a card, smiling warmly as they opened them. Brittney's contained a gift card to an upscale maternity store, while Stephanie's was for a high-end women's apparel store.

"This is amazing, Gloria," Stephanie said, grinning.

Brittney nodded in agreement. "Thank you so much!"

As the gifts were admired and laughter flowed, Brittney couldn't resist teasing her sister. "Stephanie, I think your gift card is for looking stylish while you hold my baby at the store."

Stephanie shot back with a playful glare. "Oh, I'll hold the baby while you're trying to figure out why that T-shirt won't fit over your stomach anymore."

Gloria chimed in from her spot on the couch, pretending to be deep in thought. "I'm just wondering if the baby's first words will be 'Team Brittney' or 'Team Stephanie.'"

Brian leaned back, shaking his head. "I'll teach him to say, 'Team Brian.' Problem solved."

The room erupted into laughter again, the playful banter continuing as everyone dug into the second cake. For the first time in a long while, the group felt the lightness of family, shared humor, and genuine joy.

CHAPTER 25

Two days after the birthday dates with Stephanie and Brittney, Brian and Stephanie were sharing a quiet and private moment in his room. They sat close together on the bed, their fingers interlaced. The soft glow of his desk lamp lit the room, giving a warm hue to the otherwise quiet evening. The open door lent an air of innocence to their shared moment, even as their closeness felt like a stolen fragment of time. They leaned into a kiss, a tender connection filled with the unspoken emotions that had been building between them.

When the kiss ended, Stephanie pulled away slightly, her cheeks flushed. She wrapped her arms tightly around Brian, pressing her face into his shoulder.

"That was... nice," she murmured, her voice tinged with a shy smile.

Brian chuckled softly, resting his chin on her head. "Yeah, it was."

For a moment, they simply held each other, the world outside his room forgotten. Then Brian spoke, his voice more serious.

"Steph, can we talk about Brittney's baby?"

Stephanie leaned back slightly, her expression softening with curiosity. "Of course. What's on your mind?"

Brian hesitated, choosing his words carefully. "I've been thinking about this. I know it's a big deal, and it's going to change everything. I mean, if I'm going to be her husband, and she's my wife, it's only right that I be the Daddy, too. That is if Brittney's okay with it."

Stephanie's eyes widened, surprise lighting her features. "Brian, you're serious, aren't you? That's... wow. That's amazing. You never cease to amaze me with your love."

He nodded, a faint smile on his lips. "I mean it. Anyone can be a father, but being a dad? That's something special. I want Brittney to know and believe that we're going to love that baby as if we made it — all three of us made it. I don't want her to see the baby and think of Richard and her ordeal. Before I talk with her about it, we need to be on the same page together." He rushed out, explaining from his heart.

Stephanie studied him, her admiration evident. "You're incredible, you know that? I'm okay with it — more than okay. I think it's wonderful."

"I love you, Stephanie, more than I can ever say. I know it's going to change how we do things when the little guy gets here, but I think the three of us would be more of a family than if we didn't. I'm even considering adopting him if she's up for that. Right now, that might be too much, but, in the end, he will be an over-loved, spoiled little man with a special family." He finished his heartfelt confession.

Brian reached out and hugged her tightly. "Thinking about it, it also solves a number of other issues when he's growing up, making things easier for them both—all three of us. I need to know how you feel about it. Honestly, don't hold back. What do you think?"

Stephanie looked into his eyes, seeing into the deepest parts of his soul, and could see nothing but his love and admiration for Brittney and the baby. Her eyes were wet as she hugged him tightly. "Without a doubt, I agree, my love."

Brian let out a relieved breath as he hugged her tightly. "Thank you, my love," was all he could say.

Stephanie squeezed his hand, her voice filled with warmth. "Let's talk to her tonight.

Together."

*****

Later that evening, Brian and Stephanie found Brittney sitting cross-legged on the plush couch in the living room, a sketchpad balanced on her knees. She was absorbed in her drawing, her pencil moving with practiced ease. Umi and Gloria sat at the dining table nearby, shuffling cards but occasionally casting glances toward the teens in the living room.

"Hey, Britt," Brian said, his tone gentle as he approached. Stephanie sat beside him, offering a reassuring smile.

Brittney looked up, slightly startled. "Oh, hey. What's up?"

Brian shifted in his seat, his hands clasped nervously. "I wanted to ask you something. It's about the baby."

Her pencil froze mid-stroke, and her expression grew guarded. "What about him?"

Brian met her eyes, his voice steady but sincere. "Brittney, you know I love you, world without end, and that means I love your baby. I want to be his Daddy."

Brittney blinked, stunned. "What? Brian, I..."

"Brittney, my love, I want to. Anyone can be a father, but being a dad is something special to me. It means being there every step of the way, and I want to be that man. To hold him when he's happy or sick, changing his diapers when needed — all of it."

The room was silent except for the faint clatter of cards being shuffled. Brittney looked between Brian and Stephanie, her eyes glistening. "You really mean that?"

Brian was nodding when Stephanie chimed in, her voice warm and encouraging. "He does. And I think it's a wonderful idea."

Brittney's lips trembled into a smile. "I... I don't know what to say. That's..."

Brian leaned forward slightly. "You don't have to decide right now."

Brittney's expression brightened. "Thank you, Brian. I think... I know you'd be a perfect dad."

Brian smiled softly. "I can only try," he said softly.

Stephanie placed a hand on Brittney's arm. "We're lucky to have him."

The three of them shared a hug, a silent promise forming between them. As they pulled apart, Stephanie glanced at Brittney's sketchpad.

"Hey, what are you drawing?"

Brittney beamed, holding up the pad. "It's Brian and I, our first kiss at the promise ceremony."

Umi and Gloria exchanged quiet, approving smiles at the dining table. Gloria whispered, "That boy has a heart of gold."

Umi nodded, her voice soft. "This is exactly what she needs."

CHAPTER 26

T he soft glow of a single lamp filled Brian's living room as the three of them settled into their usual spots. Jazz hummed softly in the background, a familiar comfort from many nights like this. Brian leaned back into the plush armrest, his gaze constantly drifting from his book toward the kitchen, where Gloria and Umi were quietly chatting over tea and cards.

Stephanie, seated close to his left, noticed his frequent glances and the subtle tension in his posture. She exchanged a look with Brittney, who sat on his right, mirroring her curiosity.

"You're thinking about something," Stephanie said, nudging him lightly with her elbow. Her voice was gentle but laced with playful suspicion.

Brian blinked, startled, and looked at her. "What? No, I'm not."

Brittney tilted her head, studying his face. "Liar," she said softly, her voice filled with a mix of affection and determination. "You've got that look again."

"What look?" Brian's protest sounded weak even to his own ears.

"The one you get when you're overthinking something but don't want to bring it up," Stephanie explained. "What's going on?"

Brian laughed nervously, running a hand through his hair. "You two always gang up on me," he muttered, though his smile betrayed his affection.

Brittney leaned closer, her eyes soft but insistent. "Twins plus one meeting," she declared, standing up. "We need privacy for this."

As she rose, Umi's voice floated over from the kitchen, her tone tinged with curiosity. "Everything okay over there?"

Stephanie smiled at her mother, her tone light and teasing. "Oh, nothing's wrong, Mom. Brian just has a secret we're determined to uncover."

Gloria chuckled softly, her gaze flickering to Brian with a knowing look. "Good luck with that, girls. He's stubborn when he wants to be."

Brian groaned, his cheeks flushing as Brittney grinned and tugged on his arm. "Come on, Brian," she said. "Let's make this easy for you."

Stephanie added with a wink toward Umi, "We'll have him talking in no time, Mom. Don't worry."

With mock resignation, Brian stood and allowed himself to be guided toward his room, his protests earning only giggles from the twins.

Once in his room, the space comfortable and familiar with framed photos of them and their families adorning the walls, they settled on the bed—Stephanie on one side, Brittney on the other. They turned to him expectantly.

"Okay, Mr. Cole," Brittney said, her tone gentle but firm. "Out with it."

Brian hesitated, his hands fidgeting in his lap. "It's… about the honeymoon," he admitted quietly, not meeting their eyes.

Stephanie reached for his hand, her grip warm and reassuring. "Brian, you can tell us anything," she said softly.

Brittney nodded. "We're here for each other, remember? Whatever it is, just say it."

Brian glanced at them, his cheeks flushing. "I just… I've been wondering if you'd prefer separate honeymoons. Like… one for me and Stephanie, and one for me and you, Britt." His voice dropped as he added, "Or if you'd rather we… all go together in one."

The room fell silent as the twins processed his words. Brittney broke the stillness first, her voice soft but steady. "Why would we need separate honeymoons?"

Brian shrugged, his gaze flickering toward the bed and then back to his hands. "I don't want to do something you're not comfortable with, ready for, or don't want to do. Especially you, Brittney. After everything you've been through, I don't want you to feel pressured."

Brittney's expression softened, and she placed a hand on his. "Brian, you've never made me feel pressured," she said quietly. "If anything, you've been the reason why I can love. The reason I've learned to trust again. I don't want to pull away from that; I want to build on it."

Stephanie nodded, her eyes shining with emotion. "Brian, what we shared during the promise ceremony wasn't just for show. It's who we are now. Together."

"But the bedroom..." Brian trailed off, his voice thick with uncertainty. "I know it hasn't been easy for you, Brittney. I don't want to ruin that progress."

Brittney smiled, her hand tightening around his. "Brian, I know you're worried. But you've shown me nothing but love and patience. I trust you. And I trust Steph. I want to keep growing, with both of you."

Stephanie leaned against his shoulder, her voice warm. "You've never pushed us, Brian. You've always made us feel safe. This is about all three of us together. We've already shared so much; why would we change that now?"

Brian hesitated, his throat tightening as their words sank in. "I just don't want to mess this, what we have now, up," he admitted softly.

"You won't," Brittney assured him. "Mom says this isn't about perfection. It's about us. All of us."

Stephanie smiled, placing a hand over both of them. "Let's make the honeymoon special. Someplace where we can celebrate everything we've become. Together."

Brian looked at them, his eyes misty. "Are you sure?"

"More than sure," Stephanie said firmly.

Brittney nodded, her gaze steady. "We've come too far to backtrack now. Let's plan something amazing for all of us."

A small laugh escaped Brian, the tension finally lifting. "Okay," he said, his smile growing. "Someplace special. Someplace that we can call ours."

Brian leaned back against the headboard, visibly more at ease now that the hardest part of the conversation was behind them. Stephanie shifted closer, leaning her chin on her palm as she gazed at him. "All right, Mr. Cole, now that we're all in agreement, where do you think we should go?"

Brittney perked up, a playful grin spreading across her face. "Knowing Brian, he's probably thinking of someplace ridiculous, like a private island or something."

Brian chuckled, tilting his head toward her. "And what's wrong with a private island? White sand, crystal-clear water…"

"Sand gets everywhere," Stephanie interjected with mock horror, her eyes sparkling. "No, thank you."

"Okay, fair point," Brian admitted, laughing. "What about a cabin in the mountains? Cozy, quiet, lots of hot chocolate…"

"And bears," Brittney deadpanned, grinning as she crossed her arms. "No thanks. I'd rather not get chased by a bear on my honeymoon."

Stephanie giggled. "Plus, I don't think Brian's stump would appreciate a week of hiking trails."

"Wow, you two are brutal," Brian said, feigning injury. "Fine, scratch the mountains."

"What about someplace smaller?" Brittney suggested, her tone turning thoughtful. "Like a bed-and-breakfast somewhere scenic. Simple, quiet… romantic."

Stephanie nodded in agreement. "That could be really nice. I've always liked the idea of those little places with ivy-covered walls and a garden out back."

Brian raised an eyebrow. "A little too quiet, don't you think? I'd go stir-crazy after the first day."

"You're impossible," Stephanie teased, nudging him lightly.

Brittney leaned forward, a mischievous glint in her eyes. "Okay, fine. How about something wild? Vegas?"

Brian groaned. "I love you both, but I don't think I could handle that much excitement on a honeymoon."

"Fair," Stephanie said, laughing. "So, no casinos. What about a national park? We could rent a cabin near a lake."

"More bears," Brian muttered, earning a chorus of laughter.

As their banter continued, the possibilities ranged from quaint seaside towns to bustling European cities. Each idea was met with playful critiques, vetoes, and exaggerated protests.

Finally, Brian stretched out on the bed, his head resting on the pillow. He closed his eyes, a faint smile playing on his lips. "You know what I see?" he said softly, his voice tinged with a mix of wistfulness and excitement.

"What?" Brittney asked, leaning in curiously.

"Central Park," he murmured. "The skyline stretching in the distance, the lights of the city reflecting off the buildings. Horse-drawn carriages moving slowly along the park's edge..."

Stephanie and Brittney exchanged a glance, their expressions softening as they imagined the scene he painted.

"That sounds..." Stephanie began, her voice trailing off as she smiled.

"Beautiful," Brittney finished for her, her eyes shining.

Brian opened his eyes and smiled softly, lifting a hand to motion the girls closer. "Come here," he said, his voice warm and inviting. "I want to hold you both while we figure this out."

316

Stephanie started to move but paused midway, glancing toward the door. "Wait," she said, walking over to open it a crack. She peeked out as if expecting to find one of their mothers lurking. "Just in case Mom suspects we're doing something unapproved."

Brittney rolled her eyes, stifling a laugh. "I think they trust us. Mostly."

Stephanie grinned, letting the door rest slightly ajar before joining them on the bed. "Better safe than sorry."

Brian chuckled as they settled in beside him, one on each side. His arms wrapped around them instinctively, holding them close. "You're both ridiculous," he teased.

"Ridiculously smart," Brittney quipped, snuggling against his shoulder.

"Ridiculously cute," Stephanie added with a smirk.

Brian leaned his head back against the headboard, looking down at them with a soft smile. "Ridiculously perfect," he murmured.

They stayed like that for a moment before Stephanie broke the silence. "So, New York," she began, glancing up at him. "What else would we do there besides staring at the skyline?"

Brian's eyes lit up. "Plenty," he said. "Horse-drawn carriages through Central Park, of course. And there's the Empire State Building—imagine the view from the top."

Brittney's voice was thoughtful. "And Times Square at night. All those lights… it would feel like another world."

"Ooh, and Broadway!" Stephanie added, her excitement growing. "We could see a show. Maybe a musical."

"Fancy dinners," Brian suggested. "I'm talking about the kind where I'd have to wear a suit and actually pretend to know which fork to use."

Brittney giggled. "We'd probably need a crash course in table manners first."

Stephanie nodded in mock seriousness. "Step one: don't drink from the finger bowl."

Brian laughed, his chest vibrating against them. "You're going to embarrass me in front of everyone, aren't you?"

"Definitely," Stephanie said, grinning.

Brittney tilted her head, her voice quieter but no less enthusiastic. "And what about the little moments? Like walking down Fifth Avenue, holding hands... just being together."

Brian turned his head to kiss her temple, his voice soft. "That's the best part."

The conversation flowed easily, ideas tumbling out as they imagined their adventure. They talked about street performers, late-night walks through the city, and stopping at little cafes for pastries and coffee. Every suggestion was met with smiles and laughter, the mood warm and filled with anticipation.

As the energy began to settle, Brittney turned toward Brian, her eyes searching his. Slowly, she leaned up and captured his lips in a lingering, heartfelt kiss. When she pulled back, her voice was barely a whisper. "I love you, Brian. More than words can ever say."

Brian's breath caught as his eyes locked on hers. "I love you too, Brittney," he replied softly.

Stephanie watched, her expression tender as she reached for him next. She cupped his cheek, drawing him into a kiss that mirrored Brittney's in its depth and emotion. When she pulled away, her voice was steady but full of feeling. "I love you, Brian. You've given me everything I've ever dreamed of."

Brian tightened his arms around them, his heart full. "You've both given me more than I could've ever imagined," he said, his voice thick with emotion.

They nestled closer, the rhythm of their breathing gradually evening out as the conversation faded into comfortable silence. The trio lay there, wrapped in each other's warmth and the shared promise of their future.

An hour later, the house was quiet save for the occasional clink of dishes from the kitchen as Umi and Gloria finished tidying up. Gloria glanced at the clock on the wall and frowned slightly. "They've been in that room for a while now," she murmured, drying her hands on a towel.

Umi turned, raising an eyebrow. "Brian and the girls? Maybe they're still talking."

"Maybe," Gloria replied, though a curious spark danced in her eyes. "I'll just check in. Make sure they're not planning to take off to Vegas or something."

Umi chuckled softly. "If they are, at least make sure they leave a note."

Gloria shook her head with a laugh and made her way down the hall. She paused outside Brian's door, noting the faint sliver of light spilling out where it was left slightly ajar. Quietly, she pushed it open a little more and froze at the sight before her.

The three of them were sprawled across the bed, tangled in an embrace that spoke of deep love and trust. Brian was on his back, his arms wrapped protectively around both girls. Stephanie was curled into his side, her head resting on his shoulder, while Brittney lay tucked against his other side, her face nuzzled into his chest. Their breaths rose and fell in a synchronized rhythm, peaceful and undisturbed.

Gloria's lips parted in a soft smile, and she turned back toward the hall. "Umi," she whispered, motioning for her to come over. "You have to see this."

Umi approached curiously, peeking around the doorway. Her expression softened immediately, her gaze lingering on the trio. "Well, would you look at that," she said quietly. A sly grin tugged at her lips. "Sleeping together before the marriage. Scandalous."

Gloria snorted, covering her mouth to stifle her laugh. "You're terrible."

"I'm honest," Umi replied, her tone laced with amusement. "But look at them. It's sweet."

Gloria nodded, her voice dropping to a whisper. "I don't think I've ever seen Brittney this relaxed. She's always been a worrier, even as a little girl."

"And Stephanie," Umi added, "She used to keep everyone at arm's length. But now? Look at her, completely at ease."

Umi stepped closer, her voice softening further. "It's because of him. Brian... he's good for them. For all of them."

Gloria sighed, her gaze lingering on the trio once more. "He is. And they're good for him, too. Look how he holds them. Like he'd do anything to keep them safe."

"They deserve this," Umi said quietly, her tone filled with warmth. "After everything they've been through, they deserve a little peace."

Gloria nodded again, her smile returning. "Let's let them sleep. We can cover them up and turn off the light."

Umi smirked, stepping back toward the hall. "Just don't let them catch us. We'll never hear the end of it."

Gloria rolled her eyes but couldn't suppress a chuckle as she carefully pulled a blanket from the foot of the bed and draped it over them. She turned off the lamp, leaving only the faint glow of moonlight streaming through the window.

As they tiptoed away, Gloria glanced back one last time, her heart swelling with affection. "Goodnight, my loves," she whispered, closing the door gently behind them.

As they walked away, Gloria murmured, "I have a feeling this honeymoon is going to be unforgettable for them."

Umi chuckled softly. "And for us, when we get the bill."

Their quiet laughter faded down the hall, leaving the trio undisturbed in their shared dream of the future.

CHAPTER 27

The day before the trial began, District Attorney Scott Miller and Defense Attorney Jack Hartford sat waiting outside Judge Ann Harlow's chambers. The hallway was quiet, save for the occasional click of shoes against the tiled floor. Both men had been there for quite some time, their initial patience long replaced by faint irritation.

When Judge Harlow finally appeared, her dark robe flowing behind her, she offered a wry smile. "Gentlemen, I apologize for the delay," she said, her tone warm but brisk. "Apparently, no good deed goes unpunished. Please, join me in my chambers."

The judge led them into her office, a space both imposing and serene. The soft amber lighting cast a warm glow across the rows of leather-bound legal tomes lining the walls. Judge Harlow settled behind her large oak desk, her presence filling the room with quiet authority.

Scott Miller adjusted his tie as he took his seat, carefully laying out his notes on the polished surface. Across from him, Jack Hartford leaned back in his chair, his posture relaxed but his eyes sharp, exuding an air of practiced confidence.

Finally, Judge Harlow looked up from her notes, her tone firm. "Alright, gentlemen, let's begin. We're here to address pre-trial motions ahead of tomorrow's proceedings. Mr. Miller, you've filed to clear the gallery during Brittney Welch's testimony. Present your case."

Scott stood up, his demeanor calm but deliberate. "Your Honor, the State requests the gallery be cleared for the duration of Brittney Welch's testimony. She is a minor who has endured extensive emotional and psychological trauma at the hands of the defendant. A public gallery, particularly with members of the press, would amplify her distress, potentially affecting her ability to testify accurately. Limiting the gallery to immediate family and essential personnel ensures her testimony is not unduly stressful or compromised."

Judge Harlow nodded, her expression unreadable. "And Mr. Hartford, your response?"

Jack leaned forward, his tone measured. "Your Honor, the defense strongly objects to this request. Clearing the gallery infringes upon my client's Sixth Amendment right to a public trial. Transparency is a cornerstone of justice, and while I understand the prosecution's concerns, discomfort is not a valid reason to exclude the public."

Scott looked at him. "Discomfort? We're not talking about a minor inconvenience here, Mr. Hartford. We're talking about a victim, a teenage girl, being subjected to public scrutiny while recounting the most traumatic events of her life. Surely, you can even see the value in protecting her dignity."

Scott turned to the judge. "Your Honor, Miss Welch has already been subjected to ridicule and victim-shaming to the extent she now continues her classes via remote access. Members of the community have already condemned her as a 'money-hungry liar,' causing her to only venture from her residence for medical reasons."

Jack turned to Scott. "Mr. Miller, you are presenting information about things that have already happened and are outside the scope of the court system; this isn't our concern. I'll also point out that the law doesn't prioritize comfort over fairness. If the witness is stable enough to testify, as you've assured us, she should be stable enough to do so in a public courtroom."

Judge Harlow interrupted before Scott could reply. "Enough, Mr. Hartford. I won't have you trivializing the victim's trauma in my chambers. If you're going to argue against the motion, stick to the legal grounds, not snide commentary."

Jack raised his hands as if surrendering. "Of course, Your Honor. My point is simply this: Clearing the gallery risks creating the perception of secrecy. The jury could interpret it as evidence that the witness's testimony is somehow fragile or questionable."

Scott turned to the judge, his voice unchanged. "Your Honor, Brittney Welch's testimony is far from questionable. The defense is trying to weaponize her vulnerability against her. Let me be clear: My request is not about secrecy; it's about ensuring the integrity of her testimony. The press will still have access to transcripts, preserving transparency."

Judge Harlow sighed. "This case hasn't even started, and I'm already seeing how difficult it's going to be to maintain order. Mr. Hartford, unless you can provide concrete evidence that clearing the gallery will prejudice the jury, I am inclined to side with the State on this matter."

Jack's tone sharpened. "If we're discussing concrete evidence, Your Honor, the defense has a request of its own — a competency hearing for Miss Welch. Given her documented mental health struggles, we have reason to question her ability to reliably distinguish fact from fiction, especially under the pressure of cross-examination."

Scott's eyes narrowed. "This is outrageous. Miss Welch has been preparing for this trial for months. She's demonstrated her ability to recount events clearly and consistently. A competency hearing is a thinly veiled attempt to intimidate and humiliate her."

Jack pretended to be shocked. "Intimidate? Hardly, Your Honor. Ensuring the reliability of a witness is fundamental to a fair trial. If the prosecution is so confident in her stability, what harm is there in confirming it formally?"

Judge Harlow stared at Jack coldly. "Mr. Hartford, I'm warning you: If I allow this hearing, you will keep your questions focused on her ability to understand and recount events. Any attempt to use it as a fishing expedition to discredit her character will result in immediate sanctions. Do I make myself clear?"

Jack replied, "Crystal, Your Honor. My only interest is in ensuring a fair trial."

Scott muttered softly, "Fair to whom?"

Judge Harlow snapped her attention to Scott. "Mr. Miller, that's enough. I expect professionalism from both of you; otherwise, I'll hold you both in contempt before this trial even begins."

She took a deep breath, tapping her pen on the desk as she considered what was presented.

Seconds later, she glanced between both attorneys. "Here's my ruling. Mr. Miller, I am granting your motion to limit the gallery. Only immediate family, essential personnel, and attorneys will be permitted during Miss Welch's testimony. To be absolutely clear, gentlemen, only for Miss Welch's testimony. No other aspects of the case are subject to this ruling. However, the press will have access to transcripts to ensure public accountability. This is a compromise, not an invitation for either side to make this trial a spectacle."

Judge Harlow turned toward Jack, her voice cold and sharp. "Mr. Hartford, I am granting your motion for a competency hearing, but I will be watching closely. If you overstep or deviate from the purpose of this hearing, you'll find yourself in contempt faster than Mr. Miller can object."

Jack nodded. "Understood, Your Honor."

Judge Harlow leaned forward, her tone a bit softer. "I want to be clear: This trial is already emotionally charged, and I expect both of you to conduct yourselves with the utmost decorum. That includes treating the victim and each other with respect. Do not test my patience, gentlemen."

Scott stood up, nodding. "Understood, Your Honor. Thank you."

Jack stood up slowly, a faint smirk on his lips. "As always, Your Honor."

Judge Harlow looked between the two. "It's 11:30 a.m. now; we're reconvening in the courtroom at 1:00 p.m. sharp. Be ready to proceed," her voice firm and resolute.

*****

The office at the courthouse was modest, with fluorescent lights casting a pale glow over the scuffed wooden table. Papers were scattered in front of Scott Miller, who sat across from Brittney. She fidgeted with the sleeve of her oversized sweater, her fingers tugging at a loose thread. Umi sat beside her, a steady hand resting on her daughter's shoulder. Gloria stood nearby, arms crossed protectively, while Stephanie and Brian lingered near the door, exchanging nervous glances.

Scott's voice was calm but firm. "Brittney, before the trial starts, we need to address a preliminary matter. The defense has requested a competency hearing to assess whether you're fit to testify."

Brittney froze, her brows furrowing. "What? He thinks I'm too stupid to tell the truth? Is that what this is about?" Her voice cracked with indignation as her grip tightened on the chair's arm.

Umi's hand gently squeezed her shoulder. "Brittney, he's just trying to distract you. You know the truth, and that's all that matters."

Scott leaned forward, his tone reassuring. "Exactly. This isn't about you, Brittney. It's about creating doubt. But we've prepared for this, and I'll make sure Hartford doesn't overstep."

For the next fifteen minutes, Scott explained what Brittney should expect. Every now and again, she would ask a question, her voice firm with each question. Brian and Stephanie could hear her determination as the meeting progressed.

Brittney's gaze softened as she looked at Scott. Though her voice trembled slightly, it carried determination. "Okay. Let's do this, Mr. Scott."

The room fell silent for a moment, the soft hum of the overhead vent the only sound. Gloria offered a small, reassuring smile. "You've got this, sweetheart. You're stronger than you know."

Brittney straightened her shoulders, nodding as the group stood to leave.

*****

The courtroom was vast and formal, with polished wooden benches and high ceilings that made every sound echo. Judge Ann Harlow sat at her oak bench; glasses perched low on her nose as she reviewed her notes. The cleared gallery emphasized the gravity of the hearing, with Brittney's family seated directly in front of her. Brittney's baggy sweater and oversized shirt contrasted sharply with the attorneys' formal attire.

Judge Harlow cleared her throat, her tone measured. "This is a competency hearing to determine whether the witness, Miss Brittney Rose Welch, is fit to testify in the upcoming trial. Mr. Hartford, the floor is yours."

Jack Hartford stood smoothly, adjusting his tie as he addressed the court. "Your Honor, before proceeding, the defense would like to call Dr. Alexander Myers to the stand."

A tall man with a composed demeanor approached the witness stand. Dr. Myers, dressed in a crisp suit, exuded confidence as he took the oath and settled into his seat. Hartford moved to the center of the courtroom, projecting calm authority.

"Dr. Myers, please state your qualifications for the court," Hartford began.

"My name is Dr. Alexander Myers. I hold a doctorate in clinical psychology with a specialization in trauma and PTSD.

I've been practicing for over fifteen years and am affiliated with the Beaverdam Trauma and Recovery Institute."

"Thank you, Dr. Myers," Hartford said with a faint smile. "Based on your review of the medical documentation and behavioral evaluations provided, how would you describe Brittney Welch's psychological state?"

Dr. Myers folded his hands. "Brittney exhibits signs consistent with a complex trauma profile. Her diagnoses of C-PTSD and bipolar disorder suggest she has heightened emotional reactivity and potential difficulty distinguishing emotional memories from objective events."

"In your professional opinion, could Brittney's condition affect her ability to recall events accurately, especially under the emotional strain of testifying?" Hartford's voice was measured.

Dr. Myers leaned forward slightly. "Yes, it's possible. Individuals with her diagnosis can experience memory fragmentation or heightened emotional recall that can distort their perception of events. The emotional weight of reliving trauma may unintentionally color their testimony."

Scott rose immediately, his voice firm. "Objection, Your Honor. Speculative. Dr. Myers has never evaluated Miss Welch personally and is drawing conclusions based on generalizations."

Judge Harlow nodded. "Sustained. Mr. Hartford, keep your questioning within the scope of the doctor's expertise."

Hartford gave a slight nod. "Dr. Myers, to clarify, are your statements based on the general traits of individuals with Brittney's diagnosis?"

"Yes," Dr. Myers confirmed. "These are well-documented tendencies in individuals with trauma-related conditions."

"Thank you, Doctor. No further questions." Hartford took his seat, his gaze steady.

Scott stood and addressed the court. "Your Honor, the prosecution calls Dr. Jennifer Rodriguez to the stand."

Dr. Rodriguez's warm, composed demeanor immediately filled the room with a sense of trust. She approached the stand, took the oath, and settled into her seat. After a reassuring glance at Brittney, she turned her attention to Scott.

"Dr. Rodriguez," Scott began, "can you explain your professional relationship with Brittney Welch?"

"Certainly," Dr. Rodriguez said. "I am Brittney's therapist and have been treating her since her diagnosis of C-PTSD was confirmed. We've worked extensively on coping strategies and understanding her emotional triggers."

"Dr. Rodriguez, based on your knowledge of Brittney's condition and your work with her, does her condition affect her ability to recall events accurately?"

Dr. Rodriguez's expression turned thoughtful. "No. Brittney's condition does not impair her ability to recall events. Rather, her emotional responses may be triggered by certain memories, but the events themselves remain intact in her memory."

Jack rose, his voice sharp. "Objection, Your Honor. Speculative. Dr. Rodriguez is offering subjective opinions based solely on therapy sessions."

Judge Harlow's gavel tapped lightly. "Overruled. Continue, Mr. Miller."

Scott nodded. "Dr. Rodriguez, can you elaborate on how Brittney's condition manifests?"

Dr. Rodriguez leaned forward slightly. "Brittney's condition is primarily marked by heightened emotional responses and, at times, physical reactions to triggering stimuli. These responses stem from trauma, not from a distorted perception of what happened."

Jack stood for cross-examination, his tone brisk. "Dr. Rodriguez, would you agree that C-PTSD could, in some cases, cause individuals to experience memory fragmentation or emotional interference?"

Dr. Rodriguez hesitated briefly. "In rare cases, yes. However—"

Jack cut her off smoothly. "Thank you, Doctor. No further questions."

Scott stood immediately, his voice deliberate. "Redirect, Your Honor."

"Proceed," Judge Harlow said.

"Dr. Rodriguez, earlier, you were explaining the role of emotional triggers in Brittney's condition. Could you please complete your explanation?"

Dr. Rodriguez nodded. "Of course. Brittney's condition triggers emotional or, sometimes, physical responses, but it does not alter her perception of reality. Her recollection of events remains accurate, even if recalling them is emotionally taxing."

Scott's voice was calm but firm. "And based on your work with Brittney, do you have any reason to doubt her capacity to testify truthfully and accurately in this courtroom?"

Dr. Rodriguez's voice was unwavering. "None whatsoever."

Scott smiled faintly. "Thank you, Doctor. No further questions."

Judge Harlow glanced between the attorneys before addressing the court. "Dr. Rodriguez, you are excused."

As Dr. Rodriguez stepped down, the gallery murmured softly, the weight of her testimony lingering in the air. Scott's calm but decisive demeanor spoke volumes as he returned to his seat.

Judge Harlow turned her attention back to Hartford. "Mr. Hartford, you may proceed."

Jack stood up, adjusting his tie. "The defense would like to call Brittney Rose Welch to the stand."

Brittney stood up, nervously looking at Scott as she passed him on her way to the stand. As she sat down, her hands fidgeted with her sweater.

Hartford rose smoothly, adjusting his tie as he approached the stand. His voice was calm but carried a sharp edge. "Miss Welch, do you understand the purpose of this hearing?"

Brittney's voice was steady despite her trembling hands. "Yes, it's to decide if I can testify."

Hartford nodded, his expression unreadable. "Do you also understand the importance of respecting this court? Tell me, Miss Welch, is this the attire of someone taking these proceedings seriously?"

From the gallery, Gloria's hand gripped Umi's tightly.

Scott rose immediately. "Your Honor, I object to this line of questioning. It's irrelevant and inappropriate."

Judge Harlow's eyebrows rose slightly as she addressed Hartford. "Mr. Hartford, explain how this question is relevant to the purpose of this hearing."

Hartford adjusted his tie and replied smoothly. "Your Honor, attire is the visible expression of respect for the court and its proceedings. I believe it's a relevant point, as it reflects the witness's understanding of the court's authority."

Judge Harlow turned to Scott, her gaze sharp. "Mr. Miller, do you have anything to offer that would clarify this matter?"

Scott rose, his tone calm but firm. "Yes, Your Honor. I have medical reports and a sworn affidavit from Miss Welch's physician and therapist confirming her physical condition and the necessity of minimizing her discomfort today. I can submit them to the court immediately."

He walked forward and handed over the documentation, his confidence evident. Judge Harlow took a moment to review the materials before glancing back at Hartford.

"Mr. Hartford," the judge said, her tone measured but icy, "I've reviewed the reports and affidavit, which confirm that Miss Welch's attire is entirely justified. Tread very carefully."

Hartford's jaw tightened, but he gave a curt nod. "Understood, Your Honor."

Judge Harlow answered the objection. "Overruled. The witness will answer the question."

A flush crept up Brittney's cheeks as she glanced down at her sweater. Tears welled in her eyes but didn't fall. "I wore this because I'm in pain," she said softly but firmly. "It's not about respect. I respect this court. I was asked not to take the pain pills so that the defense couldn't argue they affected my ability to tell the truth and because they make me more, um, emotional."

Hartford's expression tightened, but he pressed forward. "Miss Welch, you stopped taking your medication for six months, correct? Isn't it possible that lapse affected your ability to recall events clearly?"

Brittney inhaled deeply, her voice wavering but resolute. "It stopped because of a misunderstanding, but I've been back on my medication since the SVU interview. It hasn't changed what happened."

Hartford leaned closer, his voice low and pointed. "Are you sure it hasn't? Isn't it true that your condition makes it difficult to separate fact from emotion?"

"Objection, Your Honor," Scott interjected. "Speculative."

"Sustained," Judge Harlow said firmly. "Move on, Mr. Hartford."

"Miss Welch, can you define what it means to testify under oath?" Hartford asked, his voice sharper now.

"It means I swear to tell the truth and nothing but the truth," Brittney replied, her tone even.

"And when you swear an oath, what does it mean?" Jack pressed his point.

"Swearing an oath is like a promise; only if you break the oath, you can go to jail," she answered, her tone still even.

"And are you confident you understand the difference between the truth and a lie?" Hartford pressed further.

"Yes, I understand," she answered firmly.

Hartford's lips curved slightly, but his tone grew more pointed. "If you were to make a mistake in your testimony, would you admit it, or would you stick to what you think is right?"

Brittney's voice was calm but strong. "I would admit it. I don't want to hide anything."

Hartford's expression hardened. "Miss Welch, you've described feeling 'overwhelmed' and 'anxious' in the past. How can this court be sure your testimony isn't clouded by those emotions?"

Brittney straightened her posture, meeting Hartford's gaze. "Because I remember exactly what happened. The anxiety comes from talking about it, not from doubting the truth."

Hartford's tone grew colder. "Would you agree that someone under emotional distress might perceive events differently than they actually occurred?"

"Objection, Your Honor," Scott interjected. "Speculative."

"Sustained," Judge Harlow said firmly. "Move on, Mr. Hartford."

Hartford shifted tactics. "Miss Welch, on the day you claim one of the incidents happened, you were under extreme stress, correct?"

"Yes, but that doesn't change what he did," Brittney replied, her voice steady.

"But how can this court be certain your stress didn't alter your perception of the events?" Hartford countered.

Brittney's hands tightened on the stand, but her voice didn't falter. "Because the bruises, the pain, and the things he said weren't in my head. They were on my body; I felt the pain, and I heard his words. They are real."

Hartford's expression grew calculating. "Miss Welch, why are you here today, in this courtroom?"

Brittney rose gently, a twinge of defiance in her voice. "To make sure he can't do this to another woman."

Hartford leaned in slightly, his tone more biting. "Are you sure you're here for justice, Miss Welch? Or is it because you found out Richard is rich, and you want his money?"

Brittney's face flushed, but her voice was unwavering. "I'm here because of what he did to me. This isn't about money; it's about making sure he's held accountable."

Brittney's voice wavered slightly, but her determination shone through as she added, "Because I want the truth to be known. What Richard did to me wasn't right, and it's my responsibility to speak up to help other women."

Hartford's voice dropped, almost a whisper. "Do you feel pressured by your family or the prosecution to testify?"

"No," Brittney said firmly. "This is my choice. I need to do this."

Scott stood for redirect, his voice steady and supportive. "Miss Welch, earlier, you said you understand the difference between truth and lies. Why is it important to you to testify truthfully?"

Brittney's expression softened slightly as she answered. "Because it's the only way to make sure he doesn't hurt anyone else."

Scott nodded, his voice calm but resolute. "You've been asked a lot of questions today, and you've shown courage in answering them. Do you feel prepared to testify in this trial?"

"Yes," Brittney said, her voice unwavering. "I've told the truth here, and I'll tell the truth in the trial."

The door to the courtroom opened quietly, drawing Brittney's gaze. Captain Bishop entered, her presence calm and commanding as she took a seat in the back of the gallery. Brittney's breath hitched, but she sat up straighter, her hands steadying on her lap.

Hartford's tone sharpened. "Miss Welch, isn't it convenient that your 'truth' always makes you the victim? Isn't it possible you've convinced yourself of things that didn't happen?"

Tears slipped silently down Brittney's cheeks, but she held her composure. Her voice broke through the tension. "No. I know what happened. I know what he did to me."

Jack looked at the judge. "No more questions, Your Honor."

Judge Harlow looked at Scott. "Mr. Miller?"

Scott stood up. "No more questions, Your Honor."

Judge Harlow glanced at the documentation on her desk and then turned her attention to Brittney. Her tone was measured but carried a note of genuine concern. "Miss Welch, I have some questions for you."

Brittney sat up straighter, her hands gripping the edge of the stand. "Yes, Your Honor."

"The report Mr. Miller provided states that you have chosen not to take pain medication while on the stand to ensure your answers remain clear. Is this correct?"

Brittney nodded slightly. "Yes, Your Honor. I didn't want anything to interfere with my ability to testify clearly."

"And you don't think the pain will become too much for you?" the judge asked, her sharp gaze softening just slightly.

Brittney hesitated for a moment before answering, her voice steady. "It's not easy, Your Honor, but I've handled it before. I can manage the pain."

Judge Harlow leaned forward slightly. "And what if an unexpected event occurs—a sneeze, a coughing fit, or even if you become very upset? Do you feel prepared to handle those situations?"

Brittney's grip on the stand tightened, but her tone remained resolute. "If something like that happens, Your Honor, I'll take a moment to collect myself. I know what I need to say, and I won't let anything stop me from telling the truth."

Judge Harlow's gaze held Brittney's for a moment before she spoke again, her tone firm. "Miss Welch, I am going to give you an order that you are to follow until this case is concluded. Do you understand me?"

Brittney's eyes widened slightly, but she nodded. "Yes, Your Honor."

"I am ordering you to take your prescribed medication if you need to. If you do, you will inform Mr. Miller, and he will bring it to the court's attention when appropriate. If adjustments to the schedule are necessary, they will be made. This court will not tolerate a witness harming herself to appease its process. Am I clear?"

Brittney exhaled softly, her shoulders relaxing just a bit. "Yes, Your Honor, I understand."

Judge Harlow shifted her gaze to the attorneys. "This order is placed on the record. Mr. Miller, if informed, you will notify the court. If accommodations need to be made, so be it. Both counsels will remain flexible in scheduling. I will not tolerate attempts to exploit this order for tactical advantage. Am I clear, gentlemen?"

Scott rose immediately, his voice steady. "Crystal clear, Your Honor."

Hartford's nod was curt, his tone neutral. "Understood, Your Honor."

Judge Harlow turned back to Brittney, her voice softening. "Miss Welch, thank you for your patience. This court finds you competent to testify."

She glanced at the clock, then back at Brittney's tear-streaked face. "Given the time and the emotional toll of this hearing, the court is adjourned early. We will reconvene tomorrow at 9:00 a.m."

As the judge and bailiff exited the courtroom, Brittney moved toward her family. She wiped her tears, her voice trembling. "I didn't lose it," she whispered.

Umi hugged her gently. "I'm so proud of you, my angel. We all knew you could do it."

Captain Bishop approached quietly. "You did well, Brittney. You're braver than most people I've met."

Brittney managed a faint smile. "Thank you. It helped to see you here."

The captain nodded, her hand briefly resting on Brittney's shoulder before stepping back. The courtroom lights dimmed as the family escorted Brittney out, ready to face the next day together.

CHAPTER 28

The living room was dim, lit only by the soft glow of a table lamp in the corner. The house was still, save for the faint sound of Gloria and Umi in the kitchen. Brittney sat curled up on the couch, her arms wrapped around a pillow, her gaze distant as she stared at the blank television screen.

Brian stepped into the room quietly, holding several hairbrushes in one hand he grabbed from the bathroom. He paused, taking in Brittney's hunched form. "Hey," he said gently, breaking the silence. "Want some company?"

Brittney glanced up, her eyes tired but calm. "Sure," she said softly, shifting slightly to make room on the couch.

Brian set the brushes down on the coffee table and sat across from her. "Thought I'd keep up my tradition," he said with a small smile, picking up a brush and gesturing toward her loose, tangled hair. "How about I take care of this for you?"

She hesitated, her fingers tightening around the pillow. "You don't have to," she murmured.

"I know," Brian replied easily. "But I'd like to. It's kind of my thing, remember?"

Her lips twitched faintly, almost a smile. "Yeah. Okay."

She turned her back to him, settling into the cushions as he scooted closer. With practiced care, Brian began brushing her hair, his movements slow and deliberate. The soft sound of the bristles filled the room, a rhythmic counterpoint to the quiet tension lingering in the air.

"You handled today really well," Brian said after a moment, his tone steady. "It's been a rough one, but you stayed strong. I'm proud of you."

Brittney exhaled shakily, her shoulders relaxing slightly under his gentle touch. "I'm just tired," she admitted. "Of all of it."

"I know," Brian said, his voice warm. "But you're not alone, Britt. We're in this together."

She nodded, her fingers loosening their grip on the pillow. "Thanks," she said quietly. "For being here. For everything."

"Always," Brian replied, finishing her braid and securing it with a tie. He leaned forward to meet her gaze as she turned to face him. "You've got me, Steph, Mom, everyone. We're a team."

The sound of footsteps on the stairs drew their attention, and Stephanie appeared in the doorway, her expression soft. "Brian?" she asked, hesitating slightly. "Mind if I join you guys?"

Brian looked at Brittney, who gave a small nod. "Of course," he said, gesturing to the couch.

Stephanie crossed the room and sat down on Brittney's other side, reaching out to squeeze her sister's hand. "I just wanted to check on you," she said softly. "And see if you need anything."

Brittney shook her head, a faint smile crossing her lips. "I'm okay," she said, her voice steady. "Just… glad you're here."

Brian watched as Stephanie leaned her head against Brittney's shoulder, the two sisters sitting in a rare moment of calm. He reached out, wrapping an arm around both of them. "You know," he said lightly, "this is the quietest I've seen you two in a long time."

The twins exchanged a glance before chuckling softly. "Don't get used to it," Brittney teased, her voice tinged with warmth.

The soft clink of mugs heralded the arrival of Umi and Gloria, stepping in from the kitchen. Gloria had a knowing smile on her face, and Umi carried a tray with a bowl of popcorn and a plate of cookies.

"Well, this is cozy," Gloria said, her tone warm as she set her coffee down on the table. "Mind if we join the party?"

"Looks like we're missing all the fun," Umi added, placing the snacks on the table and sitting in the armchair. "What's the occasion? Or is it just Brian's magic touch with a hairbrush?"

Brittney smiled faintly, glancing at Brian. "He does have a knack for it," she admitted.

Gloria plopped down on the couch next to Stephanie, nudging her playfully. "So, what are we talking about? Boys? School drama? Or maybe we're all just trying to forget today?"

Brian smirked. "A little of everything, I think."

"Well, in that case," Umi said, leaning forward to grab a cookie, "how about a round of embarrassing stories? That's always good for a laugh."

Brittney groaned softly. "Mom, please don't."

"Oh, come on," Gloria teased, nudging Stephanie. "Remember that time you both tried to switch places in the sixth grade and fooled no one except poor Mrs. Kramer?"

Stephanie burst out laughing, shaking her head. "She thought we were the same person for two weeks!"

Brittney's cheeks flushed, but she couldn't help but laugh along. "That was all Stephanie's idea, by the way."

Brian leaned back, grinning. "I'm just glad I wasn't around for that. I wouldn't have been able to tell you apart either."

"Ha!" Stephanie said triumphantly. "Even Brian admits it."

"Actually," Brian said, his grin widening, "Now I can always tell the two of you apart. Doesn't matter the time, the place, or the situation."

Umi raised an eyebrow, sipping her coffee. "Oh, really? Always?" she asked, her tone dripping with playful skepticism.

"Always," Brian replied confidently, crossing his arms. "You could dress them the same, blindfold me, spin me around in circles, and I'd still know who's who."

Stephanie snorted, shaking her head. "You're full of it, Brian. There's no way you could do that."

"I'm with Steph on this one," Brittney chimed in, a mischievous glint in her eyes. "I say we put it to the test."

Umi leaned forward, clearly enjoying the challenge. "Brian, I love you like my own, but I don't even buy it. You sure you want to stake your reputation on this?"

"I don't need to stake my reputation because I'll win," Brian shot back with a grin. "Go ahead. Set it up."

Brittney's smile widened. "Okay, but let's make it interesting. If you lose, you have to do my dishes for a month."

"A month?" Brian gave her an incredulous look. "I think you're forgetting who's in charge here."

"Brittney," Gloria interrupted, shaking her head with mock disapproval. "That's absurd. If we're making bets, let's keep them fair. If Brian wins, he gets two weeks off dishes—one week during Brittney's rotation and one during Stephanie's. If he loses, he's stuck with two weeks of dishes."

Brian rubbed his chin, pretending to mull it over. "Two weeks? That's it? You're practically handing me a victory, Mom."

Stephanie laughed, nudging Brittney. "He's way too confident about this. Let's knock him down a peg."

Brittney smirked, leaning back against the couch. "You're on, Brian. Let's see what you've got."

Minutes later, Brian stood in the middle of the living room, the blindfold tied securely. "All right," he said confidently, his hands outstretched. "Mix it up, confuse me, but I'll still win. You're only delaying the inevitable."

Stephanie rolled her eyes. "You're getting way too cocky, Brian."

"Cocky? No," he shot back with a grin. "Confident? Absolutely."

Umi stepped in, her tone playful. "All right, girls, let's make this hard. Switch spots, swap clothes, do something unpredictable."

The twins exchanged mischievous glances before swapping sweaters and even slipping on mismatched socks to throw him off. Stephanie pulled her hair into a messy bun, while Brittney let hers fall loose. They took turns whispering and giggling as they moved around him.

"Are you ready for this?" Umi asked her voice light with amusement.

Brian adjusted his stance slightly. "More than ready."

"All right, genius," Gloria said. "Go for it."

Brian paused, tilting his head as though listening for some hidden cue. He reached out carefully, brushing against one of the twins' arms. He hesitated, stepping back and holding up a finger. "Hmm."

Brittney smirked. "What are you waiting for? Some divine intervention?"

"Nope," Brian said, theatrically snapping his fingers. He reached out again, this time brushing a shoulder. After a few seconds, he stepped back dramatically. "This one is Stephanie."

Stephanie's jaw dropped. "What?! How did you..."

"Easy," Brian said, pulling the scarf off with a flourish. "The shampoo. You used the peach one today, and Brittney's is lavender. I told you; I can always tell."

Brittney groaned, throwing her hands in the air. "It's rigged! You moms gave it away!"

Stephanie nodded fervently. "Totally rigged. Mom, why didn't you switch shampoos?"

Umi held her hands up defensively. "Hey, this was your challenge. You're the ones who said yes."

"Fine," Brittney huffed. "One more round. And this time, no shampoo clues."

Brian grinned as they tied the blindfold back on. "You can make it as hard as you want. I've got this."

The group retreated into the dining room, this time taking extra steps to mask their identities. The twins swapped clothes again and tied their hair identically. Umi even lent Brittney her cardigan, while Stephanie slipped on gloves and layered on a scarf.

When they returned, they circled Brian like a game of musical chairs, giggling and whispering furiously.

"All right," Gloria said, her voice barely containing laughter. "We're ready, oh mighty twin-whisperer."

Brian stood still, turning his head slightly as if listening to the room. "Okay," he said slowly. "Let's see what you've got."

He moved cautiously, brushing a hand over someone's arm. Then he paused, tilted his head, and muttered, "Interesting."

"Stop stalling," Stephanie teased. "You're just trying to look cool."

Brian smiled. "This is an art, Steph, not a science."

Brittney crossed her arms. "It's witchcraft, is what it is."

After a few more seconds of deliberate movement, Brian stopped in front of one of the girls. He reached out carefully, brushing against their hand. Then, with a confident smile, he declared, "This is Brittney."

Brittney threw her hands in the air. "No way! How?"

Brian whipped off the blindfold. "You have a softer grip than Stephanie. Plus, you breathe a little differently when you're trying to stay calm. I told you; I can always tell."

Stephanie groaned. "Okay, that's just creepy. Are you sure you're not a magician?"

Gloria laughed. "I'll say it, this is borderline magical. But I guess it just proves how much you pay attention."

Brittney pointed at him, her expression deadpan. "I'm telling you; this is rigged."

"Not rigged," Brian replied with a grin. "Just skill."

Brian leaned back, his grin widening. "Alright, double or nothing. If I win this next round, two weeks off dishes becomes four. If I lose, I take four weeks of dishes. What do you say?"

"Absolutely not," Umi said with mock sternness. "This isn't about chores anymore. It's just for fun."

Gloria nodded. "Besides, we're not about to encourage you. Your head is already big enough."

"Fine, fine," Brian relented, holding up his hands. "How about this: I'll make it even harder. Both of you join in. Let's see if I can still figure it out with all four of you trying to fool me."

The moms exchanged intrigued glances. Umi raised an eyebrow. "You think you can tell the difference between all of us, Brian? Really?"

"I know I can," he said confidently. "Blindfold me again. Make sure I can't see anything."

Gloria tied the scarf securely while Umi inspected it carefully. "Alright, no gaps. He's definitely not seeing anything."

"Good," Gloria said. "Now let's make this interesting."

The group huddled in the dining room, whispering and laughing as they got creative. Umi sprayed the same perfume on everyone. Gloria slipped on another sweater, while the twins swapped accessories. They circled Brian multiple times, changing positions to confuse him.

"Alright," Gloria called, stifling a laugh. "Show us your magic, Brian."

Brian stood still, tilting his head as though listening. Slowly, he reached out, brushing a shoulder here and a hand there. He took longer this time, pausing frequently and even sniffing the air, to which Brittney groaned. "He's stalling again!"

"Patience, Britt," Brian replied, his tone light. "This is an advanced round."

After several moments of calculated movement, Brian stopped. He reached out one last time, brushing against someone's arm. A slow smile spread across his face. "This one... is Stephanie."

Stephanie gaped at him. "Are you kidding me?"

Umi started, her jaw dropping slightly. "Brian... This is getting ridiculous. How do you keep doing that?"

Brian pulled off the blindfold, his grin triumphant. "It's not magic. It's just skill."

"You're either a genius or a wizard," Gloria said, shaking her head. "Alright, Brian. How do you do it?"

Brian leaned back, savoring the moment. "Alright, you want to know the secret? Here's how it works..."

Brian leaned back on the couch, savoring the anticipation. The group sat around him, eyes wide with curiosity and skepticism.

"Alright," he began, "it's not magic, though I like the idea of being called a twin-whisperer." He shot a wink at Stephanie, who rolled her eyes but smiled despite herself.

"First off," Brian continued, "it's all about paying attention. I've spent a lot of time with you two, watching, listening, and just... noticing. You each have tiny tells that give you away."

"Like what?" Brittney demanded, crossing her arms.

"Well," Brian said, holding up a hand to count off points, "First, your posture. Britt, you tend to stand a little straighter when you're trying to play it cool, while Steph leans ever so slightly, like she's ready to move. I noticed it even when you swapped sweaters."

Stephanie blinked. "I lean? Really?"

"Just a tiny bit," Brian said with a grin. "It's subtle, but it's there."

"Okay, that's one," Umi said, gesturing for him to continue. "What else?"

"Touch," Brian said simply. "When I brushed against your hands or arms, I could tell the difference. Brittney's touch is a little lighter, like she's holding back. Stephanie is more direct, firmer."

The twins exchanged a look, clearly surprised. Gloria chuckled. "Well, that's two. What else?"

Brian's grin widened. "Your reactions. I do little things to test you. For example, when I tapped your arm, Steph, you stiffened for a split second, like you were preparing to be identified. Brittney didn't. She just waited."

"That's ridiculous," Brittney said, though her cheeks turned pink. "You're reading too much into this."

"Nope," Brian said with a shrug. "It's all there if you pay attention. Plus," he added, pointing at Umi and Gloria, "you two helped me, whether you meant to or not."

"What?" Gloria said, laughing. "How?"

Brian smirked. "Mom Umi, you're the wild card. You were trying so hard to mix things up that you overdid it with the perfume. That was a dead giveaway for me; it was so different from what the twins usually smell like. And Mom Gloria, you swapped gloves, but your movements are more deliberate than either of the girls. You're the steady one."

Umi groaned, shaking her head. "We made it too easy for you, didn't we?"

"A little," Brian admitted. "But the real trick is this: I've known Brittney and Stephanie long enough to pick up on all these little details. Their body language, their habits, their energy — it's like second nature."

The room fell quiet as everyone processed his explanation. Finally, Stephanie broke the silence.

"That's either really impressive," she said, "or really creepy."

"Why not both?" Brian teased, winking at her.

Brittney sighed, throwing up her hands. "Fine, you win. But next time, I'm bringing in reinforcements."

"Good luck," Brian said with a grin. "I'll still win."

The room burst into laughter, the earlier skepticism giving way to genuine admiration. Even Umi had to admit, "Alright, Brian. I might have underestimated you."

Gloria smiled warmly. "I'll say it, this is borderline magical. But I guess it just proves how much you pay attention to these two."

Brian shrugged, his smile softening. "They're worth paying attention to."

The twins exchanged a look, their initial disbelief melting into grudging appreciation. "Okay," Stephanie said. "You earned your two weeks off dishes. But don't get used to it."

"Agreed," Brittney added with a smirk. "We're still going to find a way to beat you one day."

"I'm looking forward to it," Brian said, leaning back with a satisfied sigh. "But for now, I'll take the win."

Brian leaned back with a smug grin. "You're welcome to keep trying to beat me," he said, pausing for effect, "just not on our wedding day or during our honeymoon."

The room exploded with groans and laughter. Stephanie grabbed a throw pillow and playfully threw it at him. "Oh, come on, Brian! You had to go there?"

"Of course," he replied, catching the pillow mid-air and tossing it back onto the couch. "I need to enjoy at least those moments in peace."

Brittney rolled her eyes dramatically. "Fine. Wedding day is off-limits. But honeymoon? I make no promises."

Gloria wagged a finger at Brittney. "Oh, no, young lady. Wedding day, honeymoon, and every other major milestone in your lives are sacred. Save your scheming for less important days."

Umi nodded in agreement, barely hiding her grin. "We'll allow one rematch a year, maximum. And only if Brian agrees."

Brian chuckled, holding up his hands in surrender. "Alright, alright. Deal. But I'll still win."

Stephanie sighed, shaking her head with a smile. "You're impossible."

"And yet, you all love me," Brian teased, earning a chorus of groans and laughter from everyone.

The room settled into a warm, companionable quiet, broken only by the occasional soft chuckle. The tension of the day had dissolved, replaced by the easy comfort of family and shared moments of joy.

Brian glanced at the clock on the wall and let out a small sigh. "It's late," he said, standing and stretching. "And I just realized, I haven't even showered yet."

Stephanie raised an eyebrow, smirking. "That's why you were so careful about the blindfold. Didn't want us catching a whiff of your sweaty self?"

Brian laughed, leaning down to kiss her on the cheek. "Goodnight, Steph." He turned to Brittney and kissed her forehead. "Goodnight, Britt."

He stepped over to the moms, giving each of them a quick kiss on the cheek as well. "Goodnight, Mom. Goodnight, Mom Umi."

"Goodnight, Brian," Umi said warmly. "Don't forget your shower."

"Goodnight, sweetheart," Gloria added with a smile. "Don't stay up too late."

He stepped out, waving behind him as he closed the door softly.

The house fell quiet for a moment until Brittney let out a small yawn.

Stephanie caught the motion and chuckled. "Looks like I'm not the only one ready to crash."

Brittney nodded, standing and stretching as well. "Yeah. Time to call it a night."

The twins turned to their moms, hugging each of them in turn. "Goodnight, Mom," Stephanie said.

"Goodnight, Mom," Brittney echoed. "Goodnight, Mom Gloria."

"Goodnight, girls," Umi said as she hugged them back. "Sleep well."

"Sweet dreams," Gloria added, giving them each a gentle pat on the back.

The twins headed upstairs, their footsteps fading as the moms settled onto the couch.

For a moment, neither spoke. Then Umi broke the silence with a soft chuckle. "I can't believe Brian pulled that off. Three rounds, and he didn't miss a single one."

Gloria shook her head, smiling. "He pays attention in ways most people don't. That boy notices everything. It's no wonder the twins adore him."

"He's got a good heart," Umi said, her tone thoughtful. "The way he balances them, keeping things light for Brittney, steady for Stephanie... It's like he instinctively knows what they need."

Gloria nodded, taking a sip from her coffee. "They're lucky to have him. And honestly, I think he's just as lucky to have them."

For a few moments, they sat quietly, enjoying the warmth of the room and the shared satisfaction of the day's lighter moments.

"So," Gloria said, breaking the silence with a teasing grin. "What do you think they'll try next to outsmart him?"

Umi laughed softly. "Whatever it is, I hope they wait until after the honeymoon." She leaned back, her smile turning fond. "It's nice to see them all laugh like that. After everything, they deserve it."

"Don't we all," Gloria agreed, leaning back as well. "Don't we all."

The two women exchanged a warm look before letting the quiet of the house settle around them, the soft glow of the lamp casting a peaceful light over the room.

CHAPTER 29

T he courtroom buzzed with muted conversations as people settled into their seats. The gallery was packed, split between groups of students from the twins' high school. Some were there to support Brittney, their faces a mix of quiet solidarity and apprehension. Others had gravitated to Richard, their expressions confident, even smug, as if convinced of his innocence. A scattering of reporters filled one section, their notepads and recorders ready to capture every detail.

In the front row, the Welch and Cole families sat together. Umi and Gloria exchanged a brief, reassuring glance as they flanked Brittney and Stephanie, who sat silently beside Brian. Stephanie's hand rested lightly on Brian's arm, her grip tightening as the minutes stretched on.

A sharp voice rang out, cutting through the low hum of voices. "All rise," the bailiff called, his tone firm and commanding.

The room fell silent. Chairs scraped the floor as everyone stood, eyes turning to the doors behind the bench. A moment later, Judge Ann Harlow entered, her black robes flowing as she stepped to her seat. Her expression was composed but carried an air of unyielding authority. She nodded curtly to the bailiff.

"You may be seated," the bailiff announced, and the room rustled again as everyone returned to their seats.

Judge Harlow adjusted her glasses, her gaze sweeping the room, lingering momentarily on the press section and the groups of high school students. She tapped her gavel lightly, more for effect than necessity.

"This court is now in session," she began, her voice firm and resonant. "We are here to begin proceedings in the case of *The State vs. Richard Perez*. I remind everyone that Peter Lemons has already accepted a plea deal and is now a witness for the State. He will testify later in this trial."

Her gaze swept across the gallery, resting momentarily on the students. "This is a trial involving sensitive and serious allegations. I want to address the gallery and set clear expectations. This courtroom demands decorum and professionalism from everyone present. Disruptive behavior, outbursts, or disrespect will not be tolerated and will result in immediate removal. This is not a venue for gossip, speculation, or personal biases; it is a court of law."

Her attention shifted to the jury box, her voice steady but firm. "Members of the jury, you are tasked with determining the facts of this case based solely on the evidence presented in this courtroom. You are to remain impartial, setting aside personal feelings and preconceived notions. The testimony you will hear may be difficult at times. I urge you to approach it with the seriousness and care it deserves."

She turned her attention back to the attorneys. "Counselors, I expect the highest standards of professionalism. This trial is emotionally charged, but I will not allow theatrics or disrespect to compromise its integrity. You have been warned."

With a nod to the bailiff, she concluded, "Mr. Miller, opening statements."

Scott Miller stood, adjusting his tie as he approached the jury box. His movements were calm, deliberate, but there was a resolute energy about him. He paused for a moment, his gaze sweeping across the courtroom before focusing on the twelve jurors.

"Good morning, ladies and gentlemen of the jury. My name is Scott Miller, and I am honored to serve as the District Attorney for this case. This is my first case as District Attorney, and while that may be something the defense chooses to point out, let me assure you of this: I have dedicated my career to seeking justice. As a former detective, I have stood with victims, pursued truth, and presented cases in this very courtroom. And today, I stand here for Brittney Welch."

He paused briefly, letting his words settle. "This case is not about me, my experience, or my title. It is about one young woman's courage to stand up and say, 'Enough.' It is about justice and accountability."

Scott walked toward the jury box, his voice steady but impassioned. "You will hear testimony from Brittney Welch, who was manipulated, threatened, and violated by someone she trusted, someone who took advantage of her vulnerability for his own selfish desires. You will hear from Peter Lemons, who has chosen to take responsibility for his role in these events and will corroborate the victim's story. You will also see evidence—text messages, photos, and testimony—that will paint a clear and undeniable picture of the defendant's actions."

Scott's tone shifted slightly, becoming more measured but no less intense. "You will also hear from witnesses who knew Brittney before these events—a happy, thriving, and vibrant teen with hopes and dreams for her future. Through their words and testimony, you will see the stark contrast between who she was and who she is now: a young woman dealing with an undesired pregnancy and surviving through classic post-traumatic stress disorder. This condition disrupts its sufferers' lives tremendously, affecting not only their mental and emotional well-being but their ability to engage with the world as they once did."

He turned slightly, addressing the gallery for a moment before refocusing on the jury. "Now, the defense may try to distract you. They may suggest that Brittney's testimony is unreliable because of her emotional state. They may attempt to diminish her story by focusing on her struggles, her youth, or even my role in this trial. I will not speculate on their tactics. What I will do is present you with the truth. Piece by piece, you will see how Richard Perez controlled, manipulated, and ultimately harmed Brittney Welch."

He stepped closer to the jurors, his voice softening. "This will not be an easy trial to sit through. The testimony you hear will be difficult, and some of the evidence will be upsetting. But your role as jurors is to see past the noise, the distractions, and the attempts to twist the narrative. Your role is to weigh the evidence presented, listen carefully to the truth, and deliver justice."

Scott straightened, his tone resolute. "By the end of this trial, I am confident that you will see the defendant, Richard Perez, for who he truly is—not the charming young man some of you may have heard about, but someone who preyed on a

358

vulnerable young woman, leaving a trail of evidence in his wake. And when that truth becomes clear, I trust you will deliver the verdict for Brittney Welch and the justice she deserves."

With a final nod to the jury, Scott returned to his seat, his expression calm and determined.

Jack Hartford rose with deliberate calm, buttoning his jacket as he approached the jury box. His expression was one of confident composure, his voice smooth and assured.

"Good morning, ladies and gentlemen of the jury. My name is Jack Hartford, and I have the privilege of representing Richard Perez. My role here today is not just to defend Richard, but to ensure that the truth prevails, and that justice is not clouded by emotions or assumptions."

He gestured briefly toward Scott Miller. "You've just heard from the District Attorney, Mr. Scott Miller, who, as you know, is newly appointed to this role. This is his first case as District Attorney, and I commend him for his passion. However, passion alone does not make a case. It does not replace evidence, facts, or the burden of proof that rests squarely on the prosecution's shoulders."

Jack paused, pacing slightly as he continued. "The prosecution will ask you to take the word of Brittney Welch, a young woman who has endured her own struggles, yes, but whose version of events is riddled with inconsistencies. They will present witnesses and evidence that, on the surface, may seem compelling. But as we peel back the layers, as we examine the details, you will see a story that doesn't quite add up."

He turned to face the jury directly, his tone growing sharper. "You will hear that Brittney Welch has faced emotional challenges. You will also hear testimony about how these challenges may have influenced her perception of events.

Memories can blur, details can shift, especially under stress. And while we sympathize with Brittney's struggles, we cannot let sympathy replace scrutiny."

Hartford leaned slightly on the jury box railing, his voice dropping just enough to draw them in. "This case is about more than allegations. It's about evidence, or, in this case, the lack thereof. The prosecution's narrative hinges on Brittney's testimony, but where are the irrefutable facts? Where is the solid, unshakable proof that Richard Perez committed these alleged acts? Ladies and gentlemen, I submit to you that it simply does not exist."

He straightened, gesturing toward Richard, who sat composed and calm at the defense table. "Richard Perez is not a monster. He is not the manipulative predator the prosecution wants you to believe. He is a young man whose life has been turned upside down by accusations that lack substance and context. Accusations that, when examined closely, will fall apart."

Jack's tone softened, growing almost conversational. "By the end of this trial, I believe you will see that this case is not as clear-cut as the prosecution wants you to think. You will see the gaps, the doubts, and the unanswered questions. And in our justice system, doubt is not just an inconvenience; it is the standard by which you must decide this case. Because in this courtroom, the burden of proof is on the prosecution. And if they cannot meet it, then the law is clear: you must find Richard Perez not guilty."

With a nod to the jury, Jack Hartford returned to his seat, his expression one of quiet confidence.

Judge Harlow adjusted her glasses, her sharp gaze moving from the attorneys to the jury. "Ladies and gentlemen of the jury, you have now heard the opening statements from both the prosecution and the defense. I remind you that these statements are not evidence. They are intended to provide an outline of what each side expects to prove during the course of this trial. Your role is to evaluate the evidence and testimony presented with an impartial and open mind."

A murmur from the back of the gallery brought her attention to the gallery. "To those seated in the gallery, this is a reminder to maintain absolute decorum. This is a court of law, and disruptive behavior will not be tolerated. Any violations will result in immediate removal."

After pausing to allow the attorneys a moment, Judge Harlow glanced at Scott Miller. "Hearing no additional matters, Mr. Miller, you may call your first witness."

Scott Miller stood up smoothly. "The State calls Taylor Harris to the stand."

Taylor, a vibrant-looking teenager with curly hair and a confident posture, stood from her seat in the gallery. She glanced nervously at Brittney, offering a small, encouraging smile before making her way to the witness stand. The bailiff approached her.

The bailiff held a Bible under her left hand. "Raise your right hand. Do you solemnly swear that the testimony you are about to give is the truth, the whole truth, and nothing but the truth?"

Taylor answered with a firm voice. "I do."

As Taylor settled into the chair, Scott approached with a reassuring smile. "Good morning, Miss Harris. Could you please introduce yourself to the court?"

"Hi, I'm Taylor Harris. I'm a senior at Bryan Athan Senior High School, and Brittney's one of my best friends," she answered.

"How long have you and Brittney been friends?" he asked.

"Since middle school. We started hanging out because we both love making up stories and comics. Brittney's an amazing artist; she would draw, and I'd help come up with ideas for the characters and plots. It was our thing," she answered.

"How would you describe Brittney before this school year?"

Taylor answered, her voice a bit softer. "She was bubbly, super creative, and just... full of energy. She always had her sketchpad with her, and she loved coming up with new ideas. Her laugh was contagious, and she made everyone around her feel happy."

"Did you notice any changes in Brittney's behavior this year?"

Taylor's smile faded. "Yeah. She started pulling away from us. She didn't want to draw or hang out anymore. She just seemed sad all the time like she wasn't the same person. Even when we tried to talk to her, it was like she wasn't really there."

Scott pressed. "Did you ask her why?"

"We tried, but she wouldn't say much. She'd just shrug or say she was tired. I knew something was wrong, but I didn't know what. It wasn't like her to be so quiet," she answered.

Scott continued. "Have you noticed how Brittney is doing now?"

Taylor nodded, holding back tears as she answered. "She's still struggling. I don't see her smile like she used to. It's like that spark she had is gone."

Scott nodded gently. "Thank you, Miss Taylor. No further questions, Your Honor."

Jack stood up and slightly leaned on the railing. "Taylor, are you aware that Brittney has been diagnosed with bipolar disorder?"

Taylor fidgeted while she answered. "Yes, but..."

Jack cut her off. "And are you familiar with the symptoms of bipolar disorder? Such as mood swings, withdrawal, and periods of depression?"

Scott stood up. "Objection, Your Honor. Mr. Hartford is badgering the witness and asking for medical opinions she isn't qualified to give."

Judge Harlow replied firmly. "Sustained. Mr. Hartford, you are straying from the witness's area of knowledge. Move on."

Jack stood up and leaned slightly on the railing, his tone measured but probing. "Miss Taylor, you mentioned that you and Brittney enjoyed making up stories and creating comics together. Is that correct?"

Taylor hesitated, glancing briefly at Brittney before nodding. "Yes, we loved creating stories."

Jack took a step forward, his expression sharpening. "So, you and Brittney spent a lot of time coming up with fictional scenarios, characters, and plots. Would it be fair to say that Brittney has a talent for inventing things that aren't real?"

Taylor frowned, her confidence wavering. "Yes."

Jack pressed, his voice turning accusatory. "Isn't it true that someone who is skilled at creating fictional worlds might also be skilled at distorting the truth in real life?"

Scott rose swiftly, his tone sharp. "Your Honor. The defense is attempting to imply dishonesty based on the witness's hobby. This line of questioning is irrelevant and speculative."

Jack answered. "This goes directly to her ability to fabricate and provides insight into the victim's personality and credibility."

Scott rose swiftly, his tone sharp. "Objection, Your Honor. The defense is still making unfounded accusations and drawing conclusions that the witness's hobby somehow reflects dishonesty in her personal life. This is irrelevant and prejudicial."

Judge Harlow fixed Jack with a stern look. "Sustained. Mr. Hartford, I suggest you focus your questions on facts. Move on."

Jack hesitated for a moment, clearly dissatisfied, before retreating to his desk. "No more questions, Your Honor."

Judge Harlow dismissed Taylor, and Ashley Diaz was sworn in.

Ashley, a petite girl with bright eyes and an air of nervous energy, stood from her seat. She adjusted her sweater nervously as she sat down.

Scott stepped forward with a warm smile, his tone calm and steady. "Good morning, Miss Diaz. Could you please introduce yourself to the court?"

Ashley answered. "Hi, I'm Ashley Diaz. I'm a senior at Bryan Athan Senior High School."

Scott asked. "And how do you know Brittney Welch?"

Ashley smiled as she answered. "We've been friends since middle school. We bonded over comics; she would draw, and I'd write scripts. We were a great team."

Scott glanced at the jury as he asked. "How would you describe Brittney before this school year?"

Ashley's face softened. "She was... she was amazing. Brittney was one of the happiest, most creative people I knew. She could make a story come to life with just a few sketches. She loved our group, and we loved her."

Scott pressed. "Did you notice any changes in her behavior this year?"

Ashley's smile faltered. "Yes. Brittney started withdrawing from us. She didn't want to draw or talk about our projects anymore. She barely responded to texts, and when she did, it was short and... distant. She just wasn't herself."

Scott continued his line of questions. "Did you ever try to reach out to her?"

Ashley nodded. "Of course. We all did. But it was like she built this wall around herself. She never used to keep secrets, but this year, it felt like there was a whole part of her life she didn't want us to see."

Scott smiled. "Who is included in your statement, 'We all did?'"

Ashley smiled back. "Taylor Harris, Amber Stauffer, and Heather Fernandez."

Scott asked softly. "How did these changes affect you and the rest of your group?"

Jack stood up. "Objection. Speculative and hearsay, Your Honor."

Scott answered the objection. "This is firsthand information because the witness was present and is summarizing her opinion."

Judge Harlow nodded firmly. "Overruled; the witness may answer the question."

Ashley paused, her voice trembling slightly. "It hurt. We missed her so much, but we didn't know how to help. She was always the one who brought us together, and without her, it felt like something was missing."

Scott's voice was still soft and firm. "Miss Ashley, in your opinion, was this change in Brittney consistent with anything you'd seen from her in the past?"

Ashley shook her head. "No. This was different. It wasn't just a bad day or a rough week; it was like she wasn't the same person anymore."

Scott nodded. "Thank you, Miss Ashley. No further questions, Your Honor."

Jack Hartford rose, his movements smooth and deliberate. He approached the stand with a faint, almost polite smile. "Good morning, Miss Ashley."

Ashley answered cautiously. "Good morning."

Jack smiled. "You mentioned that Brittney stopped responding to texts and withdrew from your group this year. Is that correct?"

Ashley replied firmly. "Yes."

Jack leaned slightly on the railing. "And you assumed that something terrible must have happened to cause this change?"

Ashley nodded. "Well, yeah. Brittney wouldn't just stop talking to us for no reason."

Jack smiled. "You're certain of that?"

Ashley replied firmly, "Yes."

Jack paused for effect. "Miss Ashley, are you aware that Brittney's family has faced personal challenges this year? Challenges that might have affected her mood or behavior?"

Ashley frowned slightly. "I guess. But…"

Jack, interrupting smoothly, "And are you aware that Brittney has been diagnosed with bipolar disorder?"

Ashley answered a little defensively, "Yes, but that doesn't mean…"

Jack held up a hand. "Just answer the question, Ashley. Are you aware of her diagnosis?"

Ashley answered reluctantly, "Yes."

Jack smiled. "And would you agree that someone with bipolar disorder might experience mood swings or periods of withdrawal unrelated to external events?"

Scott stood sharply. "Objection, Your Honor. The defense is asking the witness to speculate on medical matters beyond her expertise."

Judge Harlow nodded firmly. "Sustained. Mr. Hartford, move on."

Jack feigned innocence. "Of course, Your Honor."

He turned back to Ashley, his tone probing. "Miss Ashley, you mentioned earlier that you and Brittney wrote scripts for comics. Is that correct?"

Ashley blinked, surprised by the question. "Yes, we did."

Jack leaned closer, his voice sharpening. "So, you and Brittney spent a lot of time creating fictional scenarios and characters. Would it be fair to say that Brittney has a talent for making things up?"

Scott rose again, his tone sharper this time. "Objection, Your Honor. This is the same line of questioning the defense asked the previous witness and was sustained. A hobby of storytelling does not equate to dishonesty in real life."

Judge Harlow's gaze hardened. "Sustained. Mr. Hartford, you were already instructed to move on from this line of questioning. This is your final warning—focus on relevant facts, or I will cut this cross-examination short."

Jack hesitated for a moment, clearly dissatisfied, before turning back to Ashley. "Miss Ashley, did Brittney ever tell you why she was acting differently?"

Ashley, frustration showing in her voice, "No, but…"

Jack cut her off. "So, to be clear, everything you've told us today about why Brittney changed is based on your assumptions, not on anything she told you directly. Correct?"

Ashley hesitated. "I guess so, but…"

Jack smiled as he turned to the jury. "No further questions, Your Honor."

Scott rose smoothly, addressing the judge. "Your Honor, rebuttal?"

Judge Harlow nodded. "Proceed."

Scott approached Ashley, his tone calm. "Miss Ashley, earlier, you mentioned that you and Brittney created stories together. Can you clarify what kind of stories these were?"

Ashley nodded, her voice firm. "They were always fiction. Sometimes, they were based on funny things that happened, or they were just daydreams we came up with together. We worked to make them sound, look, and read funny or creative. They were never meant to be taken seriously."

Scott smiled gently. "Thank you, Ashley. That's all I have, Your Honor."

Gloria Cole was sworn in and took her seat with a composed demeanor.

Scott began, "Good afternoon, Mrs. Cole. Can you introduce yourself?"

"Good afternoon. I'm Gloria Cole."

"How do you know Brittney Welch?"

"I've known Brittney since she was born. Our families have been neighbors and best friends. After the accident that took my husband's life, we became more like family," Gloria said.

"How would you describe Brittney before this year?"

Gloria's voice lightened. "She was vibrant, full of imagination, and loved sharing her ideas."

"Did you notice changes in her behavior?"

Gloria's tone grew heavier. "Yes. She became withdrawn and distant. She stopped coming over and barely spoke when she did."

"Did her behavior affect your family?"

Jack stood abruptly. "Objection. Hearsay."

"Overruled," Judge Harlow said. "The witness may continue."

"Yes. Brian and Stephanie were worried. They tried to reach out, but Brittney kept pulling away," Gloria said.

Scott nodded. "Mrs. Cole, why is it important for you to testify today?"

"Because Brittney deserves justice. The girl sitting here today isn't the same one I've known her whole life. She needs this," Gloria said.

Scott smiled. "Thank you. No further questions."

Jack approached the stand with deliberate precision, his expression calculated. "Mrs. Cole, wouldn't you agree your observations are influenced by your emotions?"

Gloria tilted her head slightly, her tone calm. "No. What I just said is only what I saw."

Jack's smile widened slightly, though it didn't reach his eyes. "Mrs. Cole, are you certain? After all, you've known Brittney her whole life. Isn't it natural that your feelings for her might color your perception?"

Gloria straightened in her seat, her voice steady. "I was asked to tell the truth, Mr. Hartford, not to let my emotions take over. What I've said is exactly what I witnessed."

Jack leaned forward slightly, his tone sharpening. "So you're saying there's no chance your emotions have affected your testimony? None at all?"

Gloria met his gaze evenly. "That's correct. I'm here to give the court facts, not feelings."

Jack's expression tightened as he tapped the edge of the railing. "No further questions, Your Honor."

Scott called Umi Welch to the stand next. She was sworn in and seated, her demeanor calm yet resolute.

Scott began, "Mrs. Welch, how would you describe Brittney and Stephanie's relationship before this year?"

"They were inseparable," Umi said. "They had this bond, their 'twins' meetings,' where they shared everything."

"Did that closeness change this year?"

Umi's expression darkened. "Yes. Brittney pulled away from Stephanie. She stopped talking, even during their meetings. It broke Stephanie's heart."

"How did these changes affect your household?"

"It tore us apart," Umi said. "The girls started fighting, especially about Brian. Brittney became jealous. It was devastating."

"Thank you, Mrs. Welch. No further questions."

Jack rose, his tone sharp. "Mrs. Welch, wouldn't you agree sibling fights are common?"

"Teenagers fight, but this was different. It changed their entire relationship," Umi replied firmly.

Jack's tone grew colder. "And yet, you admit you don't know exactly what caused Brittney's behavior. Correct?"

"I don't know everything, but I know my daughters. This wasn't just stress," Umi said.

Jack's expression remained neutral. "No further questions."

Judge Harlow glanced at the courtroom clock, then lightly rapped her gavel. "Ladies and gentlemen of the jury, we will now take a recess for lunch. Please remember my instructions: do not discuss this case among yourselves or with anyone else. Avoid any media or outside information. We will reconvene at 1:30 sharp."

The bailiff stepped forward, guiding the jury out of the courtroom as the gallery watched silently. Once the door closed behind the jury, Judge Harlow addressed the remaining audience.

"We are adjourned for lunch. Counsel, ensure you are back promptly for the afternoon session. Court stands in recess." She rose and exited through the judge's chambers.

Scott Miller sat with Gloria, Umi, Brittney, Stephanie, and Brian at the courthouse cafeteria. Trays of food sat between them, and the mood was lighter than in the courtroom.

"You're doing great so far," Scott said to Brittney, his tone warm and encouraging. "This morning went exactly as we planned. And don't worry about the defense; their arguments are thin, and we'll handle them."

Brittney offered a small smile. "Thanks. It's just... hard, you know?"

"Of course it is," Scott replied, his expression empathetic. "I know, but you're doing great."

He leaned back, suddenly grinning. "Speaking of bravery, my son tried to build a skyscraper out of pancakes last weekend. Five years old and already challenging physics."

Umi chuckled, and Gloria smiled. "And did he succeed?"

"Not a chance," Scott said, shaking his head. "But my eight-year-old daughter was there to remind him that pancakes aren't for building skyscrapers. Sibling teamwork at its finest."

The table laughed softly, and even Brittney giggled, the tension easing slightly.

Conversation flowed naturally. Stephanie and Brian discussed plans for the weekend, Gloria and Umi exchanged supportive remarks, and Brittney chimed in occasionally, a small but significant part of the group.

When the time came, Scott checked his watch. "All right, team, back to the grind." The group gathered their things and made their way back to the courtroom, settling in for the afternoon session.

*****

Judge Harlow rapped her gavel again, bringing the courtroom to order. "We are back in session. Bailiff, please bring in the jury."

The jury filed back in and took their seats. Once everyone was settled, Scott stood and addressed the court. "Your Honor, the prosecution calls Captain Ashley Bishop of the Special Victims Unit."

The gallery quieted as the side door opened. Captain Bishop entered with measured steps, her posture upright and professional. She wore her uniform, her badge gleaming under the courtroom lights. Her gaze was steady as she approached the witness stand.

The bailiff stepped forward, holding a Bible. "Please raise your right hand. Do you solemnly swear that the testimony you are about to give is the truth, the whole truth, and nothing but the truth?"

Captain Bishop raised her hand. "I do," she replied clearly. After being sworn in, she took her seat, her hands folded neatly in front of her.

Scott began, his tone respectful but focused. "Good morning, Captain Bishop. Please state your full name and title for the record."

"Ashley Elizabeth Bishop, Captain, Special Victims Unit of the Beaverdam Police Department," she replied clearly.

"Captain, before we discuss your involvement in this case, could you outline your professional qualifications and experience?" Scott asked.

Captain Bishop nodded. "I hold a Bachelor of Arts in Criminal Justice from the University of Virginia, where I focused on forensic science and *victimology*. I also earned a Master's in Public Administration from the University of North

Carolina, specializing in organizational leadership and policy development. I am a Certified Forensic Interviewer and have completed advanced training in trauma-informed policing and behavioral analysis through the FBI Behavioral Analysis Unit."

Scott continued. "And how long have you served in the Special Victims Unit?"

"I have been with the SVU for fifteen years, the last eight of which I have served as Captain," she replied.

"What are your primary responsibilities in this role?"

"My duties include overseeing investigations into cases of domestic violence, sexual assault, child abuse, and other crimes involving vulnerable individuals. I ensure that investigations are conducted thoroughly and in accordance with the law, and I also mentor my team in handling complex cases," Captain Bishop explained.

"Were you involved in the investigation of the case against Richard Perez?" Scott asked, stepping closer to the jury box.

"Yes, I was," Captain Bishop confirmed.

"Can you describe how your team became involved in this case?"

"Our unit became involved following a formal report filed by Gloria Cole and Umi Welch, under the advice of Master Deputy White. The mothers had discovered concerning information on Brittney Welch's cell phone that implicated Richard Perez and Peter Lemon in abusive behavior. Based on their report and the evidence they provided, we initiated a comprehensive investigation," she explained.

"Let's talk about the interviews conducted during this investigation," Scott prompted. "Did you personally conduct or observe any interviews with the defendant, Richard Perez?"

"Yes, I conducted the interview of Richard Perez," she replied. "From the beginning, he exhibited defiance, attempting to assert control over the situation. He repeatedly referred to me and my sergeant as 'bitch,' despite multiple warnings to remain respectful. At one point, I told him directly: 'Well, Richard, since we're on a first-name basis, let's get something straight. You call me or my sergeant a 'bitch' again, and you'll spend the night caged like the dog you're acting like.' After that, his demeanor changed slightly, though his arrogance remained. His body language — leaning back in his chair, crossing his arms, avoiding direct eye contact — was consistent with someone attempting to maintain control and dominance," she explained.

"And what about his verbal responses?" Scott asked.

"Richard frequently minimized his actions, often resorting to derogatory language and making flippant comments about the accusations against him. When I pressed him about the evidence, he attempted to downplay his behavior and only reinforced his manipulative tendencies."

Scott nodded, letting her words settle over the jury before continuing. "Captain Bishop, Peter Lemon will testify later today. Can you explain his role in this case and the importance of his testimony?"

"Mr. Lemon was present during many of the incidents captured in the footage. While his inaction is troubling, his account has been consistent and aligns with the evidence we collected. His testimony is critical in corroborating the victim's claims and providing additional context about the defendant's actions," she replied.

"Captain, let's review some of the evidence you collected during the investigation," Scott stated as he approached the witness stand.

Captain Bishop nodded, her posture straight, hands folded on her lap. "Of course," she said evenly.

Scott gestured toward the screen as the projector came to life. A grainy black-and-white video appeared, timestamped July 15th, 6:45 p.m. The footage depicted the interior of Dixie's Pop Stop, a local deli. A group of teenagers, including Richard Perez, Peter Lemon, Brittney Welch, and a few others, sat in a cluster of booths near the counter. The atmosphere was casual; empty soda cans and sandwich wrappers littered the table. Richard sat at the center, animated as he spoke, while Brittney sat off to the side, smiling faintly and occasionally glancing at him.

"This is Exhibit A," Scott began, turning toward the jury. "Surveillance footage from Dixie's Pop Stop, recorded in late July. Captain, can you describe the significance of this footage?"

"This footage captures a social interaction between the defendant and the victim before the abuse began," Bishop explained. "Richard Perez is at the center of the group, displaying his typical confident behavior, gesturing widely and maintaining the group's attention. Brittney is more reserved, but at this point, her body language is relaxed, and she seems to engage willingly with the group. This contrasts sharply with her demeanor in later footage, where signs of fear and withdrawal are evident."

Scott allowed the jury to observe as the video continued. Richard leaned across the table, speaking directly to Brittney, who nodded slightly in response. The interaction appeared casual but hinted at an imbalance, with Richard taking up more space and energy in the group.

"Captain, does this footage provide any early insight into the dynamic between the defendant and the victim?" Scott asked.

"Yes," Bishop replied. "While this interaction appears friendly, it's notable that Richard is already positioning himself as a dominant figure within the group. He directs much of the conversation, and Brittney appears drawn to his charisma. This footage also establishes that their association began before the start of Brittney's senior year, which is consistent with her account of events leading up to the later abusive behavior."

Scott paused, letting the jury process the context, before advancing to the next clip. The timestamp read July 28th, 4:30 p.m., showing the exterior of the Mifflet Gas and Go. The grainy footage revealed Richard walking toward Brittney, who stood near a car. His strides were deliberate, and Brittney's demeanor had shifted; her arms were crossed tightly, and her gaze was directed downward.

"This is Exhibit B-1," Scott continued, turning toward the jury. "Surveillance footage from the Mifflet Gas and Go. Captain, can you describe what we're seeing here?"

"This footage captures the defendant approaching the victim, and you can already see a significant change in Brittney's behavior," Bishop explained, her tone firm. "Unlike in the earlier footage, her posture here is defensive—arms crossed, shoulders hunched, and head down. The shift in her demeanor reflects the beginning of the controlling and intimidating behavior described in her testimony."

Scott nodded. "This footage was independently verified, correct?"

"Yes," Bishop replied. "The timestamp matches transaction records from the store, and the cashier confirmed seeing both individuals at the location. The footage is authentic and unaltered."

Scott approached the evidence table, his voice measured and deliberate. "Your Honor, the next video to review is marked as Exhibit B-2. This video was captured on Halloween day, October 31st, at 5:30 p.m., at the Mifflet Gas and Go. It depicts the victim, Brittney Welch, and the defendant, Richard Perez, inside the store."

The courtroom remained silent as Scott turned to the witness stand. "Captain Bishop, as part of your analysis, you reviewed this footage. Is that correct?"

Captain Ashley Bishop nodded, her tone professional. "Yes, I did."

Scott pressed a button on the control panel, and the video began to play. The grainy footage showed the brightly lit interior of the gas station. Brittney stood near the counter, dressed in what could barely be called clothing—thin straps that exposed much of her body. The marks on her chest, both old and new, were clearly visible, with some disappearing under the strap that crossed her torso. Around her neck was a black leather collar, a long dog chain dangling from it. The chain led to Richard, who stood beside her, holding it tightly in his hand.

As the footage played, the cashier leaned forward, their body language suggesting concern as they appeared to address Brittney directly.

Scott paused the video. "Captain Bishop, based on your expertise, what stands out to you in this footage?"

Bishop leaned forward slightly, her tone even but firm. "There are several significant details. First, the victim's attire is both revealing and inappropriate for public settings, particularly given the visible injuries on her chest. The bite marks, some healed, others fresh, are evident, suggesting ongoing physical abuse. Additional bite marks are just visible on other areas of her body, likely her buttocks and thighs. Furthermore, bruises are clearly discernible on multiple portions of her body, further corroborating evidence of repeated physical harm. The collar and chain are indicative of coercion and control, reinforcing the defendant's dominance over the victim. Finally, the cashier's body language strongly implies concern for the victim's condition. It is likely they were attempting to offer assistance."

Scott resumed the video. The cashier leaned closer, saying something to Brittney that wasn't audible on the footage. Brittney's head turned slightly toward them, her lips parting as if to respond. At that moment, Richard yanked the chain sharply, causing it to tighten around her neck. Brittney flinched, her body jerking slightly as her hands moved toward the chain.

Suddenly, the video feed glitched. The image grew distorted, lines of static cutting across the screen. Within seconds, it went black.

Scott paused the playback. "Captain Bishop, what does the abrupt end to this video suggest?"

Bishop's expression remained neutral, though her voice carried a sharp edge. "In my experience, this type of malfunction is unusual. It could indicate tampering with the recording system or an equipment failure."

Scott nodded. "Were you able to recover any footage from after this point?"

"No," Bishop replied. "The store manager confirmed that all video feeds went offline shortly after this moment and were unavailable for the rest of the week."

Scott turned to the judge. "Your Honor, this evidence highlights not only the defendant's control over the victim but also the suspicious circumstances surrounding the missing footage."

Jack Hartford, the defense attorney, rose to his feet. "Objection, Your Honor. This line of questioning regarding video tampering is speculative."

Scott countered quickly. "Your Honor, this observation is based on Captain Bishop's professional experience. Furthermore, it establishes the context for the chain of events."

The judge nodded. "Overruled. Proceed."

Scott turned back to Bishop. "Captain, was the cashier interviewed in the video?"

"Yes," Bishop replied. "The cashier stated that they were about to ask Brittney if she needed help when the defendant yanked the chain. They described Brittney's expression as fearful and noted that the chain tightening seemed to silence her."

Jack stood again. "Objection, hearsay."

Scott didn't hesitate. "Your Honor, the cashier is on the witness list and will testify later in this trial."

The judge waved Jack down. "Overruled. The witness will have an opportunity to provide direct testimony."

Scott nodded. "Thank you, Captain Bishop. Let's move to the next video."

The screen shifted to a new video; the camera angle focused on the interior of a garage-like space. The timestamp was August 3rd, 5:15 p.m. The room was dimly lit and cluttered with discarded furniture, tools, and old equipment. In the center were a worn couch and a coffee table, the space arranged like a makeshift lounge.

"This is Exhibit C," Scott announced. "Security footage recovered from cameras installed at the defendant's shop. Captain Bishop, can you describe the significance of this footage?"

"This footage provides critical context for the events described by the victim," Bishop explained, her tone firm but careful. "The shop appears to be a meeting place where the defendant exerted control over Brittney. Multiple interactions between the defendant, Brittney, and others were recorded here, totaling 66 scenes over several weeks. The majority of these show the defendant engaging in behaviors consistent with coercion and intimidation and confirm the charges of sexual and physical assault."

Scott's tone grew heavier as he continued. "These interactions, along with the victim's testimony and corroborating evidence, form a clear and escalating pattern of coercion, ultimately culminating in charges of sexual and physical assault."

As the gravity of Scott's words settled over the courtroom, a muffled sob broke the silence. All eyes turned toward the gallery, where Brittney Welch sat, her head bowed and her shoulders trembling as she lost her composure. Her visible distress sent a ripple of emotion through those watching, and the judge raised a hand to signal for order.

Judge Harlow's voice was calm but firm as she addressed the court. "We will take a brief recess to allow everyone a moment to collect themselves. The court will reconvene in ten minutes."

The judge's gavel struck lightly, and the courtroom began to stir as attorneys shuffled their papers and spectators murmured quietly. Brittney's mother moved to comfort her, wrapping an arm around her shoulders as they quietly exited to a nearby hallway.

The courtroom gradually emptied, leaving only a few court officers and staff. Captain Bishop remained on the witness stand, her expression composed but somber. Scott Miller and the defense attorney used the pause to confer with their respective teams.

Ten minutes later, everyone was seated in the courtroom as the judge returned to the bench, signaling the bailiff to restore order. The courtroom settled quickly as the gallery filled once more. Brittney returned to her seat, visibly calmer, her mother seated beside her with a reassuring hand on her arm.

Judge Harlow cleared her throat and addressed the court. "Thank you for your patience. We will now resume the proceedings."

Scott rose again, his tone measured as he gestured toward the screen. "Your Honor, with the court's permission, I'd like to continue our review of Exhibit C, security footage recovered from the defendant's shop."

"Proceed," Judge Harlow said, her voice steady.

The video played, showing Richard seated on the couch, leaning forward as he spoke to Brittney. Although the audio was unclear, his aggressive gestures and Brittney's withdrawn posture spoke volumes. In one frame, he pointed sharply toward the door while she hesitated, her body language stiff and reluctant. Another clip showed Richard pacing while speaking to another male present; his movements were animated, and his tone was clearly commanding.

Scott let the video pause on a still frame of Richard standing over Brittney, who was seated on the couch, her arms crossed defensively. "Captain, what stands out to you in this interaction?"

Bishop glanced at the screen. "This frame highlights the power imbalance. The defendant is standing over the victim, using his physical presence to intimidate her. Her posture—arms crossed, head down—further indicates that she felt threatened or powerless in this situation."

Scott paused, advancing to another segment of footage. The timestamp showed August 15th, 6:00 p.m., but the setting was the same. This time, Richard gestured emphatically toward Brittney as she moved hesitantly across the room.

Scott nodded. "Thank you, Captain Bishop. Let's move to the next video."

The screen shifted to a new video, the timestamp marking it as the evening of Halloween. The camera showed the exterior of Richard's shop. Snow was visible on the ground, and Brittney, completely nude, stood trembling in front of the locked door. She pounded on it with both fists, her breath visible in the cold air.

A man appeared on the left side of the frame, walking toward the scene. His hesitant movements suggested confusion or concern as he approached.

Scott paused the footage. "Captain Bishop, what stands out in this scene?"

Bishop's voice softened slightly but retained its professional tone. "The victim is in a state of extreme vulnerability, exposed to freezing conditions while unclothed. Her movements—pounding on the door and turning toward the approaching man—indicate desperation. The visible bruises and faint bite marks across her body further reinforce the pattern of physical abuse. This situation is consistent with psychological abuse, placing the victim in a humiliating and dangerous position."

Scott resumed the video briefly. The man on the left drew closer, but before he reached Brittney, the door to the shop opened abruptly. A hand, later identified as Richard's, yanked Brittney inside, and the door slammed shut.

Scott stopped the video. "Captain, was the man seen in this video interviewed?"

"Yes," Bishop replied. "He stated that he saw a young woman in distress and began walking over to help. Before he could reach her, the defendant pulled her inside."

Jack stood again. "Objection, hearsay."

Scott met his gaze. "The man is on the witness list, Your Honor."

The judge nodded. "Overruled. Proceed."

Scott turned back to Bishop. "Based on your analysis, what does this scene suggest about the defendant's treatment of the victim?"

Bishop's expression hardened. "This scene demonstrates calculated psychological abuse. The defendant created a situation where the victim was entirely reliant on him while simultaneously isolating her from potential help. It is emblematic of coercion and control."

Scott paused to let the jury absorb the scene before turning toward the judge. "Your Honor, permission to introduce Exhibit D, a timeline summarizing the interactions captured in the shop's security footage."

"Granted," Judge Harlow replied.

A timeline appeared on the screen, listing key dates and interactions, each one noted with a brief summary of the observed behaviors. Scott allowed the jury a moment to study the timeline before continuing.

"Captain Bishop, can you elaborate on what this timeline represents?" Scott asked.

"This timeline outlines 66 separate scenes recorded in the defendant's shop over the course of several weeks," Bishop explained. "It highlights key interactions, including the defendant's repeated use of verbal intimidation, sexual and physical assault, and coercive behavior. Each entry is corroborated by the footage we reviewed."

"Captain, before we move to our final question, could you explain the process followed to obtain, secure, and verify this footage, ensuring the chain of custody was preserved?" Scott asked.

Bishop nodded. "Absolutely. Once we identified the relevant locations—Dixie's Pop Stop, the Mifflet Gas and Go, and the defendant's shop—we issued subpoenas to obtain their surveillance footage. Each source provided the raw footage directly to law enforcement. We then logged and secured the data using evidence-handling protocols, ensuring it was only accessible to authorized personnel. The footage was reviewed and cross-referenced with timestamps, transaction records, and witness statements to confirm its authenticity. Throughout this process, chain-of-custody documentation was maintained, and copies of the footage were stored securely to prevent tampering."

Scott turned back to the jury, his voice steady. "So, to be clear, is the footage we've viewed today the same footage that was retrieved from these locations?"

"Yes," Bishop confirmed. "The footage was analyzed, logged, and preserved without alteration."

"Thank you, Captain. One final question: based on your professional experience, how would you characterize the behavior exhibited by the defendant in the footage?"

"The defendant's behavior is consistent with patterns of coercive control and physical abuse. He used fear, manipulation, and violence to dominate and silence the victim, a hallmark of prolonged and calculated abuse," she stated firmly.

Scott paused, allowing the weight of her testimony to settle before addressing the judge. "Your Honor, I have no further questions for this witness."

Judge Harlow turned to the defense table. "Mr. Hartford, your witness."

Jack Hartford rose, buttoning his suit jacket as he approached the stand. His tone was smooth but edged with skepticism. "Captain Bishop, while you've provided an overview of the investigation, can you confirm that you were physically present during any of the incidents involving my client?"

"That is correct," she replied evenly.

"So, your testimony relies entirely on the interview and the evidence, all collected after the fact?" Hartford pressed.

"Yes, as is standard in most criminal investigations," she countered.

Hartford's lips tightened briefly before he continued. "You mentioned that Mr. Lemon's account aligns with the evidence. Isn't it true that he failed to intervene during any of these incidents?"

"Yes, that is true," Captain Bishop acknowledged.

"And yet, you've characterized his testimony as critical. Isn't it possible that Mr. Lemon's account is an attempt to deflect responsibility?" Hartford asked.

"It is always possible to question a witness's motives. However, Mr. Lemon's cooperation from the outset of our investigation and the corroboration of his statements with physical evidence lend credibility to his account," Captain Bishop said firmly.

Hartford's tone grew sharper. "Captain, wouldn't you agree that someone who sits idly by during such incidents might not be the most trustworthy witness?"

"Mr. Lemon's inaction is concerning, but it does not negate the truth of his testimony or the importance of his perspective in understanding the full scope of the defendant's actions," she responded.

Hartford hesitated briefly, then stepped back. "No further questions, Your Honor."

Judge Harlow turned to Captain Bishop. "Thank you, Captain. You are excused."

Judge Harlow waited until Captain Bishop exited the witness stand before turning to Scott Miller. "Mr. Miller, you may call your next witness."

Scott rose, his tone measured. "The prosecution calls Sergeant Mary King to the stand."

The gallery stirred slightly as Sergeant King entered, her uniform crisp and her demeanor calm but alert. She approached the witness stand with purpose, her sharp eyes scanning the courtroom briefly before focusing ahead. The bailiff stepped forward with the Bible.

"Please raise your right hand. Do you solemnly swear that the testimony you are about to give is the truth, the whole truth, and nothing but the truth?"

"I do," King replied, her voice clear and steady. She took her seat, sitting upright with her hands resting lightly on the stand.

Scott began. "Good afternoon, Sergeant King. Please state your full name and title for the record."

"Sergeant Mary Ann King, Special Victims Unit of the Beaverdam Police Department," she replied.

"Sergeant, could you describe your professional background and experience?" Scott asked.

"I hold a Bachelor of Science in Psychology from the University of Mississippi, with a focus on behavioral psychology and conflict resolution. I graduated top of my class at the Law Enforcement Academy, specializing in crisis negotiation and interrogation techniques. I am also certified in behavioral analysis and *kinesics*, and I'm currently pursuing a Master's in Forensic Psychology at the University of Alabama," King explained.

Scott nodded, impressed. "And how long have you served with the Special Victims Unit?"

"I've been with SVU for six years, and I was recently promoted to sergeant," King answered.

"What are your primary responsibilities in this role?" Scott continued.

"I assist in conducting and overseeing interviews, analyzing behavioral cues during interrogations, and supporting victims throughout the investigative process. My role also involves helping to build psychological profiles of suspects," she explained.

"Were you involved in the investigation of Richard Perez?" Scott asked, his tone sharpening slightly.

"Yes, I was," King confirmed.

"Can you describe your observations during Mr. Perez's interview?"

King's expression didn't waver. "He immediately began using derogatory language, referring to me as 'bitch' more than once. At one point, he snarled, 'Stop yanking me, bitch. I'll file charges on you for this.' My response was simple: 'Keep calling me that, and you'll find out just how tough I can be.' After securing him to the table, he leaned back, smirking, and said, 'You're all the same. Loud until someone fights back.'"

"And how did you handle that situation?" Scott asked.

"I maintained professionalism, letting him know that his behavior would not intimidate me or derail the interview. His attempts to assert dominance were consistent with the controlling behavior observed throughout the investigation," King stated.

"What was his demeanor during questioning?"

"Defensive and dismissive. He avoided direct answers and often attempted to redirect blame onto the victim, claiming she exaggerated the incidents or 'wanted things rough.' His body language — leaning back, sneering, and crossing his arms — was indicative of someone attempting to project control despite feeling cornered," King explained.

Scott nodded. "Thank you, Sergeant. Now, did you observe the interview with Peter Lemon?"

"Yes, I did," she confirmed.

"Peter Lemon entered the interview room looking apprehensive. His shoulders were hunched, his hands fidgeting, and his eyes rarely met ours," King described. "From the outset, his body language conveyed nervousness but also a willingness to cooperate."

Scott leaned closer to the jury box. "How did his attitude compare to Richard Perez's?"

"It was a stark contrast," King replied. "Unlike Mr. Perez, who was defiant and dismissive, Mr. Lemon expressed genuine remorse. He admitted to being present during many of the incidents and provided details that corroborated both the victim's account and the evidence we had collected. He seemed eager to help once he realized the full gravity of the situation."

Scott asked, "Did you notice any inconsistencies in his statements?"

"No," King answered. "His account was consistent throughout, and his willingness to acknowledge his failures to act lent credibility to his testimony. While he expressed guilt for not intervening, he did not attempt to excuse or justify his inaction."

Scott nodded thoughtfully. "What specific behaviors or cues convinced you that Mr. Lemon was being truthful?"

"His fidgeting decreased as the interview progressed, indicating he felt more comfortable speaking openly. He also maintained a steady tone and was quick to provide details when asked. These behaviors align with someone attempting to be honest rather than deceptive," King explained.

"Thank you, Sergeant. One final question: based on your expertise, how would you characterize Richard Perez's behavior throughout the investigation?"

"Richard Perez exhibited a pattern of coercive control and defiance. His use of derogatory language, attempts to intimidate, and consistent minimization of his actions are hallmarks of someone accustomed to manipulating and dominating others. His behavior was calculated and predatory," King stated firmly.

Scott paused, letting the jury absorb her words. "No further questions, Your Honor."

Judge Harlow turned to the defense table. "Mr. Hartford, your witness."

Jack Hartford rose, buttoning his suit jacket as he approached the stand. His tone was measured, but there was a sharpness beneath his words. "Good afternoon, Sergeant King," he began.

"Good afternoon," King replied, her voice steady.

"You've described Mr. Perez as manipulative and controlling during his interview," Hartford started. "Would you agree that interviews, by their very nature, can sometimes provoke exaggerated responses due to the stress of the situation?"

"Interviews can be stressful," King acknowledged. "However, Mr. Perez's behavior during questioning was consistent with the controlling tendencies observed throughout the investigation, not a singular reaction to the interview setting."

Hartford raised an eyebrow. "Consistent, you say. But wouldn't you agree that interpreting behavior is, at its core, subjective?"

"Behavioral analysis involves both objective evidence and professional interpretation," King countered. "While subjectivity can play a role, my conclusions are grounded in training, experience, and corroborating evidence."

Hartford nodded slowly, pacing near the jury box. "Let's talk about Peter Lemon for a moment. You've described him as cooperative and remorseful. Isn't it possible that Mr. Lemon's cooperation was motivated by self-preservation? After all, cooperating with law enforcement can often result in leniency, can it not?"

"Cooperation is always considered in the context of evidence," King replied evenly. "Mr. Lemon's statements aligned with the facts of the case, and his body language indicated genuine remorse, not opportunism."

"And yet, you admit he failed to act during these incidents. Doesn't his inaction raise questions about his reliability as a witness?" Hartford pressed.

"Mr. Lemon's failure to intervene is troubling," King admitted. "However, his consistent testimony and the details he provided—details corroborated by other evidence—lend credibility to his account."

Hartford stopped and faced King directly. "Sergeant, wouldn't you agree that behavior, especially in high-pressure situations, can be misinterpreted?"

"Behavior in high-pressure situations can vary," King answered. "But as an investigator trained in *kinesics* and behavioral analysis, I assess patterns and corroborate them with other evidence to reach conclusions."

Hartford's lips tightened briefly. "In other words, we're relying on your professional judgment."

"We're relying on my training, experience, and the evidence," King corrected.

Hartford let the room sit in silence for a moment before stepping back. "No further questions, Your Honor."

Judge Harlow nodded, her gaze steady. "Thank you, Sergeant. You are excused."

King rose from the stand, her movements calm and deliberate as she exited through the side door. The gallery murmured softly, the weight of her testimony settling over the courtroom.

Judge Harlow looked at Scott. "Mr. Miller, your next witness on your list is Peter Lemon. Do you still wish to call him at this time?"

Scott stood up. "Yes, Your Honor."

Judge Harlow looked at the bailiff. "Please bring in Mr. Lemon."

The side door to the courtroom opened, and Peter Lemon stepped in, escorted by an officer. He was dressed in a suit jacket and neatly pressed pants, his hair carefully groomed. Despite his polished appearance, his face betrayed his inner turmoil. His eyes were heavy with guilt, and he avoided looking at the gallery as he was led to the stand.

The bailiff approached him. "Raise your right hand. Do you solemnly swear that the testimony you are about to give is the truth, the whole truth, and nothing but the truth?"

Peter's voice was barely audible but steady. "I do."

He took his seat, his hands clasping the edge of the witness stand tightly as if to anchor himself.

Scott Miller rose, his expression calm but serious as he approached the stand. He stopped a respectful distance away, his voice steady. "Good afternoon, Mr. Lemon."

Peter glanced up briefly, his voice low but clear. "Good afternoon, sir."

Scott asked, "Can you please state your name for the record?"

Peter Lemon sat stiffly in the witness chair, his hands clasped tightly in his lap. His eyes darted nervously between the District Attorney, Scott Miller, and Richard Perez, who sat at the defense table with an air of smug indifference. The tension in the courtroom was palpable, thick enough to feel.

Peter cleared his throat. "Peter Michael Lemon," he said, his voice barely audible.

The projector flickered to life as Scott displayed the first frame of the security footage. It showed Richard, Peter, and Brittney in the back room of a shop. The timestamp in the corner read July 14, 9:37 PM.

"Mr. Lemon, do you recognize the location shown in this image?" Scott asked.

Peter nodded. "Yes. That's the back room of Richard's shop where we liked to hang out."

"And the individuals in this image?"

Peter pointed weakly at the screen. "That's me on the left, Richard in the middle, and Brittney on the right."

Scott advanced the footage to the next frame, which showed Richard gripping Brittney's arm tightly. Her expression was tense, her discomfort unmistakable.

"What's happening in this frame?" Scott asked.

"Richard grabbed her," Peter said hesitantly. "She wanted to leave, but he wouldn't let her."

Scott moved to another clip. Brittney was cowering on a couch; you could see small blood stains on her white T-shirt while her hands covered her chest. Richard stood over Brittney, yelling, while Peter sat on the couch, his gaze averted.

"Mr. Lemon, do you remember exactly what happened right before this image?" Scott asked with a firm, measured tone.

Peter nodded. "Yes."

Scott turned to the jury. "Ladies and gentlemen of the court, I should warn you the following testimony and its accompanying images and/or video are extremely graphic. They are being presented to provide an exacting and precise explanation of the depth and depravity the defendant inflicted on the victim." He turned to Peter. "What, exactly, did you see, Mr. Lemon?"

Just before Peter could answer, Jack stood up. "Objection, Your Honor. The prosecution is giving a summation that is leading the jury."

Scott immediately shot back. "Your Honor, it's not a summation; it's giving the jury a chance to prepare to see the details of the defendant's brutal attacks on the victim."

Judge Harlow considered the objection and the rebuttal. "Overruled. The images and videos have been accepted as allowable evidence. Mr. Miller, continue."

Scott looked back at Peter. "Mr. Lemon, what exactly did you see?"

Peter hung his head, shaking it. "I can't say it…"

Scott spoke firmer. "Please tell the court what you saw, Mr. Lemon."

There was a long pause, and then Judge Harlow looked at Peter. "Mr. Lemon, answer the question, please," she directed him.

Peter's mouth opened and shut immediately, words failing to come out.

The scene on the screen played out, in graphic detail, how Richard drew blood from, on, and all over her chest. Long moments played as Brittney screamed, sobbed, and begged Richard to stop played out on the screen. Gasps from the jurors and most of the gallery showed their shock as they watched the video. The video came to the point where he started the question.

Brittney started sobbing, tears rolling down her face.

"Ladies and gentlemen, I apologize for the graphic detail; however, it explicitly demonstrates the type of abuse the victim received. Please note, the defendant's face is clearly visible in the second camera view," Scott said softly.

Scott looked at Peter. "Now, Mr. Lemon, what's happening here?"

"He was shouting at her," Peter said, his voice cracking. "Saying he owed her. That she'd regret it if she didn't listen to him."

The gallery murmured, and Brittney, sitting between Stephanie and Brian, clutched her chest tightly, her breath ragged. Her shoulders shook as tears streamed down her face. Stephanie leaned closer, whispering words of comfort, but Brittney's trembling hand moved slowly into the air.

The judge noticed immediately, rapping her gavel. "Miss Welch, is there something you need to say?"

Brittney tried to respond, but her words were choked sobs. Stephanie turned toward the judge, her voice trembling but clear. "Your Honor, my sister says she's in pain and needs to take her medication. She's asking to be excused from the courtroom."

Scott stepped forward, his expression one of genuine concern. "Your Honor, may I approach?"

The judge nodded. Scott walked to the gallery, kneeling to speak with Brittney. After a moment, he stood and addressed the bench. "Your Honor, Miss Welch is experiencing significant physical distress. I request that she be excused for the remainder of this line of questioning and permitted to take her prescribed pain medication."

Jack Hartford was on his feet instantly. "Objection, Your Honor! My client has the right to see his accuser during critical testimony. Allowing her to leave violates that right and could unfairly influence the jury by suggesting my client is causing her current distress."

Scott's tone was measured but firm. "Your Honor, the victim's distress is not speculative; it is a fact supported by the footage and testimony. I will add that Miss Welch is not on the stand now; therefore, her presence isn't legally required. Her absence during this limited questioning does not deprive the defense of its right to cross-examine her on her own testimony. This request ensures the well-being of the victim without compromising the integrity of these proceedings."

The judge considered the arguments before speaking. "Miss Welch is excused from the courtroom for the remainder of this testimony. Bailiff, please assist Miss Welch and her siblings in leaving the courtroom."

The gallery watched as Brittney, Stephanie, and Brian exited. Stephanie wrapped an arm protectively around Brittney, who leaned into her twin as they walked out. The tension in the courtroom remained palpable.

Judge Harlow rapped her gavel softly, commanding the attention of the courtroom. She leaned forward, her expression steady but firm, her gaze settling on the jury.

"Ladies and gentlemen of the jury," she began, her voice carrying an air of authority tempered with understanding, "you have just witnessed an unusual but necessary step in these proceedings."

The jurors sat attentively, their eyes fixed on the judge. She paused, ensuring her words carried the appropriate weight.

"The court has excused Miss Welch from the courtroom for the remainder of this testimony due to her physical distress. Please be advised that this decision was made solely to accommodate her immediate needs and should not influence your assessment of the evidence or the credibility of any testimony."

Her gaze swept across the jury box, ensuring each juror heard her clearly. "Your duty remains to evaluate the evidence impartially and without regard to the temporary absence of the victim."

The room remained silent, the gravity of her words settling like a heavy blanket. The judge straightened, her voice regaining its formal tone. "We will now proceed. Mr. Miller, you may continue."

Scott returned to the screen, advancing to the next clip, which was timestamped August 3, 8:15 PM. The footage showed Richard pinning Brittney against the wall, his hand gripping her wrist as she flinched.

"Mr. Lemon, can you describe what's happening in this clip?" Scott asked.

Peter hesitated, his voice faltering. "He was threatening her. He said she'd better do what he wanted, or her family would pay for it."

"And what did you do?" Scott pressed.

Peter's gaze dropped. "I didn't do anything. I just sat there. I didn't stop him."

Scott advanced again, this time to a clip from August 18, 8:57 PM. The footage showed Richard hitting Brittney, her head snapping to the side. Peter winced at the image.

"Do you remember this night?" Scott asked.

Peter nodded, tears streaming down his face. "He slapped her. She cried, and he just laughed. He said no one would believe her."

Scott looked squarely in his eyes. "Mr. Lemon, did Brittney ever ask for Richard to stop?"

Peter shook his head, answering softly, "Yes."

Scott paused for a moment. "Mr. Lemon, speak louder so the jury can hear you, please."

Peter looked up. "Yes, she asked him to stop. She pleaded, begged, cried, and screamed for him to stop," he said, tears running down his face.

Scott's look didn't change; his voice was firm when he asked, "And did he?"

Peter shook his head, tears raining onto the hardwood floor. "No."

Scott's voice softened a small amount when he asked, "And what did you do when you heard these pleas, screams? Or the crying, begging?"

Peter's voice was almost a whisper; the microphone caught it and echoed his answer. "Nothing."

Before Scott played the next clip, he paused and turned to the judge. "Your Honor, may I approach?"

The judge gestured for both attorneys to join him. Scott and Jack approached the bench, their voices low but firm.

"Your Honor," Scott began, "This timeline outlines 66 separate scenes recorded, each showing similar acts of battery and abuse committed by the defendant. If the defense will concede that the footage accurately depicts their client committing these acts, I am willing to summarize the remaining evidence for the record. This will save the court and the jury from having to view each disturbing clip individually."

The judge turned to Jack Hartford. "Mr. Hartford, do you wish to concede this point?"

Jack frowned, visibly weighing his options. "Your Honor, while I acknowledge the footage shows what my client visibly did, we reserve the right to contest the interpretation of these acts. Concession could unduly influence the jury."

Scott's tone sharpened. "Your Honor, if I'm forced to continue presenting this footage, it will only highlight how many times and how severely the defendant battered and abused the victim. Conceding spares the court and the jury from reliving these horrifying events repeatedly. It's in everyone's best interest to accept this summary."

Judge Harlow tapped her gavel lightly. "Mr. Hartford, do you concede?"

Jack hesitated but finally nodded, his shoulders sagging. "Yes, Your Honor. The defense concedes the footage depicts my client as shown."

The judge turned to Scott. "Summarize the remaining footage for the record, Mr. Miller."

Scott returned to the stand and addressed the jury. "For the record and the jury, there are an additional 62 clips depicting a consistent pattern of battery and abuse by the defendant,

Richard Perez, toward Brittney Welch. The acts include verbal threats, physical aggression, and controlling behavior, spanning a period of two months. This evidence supports the victim's testimony and demonstrates the severity of the defendant's actions."

The judge nodded. "Noted for the record. Proceed."

Scott turned to Peter, his expression resolute. "No further questions, Your Honor."

Jack Hartford stood, adjusting his jacket as he approached the witness stand. His movements were sharp and deliberate, his tone cutting as he began his cross-examination. "Mr. Lemon, you admit you sat there and did nothing during these events. Why should the jury believe you now?"

Peter looked down, his shame etched into his features. "Because it's the truth."

Jack leaned closer, his voice sharp. "The truth? Or a convenient story to save yourself? Aren't you testifying in exchange for leniency in your own charges?"

Peter straightened slightly, his voice firm despite the tears in his eyes. "No. I wasn't offered a deal until after I said I would testify. I asked to testify because it's the right thing to do."

Jack's tone grew icy. "And how do we know you weren't complicit? You were there for every incident, sitting silently. How do we know you didn't participate?"

Peter's voice rose, trembling with emotion. "Because I didn't! I never touched her. Ask Brittney! I didn't want this to happen, but I didn't stop it either. That's my failure, not hers."

The courtroom fell silent, and the judge rapped her gavel once. Jack stepped back, his expression unreadable. "No further questions, Your Honor."

Scott rose again, his tone calm but purposeful. "Mr. Lemon, earlier, you said Brittney deserves justice. Why do you believe your testimony will help her?"

Peter looked back at Brittney, his voice steady. "Because it shows the truth. Richard hurt her, controlled her, and made her suffer. I saw it. I was there. And now everyone else can know it too."

Scott continued. "When did you plead guilty to your charges?"

Peter answered softly. "Two days after I was arrested."

Scott pushed for the answer he wanted. "And when was a plea deal offered to you?"

Peter answered, his voice still soft. "About a week later."

Scott concluded. "So you chose to plead guilty and take responsibility before any deal was offered. Is that correct?"

Peter answered with a firm voice. "Yes."

Scott pressed so the jury knew all of the details. "Have you asked for anything in return for your testimony?"

Peter looked up, his voice firm. "No."

"When you met me in person, with your lawyer present, why did I offer you a deal?" Scott asked him.

"You said it was because I came clean right away, that I cooperated with the detectives from the beginning, and you wanted me to be a witness for the state. You added it was the only way to help Brittney get justice," Peter explained.

Scott pushed gently. "And how did you reply?"

Peter looked at the jury. "I said that if it helps Brittney, I'll do it."

Scott paused, then asked gently. "Mr. Lemon, is there anything you'd like to add before you leave the stand?"

Peter, tears welling in his eyes, his voice cracking while he spoke, "I just... I just want to say how sorry I am. To Brittney. To her family. I should have stopped him. I should have done something. I'll never forgive myself for what I didn't do."

The courtroom fell silent, the weight of Peter's words hanging heavy in the air. He wiped his eyes and looked down, unable to meet Umi's gaze.

Judge Harlow's voice was soft and firm. "Thank you, Mr. Lemon. You are excused."

The bailiff stepped forward, guiding Peter out of the courtroom through the same side door he entered. Judge Harlow waited until the door clicked shut before addressing the room.

Judge Harlow adjusted her glasses and addressed the courtroom. "Bailiff, please bring Miss Welch and her siblings back into the court."

Moments later, Brittney, Brian, and Stephanie were walking down the central walkway of the courtroom. Before Brittney could turn into a row, Judge Harlow addressed Brittney. "Miss Welch, please approach the bench. Counselors, you as well."

Moments later, all three were standing in front of Judge Harlow's bench. Harlow looked down, looking at Brittney's face, her voice soft and authoritative. "Miss Welch, did you take your prescribed medication?"

Brittney nodded. "Yes, ma'am. I took the one for anxiety and one for the pain," she answered softly. "I'm sorry, Your Honor..."

Judge Harlow gently cut her off. "Miss Welch. Do not apologize for doing what I told you to do. You can return to your seat with your siblings."

A moment later, Brittney was sitting between Brian and Stephanie.

Judge Harlow looked at Scott. "Mr. Miller, I understand you intended to call Miss Welch this afternoon. Due to the hour and, more importantly, her current emotional state, is there another witness you can call now?"

Scott paused for a moment. "Your Honor, the other two witnesses would be hard-pressed to be here in under two hours," his voice firm and measured.

Judge Harlow weighed her options. "Thank you, gentlemen, please return to your places," her normal air of authority back.

Once they were in place, Judge Harlow addressed the jury. "Ladies and gentlemen, due to conditions outside the procedural norm, we will adjourn for the evening. Before you leave, I must remind you of your responsibilities during this recess."

She paused, ensuring her voice carried authority but remained approachable. "Do not discuss this case with anyone, including your fellow jurors, family members, friends, or anyone else. It is essential that you keep an open mind and reserve your judgment until all the evidence has been presented and you have received my instructions on the law."

Her gaze moved steadily across the jury box. "You must also avoid any exposure to media coverage, social media, or any other source of information about this case. This includes television, radio, newspapers, and online platforms. It is critical that your verdict be based solely on the evidence presented here in this courtroom and nothing else."

She leaned forward slightly, her tone firm but understanding. "If anyone attempts to speak to you about this case, or if you inadvertently come across information outside this courtroom, please report it to the bailiff immediately."

Straightening in her seat, she nodded at the jury. "Thank you for your service and attention today. We will reconvene tomorrow morning at nine o'clock. Please have a restful evening."

With a light rap of her gavel, she concluded. "Counselors, please remain. The court is adjourned."

As the last echoes of the gavel faded, Judge Harlow motioned for the attorneys to approach the bench. Her expression was firm, a quiet authority radiating from her as Scott Miller and Jack Hartford stepped forward.

"Gentlemen," Judge Harlow began, her voice low but resolute, "what happened with the victim today was unusual but unavoidable. Miss Welch was excused from the courtroom due to physical and emotional distress, and by my orders, she took her prescribed medication to stabilize herself. I want to make myself perfectly clear: this incident is not to be *weaponized* in any way when she testifies tomorrow."

She leaned forward slightly, her sharp gaze shifting between the attorneys. "Mr. Miller, Mr. Hartford, neither of you will refer to Miss Welch's excusal from the courtroom today or her need for medication. This includes any mention of her condition to belittle her testimony, question her credibility, or attempt to gain a tactical advantage."

Jack Hartford opened his mouth to respond, but Judge Harlow cut him off with a raised hand. "Let me finish, Mr.

Hartford. I will not tolerate any implication that the events of today reflect on her ability to testify. She was excused at the court's discretion, and her actions were following my orders."

Scott Miller gave a slight nod of understanding, but Hartford's expression tightened. "Your Honor, I..."

"You will listen carefully," Judge Harlow interrupted, her tone icy. "This directive applies equally to both sides. If either of you attempts to use what happened today, directly or indirectly, you will find yourself on the receiving end of a very harsh reprimand. Is that understood?"

"Yes, Your Honor," Scott said, his tone measured.

Hartford hesitated for a moment, then nodded reluctantly. "Understood, Your Honor."

Judge Harlow straightened in her seat, her voice softening just slightly. "Good. Let's keep tomorrow's testimony focused on the facts and the evidence. The victim has a right to be treated with respect, and the court has a duty to maintain the integrity of these proceedings."

She dismissed them with a wave of her hand. "You're excused for the evening. I suggest you both prepare for tomorrow."

Scott and Hartford stepped back, their expressions unreadable as they returned to their respective tables. Judge Harlow watched them with a keen eye as they gathered their belongings. They stood there as she finally stood up and exited the courtroom; firm resolve remained, ensuring that the trial would proceed with fairness and decorum.

Outside the courtroom, Scott turned to Jack, his face betraying a mix of determination and fatigue. "Got a few minutes?"

Jack, already loosening his tie, raised an eyebrow. "Sure. What's on your mind?"

Scott leaned against the desk, his posture weighed down by the gravity of the case. Jack stepped fully into the room, closing the door behind him, his expression unreadable but tinged with the weariness of the day.

"I'm not here to push," Scott began, his tone measured but steady. "But after everything we've laid out today, I think it's time to discuss a deal."

Jack folded his arms, leaning back against the wall with a skeptical look. "And what do you think my client would consider fair? Because I can tell you right now, Richard still believes he's walking out of this *scot-free*."

Scott didn't react, his voice steady as he outlined the terms. "Fifteen years. No parole. After release, fifteen years' probation with GPS monitoring. Thirty-five percent of his disposable income goes to the victim recovery fund. Permanent placement on the registry. And he surrenders all parental rights to the child."

Jack let out a dry laugh, though his clenched jaw betrayed his frustration. "You're piling on, Miller. That's not a deal. It's a life sentence by another name."

Scott stepped forward slightly, his tone remaining calm but firm. "It's a chance, Jack. More than he deserves, and we both know it."

Jack's eyes narrowed. "You might think that, but he won't. You're asking him to admit guilt for things he still insists he didn't do."

Scott leaned forward, his voice dropping, quiet but unyielding. "Let's cut through the noise. You and I both know he's guilty. Peter's testimony was clear. Captain Bishop's report backs it all up. And Brittney? You saw her today. That girl's barely holding on. This isn't just about a conviction. It's about closure for her and for everyone else he's hurt."

Jack sighed heavily, rubbing the back of his neck as he absorbed Scott's words. "And if he refuses?"

Scott's expression hardened. "Then we continue. And I'll make sure the jury sees every piece of evidence—every bite mark, every moment of testimony that makes their skin crawl. If this goes to the jury, I'll push for consecutive sentences. He won't see daylight until Brittney's grandkids are grown."

The weight of the statement hung in the air as Jack studied Scott, the tension between them thick. Finally, Jack exhaled sharply, his tone resigned. "I'll talk to him. But I'm not making any promises."

"That's all I'm asking," Scott replied, his tone softening slightly. "You know where to find me."

Jack gave a curt nod before turning on his heel and leaving the room. As the door clicked shut behind him, the exhaustion in his posture deepened, the weight of the conversation pressing heavily on his shoulders.

*****

On the way home, the car was unusually quiet. Brittney sat by the window, her face turned toward the glass, where soft tears rolled down her cheeks, catching the dim glow of passing streetlights. Stephanie and Brian spoke in hushed tones in the backseat until a faint sniffle interrupted them. Brian leaned over the bench, gently placing his hand on Brittney's shoulder.

"Are you okay, sweets?" he asked, his voice low and tender.

Through her soft sobs, Brittney murmured, "I'm sorry."

Brian's brow furrowed, and his tone became even gentler. "Sorry about what?"

Brittney hesitated before turning to look at him. Her tear-streaked face was pale, and her eyes brimmed with guilt. "Because I let everyone down," she whispered.

Brian's eyes softened, and before he could respond, Umi's voice floated gently from the front seat. "Angel, you didn't let anyone down. What happened today wasn't a failure. It was truth. Honest and raw."

As Umi reached back and squeezed Brittney's hand, Brian leaned in, pressing a soft kiss to her cheek. "Not me, and I know it wasn't Stephanie either. Who do you think you let down?"

Brittney hesitated, glancing nervously at Stephanie before answering. "Myself. I... I tried so hard, but when the pictures came up, and then Peter started talking..." Her voice broke, and her gaze fell to her lap. "I couldn't stop seeing it all. It was like I was back there."

Brian gently turned her face toward his. "Love, listen to me. You're still healing, and nobody expects you to get through all of this without feeling the weight of it." His tone was firm but kind, brimming with conviction. "What you showed today wasn't weakness; it was courage. It's okay to feel upset. You're going to get through this."

Gloria glanced at Brittney through the rearview mirror, her voice soft but practical. "Brian's right. Don't be too hard on yourself, Brittney. For now, just promise that you'll believe in your own strength to get through this, okay? One day at a time."

Umi nodded, adding quietly, "Gloria's right, Angel. It's not about perfection. It's about giving yourself permission to be human."

Stephanie leaned forward and kissed Brittney's other cheek. "Sis, you didn't let anyone down—not me, not Brian, and not our Moms. We love you, and we're here, okay?"

For the first time that night, Brittney's lips quivered into a faint smile. "Okay."

Stephanie grinned, wiping away a stray tear from Brittney's cheek. "You know what? Let's do dessert before dinner. Chocolate fixes everything. Right, Brian?"

Brian chuckled softly. "Chocolate and pizza, maybe. How about Andy's? They make your favorite, the one with pineapple and black olives."

Stephanie shuddered dramatically, laughing. "Yuck! That's disgusting. You and your weird taste, Brittney."

"Don't knock it till you've tried it," Brittney teased.

Brian let out a soft laugh, and Gloria smiled in the mirror. "Andy's it is. Let's make tonight better."

The car settled into a more relaxed atmosphere as laughter and playful banter filled the space. For a brief moment, the heaviness of the day eased, replaced by the comfort of family and hope.

*****

Later that night, after a game of 'Sushi Go Party!', it was obvious Brittney wasn't feeling good. After the game, Stephanie suggested they take their showers to see if it would help Brittney relax and feel better. In the background, a soft jazz channel played on the TV. Gloria and Umi sat at the kitchen table, their quiet laughter and the shuffle of cards adding a soothing, family quality to the house. On the couch, Brian was immersed in a thick technical book, its dense diagrams and notations providing him with a temporary distraction.

The faint creak of the stairs drew Brian's attention. Brittney and Stephanie descended; their oversized bathrobes wrapped tightly around them. Their damp hair clung to their cheeks, the smell of fresh shampoo following them.

Brian set his book aside and smiled. "Hey, Britt," he said, his voice warm but careful. "Come sit by me."

Brittney hesitated at the base of the stairs, glancing toward the kitchen where Gloria and Umi were engrossed in their game. Stephanie gave her sister's arm a gentle nudge. Slowly, Brittney shuffled to the couch and perched on the edge of the cushion beside Brian, her hands tucked deep into the folds of her robe. Stephanie settled on Brittney's other side, watching her closely.

"How are you feeling, any better?" Brian asked gently, leaning slightly toward her.

Brittney glanced at her hands, her voice barely above a whisper. "Not really."

Brian nodded, his expression patient. "Do you want to talk about it?"

There was a long pause before Brittney shook her head. "No, I'm just worrying about things."

Stephanie reached over, resting a hand on Brittney's knee. "You don't have to go into details, Britt. But sometimes it helps to talk, even just a little."

Brittney's shoulders tensed, and her gaze flicked between her sister and Brian. Finally, she sighed. "It's... tomorrow. The testimony. I keep thinking about it—about what I have to say, about what they'll ask me. And... those pictures. They won't leave my head."

Brian's brows knitted in concern, but he kept his tone calm. "That's a lot to worry about, Britt. No wonder you're feeling overwhelmed."

Brittney's hands tightened into fists beneath her robe. "I feel like I'll freeze up. Like I'll forget everything or say something wrong."

Stephanie squeezed her knee gently. "You've done awesome so far—talking to the detectives, standing up to help other women. Tomorrow is just another step. And we'll all be right there with you."

Brittney's voice cracked as she whispered, "What if they don't believe me?"

"They will. They already heard Peter's story, which is the same as yours. You're telling the truth, Britt. And that's all that matters," Brian said, his voice steady and reassuring.

Another pause stretched between them, the soft strains of a smooth trumpet filling the silence. Finally, Brian spoke again, his tone softer.

"Can I try something that might help?" he asked, his eyes warm and steady.

Brittney hesitated, searching his face for a moment before nodding cautiously. "Okay."

Brian's smile was small but reassuring. "Let's start simple. Can you take your arm out of your robe? Just this one." He gestured to the arm nearest to him.

Brittney stiffened, glancing at Stephanie, who gave her an encouraging nod. "It's okay, Britt."

Slowly, Brittney slipped her arm free, her movements hesitant. Her fingers trembled slightly as they rested on the cushion between her and Brian.

"Good," Brian murmured. "Now, I want you to focus on my voice. Just my voice. Nothing else matters right now. Can you do that?"

Brittney nodded, her breathing uneven.

Brian took her hand gently, his thumb tracing slow circles over her knuckles. "Close your eyes if you want to," he said softly. "Just listen."

He leaned down, brushing his lips lightly over her wrist. The touch was feather-soft, more a whisper than a kiss. "You're strong, Britt. Stronger than you know."

Stephanie shifted closer, wrapping her arm around Brittney's shoulders and pulling her into a loose embrace. Her fingers combed gently through her sister's damp hair, her voice a quiet murmur. "You're doing so well, Britt. Just let yourself be here, with us."

As Brian trailed soft kisses along her forearm, Brittney's breathing began to slow. The tension in her shoulders eased, her body leaning slightly into Stephanie's hold.

"You're home and in my arms," Brian said between kisses, his voice steady and grounding. "I love you."

When his lips reached her shoulder, Brittney shivered slightly, the sensation pulling her further into the present. Brian kissed her neck softly and whispered, "You're not alone, Brittney. I love you."

Brian trailed the kisses back down her arm. At her upper arm, he whispered, "I'm here, with you, and I will always be here with you."

Brittney relaxed into Stephanie's embrace, her breath slow and steady. Umi and Gloria paused their conversation, looking over at the teens, watching with keen interest.

Brian continued down her arm and stopped at her knuckles, kissing each softly. "You can feel us here, with you. We can feel you, your love," he started back up her arm, pausing frequently to gently touch the skin, then kiss the same spot. He paused at her elbow, his voice soft and gentle. "Feel our love, Britt. Feel Stephanie as she holds you, my little kisses, and know in your heart we love you."

When his lips came to her shoulder, Brittney turned toward him, her eyes fluttering open. For a moment, the room seemed to hold its breath as their gazes met. Then, slowly, their lips met in a tender, lingering kiss. The warmth of his touch and the quiet reassurance in his embrace melted her lingering tension. Moments later, the kiss was done.

Brittney had a soft red glow on her cheeks as she looked into his blue eyes.

"That was..." Brittney began, her voice soft. "Amazing. I feel... better. A lot better," a small smile on her lips.

Stephanie smiled at her sister, her tone warm and affectionate. "You look like you feel better," she said softly, brushing a stray strand of Brittney's hair back. "It's nice to see you smile again."

She glanced at Brian, her eyes sparkling. "Well, that looked like it was fun, and now I want some, too." Her tone turned playful as she nudged him lightly.

The three of them laughed, the sound light and unrestrained. Brittney leaned back into Stephanie's embrace, her smile widening.

Stephanie leaned forward, her eyes sparkling. "I've got an idea," she said, hopping up from the couch. She disappeared down the hall and returned moments later with Brittney's drawing pad and a pencil.

Handing them to Brittney, Stephanie's voice was gentle but excited. "Draw what you just felt. All of it—the calm, the warmth, the love. Put it on the page."

Brittney hesitated, her fingers brushing over the textured paper of the sketchpad. Slowly, she took it, nodding. "Okay. I'll try."

As Brittney began sketching, Stephanie moved to the other side of the couch and settled beside Brian. Her smile turned playful as she nudged him. "Come here," she said, her voice soft but teasing. "My turn."

Brian chuckled, wrapping an arm around her shoulders as he leaned in. Their lips met, the kiss deep and unhurried, a mirror of the tenderness he had shown Brittney moments before. When they pulled apart, Stephanie's cheeks were tinged pink, and her expression was blissful.

"Wow," Stephanie said with a laugh, her voice still breathless. "I see why she liked that."

Brian grinned, brushing a stray lock of hair from her face. "Glad I could help."

In the background, Gloria shuffled the deck of cards. "Last round?" she asked Umi.

Umi nodded. "Only if I win," she replied with a small grin.

As the movie began playing on the TV, the room fell into a comfortable quiet. Brittney scratched away on the sketchpad, drawing a sun rising over a breaking wave on the beach. Three silhouette characters sat in the center of the page, the two ends kissing the one in the middle. A ribbon tied around the trunk of a tree woven between the three silhouettes, ending in a heart shape on sand. Sometime later, she set the pad and pencil down, cuddled into Brian, and watched the movie. A while later, Brian noticed Brittney's breathing slow and even out. He glanced down and realized she had fallen asleep in his embrace. He gently poked Stephanie and then pointed at Brittney.

Steph nodded, whispering, "I'll get her bed ready," before quietly moving away. As she passed Umi, she paused to say softly, "Britt's fallen asleep. Brian's going to bring her up to bed," before continuing up the stairs to Brittney's room.

Brian carefully shifted Brittney onto his lap. She stirred for a moment, murmuring softly, and instinctively wrapped her arms around his neck as he stood. Slowly and carefully, he walked past the kitchen table where Gloria and Umi sat, and then up the stairs. In Brittney's room, he gently laid her down on the bed and tucked the blanket around her snugly. Leaning down, he pressed a soft kiss to her forehead, whispering softly, "Good night, my princess."

As Brian stepped out of the room, Stephanie wrapped her arms around him in the hallway. "Please tuck me in, my prince," she said with a playful grin.

Brian followed her to her room and stood at the bedside as she climbed in. Bending over, he tucked her in, brushing a soft kiss across her lips. "Good night, my princess," he whispered.

"Sweet dreams, my prince," Stephanie replied softly, her voice laced with contentment.

Back downstairs, as Brian passed Umi and Gloria, he said, "I'm heading home to shower and go to bed. Good night, Moms."

"Good night," Gloria called after him, smiling warmly.

When the door clicked shut, Umi glanced at Gloria. "Did you see that?" she asked softly.

Gloria nodded, her expression thoughtful. "I did. And it makes me happy… and a little nervous."

Umi tilted her head, curiosity flickering in her eyes. "Why nervous?"

Gloria set her cards down, taking a moment before answering. "It's not just them being so close, though that's part of it. Brittney is still so fragile right now, emotionally and mentally. Brian's helping her feel safe, but it's a lot for him to carry. If Brittney starts relying on him too much, it could strain him, or their relationship."

Umi nodded slowly, absorbing Gloria's words. "And Stephanie?"

Gloria smiled faintly. "She's strong, but she's young, too. She trusts Brian completely, but with Brittney needing him so much… it might be hard not to feel left out sometimes."

Umi leaned back in her chair, her fingers drumming lightly on the tabletop. "You're not wrong. But I think they're navigating this better than I expected. Brian's steady, and Stephanie knows her own strength. They're figuring it out."

Gloria sighed, a mix of pride and lingering concern in her voice. "You're right. They're amazing kids, young adults, really. I just don't want to see them hurt."

Umi went into the living room. "I want to see what she drew," as she bent down and picked up the pad. Her eyes went wide when she saw it. Slowly, she turned the image so Gloria could see it as she walked back and placed the pad on the table.

She placed her hand on Gloria's hand. "None of us do. But we also can't shield them forever. They're growing into something wonderful and beautiful. We just have to trust them."

Gloria chuckled softly. "True. But I'll still keep an eye on them. Just in case."

Umi smiled, a warmth in her gaze. "That's what we do. We're moms, after all."

Gloria sighed again, this time with a mix of pride and nostalgia. "Yeah... moms."

Umi sat back down and shuffled the deck of cards, her tone reflective. "They're growing up. But at least they're growing into something beautiful."

Gloria nodded, her smile returning. "Something really beautiful."

CHAPTER 30

The courtroom hummed with muted conversations as spectators settled into their seats. Precisely at 9:00 a.m., Judge Ann Harlow entered, her robe flowing as she ascended the bench with her usual poise. She tapped her gavel twice, bringing the room to order.

"Good morning, ladies and gentlemen," Judge Harlow announced, her voice firm yet composed. "The court is now in session. Mr. Miller, please call your next witness."

Scott Miller stood, his movements deliberate as he adjusted his jacket. "Your Honor, the State calls Dr. Olivia Hayes to the stand."

Dr. Hayes, a tall woman with sharp features and an air of quiet authority, rose and approached the witness stand. Her steps were measured, and her professionalism was evident in every movement.

The bailiff stepped forward with a Bible in hand.

"Dr. Olivia Hayes," the bailiff intoned, "please raise your right hand."

Dr. Hayes complied, her gaze steady.

"Do you solemnly swear or affirm that the testimony you are about to give in this court is the truth, the whole truth, and nothing but the truth, so help you God?"

"I do," she replied with quiet confidence and took her seat in the witness chair.

Scott approached, his tone respectful. "Good morning, Dr. Hayes."

"Good morning," she responded evenly.

"For the record, please state your name and professional qualifications."

Dr. Hayes adjusted her glasses slightly. "My name is Dr. Olivia Hayes. I hold a PhD in forensic biology and have over fifteen years of experience specializing in DNA analysis and forensic odontology. I currently serve as the lead forensic scientist at the Beaverdam Forensic Laboratory."

Scott nodded. "In your role, do you routinely analyze evidence collected during criminal investigations?"

"Yes. My responsibilities include examining biological evidence, conducting DNA analysis, and preparing expert reports for use in court."

"Dr. Hayes, did you analyze evidence related to this case?"

"Yes, I did," she confirmed.

Scott turned to the clerk, who handed him a sealed evidence bag. Holding it up, he addressed the court. "Your Honor, I move to submit Exhibit E into evidence: the shirt worn by the victim at the time of one of the alleged assaults."

Judge Harlow reviewed the bag briefly before nodding. "Exhibit E is admitted."

Scott approached Dr. Hayes, offering her the evidence bag. "Dr. Hayes, is this the item you examined?"

Dr. Hayes inspected the seal before nodding. "Yes, this is the shirt provided to me by the Beaverdam Police Department."

"Could you describe the analysis you performed?" Scott asked.

"I conducted DNA extraction and amplification on bloodstains and saliva found on the shirt. Using polymerase chain reaction, or PCR, I compared these DNA profiles to those of the victim, Brittney Welch, and the defendant, Richard Perez."

"And what were your findings?"

Dr. Hayes delivered her answer with precision. "The bloodstains matched the victim, consistent with injuries sustained from bite marks. The saliva found on the shirt matched the defendant, with a probability of 99.9%, indicating direct contact."

Scott turned toward the jury, emphasizing her words. "Dr. Hayes, was this the only analysis you conducted?"

"No. I also examined documented bite marks on the victim's body."

The room seemed to be still, the gravity of the statement palpable.

"Could you explain that process?" Scott pressed.

Dr. Hayes leaned forward slightly, her tone instructional. "Using high-resolution images and silicone impressions of the bite marks provided by the medical examiner, I compared these to dental impressions from the defendant. Overlay analysis confirmed that the bite marks were consistent with the defendant's dental pattern."

"What conclusion did you reach?"

"The bite marks on the victim's breasts, shoulder, back, rib cage, and upper arm matched the defendant's dental impressions. The unique features, such as alignment and spacing, were conclusive."

"Were these injuries consistent with the victim's account of the assault?" Scott asked.

"Yes," Dr. Hayes affirmed. "The depth and pattern of the bite marks align with the description provided by the victim."

Scott shifted slightly, addressing the jury directly. "Dr. Hayes, can you elaborate on the significance of finding both blood and saliva on the shirt?"

Dr. Hayes spoke with authority. "The blood corroborates the victim's injuries. The defendant's saliva supports the claim of direct physical contact, consistent with an aggressive encounter. Together, these findings substantiate the victim's account."

"Dr. Hayes, are you confident in the chain of custody for these samples?"

"Entirely. All evidence was handled according to strict forensic protocols, with no breaches reported."

Scott nodded, his tone conclusive. "Your Honor, I have no further questions."

Judge Harlow turned to the defense attorney. "Mr. Hartford, your witness."

Jack Hartford rose smoothly, his demeanor controlled. "Dr. Hayes, bite mark analysis has faced criticism for its subjectivity. Would you agree?"

Dr. Hayes maintained her composure. "While it has been debated, advancements in imaging and analytical methods, such as those I employed, have greatly enhanced reliability."

Jack's tone sharpened. "Can DNA evidence be unintentionally transferred?"

"In rare instances, yes. However, the placement and context of this evidence strongly suggest direct transfer," Dr. Hayes responded without hesitation.

Jack paused briefly before retreating. "No further questions."

Scott stood for the redirect. "Dr. Hayes, how confident are you in your findings?"

"Extremely confident. The evidence supports the victim's account and implicates the defendant directly."

Judge Harlow addressed Dr. Hayes. "Thank you for your testimony. You may step down."

Dr. Hayes left the stand, her professionalism unshaken, as Judge Harlow addressed the courtroom. "Mr. Miller, please call your next witness."

Scott Miller stood, his posture confident but professional. "Your Honor, the prosecution would like to call Dr. Elise Markham to the stand."

As the bailiff turned toward the door, another uniformed court officer hurriedly entered and approached the bench, whispering something to the judge. Judge Harlow's brow furrowed slightly, then relaxed as she nodded and addressed the court.

"It appears we need a moment to address an unforeseen matter," she announced. Her gaze swept the room, settling briefly on the attorneys. "Mr. Miller, Mr. Hartford, please approach."

The two lawyers exchanged curious glances before walking to the bench.

In a low voice, the judge explained, "Dr. Markham has just informed us through the bailiff that she has a pressing family emergency. She is not available for testimony today."

Scott's expression shifted to one of understanding, tinged with concern. "I see, Your Honor. This is unfortunate. Dr. Markham's testimony is critical to our case. Unfortunately, I am unable to call Brittney Welch, who is not prepared to testify, because she is currently following the court's directive to take her prescribed medications as scheduled."

Jack's eyes narrowed as he leaned slightly forward. "Your Honor, if the prosecution claims their witness is unable to testify due to medications, this raises serious questions about her overall reliability and mental state. The defense must reserve the right to scrutinize her testimony thoroughly."

Scott's demeanor stiffened, his tone firm. "Your Honor, Brittney Welch's competence has already been established in the pre-trial hearing. This court deemed her fully capable of providing testimony. Mr. Hartford's insinuations are baseless and serve only to disparage a credible witness unnecessarily."

Judge Harlow's gaze turned sharp as she addressed Hartford. "Mr. Hartford, the court's prior ruling on Brittney Welch's competence is not up for debate. I will not tolerate any attempts to undermine her credibility based on her compliance with medical directives or this court's orders. You will proceed with professionalism and respect."

Hartford raised his hands slightly in a gesture of acquiescence. "Understood, Your Honor. My apologies if my remarks were misinterpreted."

Judge Harlow's tone remained firm. "See that they are not repeated." She turned her attention back to Miller. "Mr. Miller, are you prepared to proceed with another witness today?"

Miller hesitated, his expression a mix of resolve and consideration. "Unfortunately, Your Honor, I must request an adjournment for today. Neither Dr. Markham nor Ms. Welch are available, and the following witness is scheduled for Friday morning, Your Honor."

The judge nodded thoughtfully. "A reasonable request. The court will adjourn early today and resume tomorrow at 9:00 a.m. sharp."

The attorneys returned to their tables as the judge struck her gavel lightly. "Court is adjourned."

As the families exited the courtroom, Scott stepped near the door, waiting for Jack.

"Got a minute?" Scott asked as Jack turned toward him.

Jack turned to face him. "Only if you're not going to gloat."

Scott shook his head, his tone measured and even. "Not gloating. Just a reality check. You know how everything is going. Between Dr. Hayes, the pictures you know are coming, the video, all of it. And we both know if your client takes the stand, with his attitude, he's going to dig himself so deep no one's going to save him. Richard can't wiggle out, no matter how he acts on the stand. We both know how this ends, right?"

"Do we really? Trials can be unpredictable," Jack answered uneasily.

Scott nodded. "In some cases, but we both know this isn't one of them. We have the specialists in the rest of the reports; there's no ambiguity here. Jack, if this goes to verdict, Richard's staring down at least forty years, conservatively."

"And what? Are you feeling generous?" Jack asked sharply.

"Something like that. I don't want to drag Brittney through any more than she's been through. We both know that cross-examination is going to be grueling for her, even if she can handle it. Here's a deal: twenty-five years, no parole, followed by twenty-five years of probation, GPS monitoring, permanent residence on the sex registry, and he permanently surrenders all parental rights to the child he created with his acts."

"Scott, that's a hard sell. You know my client doesn't even think he's done wrong," Jack replied.

"Yeah, I know, and that doesn't even include the aggravated assault charges. If we factor that into everything, he's looking at sixty or so years. How about this: twenty years, no parole, twenty years' probation, thirty-five percent of disposable income into the victim's recovery fund, the registry for life, and he still surrenders all parental rights to the child?"

"You want him to pay child support for a child he has no rights to? Really?" Jack asked astonishment in his voice.

"No, not child support. The victim's recovery fund will make sure Brittney's medical expenses and long-term care are covered, especially if she needs surgeries to repair the damage from Richard. It also covers the cost of raising a child. We know the program is very strict on amounts collected from offenders, often ending at 55 percent of their disposable income. I'm offering a big break here, and you know it. Jack, just think for a moment: what if Brittney was your girl, Tammy? What would you want?" Scott asked with a serious tone.

While Jack considered what Scott was saying, the weight of his professional duty to Richard weighed heavily on his mind.

Scott added, "We both know he took a fragile young woman and messed her life up, and it's going to be hell for her for a very long time."

Jack hesitated, seriously considering what was being offered. "Okay, Scott, I'll talk with him, but I can't make any promises. You know this is going to be like pulling teeth from a wild dog," Jack finally answered reluctantly.

"I never do, but here's a bit of incentive. The moment we reconvene tomorrow morning, if he hasn't accepted the plea, all deals are off the table, and I'll make sure this goes to jury," Scott added.

"There's no wiggle room, Scott. Almost nothing to work with," Jack complained, knowing it would be a hard sell to Richard.

"Jack, I'm here to get Brittney justice and to stop your client from doing it again. Here and now, nothing else matters. I'll let you know this: I will be going for the maximum for each charge of rape in the first degree, aggravated assault, witness intimidation, and tampering—all 67 confirmed charges. I'll be pushing for consecutive sentences, not concurrent," Scott added with a calculated tone.

"And your offer?" Jack asked.

"One sentence, done and over. If he agrees to the settlement option for the victim's fund, it's a closed case," Scott reassured him.

"Okay, Scott, you've convinced me. I'll try; that's all I can do," Jack surrendered.

"You have my number. I hope to hear from you tonight, and if not, then before we reconvene," Scott said, extending his hand.

Jack shook his hand. "I really hope he takes the deal. I'll call one way or another when I'm done with him tonight."

Scott walked away in his measured stride. Once he turned the corner and was out of sight of Jack, he let a small smile creep onto his face.

*****

Later that afternoon, as Scott was leaving his office for the night, his cell phone rang.

"Miller," he answered.

Moments later, he answered, "Thanks for letting me know. See you tomorrow morning," and hung up.

Scott thought for a few minutes as he walked toward his car. A smile came across his face as he decided to call Umi.

Umi answered the call. "Hello?"

"Good afternoon, Umi. It's Scott Miller."

After she greeted him, "I'd like to have a quick meeting with you and Brittney this evening if we can."

As she replied, Scott smiled. "Actually, I have some good news this time," he replied.

"Okay, I'll see you in about twenty minutes," Scott said as he hung up the phone and dialed Captain Bishop.

"Hey, Bishop, good news for a change," he said after she answered.

A moment later, "Yup. I'm heading there now. Meet me there in twenty minutes?"

"Great, see you there," Jack answered, his smile big as he hung up the phone.

Scott picked up his pace. For the first time in a long time, he was going to deliver some long-overdue good news to Brittney.

*****

That afternoon, everyone was in the living room, waiting for Scott and Captain Bishop to arrive.

Stephanie bumped Brittney's shoulder with hers. "How was art class today? I can see you're really interested in it. Is it helping?"

Brittney answered softly. "I like it a lot. My instructor says I have natural talent. I know I'm drawing dark things now, but Doctor Jenny says to expect it, and we'll focus on happier things later. I love working with Ashley; she really helps me to think about tomorrow. Do you think I should bring it up to Mr. Scott or Captain Ashley?"

Stephanie smiled as she whispered back. "I would. It's part of how you're recovering. Or, better yet, how well you're doing."

Everyone talked lightly for a while until there was a knock at the door. When Brian opened the door, Captain Bishop and Scott saw everyone sitting in the living room, looking at them.

"Good afternoon, everyone," Captain Bishop greeted them with a warm and professional voice.

Brian looked at him. "It's a captive audience, Mr. Scott."

"It sure does look like that. I'm glad I've got good news for a change," Scott replied with a smile.

After the greetings were done, Scott sat in the only remaining chair in the living room while Captain Bishop stood nearby.

Gloria's hand rested gently on Umi's hand, gently squeezing it as Scott started to talk.

Scott looked at Brittney. "For the first time since we've started this, I've got some good news for everyone."

Brittney looked up. "What?" Her face showed confusion, not sure what would be good news.

"Mr. Hartford and I had a good and long conversation and came up with a deal for Richard," Scott started.

Scott smiled. "Before I get into all of that, I want everyone to know that Richard really didn't have a choice. Between the testimonies today, his attorney, and how I presented my intentions to him, Richard knew he was going to be very old if he ever got out of jail."

"What kind of deal?" Gloria asked, leaning forward and gently squeezing Umi's hand.

"He understood that, even without Brittney's testimony, we've already won the case. So, I gave them an offer so Brittney didn't have to testify, one that secured justice for her and the baby."

Brittney's face brightened up. "I don't have to testify tomorrow?" The worry on her face was replaced with disbelief.

Jack smiled. "That's right, Brittney. Richard is going to spend the next twenty years in jail, and then he's going to spend the next twenty years on parole, with GPS monitoring to ensure he doesn't come near you or the baby. He's also got to register on the sex offenders list."

Brittney asked, her hands going around her belly, "And he's going to stay away from me and my baby?"

Jack's smile grew. "Even better. He's agreed to surrender all parental rights. It's as if he doesn't exist. There's more good news. He's also agreed to thirty-five percent of his monthly income. What that means to you is a check every month for you and your baby. All of this is automatic; the state takes care of everything."

"And he can't come after my baby or me, ever?" Brittney asked, her voice sounding doubtful about what she heard.

"That's right. And if his income changes, the distribution doesn't. Let me explain how this works: it's not child support; it's from the victim's recovery fund. This fund is specifically set up to help victims of violent crimes rebuild their lives. The payments ensure that you'll have financial stability to cover medical bills, therapy, and raising your baby. Once this is finished, you won't have to deal with him directly. The state handles everything, so you can focus on healing and moving forward," Scott said.

"I don't understand," Brittney said softly, her hands fidgeting.

"Sis, basically, it means no matter what happens to him, you're going to get what you need to take care of your baby and yourself, and he can't stop it. Is that right, Mr. Scott?" Stephanie asked.

Jack smiled. "That's about it. If he stops paying, you keep getting your check, and you don't do anything. It's to protect you from having to deal with him," Jack explained.

Brittney started fidgeting with the hem of her shirt. "Is this real? Is it really over?" she asked softly, gently rubbing her belly, still not believing what Scott was telling her. A mix of relief and other emotions was visible on her face, her hands shaking. Stephanie reached over and gently took her hand, squeezing it.

Umi gently squeezed her shoulders, silently reassuring her daughter.

Brian looked over. "If I'm out of line, tell me, please, but how long does this distribution go on for?" His worry and concern for Brittney's future were clear in his tone.

"Good question, Brian. It's designed to be an income for victims drastically affected by the crime committed against them. With cost-of-living raises, Brittney will have income until she's no longer disabled, which means the rest of her life," Scott explained.

Scott looked back at Brittney. "Tomorrow, all of this will go on the record. You have to be there in case the judge asks you any questions, but you won't be testifying. Then, everything has to be written up and signed. I figure in one or two months, everything will be set up and done. Between now and then, you have one more courtroom visit tomorrow, and either I come and see you, or you can come to my office to sign the papers," Scott answered Brittney's question.

Umi looked up, her eyes wet. "That's more than we could have hoped for, Scott. I don't know what to say."

Captain Bishop looked at Umi. "This is exactly what the fund and program were designed for," she answered warmly. "I've never seen a case that was as deserving as Brittney's is."

Brittney struggled to stand, wincing in pain as she moved. Brian, being watchful, put his hand out and let her pull against him as she stood up, her gaze moving to him briefly as she mouthed, "I love you," without a sound. As she approached

Scott, she extended her hands to hug him. "Mr. Scott, may I?" she asked, her voice shaky.

Scott stood up, and Brittney gently wrapped her hands around him, holding him loosely. "Thank you for everything. I almost gave up. If Captain Ashley hadn't convinced me to talk with you, Brian, and Stephanie, none of this would have happened. I owe you so much," she said, her voice catching as tears started to roll down her cheeks.

Scott gently hugged her back. "Brittney, I've never seen such a brave young woman as I've seen in you. You have the strength to conquer anything that happens to you, and you've proven it to yourself and all of us these past few weeks."

"For the first time in a long time, it feels like things might get better. Thank you," her voice was just a whisper as that small ember of hope that started months ago started burning brighter in the pit of her stomach as Scott hugged her back.

A few seconds later, Scott let Brittney go, and Brittney walked over to Captain Bishop and hugged her. "Thank you for convincing me, Captain Ashley."

Brittney looked up into Captain Bishop's eyes. "You were right; trusting Mr. Scott was hard, but I'm glad you convinced me to do it."

"Brittney, we both knew things were going to get better; all you had to do was believe in yourself. You're very welcome. Any of you, if you need anything, please don't hesitate to call me," Captain Bishop said as she hugged Brittney.

Gloria added, "We're so proud of you, sweetheart," wiping her eyes dry.

Scott stood up, his smile growing. "I need to get home; my five-year-old is waiting to watch *Frozen* with me for like the tenth time."

Stephanie smiled back. "That's one of our favorites. We've seen it hundreds of times, right, Brittney?"

Brittney giggled as she sat down, feeling something different deep within her. "Something like that."

Brian looked at Brittney. "Now, that's something I haven't heard in a while."

Stephanie looked up. "What?"

"Brittney's giggle. It's music to my ears," Brian said with a big smile.

Brittney's cheeks turned a soft red, with a small smile. "Thank you, Brian."

Umi glanced toward Brittney, her voice shaky. "Angel, you've been so strong, and seeing you smile like this again, it's all we could have prayed for."

Captain Bishop turned. "Oh, before I leave, Brittney, how are your drawing classes going?"

Brittney looked up, her eyes bright. "Great. Would you like to see my workbook? Wait. How did you find out about that?"

Stephanie got up. "I'll get the workbook, Steph."

"I checked into the status of your case, and it was listed in the report as a suggestion by your therapist. I'm really happy you're taking an interest in it," Captain Bishop answered.

"My teacher keeps telling me I'm good, but I'm not so sure," Brittney said softly, her voice just above a whisper.

As Brittney finished speaking, Stephanie handed the drawing pad to Brittney.

"Doctor Jenny says this one," Brittney flipped and pointed to a picture of a dark hooded figure with vampire teeth that appeared as if it were jumping off the page, "is what she says is a result of what I'm living, um, lived through."

Brittney rapidly flipped to another image of a bed in a brick-lined room with prison bars all around it. "And this one too. They are the darkest, meanest. She says that, over time, they won't be so 'dark,' like this one," as she flipped to the image of the three silhouette figures kissing on the beach.

"Brittney, these are really good," Scott said.

"I think Scott's right, Brittney. These drawings are better than some that I've seen in stores," Captain Bishop added.

Scott looked at Brittney, his voice serious. "These aren't just pictures you've drawn. It's your story. They're telling everyone what you survived and how you are starting to rebuild your life. Doctor Jenny is right; this is you taking control of your narrative."

Captain Bishop studied the images, then nodded in agreement. "It's incredible, Brittney. You've turned some of your hardest experiences into something that's not only helping you but could inspire others someday. Please, don't stop. You are showing the strength it takes to heal. Seeing how many drawings you've made is proving how much progress you've made."

"I don't think so, Brittney; I know so," Scott said, his voice still serious.

"And you've been in classes for a few months? You have some talent," Captain Bishop said.

Brittney's cheeks were a soft rose color. "I'm not sure..." she started, unsure if she should point out the last page. In the back of her head, she made the decision.

"Flip to the last page. That's today's work," her voice edged on happiness.

The last image in the book was a striking resemblance to Scott's face in knight's armor.

"Thank you, Brittney. I'm honored to be included in your images," Scott said as he recognized his likeness.

"I agree with Captain Bishop. These are excellent. Don't give it up; you could be on to something big here," Scott said.

"Okay, everyone, I have to get out of here before I have a very mad five-year-old after me," Scott said as he headed to the door.

"I've got some dinner plans with my son, too, so I'd better be getting out of here also. Remember, call me if you need anything, okay?" Captain Bishop asked.

Brian reached out to Scott. "Mr. Scott, I want to personally thank you for everything. I don't think I could ever express my gratitude for what you've done for my fiancé, best friend, and our families."

Scott smiled. "I'm really happy with how things turned out. My only wish is that we could have met under different circumstances."

While the two were talking, Stephanie walked over and hugged Captain Bishop. "Captain Ashley, thank you for making my sister and my family whole again," her eyes wet as tears started to roll down her cheeks.

Captain Bishop hugged her back. "You're very welcome. Like Scott just said, the only thing I would change is how and why we met in the first place."

Scott turned at the door. "Remember, you still have to be in the courtroom tomorrow morning, 9:00 a.m."

Umi assured them they would all be there as Scott and Captain Bishop walked out the door.

Umi's and Gloria's faces were streaked with tears as they watched them leave the house. "What a day!" Gloria said, squeezing Umi's hand tightly.

While Scott and Captain Bishop walked toward their cars, Scott paused for a moment. "Ashley, this is why we do this job," he commented.

Captain Bishop nodded. "Scott, and I know this time, the justice couldn't feel any better."

CHAPTER 31

Dinner had been a quiet, comforting affair, good news and the tension of the day gradually giving way to soft laughter and shared stories. Now, the family gathered in the living room, the hum of togetherness filling the space. Gloria and Umi sat on the couch with steaming mugs of tea, their relaxed postures reflecting the peace slowly settling over the household.

"So," Stephanie said, nudging Brittney's arm with a grin, "how's that comic you've been working on with Ashley? You've been so secretive about it."

Brittney's cheeks flushed a soft pink. "It's not done yet," she said shyly, "but... I guess I could show you if you really want to see it."

"Absolutely!" Stephanie beamed, her enthusiasm contagious.

Brittney stood up, careful of her healing body, and retrieved a large sketchpad from her room. When she returned, all eyes were on her. She settled into a chair and opened the book, revealing the first painted image of the story: a clumsy but endearing depiction of a first kiss between two young characters, the background a swirl of colors evoking nervous excitement.

"Oh wow," Brian said, leaning forward. "That's really good."

"Thanks," Brittney murmured. "Ashley Diaz helped me with some of the ideas. This one's about a first kiss, but it's kind of funny. The guy here ends up accidentally knocking over a lamp when he leans in too fast."

Gloria chuckled from the couch. "That sounds adorable. Show us more."

Brittney turned the page, revealing a mix of finished illustrations and rough pencil sketches. Some panels were vibrant and polished, while others had raw outlines with notes scribbled in the margins. Each page captured the charm and humor of the story.

"This one here," Brittney said, pointing to a sketched panel of the male character tripping over his own feet, "is still rough, but I wanted to show how awkward he is. Ashley said it's relatable."

Stephanie laughed. "It totally is. Britt, this is amazing."

The siblings and Brian admired the work, and Gloria and Umi exchanged glances, their smiles warm and content. Gloria leaned back with her mug cradled in her hands. "It's good to see this," she murmured to Umi. "Them laughing, being themselves again. It's been so long."

Umi nodded, her eyes misty. "It really has. Brittney's starting to heal, Gloria. We all are."

The room filled with laughter as Brittney flipped to the final page she had worked on. "This one's from today," she said softly, revealing a beautifully detailed scene of the characters sitting together under a tree, their hands intertwined, a soft glow surrounding them. "It's the moment they realize they don't have to be perfect to be happy."

Brian reached over, squeezing Brittney's hand gently. "That's a great message."

Brittney smiled a genuine, hopeful smile. For the first time in a long time, the weight on her shoulders felt just a little lighter.

*****

Later that night, after all the excitement had settled down, Stephanie snuck into Brian's bedroom. They sat there on his bed with their fingers interlaced. The soft glow of his desk lamp lit the room, giving a warm hue to the otherwise quiet evening. They leaned into a kiss, a tender connection filled with the unspoken emotions that had been building between them.

When the kiss ended, Stephanie pulled away slightly, her cheeks flushed. She wrapped her arms tightly around Brian, pressing her face into his shoulder.

For a moment, they simply held each other, the world outside his room forgotten.

When Brian and Stephanie went into the living room, they found Brittney sitting cross-legged on the plush couch, a sketchpad balanced on her knees. She was absorbed in her drawing, her pencil moving with practiced ease. Umi and Gloria sat at the dining table nearby, shuffling cards but occasionally casting glances toward the teens in the living room.

"Hey, Britt," Brian said, his tone gentle as he approached. Stephanie sat beside him, offering a reassuring smile.

Brittney looked up, slightly startled. "Oh, hey. What's up?"

Stephanie glanced at Brittney's sketchpad. "Hey, Britt, what are you drawing now?"

Brittney beamed, holding up the pad. "It's us. That kiss you asked me to draw about how I felt—well, I wanted to make it better."

At the dining room table, Gloria reached over, nudging Umi playfully. "Ready for this?"

Umi raised a curious eyebrow. "Ready for what?"

Gloria grinned mischievously. "It's time to talk about a baby shower."

Umi chuckled, catching on. "Oh, that's an awesome idea. And with them all together, now is the perfect time."

Gloria stood, her movements deliberate. "Hey, you three, can we join you for a fun discussion?" she called out as Umi followed her lead.

Brittney looked up from her drawing, a smile tugging at her lips. "Okay," she replied, her voice tentative but warm, unsure of what they were about to bring up.

As Gloria and Umi settled into seats around the living room, Gloria clapped her hands together. "So, we were thinking… it's time to start planning a baby shower!"

Brittney's eyes widened, her pencil pausing on the page. "A baby shower?" she echoed, almost as if the words were foreign.

Stephanie chimed in, her voice full of excitement. "We can invite our friends, decorate the house, and make it all about you and the little one."

Brian leaned back, his voice steady and reassuring. "It's going to be fun—food, music. Whatever makes you feel happy."

Brittney's lips trembled as her eyes filled with tears. She quickly wiped at her face with her sleeve, her voice shaky. "I... didn't think about a baby shower."

Stephanie placed a comforting hand on Brittney's arm. "Well, you're going to have one."

For the first time, Brittney let herself smile through her tears. "I don't even know what to say. This is... Thank you."

"Say you'll help us plan it," Gloria said, her tone light and encouraging. "We want it to be perfect for you."

Brittney hesitated before nodding, her voice growing stronger. "Okay. I'd like that."

The conversation flowed naturally, ideas bouncing between them. Brian suggested a theme based on Brittney's love for drawing, perhaps incorporating her artwork into the decorations. Stephanie brought up the idea of personalized thank-you cards Brittney could design. Umi and Gloria debated over menu options while Brittney listened, her smile growing wider with each passing moment.

Brittney wiped at her eyes again, this time with a wide grin. "I'm glad to be part of the family again. I really am."

"Brittney, you *were* always a part of the family. You just took a small vacation, that's all," Stephanie joked.

The room filled with laughter and shared excitement as the plans took shape. Brittney joined in eagerly, suggesting color schemes and game ideas, her shy demeanor giving way to a genuine excitement that lit up her face.

As the night went on, the family's love and support enveloped Brittney, making her feel, for the first time in a long time, truly whole and part of the family.

CHAPTER 32

The courtroom was alive with a low murmur as Judge Harlow entered, her dark robes flowing as she ascended to her seat. The bailiff called for order, and the room fell silent.

"We are here today to finalize a plea agreement in the case of *State* vs. Richard Perez," Judge Harlow began, her voice steady and authoritative. "Mr. Hartford, Mr. Miller, are we ready to proceed?"

Jack Hartford rose, adjusting his tie, his face taut with tension. "Yes, Your Honor. My client has agreed to the terms of the plea deal as negotiated with the prosecution."

Scott Miller nodded from his place at the prosecution's table. "Ready, Your Honor."

Judge Harlow's sharp gaze shifted to Richard Perez, who sat slouched in his chair, his jaw tight and eyes defiant. "Mr. Perez, please stand."

Richard rose slowly, his movements deliberate, and stared at the judge with barely concealed disdain.

"Mr. Perez, do you understand the terms of this plea agreement?" Harlow asked.

Richard's lips twisted into a sneer. "Yeah, I understand. She's just after my money," he spat, his voice dripping with contempt. "That's all this is about, right?"

"Mr. Perez," Harlow warned, her tone icy, "I will not tolerate disrespect in my courtroom. This agreement was reached to provide justice and closure. It is not up for debate."

"Justice?" Richard scoffed. "This is a joke. She's a liar, and you're all eating it up. She just wants a payday."

Jack Hartford placed a hand on Richard's arm, his voice low and urgent. "Richard, stop. This isn't helping."

Scott Miller interjected, his tone calm but firm. "Your Honor, the terms are more than generous. The state stands by its agreement and expects compliance."

Judge Harlow's expression hardened. "Mr. Perez, you are being given an opportunity here. I suggest you take it. Another outburst will result in contempt of court charges. Do you understand me?"

Richard's mouth twisted, but he nodded curtly. "Fine."

"Good," Harlow replied, her tone clipped. "To reiterate, the plea agreement includes twenty years of incarceration without parole, followed by twenty years of probation with GPS monitoring, lifetime registration as a sex offender, and a financial contribution of thirty-five percent of your monthly disposable income to the victim's recovery fund, with an optional settlement clause. You also agree to surrender all parental rights to the child resulting from your actions. Do you understand and accept these terms?"

Richard's nostrils flared. "I get it. Just sign the damn thing."

Harlow's patience snapped. "Mr. Perez, you are now in contempt of court. That's an additional six months added to your sentence. Watch your language. Do you have anything further to add?"

Richard rolled his eyes. "Unbelievable," he muttered.

"Mr. Perez, you are now in contempt of court for a *second* time. That's an additional six months added to your sentence. Do you have anything further to add?" Her tone and look were as if they were chiseled out of stone.

Jack Hartford's face turned ashen as he leaned toward his client. "Richard, please. Stop. Just accept the deal and be done with it."

Richard's defiance flared anew. "Oh, so now I'm supposed to grovel? Fine. Take all of it," he snapped, his voice dripping with sarcasm. Under his breath, he muttered, "Bitch."

The courtroom froze.

Judge Harlow's eyes narrowed as her voice cut through the air like steel. "Excuse me, Mr. Perez? Did you just call me a bitch?"

Richard's face paled, but he didn't answer.

"Very well," Harlow said, her tone frosty. "For your blatant disrespect and continued defiance, I am modifying the financial terms of your plea agreement. You will now contribute fifty-five percent of your monthly disposable income to the victim's recovery fund. Additionally, I am imposing consecutive sentences for your contempt of court charges. That's six months for each instance, for a total of one and a half years, to be served *after* your initial twenty-year sentence."

Jack Hartford's voice was almost a whisper. "Your Honor, may I have a moment to confer with my client?"

Harlow's gaze didn't waver. "You may, but my decision stands."

Jack turned to Richard, his voice desperate. "Richard, stop this now. You're only making it worse."

Richard glared at him but remained silent.

Scott Miller stood, his voice measured. "Your Honor, the state is satisfied with these modifications and supports your decision."

Harlow nodded curtly. "Mr. Perez, now do you understand the gravity of your actions and accept the terms of this plea agreement?"

Richard's shoulders sagged. "Yeah, I get it. Whatever."

"Let the record show that the defendant has accepted the plea agreement," Harlow stated firmly. "This court is adjourned."

The gavel came down with a resounding crack, and the courtroom buzzed with whispers as Richard was led away, his defiance now subdued.

Two officers flanked Richard as the bailiff guided him to the exit. As one opened the door, Richard jerked violently, forcing the officers to grab him by the arms. "This isn't over!" he yelled, his voice echoing in the courtroom. He glared over his shoulder at Brittney and her family. "You're all liars! You'll pay for this!"

The officers tightened their grip, dragging him out as his protests continued. The door slammed shut behind him, leaving the courtroom in silence.

A collective sigh of relief filled the room. Jack turned to Scott, extending his hand. "Well, that was… something. No hard feelings, Scott."

Scott shook his hand firmly, his expression a mix of exhaustion and satisfaction. "None at all, Jack. You did what you could. Sometimes, clients just don't listen."

Jack nodded, his voice soft. "Good luck with everything."

As Jack turned to leave, he paused beside the bench where Brittney sat, her hands trembling as she clutched the charms around her neck. His expression softened, and he hesitated for a moment before speaking.

"Miss Brittney," he began, his tone careful and measured, "I truly hope everything works out for you. I can't express enough how hard…" He paused, searching for the right words. "How hard this has been for everyone. You've shown remarkable strength. I wish you and your family the best."

Brittney looked up, startled, but managed a small nod. "Thank you, sir," she whispered.

Jack gave a brief nod in return and walked away, his shoulders heavy with the weight of the case.

Scott turned toward Brittney, kneeling to her level. "Brittney, it's over now. Really over. You were brave, and you've done more than anyone could have asked of you."

Brittney's eyes filled with tears as she whispered, "It's really over?"

Scott nodded. "Yes. He can't hurt you or your family anymore."

Stephanie and Brian leaned in, wrapping their arms around Brittney as she broke into soft sobs. Brian gently stroked her hair, his voice soothing. "Because of you, we're all safe, and he can't hurt another woman, Brittney."

Judge Harlow quietly exited the bench, her face softening as she glanced toward the family. Gloria and Umi exchanged looks of quiet relief, their hands clasped tightly as they rose to leave.

Scott stood and stepped back, allowing the family their moment. As the courtroom emptied, Brittney's sobs quieted, replaced by a small, shaky smile as she looked at Stephanie and Brian. "Thank you," she whispered, her voice barely audible.

Brian squeezed her hand. "You're stronger than you think, Britt."

The group slowly made their way out, the weight of the trial lifting with every step. Outside the courtroom, the sun broke through the clouds, casting a warm glow over the steps. For the first time in months, Brittney felt more than just a flicker of hope.

*****

Later that night, at Umi's house, the twins took their showers and then sat on the floor. Brian braided their hair while they talked. Umi and Gloria played cards at the table, giving the room to the teens. After he finished with Stephanie, Brian excused himself and went to the bathroom. When he returned, he stepped into the kitchen. The soft strains of jazz floated through the living room, setting a calm and easy mood. Stephanie and Brittney were on the couch, their heads close together as Brittney sketched something on her notepad.

"No, no," Stephanie said, waving a hand for emphasis, "make it flowier. Like it's caught in the breeze. See?"

Brittney laughed and nodded, erasing a small line. "Like this? Or do you want more detail on the edges?"

"Perfect! Maybe some flowers around the hem, you know, just to give it that little extra something." Stephanie's grin widened as she saw her idea come to life.

Brian walked in from the kitchen with three cans of soda balanced precariously in his hands, his expression exaggeratedly focused. He made a dramatic show of setting them on the table without spilling and plopped down on the couch with a groan of mock exhaustion.

"Loves, we need a serious discussion about some of the wedding details," he began, leaning back into the cushions.

Brittney and Stephanie looked at him, small smiles on their faces as Brittney asked, "What's up?"

He folded his hands as if ready to give a presentation. "The moms are all over me about wedding details. I'm going to need you two to step up and save me."

Stephanie raised an eyebrow, smirking as she leaned back. "Oh, so now you need our help? Big guy can't handle a little planning pressure?"

"It's not pressure," Brian replied, placing a hand on his chest as if wounded. "It's the interrogations. 'What's the color scheme? What theme? What's the vibe?' It's relentless."

Brittney giggled, setting her sketchpad aside. "And here I thought you were the calm and collected one. Picking colors can't be *that* hard, Brian."

Brian pointed dramatically at her sketchpad. "Says the artist! You could do this in your sleep. Me? I'm just trying not to drown in the sea of questions!"

Stephanie laughed, leaning forward. "All right, Mr. Groom, let's start simple. Do you have any ideas? Or do we need to swoop in and rescue you?"

Brian sighed in mock relief. "Rescue sounds great. I'm thinking something classy but nothing over the top."

Brittney tapped her pencil against her lips thoughtfully. "How about a warm palette? Burgundy, cream, and gold. It's elegant but still cozy."

Brian nodded slowly, considering her suggestion. "Does that fit in with a sunset at Kensington Lake? Last week, you both mentioned it, so I checked, and it's free for the first weekend in August—the 6th. I was thinking we could have the day at the lake with fun and games, use the yurts for changing, and then have the ceremony at dusk."

Brittney's eyes took on a dreamy glow. "That's a perfect setting, Brian. Those colors would look incredible with the sunset."

Brian raised his eyebrows in approval. "Not bad, Britt. I like that. Steph?"

Stephanie beamed, her excitement palpable. "I'm in. That sounds gorgeous. Britt's got an eye for this stuff."

Footsteps approached from the dining room. Umi and Gloria entered, their curiosity clearly piqued by the lively conversation.

"What's all this about a warm palette? Burgundy, cream and gold colors?" Umi asked, crossing her arms with a playful smile.

Gloria chuckled, sitting down on the armrest of the couch. "Sounds like the kids are making wedding plans without us."

Brittney waved them in enthusiastically. "We're brainstorming! Brian needed help with ideas, so Steph and I swooped in to save the day."

Stephanie gestured toward Brian with a teasing grin. "Apparently, he's drowning in color schemes and vibes."

Brian leaned forward, tapping his fingers lightly on his soda can. "All right, since everyone's here, let me throw something out for discussion. I've been thinking about how to structure the actual ceremony, and I wanted your opinions before making any decisions. Here's what I'm considering: one big ceremony with everyone together; two smaller ceremonies, one in the morning and one in the evening, but with a single reception; two completely separate ceremonies and receptions, one for each family; or two back-to-back ceremonies, one immediately following the other, with a single big reception for everyone. What do you think?"

Brittney's pencil hovered mid-sketch, her brows furrowing. "Separate ceremonies? That feels disconnected. Wouldn't it feel like two completely different weddings?"

Stephanie nodded. "Yeah, that's a good point. It might be weird to split it up that much."

Umi folded her hands in her lap, her expression thoughtful. "I can see the appeal of two smaller ceremonies, though. It gives each of you your own moment, which might be nice."

"But," Gloria interjected, "that also means more logistics. You'd need to plan two sets of vows, coordinate timing, and make sure guests aren't running back and forth all day. It might make the day feel disjointed."

Brian nodded, staying quiet as the discussion flowed around him.

Brittney tapped her pencil against her lips. "What about the one big ceremony option? It's simpler, and everyone gets to share the same moment. It feels more unified."

Stephanie hesitated, leaning back against the couch. "True, but one big ceremony might mean it's harder to personalize things. If we're doing this at the lake, would the timing work for everyone? And what about the weather? A single outdoor event could be risky."

Gloria gestured with her soda can. "That's why the combined smaller ceremonies could work. You could have one early, with just immediate family, and the second in the evening for everyone else. It splits the focus but keeps it manageable."

Umi nodded slowly. "And you'd only need one reception. That way, the day doesn't feel overcrowded, and you still get the intimacy of smaller gatherings."

Stephanie brightened suddenly. "What about the back-to-back ceremonies idea? We could have one ceremony first, take a short break, and then go straight into the second one. Then it's one big reception after."

Brittney's eyes lit up. "Ooh, I like that! It gives everyone a chance to see both ceremonies but keeps the flow smooth. We don't have to worry about guests coming and going all day."

Gloria nodded thoughtfully. "That could work. It's simple but still lets you make each ceremony unique."

Umi smiled. "And it avoids the logistical nightmare of two separate events while still making space for personalization."

Brian smiled and leaned in. "I really like that. We could use the same theme and decorations for both. I could change my lapel flower to match your dresses unless you both decide on white. Then we'd personalize each ceremony with different vows, the first kiss, and the walk down the aisle."

Brittney grinned. "And some instrumental music between the two ceremonies to signal the transition."

Stephanie clapped her hands together. "And then the music could change to cue everyone that the second ceremony is starting. It's smooth, and it keeps people engaged."

Brian sat back, his posture relaxed. "I was thinking of something like a catered, buffet-style table with a range of choices for everyone, plus an open bar during the reception."

Brittney perked up. "And a dessert bar! Like, different cakes, cookies, pies, and maybe those fancy chocolate fountains."

Stephanie grinned. "Yes! And no birds or rice. We're doing bubbles. It's way more fun, and no one gets hit in the head."

Gloria chuckled. "A dessert bar could be fun. But remember, Brian, you need to make sure there's something for everyone, like vegetarian and gluten-free options."

Umi nodded. "And don't forget the drinks. Are you thinking of signature cocktails or just a mix of everything?"

Brian grinned. "A mix sounds good, but maybe one or two signature drinks to make it special."

Stephanie smirked. "We should name them something wedding-themed. Like, I don't know, 'Happily Ever After Martini' or 'Forever Punch.'"

Brittney laughed. "Ooh, or something cheesy like 'the Knotted Margarita.'"

Brian shook his head, laughing along. "I'll leave the drink names to you two."

Brian added with a sheepish grin. "I've actually already started writing my vows for each of you."

The room fell silent for a moment before Brittney gasped. "You have? Already? Brian, that's so sweet."

Stephanie leaned forward, her expression playful but warm. "What, are you trying to make the rest of us look bad?"

Gloria laughed, giving Brian a teasing nudge. "Overachiever, huh? Umi, we might need to start a betting pool on whether he cries while reading them."

Umi smirked. "Oh, he's definitely crying. I'll put money on him tearing up by the second line."

Brian groaned, covering his face. "I'm glad you're all so supportive."

CHAPTER 33

The spacious family room of the Welch residence buzzed with energy as balloons and banners proudly announced, "It's a Boy!" A long table draped in baby-blue cloth held an array of treats, drinks, and a centerpiece cake adorned with baby booties made of fondant. Brittney, wearing her "Loading Baby: Please Wait" T-shirt, sat on a cozy armchair surrounded by wrapped gifts and a growing pile of opened ones. Laughter and chatter filled the room as guests mingled and celebrated.

Stephanie had dashed upstairs for a moment and now stood in the living room doorway, her T-shirt proclaiming, "I'm the kind of woman that when my feet hit the floor, the devil says, 'Oh crap, she's up.'" She leaned over to give Brian a kiss. "No peeking, and definitely no boys permitted," she teased.

Brian, lounging on the couch with a book in one hand and the TV tuned to his smooth jazz channel, smirked. "No boys permitted? A travesty. But don't blame me when your party's

IQ level drops by at least ten points without my dazzling commentary."

Stephanie rolled her eyes, a smile tugging at her lips. "Just keep answering the door, Einstein. And don't scare off the guests with your dazzling wit." She walked back downstairs, her laugh carrying into the party.

Brian adjusted his posture and opened the front door to welcome a group of familiar faces. "Ashley, Taylor, Amber, Heather," he greeted, stepping aside to let them in. "The stairway to Gift Central is right down there. Just follow the sound of Brittney's giddy squeals."

Heather grinned. "Thanks, Brian. Nice jazz mix you've got going. Classy."

Brian shot her a mock serious look. "Only the best for our sophisticated guests."

Ashley piped up. "You know, Brian, you're like the concierge every party needs."

Brian shrugged, deadpan. "I aim to please, and my tipping jar is right next to the entryway." The girls laughed as they descended to the family room.

A group of older women from Umi and Gloria's church arrived next, exchanging warm greetings with Brian. He recognized some and welcomed others with polite curiosity. "Ladies, down the stairs and to the right. Don't worry; it's the most festive room in the house."

Downstairs, the party was in full swing. Gloria handed out slices of cake while Umi ensured everyone's glasses were filled. Brittney beamed as she unwrapped a tiny pair of baby sneakers, eliciting coos and "Awws" from the crowd.

"Look at these! They're so adorable," Brittney said, holding them up.

Taylor leaned over, grinning. "Now, the baby's wardrobe will be better than ours."

"Speak for yourself," Ashley quipped, popping a mini quiche into her mouth.

Umi chuckled from her seat. "Just wait until he's actually here. You'll be competing for the best-dressed title in no time."

Stephanie appeared with a fresh plate of snacks. "Brittney, don't forget this one. It's from Heather."

Brittney tore into the wrapping paper, revealing a hand-knitted blanket. "Heather, this is beautiful! Did you make this?"

Heather nodded, a blush creeping up her cheeks. "Yeah, my grandma taught me. I figured it'd be something special."

"It's perfect," Brittney said, her voice warm. "Thank you so much."

The group continued their lively conversation, exchanging anecdotes and teasing each other over gift selections. Amber's gift of a "Baby's First Rock Band" set earned laughter and an immediate quip from Gloria: "Brian might steal this for himself."

"I heard that," Brian's voice called from upstairs, causing another round of laughter.

As the party wound down, Brittney stood and raised her glass of sparkling cider. "Thank you all for being here today. I want to share something special with you all. I've decided to name my son Thomas Kaito Cole. Thomas, after Brian's dad, and Kaito, after mine. You've all made this day unforgettable. It means so much to my little one and me."

Cheers erupted, and the group clinked glasses. Upstairs, Brian shook his head with a smile. "No peeking and no boys allowed? I'll just stay here with my jazz and books. Best job ever."

*****

A week later, in the quiet, early hours of the morning, a faint, pained groan broke the silence in Brittney's bedroom. The clock on her nightstand glowed faintly, displaying 4:17 a.m. She stirred the sharp twinge in her abdomen pulling her fully awake. A low gasp escaped her as another contraction rippled through her body. Blinking in the darkness, she realized with a sinking feeling that her bed was damp.

"Oh no," she whispered, struggling to sit up. Her movements were clumsy, hampered by her discomfort. As she swung her legs over the side of the bed, her knee bumped into the nightstand, sending her water glass shattering on the floor. The sound seemed jarringly loud in the quiet house.

A moment later, soft but quick footsteps padded down the hallway, and Umi appeared in the doorway, her face immediately alert. "Brittney, are you okay? What happened?"

"Mom," Brittney said, her voice shaky, "I think… I think my water broke."

Umi's expression shifted instantly to one of calm determination. She stepped into the room, flicking on the bedside lamp. "Okay, we need to get you dressed and ready to go." She glanced at the damp sheets and the shattered glass on the floor. "Don't worry about the mess. Let's focus on you."

"But, Mom," Brittney protested weakly, gesturing at the mess, "I can't just leave this here. I should clean it up."

"Brittney," Umi said firmly, already pulling open a drawer to grab clean clothes, "The mess can wait. The baby cannot. You need to get dressed."

Before Brittney could argue further, Stephanie's voice came from the hallway. "What's going on? I heard a crash." She stepped into the room, rubbing her eyes and taking in the scene.

"Brittney's water broke," Umi explained quickly. "I'm trying to get her ready, but she's worried about cleaning up this mess."

Stephanie's eyes widened for a moment before she quickly moved into action. "I'll take care of it," she said, her voice steady. "You two focus on getting dressed."

Brittney hesitated, then nodded. "Okay. Thanks, Steph."

With Stephanie already grabbing a towel and cleaning supplies, Umi helped Brittney to her feet. Together, they carefully selected comfortable clothes for her to wear. Brittney winced as another contraction tightened her abdomen, leaning heavily on her mother for support.

"Stephanie," Umi called over her shoulder, "please text Gloria and let her know what's going on. Tell her to come over as soon as she can."

"On it," Stephanie replied, her phone already in hand.

By the time they made it downstairs, Gloria was stepping through the front door, fully dressed and ready, her coat buttoned securely. Brian followed close behind, looking both concerned and half-asleep. "How close are the contractions?" Gloria asked, her sharp gaze taking in Brittney's pale face and the way she leaned against Umi.

"We're heading to the hospital; her contractions are about ten minutes apart, and her water broke. How she lasted this long with the contractions, I don't know," Umi said. "I wanted to let you know so you could decide what to do about Stephanie and Brian. It's going to be a long process, so it might be better if they stay here."

"What?" Stephanie cut in, her voice indignant. "I'm not missing this!"

"Me neither," Brian added, stepping forward.

Gloria raised a hand, cutting off the growing debate. "Hold on. Umi's right. It's early labor. It'll be hours before the baby comes. There's no reason for both of you to sit in a hospital waiting room all day."

"But..." Stephanie began, only for Umi to gently rest a hand on her arm.

"We'll call you the moment things start moving quickly," Umi assured her. "You can come to the hospital then."

"I'm not happy about this," Stephanie muttered, crossing her arms.

Before the conversation could escalate, Brittney gasped, doubling over slightly as another contraction hit. "Okay," she panted, "this... this one was worse."

Umi's attention immediately shifted to her daughter. "It's all right, sweetie. Just breathe through it. Gloria, let's get her in the van."

Stephanie and Brian watched as Gloria and Umi supported Brittney out the door and into the waiting vehicle. As they settled her into the backseat, Umi turned to Gloria. "Ready?"

Gloria nodded, glancing back at Brittney with a reassuring smile. "Let's go meet this baby."

With a final wave to Stephanie and Brian, they climbed into the van and pulled out of the driveway, heading for the hospital.

As the door clicked shut, Stephanie sighed and turned to Brian. "I'll go clean up Brittney's bed. It's the least I can do."

Brian nodded. "I'll help."

The two walked upstairs together, the house unusually quiet after the commotion. In Brittney's room, Stephanie began stripping the damp sheets while Brian picked up the shards of glass from the spilled water.

"You think she'll be okay?" Brian asked softly, placing the glass pieces carefully into a trash bag.

Stephanie paused, clutching the bundled sheets. "Yeah. Mom and Gloria have got this. And Brittney's strong, even when she doesn't think she is."

Brian smiled faintly. "She's lucky to have you. You're always there for her."

Stephanie glanced at him, her expression softening. "That's what sisters do. And Brittney's lucky to have all of us. You included."

They worked in comfortable silence for a few moments before Brian spoke again. "Do you think the baby's room is ready? You know, just in case something was missed?"

Stephanie raised an eyebrow. "It should be. But let's check."

Brian popped his head into the guest room that had been converted into a nursery. "It's all coming together. Let's make sure it's perfect."

They stepped inside, the faint scent of baby powder in the air. Stephanie adjusted a stack of diapers on the changing table while Brian straightened a small stuffed animal on the crib. When everything seemed in place, Brian turned to her, his expression tender.

He reached out and pulled her gently into an embrace. "You've been amazing through all of this," he murmured, looking down into her eyes. "Brittney, the baby, everything. I don't know what any of us would do without you."

Stephanie's cheeks flushed as she met his gaze. "I could say the same about you, Brian. You've been my rock through all of this."

Their breaths mingled as Brian leaned closer, their lips meeting in a long, soft kiss that seemed to stretch time. The embrace deepened, both of them lost in the moment until Brian gently broke away, his face flushed.

"Wow," he said, stumbling over his words. "That was... I mean... we should... um, calm down."

Stephanie's heart raced as she nodded, equally flustered. "Yeah. Calm. Definitely."

Without another word, they exchanged a silent agreement and headed downstairs. Curling up together on the couch, Brian turned on the TV, settling on his favorite smooth jazz channel, providing a gentle soundtrack to their quiet, shared moment. Stephanie rested her head on his shoulder, their fingers intertwined as the soothing music filled the room. Gradually, the tension of the early morning melted away, and the two drifted off to sleep, wrapped in each other's warmth.

*****

Hours later, a faint buzzing broke the peaceful quiet of the room. Stephanie stirred but didn't fully wake until the buzzing turned into a persistent ringtone. Groaning softly, she fumbled to find her phone, eventually pulling it from underneath her. Blinking at the screen, she answered groggily.

"Hello?"

"Stephanie, it's Gloria," came the warm but slightly hurried voice. "Everything's fine, but it's time for you and Brian to come to the hospital. Brittney's progressing, and it won't be too much longer."

Stephanie sat up, her heart racing despite Gloria's reassurances. "Okay, we'll get ready and head over now. Thanks for letting us know."

As she ended the call, Brian stirred beside her. "What's up?" he asked, his voice thick with sleep.

"That was Gloria," Stephanie replied, nudging him gently. "We need to head to the hospital. It's almost time."

Within minutes, they were in Umi's car, Brian at the wheel. The tension in the air was palpable, but Brian, ever the optimist, broke the silence. "I was never officially told, so what's the baby's name going to be?"

"Thomas Kaito Cole," Stephanie answered, a small smile tugging at her lips. "Thomas for your dad and Kaito for ours. Brittney told us at the baby shower."

Brian nodded, a wistful look in his eyes. "Tommy... I like it. I'll teach him how to ride a bike, play catch, maybe even show him how to rebuild a car engine."

Stephanie giggled, her nerves momentarily forgotten. "He'll be a newborn, Brian. You've got a few years before all that."

Brian shrugged, grinning. "Never hurts to plan ahead. I'll be the dad..." He trailed off, leaving the thought unfinished as they approached the hospital parking lot.

Gloria met them at the entrance, her expression a mix of calm and excitement. "Right on time," she said, ushering them inside. "Come on, Brittney's doing great." Glancing at Brian, "She's been asking for you."

They followed her through the sterile corridors to Brittney's room. Inside, Brittney lay propped up against the pillows, her face pale but glowing with anticipation. Umi sat by her side, holding her hand and speaking softly.

"Hey, you made it," Brittney said weakly, her eyes lighting up at the sight of them.

Stephanie rushed to her side, squeezing her other hand. "Of course. How are you feeling?"

"Tired. Excited. A little scared," Brittney admitted.

Brian stood back, his hands in his pockets, offering her a reassuring smile. "You're doing amazing, Britt. You've got this."

Just then, Brittney's face twisted in pain, and she clutched the sheets tightly. "Another one," she gasped, her breath coming in short bursts.

The door opened, and a nurse entered, clipboard in hand. "How's our mama doing?" she asked brightly, moving to Brittney's side.

"She's hanging in there," Umi replied.

The nurse checked Brittney's stats and adjusted the monitor. "You're doing just fine," she said reassuringly. "It won't be long now. Keep breathing through those contractions. You're almost there."

When the nurse left, Brittney turned her gaze to Brian. "Brian," she said softly, reaching out her hand.

He stepped closer, taking her hand in his and pressing a gentle kiss to her knuckles. "Yes, my love?"

Their eyes locked, and Brittney's voice wavered with emotion. "I have one wish."

Brian leaned in slightly, his voice low and steady. "Anything. You know I'll do anything for you."

She took a deep breath, her fingers tightening around his. "I know you said you would be the Daddy, and I love that. But, umm, would you... would you be the father of our baby?"

Brian's eyes widened, and his breath caught in his throat. "Brittney... are you sure?" he asked, his voice thick with emotion.

A soft smile curved her lips as she nodded. "Yes. I've never been more sure of anything."

Before he could respond, another contraction rippled through her, and she winced, gripping his hand tightly. Brian held her gaze, his heart pounding.

"You know it, I'll be the father, the daddy, and all of the other titles that come with being a parent," he said, his voice trembling but resolute. "I'll be there for both of you. Always."

Tears filled Brittney's eyes, and she whispered, "Thank you," as another contraction claimed her focus. Stephanie and Umi exchanged glances, their own eyes glistening as the gravity of the moment settled over the room.

A few minutes later, the door opened again, and a different nurse entered. She was slightly older, with a calm demeanor that instantly reassured everyone in the room. "Hello, everyone. I'm just here to check on our mama," she said with a warm smile, moving to Brittney's side.

She carefully examined Brittney's stats and adjusted the monitors. Satisfied, she turned to Brittney. "Everything looks good. You're progressing nicely. Now, before things move along too much, let's get a couple of details squared away. Have you decided on a name for the baby?"

Brittney's face lit up despite her exhaustion. Soft, happy tears glistened in her eyes as she answered, "Thomas Kaito Cole." She paused for a moment, glancing at Brian, and added, "And the father is Brian Richard Cole."

As she spoke, she gave Brian's hand a gentle squeeze, her emotions radiating through the simple gesture. Just as she finished speaking, another contraction surged through her, and her grip on Brian's hand tightened considerably.

Brian winced, his eyes widening slightly. "Wow, Britt, you're stronger than you look," he said with a forced chuckle, shaking his hand out as the contraction subsided.

The nurse chuckled softly. "That's just a preview, Dad. You might want to prepare yourself."

At that moment, the head nurse walked in, her authoritative yet kind presence filling the room. She took a quick survey of the situation and asked, "So, Miss Brittney, your contractions are about three minutes apart, which means it's about that time. Who's staying in the room with you?"

Umi's eyes flicked to Brian, a knowing smile playing on her lips. "Not Brian," she said teasingly. "He'll either lose it the moment Brittney makes a noise or pass out when it's time to cut the cord."

Everyone burst into a nervous laugh, and Brian raised his hands defensively. "Hey, I can handle more than you think!" he said, though the faint flush on his cheeks betrayed his nerves.

Umi patted his shoulder affectionately. "I think we'll play it safe. Gloria and I will stay with her."

The head nurse nodded. "Perfect. Everyone else, you'll need to wait in the lounge. We'll let you know as soon as there's news."

With that, the room began to clear. Stephanie gave Brittney's hand a final squeeze and whispered, "You've got this," before stepping out. Brian lingered for a moment, his gaze steady on Brittney. "I'll be right outside if you need me," he said softly.

Brittney managed a small, grateful smile. "Thank you, Brian."

As the door closed behind them, the room grew quieter, leaving Umi, Gloria, and Brittney to prepare for the final stages of labor.

*****

Two hours later, the head nurse emerged into the waiting area where Brian and Stephanie sat, their expressions a mix of nerves and anticipation. The nurse's face broke into a wide smile as she approached them. "Well, Mr. Cole," she announced warmly, "congratulations! You're the proud papa of a brand-new, bouncing baby boy!"

Brian's grin stretched ear to ear as he shot to his feet. "Wow! That's incredible! How's everyone doing?"

The nurse nodded reassuringly. "Mama is doing just fine. She's absolutely exhausted and ready to sleep, but she's healthy and happy. And little Thomas is in perfect health. He's got a good set of lungs, let me tell you!"

Stephanie let out a relieved laugh, clasping her hands together. "That's wonderful news."

The nurse's eyes sparkled as she continued. "We'll need a little time to finish cleaning up and getting everyone settled. Once that's done, I'll bring you back to visit for a few minutes. But just a few; both Mama and Thomas need their rest."

Brian nodded eagerly, his excitement palpable. "Of course, whatever they need. Thank you so much!"

The nurse gave them a final reassuring smile before heading back through the doors, leaving Brian and Stephanie to share a moment of joy and anticipation.

*****

Inside the hospital room, Brittney lay propped up against a mountain of pillows, her face radiant despite her exhaustion. She cradled baby Thomas in her arms, her gaze fixed lovingly on his tiny features. Umi sat close on one side, her hand resting gently on Brittney's shoulder, while Gloria stood at the foot of the bed, a soft smile lighting her face as she observed the tender scene.

A soft knock on the door signaled the arrival of Stephanie and Brian, who entered quietly, their movements careful as if not to disturb the tranquil atmosphere. Stephanie's eyes widened as they fell on the baby, her hands flying to her mouth.

"Oh, Britt," Stephanie whispered, her voice thick with emotion, "He's... perfect."

Brian stood frozen for a moment, his gaze locked on the tiny bundle in Brittney's arms. "Wow," he said softly, stepping closer. "Look at him."

Brittney's smile grew as she glanced up at them. "Come meet your nephew," she said, her voice full of warmth.

Stephanie moved to the bedside, peering down at Thomas, her eyes shimmering with tears. "Hi, Tommy," she murmured, reaching out to gently stroke his tiny hand. "Welcome to the world, little one."

Brian stood beside her, his gaze soft and reverent. "He's so... small," he said, his voice barely above a whisper.

Brittney chuckled softly. "Not so small when you're the one delivering him," she said with a tired but playful grin, earning a laugh from everyone in the room.

Umi leaned in, her voice gentle. "He has your nose, Brittney."

Gloria added with a knowing smile. "And your stubborn little chin."

Brittney looked down at her son, brushing her thumb lightly over his cheek. "Our son is perfect," she whispered.

Brian reached out hesitantly, glancing at Brittney for permission. She nodded, and he gently touched the baby's tiny hand, which reflexively wrapped around his finger. "Strong grip already," Brian said with a quiet laugh. "He's going to be a fighter, just like his mom."

Stephanie wrapped an arm around Brian's waist, leaning into him as they both stared down at Thomas. "You're going to do amazing things, little guy," she said softly, her voice filled with hope. She looked up at Brian. "Now I want one of my own," she said softly.

Gloria and Umi looked at each other, then at Stephanie. "That would be awesome. Just wait a bit, okay?"

There was a small round of light laughter from everyone as Stephanie blushed. Slowly, the room was filled with a comfortable silence, the kind that only comes from shared love and joy. Brittney's smile never wavered as she held her son close, surrounded by the people she loved most in the world.

CHAPTER 34

The gravel crunched under the car tires as Umi parked Gloria's van near the designated parking area. Stephanie sat in the passenger seat, her hands fidgeting nervously with the hem of her dress, while Brittney leaned forward between the seats, craning her neck to get the first glimpse of the venue.

Brittney looked at her mom in the mirror. "Mom, is Tommy going to be okay?"

Umi smiled. "Yes, dear, he'll be fine. I've known Vicky Johnson for years; she's raised her family of five. Little Tommy is in safe hands. And when we get him, Gloria and I will take care of him until you get back from your honeymoon. Now, sweetheart, stop worrying about your little man and enjoy yourself, okay?"

Brittney leaned up to Umi's cheek, kissing her. "Thank you, Mom," she said in a soft voice.

"Wait," Stephanie said, her brows furrowing. "Isn't that your car over there, Mom? I wonder when they got here."

472

Umi chuckled as she put the minivan in park. "All I know is Brian said he'd have to be here real early when Gloria and I talked about me using the van."

As the doors opened and they stepped out, a cheerful voice greeted them. "Good morning, ladies!"

Turning, they spotted a familiar face, Mr. Lyle, one of their favorite teachers from high school, dressed in medieval-themed garb, complete with a dark green tunic and a leather strap holding a camera.

"Mr. Lyle!" Stephanie exclaimed, her surprise quickly giving way to a smile. "What are you doing here?"

He laughed, lifting his camera slightly. "Today, I'm not Mr. Lyle; I'm your photographer. Brian recruited me to capture everything: your reactions, your moments, and, honestly, as much as I can without getting in trouble with the brides."

Brittney giggled. "Trouble? With us?"

"Brian was very clear," Mr. Lyle replied with mock seriousness, "that I'm to document the day without interfering with the ladies of the hour. You two are intimidating, you know."

The girls laughed, and Umi chuckled softly. "It's wonderful to see you, Mr. Lyle. Brian's lucky to have you."

Mr. Lyle adjusted his camera strap, stepping aside with a slight bow. "Shall we begin? I'll lead the way, capturing the magic as we go."

They approached the "Troll" station first, an intricately decorated booth manned by Deputy White in medieval garb, complete with a comical faux sword at her side. On the table lay a large leather-bound guest book, its pages marked with delicate calligraphy. Beside it was a small basket holding gold medallions on ribbon necklaces.

"Welcome!" Deputy White said with a grin, gesturing grandly toward the guestbook. "Please sign in, and don't forget your medallions. These mark you as honored members of the wedding party."

Stephanie picked up one of the medallions and turned it over in her hand. The polished gold shimmered in the sunlight, and an elegant engraving read, "Stephanie & Brittney's Wedding." When she flipped it over, it read "Brittney & Stephanie's Wedding."

Brittney picked up one. "These are gorgeous," Brittney murmured.

Stephanie looked up. "Did Brian arrange for you to be here?"

Deputy White smiled. "Well, sort of. He told us that the event needed security and suggested for us to attend; Grace and I volunteered for security detail for the entire event."

As the group leaned over to sign the guestbook, Stephanie noticed the first few names scrawled at the top of the page. "Look at this," she said softly, pointing. "Gloria signed first. And Brian's name is right after hers."

"Symbolic," Umi said with a smile. "He wanted to honor her, even in the little things."

The twins exchanged a glance, their smiles warm as they wrote their names below.

Deputy White gestured to a small, festively decorated cart parked nearby, loaded with neatly wrapped wedding gifts. "And over here, we have the gift procession cart. Everything you see will be part of a ceremonial parade later before it's secured in Gloria's van."

"It's amazing," Stephanie said, her eyes scanning the cart, which was adorned with flowers, ribbons, and small pennants waving in the breeze. "Brian really thought of everything."

As they began their tour of the venue, Stephanie and Brittney's amazement only grew. They stopped to peek into the "Yea Bridal Princes" yurt first, marveling at the plush cushion chairs, small medieval-style tables, and lanterns that gave the space a warm, inviting glow.

"This is so cool," Stephanie said, running her fingers along the edge of a table. "Even the little details are perfect."

They moved on to the "Yea Bridal Tavern" yurt, where a variety of medieval-inspired snacks and drinks were already set up. Brittney grabbed a small goblet filled with fruit-infused water. "It's like stepping into a movie," she said, grinning.

When they opened the flap of the next yurt, they were surprised to find a woman arranging decorations inside. She was dressed in a simple yet elegant medieval gown, her hair tied back with a decorative ribbon.

"Hello there!" the woman greeted with a warm smile. "You must be Stephanie and Brittney."

Mr. Lyle stepped forward, gesturing toward her. "Girls, this is my wife, Hannah. She's assisting me today."

"It's nice to meet you," Stephanie said, extending her hand.

Hannah shook her hand with a laugh. "The pleasure's mine. You've got quite the groom; he's been so detailed about every part of this day. He even hired me to document the guests and everything happening behind the scenes. And of course…" she added with a conspiratorial smile, "Brian himself."

Brittney raised an eyebrow, smirking. "Brian let himself be documented? That's surprising."

Hannah chuckled. "Let's just say he didn't have much of a choice. We're capturing the whole story today."

As they left the yurt and continued their tour, Mr. Lyle kept snapping photos and pointing out details Brian had meticulously arranged: the scroll signs, the lanterns in the trees, and the bubble machines set up near the ceremony platform — everything they talked about having.

They could also see parts of the adjacent medieval event. The marketplace buzzed with activity, offering handmade garb, jewelry, and trinkets while a fighting demonstration took place in a cleared area. The clanging of swords and the cheers of spectators added to the lively medieval ambiance. Nearby, a herald's voice rang out, announcing an upcoming contest. "Let it be known that a tournament is to be held!"

Finally, they reached the "Yea Brides" yurt. Brittney opened the flap and gasped. Inside, the yurt was breathtakingly elegant. The soft cushions, gilded mirror, carved vanity, and draped tapestries created a space fit for royalty. But what caught their eyes immediately were three covered shapes hanging from a nearby rack. Large blankets emblazoned with the words "Contents are Top Secret" were draped over the dresses.

Stephanie burst into laughter. "Seriously? Top secret?"

Brittney joined in, crossing her arms with a mock pout. "We can't even see our own dresses? Brian's gone all out on this secrecy thing."

Umi stepped closer, her gaze softening as she took in the sight of the space. "He really thought of everything. It's like he's woven all your dreams together." For a moment, quietly marveling at how much Brian had done, "I underestimated him."

Stephanie looked at her mom. "And now I know why he was so secretive, so we'd be surprised. Well, I am for sure."

Mr. Lyle lowered his camera briefly and smiled. "Brian wanted this space to be special, a little retreat for you both and the moms."

Stephanie walked over to the dresses and lightly touched the edge of one of the blankets. "I wonder if he actually picked these out. What do you think, Britt?"

"If he did," Brittney said with a grin, "then I'm sure they're perfect. Brian wouldn't go this far without nailing every detail."

Just as they were about to sit down, a soft knock came on the yurt's frame. Turning, they saw an older woman dressed in a regal medieval gown, complete with a delicate crown that gleamed softly in the filtered light.

"Good morning, Baroness, Princesses," she said warmly. "May I come in?"

Stephanie and Brittney exchanged a look before Brittney answered with a smile. "Of course! Please come in."

The woman stepped inside gracefully; her gown was a rich emerald green fabric, adorned with gold and silver embroidery, bell-shaped sleeves, and a tight-fitted lace bodice. Her hair, blond and braided with green ribbons, matching her gown. Her coronet, crowned with four points, sparked with gemstones that mirrored the colors of her dress.

She smiled brightly and introduced herself. "I am the Crowned Princess Rowan of Bitter Goose Swamp. It's my honor to be your Second Woman for your wedding day. My job is to assist you in getting ready for your big day."

"Second Woman?" Stephanie asked, her curiosity piqued.

Rowan chuckled lightly. "In medieval traditions, the Second Woman, my honorary title for today, is akin to a chief lady-in-waiting. My role is to ensure everything runs smoothly for the Baroness and the Princesses so you can focus on enjoying your day. I'll also help explain some of the customs and courtesies you will encounter today," she explained to everyone.

"Wow," Brittney said, sinking into one of the cushions. "He really has thought of everything. Yeah, Steph, he surprised me too."

Rowan's gaze softened. "He loves you both dearly. Now, how about we get you into something more fitting for mingling with your guests?"

With that, Rowan approached the rack and dramatically pulled back the blankets, revealing two stunning gowns and a royal robe set. One was a rich lavender, the other a pale, shimmering blue. Both were adorned with delicate embroidery and jeweled accents.

Stephanie and Brittney squealed in delight, rushing forward to inspect the dresses. "They're perfect!" Stephanie said, running her fingers over the fabric.

"Absolutely gorgeous," Brittney agreed. "How does he always know?"

Rowan smiled knowingly. "Shall we get you changed?"

While the twins started changing, Princess Rowan explained some of the customs and courtesies to expect and do, explaining titles and names that should be used when addressing apparent nobility and royalty. Their introduction included a brief summary of some of the activities planned for the day and highly recommended events they should attend.

Sometime later, the girls were dressed, their gowns fitting them perfectly. Rowan carefully pinned small, sparkling tiaras into their hair, stepping back to admire her work. "There," she said with satisfaction. "Now you look the part."

"This is incredible," Stephanie said, turning to catch her reflection in the mirror.

Brittney spun in place, the skirt of her gown twirling elegantly. "I feel like a real princess."

Rowan laughed softly. "Today, you *are* a real princess. Now, you should mingle with your guests, meet people, and enjoy yourselves. There's an appointment at the hairdresser at 4 PM sharp. One of the important events today is the Knights' Challenge, where your ring bearers will be decided. Don't forget to eat something while you're mixing. It's going to be a long, wonderful day."

Rowan then turned to Umi with a smile. "And as for you, Baroness," she said, producing a simple four-point crown and royal blue robes accented with silver trim and delicate embroidery. The outfit radiated a quiet elegance fitting for someone in a noble role.

Umi blinked in surprise, then laughed. "I love the gown; it's beautiful, but Baroness? Oh no, this is too much!"

"Nonsense," Rowan replied with a playful wink. "Your role is just as important as your daughters'. You're their bridge to the guests and royalty. Shall we get you ready?"

Stephanie and Brittney giggled as Umi reluctantly donned the royal garb. "Mom, you look amazing," Stephanie said.

"Very regal," Brittney added. "You're the queen of all moms."

The lighthearted banter continued as Rowan adjusted the crown on Umi's head and straightened her robes. "Perfect," Rowan said. "Now you're ready to mingle as well. If you need anything or can't find something, ask any of the young men with the red tunics or for me. Okay?"

Both twins nodded. "Yes, Princess," they said in unison.

With that, the girls stepped out of the yurt, their gowns glimmering in the light as they prepared to greet their guests. Umi followed, her confidence growing with each step, as the lively sounds of the medieval event and wedding guests mingling created an atmosphere of joy and anticipation.

*****

The lively sound of the marketplace surrounded them as Umi, Stephanie, and Brittney strolled through rows of stalls brimming with medieval-inspired wares. Vibrant banners fluttered in the light breeze, and the air was alive with the mingled scents of spiced wine, roasted meats, and fresh bread. Vendors called out to passersby, their voices blending with the faint clinking of swords and the distant tune of a minstrel's lute.

"This is unbelievable," Stephanie said, her eyes wide as she surveyed the scene. "It's like stepping into another world."

Brittney giggled, lifting the edge of her lavender gown as they stepped over a small cobblestone path. "Brian didn't just plan a wedding. He planned a full medieval adventure."

"Milady, might I interest you in a fine necklace to match your attire?" a vendor called, holding up a glittering chain of polished stones.

Stephanie flushed, smiling shyly. "Oh, no, thank you, but it's beautiful."

"A fine choice for a princess," the vendor said with a bow, making Brittney burst into laughter.

"Princess?" Brittney teased, nudging Stephanie. "It sounds different from when Brian calls us that. It makes it sound even better."

Stephanie paused and looked at her sister with a small smile. "Did you tell him about our pretend sessions?"

Brittney giggled, a small blush coming to her cheeks. "It may have come up once or twice when you were showering."

Stephanie placed a hand on Brittney's shoulder. "This is him listening to our daydreams!" she said excitedly.

Brittney's blush deepened. "I guess he really does pay attention to us," she answered with a giggle, adding, "Our private twin-whisperer."

Stephanie giggled, nudging Brittney. "Too close. But I can't wait to put that to the test with a kiss," she said in a soft whisper.

Umi chuckled softly, her royal blue gown catching the light as she glanced at a nearby booth adorned with colorful tapestries. A pair of young children dressed as pages hurried past, pausing only to gasp and bow dramatically before her.

"Your Majesty!" one of them exclaimed before running off again, giggling.

"Your Majesty?" Umi repeated, raising a brow at her daughters. "Now I've truly arrived."

The trio dissolved into laughter as they continued weaving through the bustling market. They paused at a leatherworker's stall where Brittney admired intricately tooled belts and then at a baker's cart where Stephanie sampled a sweet, honey-glazed pastry. Everywhere they went, garbed players addressed them with terms of respect, from "Milady" to "Your Grace," adding an enchanting layer of immersion to the experience.

It wasn't until they stopped at a fabric merchant's stall that Stephanie suddenly froze, her eyes narrowing as she stared at a banner hanging nearby. It bore a striking emblem that she recognized from something at school.

"Wait a minute," she said, nudging Brittney and pointing at the banner. "That's Aaron Fitzgerald's!"

Brittney's brow furrowed. "Aaron? You mean Brian's best man?"

"Yeah," Stephanie said, a dawning realization lighting her features. "He's part of the SCA. This isn't *all* Brian; Aaron must have helped with the SCA side of things."

Brittney's jaw dropped before she burst into laughter. "Of course! That sneaky mastermind. No wonder it's so real!"

Umi crossed her arms, a smile tugging at her lips. "Brian probably handled the wedding venue, but Aaron clearly brought the SCA flair. Those two make quite the team."

The realization settled over them as they exchanged amused glances. They wandered further, passing a jeweler's stall where Stephanie tried on a delicate circlet before setting it back with a smile. As they approached another line of stalls, Umi's gaze drifted ahead, catching sight of Gloria near a garb vendor down the way.

"You two keep exploring, have fun, and don't let Brian see you," Umi said, gesturing toward the shops. "I'll catch up with you at that fabric booth over there."

"Got it, Mom," Brittney said with a grin.

Stephanie waved her off, already eyeing a nearby pottery stall. "We won't go far."

Umi made her way toward Gloria, the sound of the market's bustling energy filling the air around her. Gloria stood near a rack of embroidered cloaks, chatting animatedly with a vendor who was gesturing to a bolt of crimson fabric.

"Gloria," Umi called, her smile growing as she approached.

Gloria turned, her face lighting up. "Umi! Isn't this incredible?" Her gown mirrored Umi's royal blue in color, but the accents were distinct; elegant gold embroidery swirled along the edges, giving it a regal yet understated charm. The simple four-point crown she wore matched Umi's perfectly, solidifying their complementary roles for the day.

"It's beyond anything I imagined," Umi said, glancing around. "Brian and Aaron really pulled off something extraordinary."

Gloria laughed, adjusting the edge of her sleeve. "Brian's attention to detail is unmatched. But I think Aaron's passion for the SCA brought everything to life."

Umi nodded, her gaze softening. "He's done so much for the girls. This entire day feels like their dreams come true."

"He wanted it to be perfect," Gloria said warmly. Then, with a mischievous smile, she added, "And speaking of Brian..." She gestured toward the archery field by the lake, where figures dressed in rich medieval garb were gathered.

As she was talking, the twins walked up, following Gloria's gesture.

Umi followed Gloria's gesture, her eyes landing on a tall figure in princely attire, complete with a flowing red cape.

483

Brian stood confidently, a bow in hand, speaking with a group of other garbed participants.

"The archery field?" Umi said, her brow arching in surprise.

Gloria's expression softened. "I think when he explained why he stopped shooting in the van, I guess he started thinking about it again. On the way here, he confessed that if Brittney could be as strong as she was, then he could be strong too."

Umi's throat tightened as she watched Brian draw back the bowstring, releasing an arrow that flew true toward the target. The sun caught the edge of his cape, and for a moment, he looked every bit the prince of the day.

"He's remarkable," Umi murmured.

Stephanie smiled. "Wow. It's wonderful he's shooting again."

Gloria smiled knowingly. "Yes, it is. I was told there are a number of events we should catch and some foods we should try. We've got plenty of time to keep Brian from seeing you two," as she winked at the twins.

For the rest of the morning and into the afternoon, the four of them moved through the marketplace and the food court. Most of the food vendors had samples for them to try.

The booming voice of a herald echoed across the field and into the marketplace. "Come one! Come all! The Knight's Challenge is soon to start! Make your way to the field of arms and watch as these fearless knights fight for their heirs to bear the title of ring bearer at the handfastings to come this evening!" his voice boomed through the market.

Brittney smiled. "I love it that Brian had this idea. When he said that he had the ring bearers, I didn't imagine anything like this."

Gloria led the group toward the battlefields. "Yeah, I'm surprised about how much he didn't tell me." Umi and Gloria shared a glance before falling into step together behind the twins. All four felt the anticipation buzzing in the air as the festivities continued.

*****

The archery field was alive with energy, a symphony of laughter, cheers, and the occasional clanging of metal from the nearby battle demonstrations. Vibrant pennants fluttered against the clear sky, and the lake shimmered in the background, casting its reflection onto the bustling competition grounds.

Spectators gathered along the roped-off area, parents and children alike chattering excitedly as they awaited the start of the Knight's Challenge. Vendors moved through the crowd, offering mugs of spiced cider and small pastries, adding to the festive atmosphere. At the center of it all stood the herald, a rotund man in a flamboyant crimson tunic who raised his staff to command attention.

"Lords and Ladies, gathered nobility and honored guests!" the herald boomed. "Today, we will witness a spectacle of courage, skill, and comedy as noble knights fight for the honor of their chosen heirs!" He gestured grandly toward a group of men, women, and young adults dressed in various levels of medieval attire.

At his words, the crowd erupted into cheers, and the participants waved theatrically, some offering exaggerated bows or flexing their "strength" to the delight of the audience.

The herald continued. "The victors of this grand challenge shall earn for their chosen youths the honor of serving as bearers of the handfasting rings for our noble Princess

Stephanie and Princess Brittney later tonight! Let the challenge commence!"

The spectators clapped and cheered as the judges were announced. "Presiding over today's event, we are honored by the presence of Princess Stephanie and Princess Brittney, Baroness Umi and Baroness Gloria, and the Crowned Princess Rowan herself!" Each judge stepped forward with a wave, their titles earning applause and delighted murmurs from the crowd.

Stephanie leaned toward Brittney with a grin. "It feels like we're in a movie."

"We *are* the movie," Brittney quipped, waving like royalty to the crowd.

Umi adjusted her four-point crown and glanced at Gloria with a smile. "I hope they don't expect us to knight anyone."

Gloria laughed. "I'll knight someone if they hand me a foam sword."

The competitors lined up for the first challenge, their targets positioned at varying distances. Lightweight bows and child-safe arrows were provided, much to the relief of several novices. The herald raised his staff. "Test your aim, noble knights! Steady your hand, for accuracy, shall win this trial!"

A tall man in flowing green garb stepped up first, dramatically raising his bow. "For the honor of my daughter!" he declared, earning a mix of cheers and giggles.

His shot wobbled midair and landed just outside the target. He clasped his chest theatrically. "Alas, my courage outweighed my aim!"

The crowd roared with laughter as the next competitor stepped up. Some proved surprisingly adept, sending their arrows close to the bullseye, while others created comedic chaos: one shot went so far astray it nicked a nearby pennant, and another arrow bounced harmlessly to the ground after an enthusiastic but poorly aimed release.

The judges exchanged amused glances, jotting down notes and chuckling as the herald declared the end of the first round.

The energy in the crowd doubled as competitors stepped into the makeshift arena, wielding foam swords with varying levels of confidence. The herald stepped forward, his voice booming. "Knights! Prove your valor with a clash of arms! Remember, no quarter need be given, but dramatic deaths are highly encouraged!"

The first match saw two burly participants circling each other, their foam swords raised. One let out a battle cry that was equal parts intimidating and ridiculous, charging forward only to trip over his own feet. His opponent froze for a moment before dramatically "falling" to the ground, declaring, "Your sheer willpower has undone me!"

The crowd erupted in laughter as the "fallen" knight offered a hand to his "victor."

Other matches followed, filled with over-the-top theatrics and good-natured antics. One participant flailed wildly, pretending to be outmatched, while another knighted a "fallen" opponent mid-battle, declaring them "an honorary hero of foam." The judges could barely contain their laughter, with Brittney wiping tears from her eyes.

The final challenge brought a mix of skill and comedy as competitors donned practice foils. The herald raised his voice once more. "Knights! Let your blades sing, and may the spirit of chivalry guide your hands!"

A wiry competitor with surprising finesse quickly became a crowd favorite, weaving and dodging with flair. His opponent, meanwhile, spun in circles, claiming to be "summoning the winds of valor" before "succumbing" to a single tap.

Another match featured an opponent who refused to attack, instead delivering a heartfelt monologue about "the futility of war" until their foil was gently plucked from their hands by a chuckling judge.

As the fencing round concluded, the crowd gave a standing ovation. The judges convened, deliberating amid light-hearted banter before finally reaching a decision.

The herald stepped forward, raising his arms. "Lords and Ladies! The judges have spoken, and four valiant youths shall bear the honor of carrying the fasting rings!"

The children, now outfitted in shimmering garb fit for royalty, joined their victorious sponsors in the arena. The crowd cheered as the winners bowed theatrically, their smiles wide as they looked toward the brides.

Umi leaned toward Gloria, her voice warm. "This was perfect. Brian and Aaron couldn't have planned it better."

Gloria smiled knowingly. "They do have their moments."

As the winners were escorted off to prepare for their roles, the herald's voice echoed once more. "The Knight's Challenge is concluded! Let the festivities continue!"

The field transformed into a scene of joyful mingling as the next phase of the wedding celebration began.

*****

Soft chatter and laughter filled the air as Stephanie, Brittney, and the two young girl ring-bearers sat in a cozy corner of the bridal tent. The hairstylist, a friendly woman with a knack for calming nerves, expertly worked her fingers through Stephanie's long hair, braiding it into an intricate crown around her head. Tiny flowers and ribbons in shades of burgundy, cream, gold, and lavender, the wedding's theme colors, were deftly woven into the braids, adding a delicate, ethereal touch.

Brittney sat beside her sister, her own hair already done in a matching style but with a blue ribbon. She turned to the young girl, who fidgeted excitedly in her chair. "You're going to look beautiful," Brittney said with a warm smile. "A mini princess."

The girl's eyes widened with delight as she clutched her hands in her lap. "Really?"

"Absolutely," Stephanie added. "You're part of the wedding party now, so you get the royal treatment."

The girl's mother, standing nearby, beamed with pride. "Just remember what we talked about. Walk slowly, keep your hands steady, and smile big when you get to the altar."

Umi, sitting in her elegant gown nearby, chuckled softly. "And don't worry. If anything goes wrong, it'll be the kind of thing we laugh about later."

The hairstylist moved on to the last of the young girls, who sat straighter in her chair, her excitement barely contained. Nearby, the second girl admired her freshly braided hair in the mirror, turning her head side to side with a delighted grin. As the ribbons and flowers were woven into her hair, her giggles filled the tent, blending with the soft rustle of gowns being adjusted and last-minute touches being made to everyone's garb.

Meanwhile, in the groom's tent, Brian stood before a mirror, adjusting the deep burgundy sash that draped across his princely tunic. The air was filled with the sound of cheerful banter as Aaron helped one of the young boy ring bearers into a tailored tunic that matched the wedding theme. The boy's father offered advice, his tone equal parts proud and amused.

"Now remember, kiddo, you're carrying something very important. No tossing it like a frisbee," he teased, earning a round of laughter from the tent.

Aaron turned, a grin tugging at the corner of his mouth. "I'd love to see that happen. It'd make this wedding unforgettable."

Brian groaned, shaking his head with a laugh. "Please don't give them ideas. I've worked way too hard to see this go off the rails."

"Relax," Aaron said, clapping Brian on the shoulder. "You've thought of everything. The whole day's been perfect so far."

Brian looked at his best friend. "Have you seen them? Do you know if they had a good day?" His voice showed concern.

Aaron gently slapped his shoulder. "Yes, and yes. Okay? I even checked with your mom; she said the girls are having a day they will never forget."

The second young boy ring bearer stood on a small stool as his mother carefully adjusted his cape. "All right, my knight. Stand tall and look sharp," she said, tapping his chin playfully. "You've got an important job today."

The boy puffed out his chest, grinning as he practiced his most serious expression.

The mood in the tent was lively, full of warmth and humor. Brian adjusted his cuffs, a faint smile playing on his lips as he listened to the camaraderie around him. Just then, the tent flap opened, and Gloria stepped inside, her face glowing with pride.

"There's my son," she said softly, walking over to Brian. Her voice was filled with affection, though her eyes were subtly scanning his face for any signs of nerves. "How's the groom holding up?"

Brian chuckled, running a hand through his hair. "A little anxious, but mostly excited. Everything's gone so smoothly so far."

"Of course it has," Gloria replied, placing a gentle hand on his arm. "I've been watching the girls all morning. They're having the time of their lives. And that's thanks to you."

Brian's smile softened. "They deserve it. Both of them. And it was also because of an army of people helping."

Gloria leaned closer, lowering her voice. "And how about you? Do you need anything? A moment to yourself? I can make something up if you need an escape."

He laughed quietly. "I'm good. This is exactly where I want to be."

"Good," Gloria said, her voice lighter now. "Because the last thing we need is the groom running off to join the archery contest."

Aaron interjected with a laugh. "Oh, I don't know. He'd probably win that, too."

The tent erupted in laughter, and Gloria joined in, her tension melting away as she saw how at ease Brian was. She gave his arm a gentle squeeze. "You're doing wonderfully. Now, I'll leave you to finish up. Just don't keep my girls waiting too long."

"Yes, ma'am," Brian said with a mock salute, earning another laugh from the group.

A few minutes later, as the laughter subsided and the groomsmen busied themselves with last-minute adjustments, the yurt's flap rustled. Father Mike stepped inside, his familiar smile brightening the room. "Good evening, gentlemen. I hope I'm not intruding on a top-secret meeting of knights and squires."

The group chuckled, and Brian turned toward him, grinning. "Not at all, Father. You're just in time."

Father Mike scanned the room, taking in the carefully organized chaos. "Well, Brian, I have to say, you've really created something here, a big, beautiful, heartfelt… mess," he teased, gesturing to the assortment of items strewn across the yurt.

Aaron, standing near the edge of the room, chimed in with a smirk. "If you think *this* is a mess, you should've seen the planning stages. Brian here was drowning in details."

Brian laughed, shaking his head. "He's not wrong, Father. I had a lot of help from Aaron and the rest of the guys to make this work."

Father Mike raised an eyebrow, crossing his arms in mock seriousness. "A lot of help, you say? So you're not the master planner we all thought you were?"

Aaron leaned forward, grinning. "Oh, no. He's just the dreamer. We were the ones running around making his dream happen."

The room erupted into laughter, and Father Mike shook his head, chuckling. "Well, Brian, it sounds like you owe your merry band of knights a round of drinks, after the wedding, of course."

Brian shot Aaron a look of mock betrayal. "Thanks for exposing me, man. I'll remember this."

Aaron clapped him on the shoulder. "You love it, and you know it."

As the laughter died down, the mood shifted. The room grew quieter, the weight of the moment settling over everyone. Father Mike stepped closer to Brian, his expression softening as he placed a hand on his shoulder.

"Brian," he began, his tone steady and sincere, "what you're doing today isn't just unconventional, it's extraordinary. It's a testament to the kind of love that's willing to step outside the ordinary, to take risks for something real and meaningful."

The groomsmen watched in respectful silence as Father Mike continued, his voice taking on a reflective note. "It won't always be easy. There will be days when you feel pulled in a hundred directions, when doubt or exhaustion creeps in. But those are the days when the promises you make today will matter the most."

Brian nodded, his gaze steady, the weight of Father Mike's words sinking in. "Thank you, Father. I'll hold onto that."

Father Mike's hand lingered on Brian's shoulder for a moment before he stepped back, his smile returning. "Good. Now, enough of my wisdom. Let's get you tethered before these princesses decide they need to rescue you instead."

The room erupted into chuckles, the tension easing as the groomsmen resumed their preparations. Father Mike gave Brian a final pat on the shoulder and nodded to Aaron before turning to leave. His presence left behind a calming energy, grounding Brian for the momentous occasion ahead.

*****

Back in the bridal tent, the finishing touches were being made. Umi adjusted Stephanie's gown while Brittney helped one of the young girl ring bearers practice holding a small bouquet.

"Just like that," Brittney said encouragingly. "You've got this."

Stephanie glanced at her reflection in the mirror, her braided hair glimmering with flowers and ribbons. Her voice was soft but full of emotion as she turned to her mother. "Thank you, Mom. For everything."

Umi paused, her hands resting on Stephanie's shoulders. "You don't have to thank me, sweetheart. This is *your* day. And you both deserve every bit of happiness it brings."

As the group prepared to head toward the ceremony, the air was thick with anticipation and joy, each moment building toward the promise of what lay ahead.

Outside the bridal tent, the herald's voice rang out, carrying across the festive grounds. "Lords and Ladies, honored guests, and noble companions! The ceremony is soon to begin! All are invited to witness the handfasting of a Prince to two Princesses in a union of love and destiny!"

CHAPTER 35

T he main ceremony tent was a picture of medieval elegance. Lanterns hung from the tent's supports, casting a soft golden glow over rows of neatly arranged chairs. A rich burgundy runner stretched down the aisle, bordered with scattered petals in cream and gold. The white wooden stage stood at the front, its ivy-draped arch adorned with ribbons in the theme's warm palette. Guests murmured in anticipation as the soft strains of instrumental music filled the air, mingling with the rustle of gowns and tunics.

At the back of the tent, the herald stepped forward, his vibrant voice resonating with ceremonial gravity: "Lords and Ladies, honored guests! The moment has arrived for the union of our noble Prince Brian and Princess Stephanie. I ask you to rise at your seats and prepare to witness this grand handfasting."

The tent filled with the rustling of guests rising, their anticipation almost palpable. At the far end of the aisle, Princess Rowen appeared, resplendent in a gown of flowing emerald and gold. She was escorted by Father Mike, whose robes of burgundy and gold accents seemed to glow softly in the candlelight. The herald's voice rang out again, carrying their names like a fanfare: "Your Majesty, Princess Rowen of Bitter Goose Swamp, escorted by our esteemed Father Mike McGovern!"

A soft murmur swept through the crowd as the pair began their stately walk. The delicate strains of a harp played, its melody cascading through the air like a gentle breeze. All eyes were on the duo as they ascended the stage, their presence a perfect blend of calm and command.

Father Mike took a moment to warmly greet the assembled guests, his voice rich and steady. "Welcome, friends and family, to this joyous occasion. Today, we gather to celebrate love, unity, and the joining of hearts in their eternal bond of love."

He gestured toward the aisle, a signal for the procession to continue, then took his seat next to Princess Rowen. The harpist's tune shifted seamlessly as the tent's rear doors opened once more.

A cart adorned with floral garlands emerged, its wheels creaking softly on the wooden floor. It was pulled by a short, rotund man with rosy cheeks, his good-natured demeanor earning a few chuckles. Deputy White walked beside him, her uniform lending an air of dignity to the whimsical image. The cart bore an array of elegantly wrapped gifts, their ribbons gleaming like jewels in the low light. The crowd clapped politely as the cart came to rest near the stage. The deputy took her seat at the front row while the man perched nearby, beaming.

With a subtle nod from Princess Rowen, the harpist began a bright and cheerful melody. Gloria and Umi appeared next, walking arm in arm. The crowd offered soft applause as they moved gracefully down the aisle, their expressions a blend of pride and joy. Upon reaching the front, they nodded respectfully toward Rowen before taking their seats on opposite sides of the aisle.

The melody shifted yet again, signaling the arrival of the next pair. Brian and Aaron appeared, their princely attire commanding attention. The burgundy sash across Brian's chest shimmered in harmony with the tent's decor. Their steps were measured, the crowd's soft applause swelling into a wave of admiration. Both men paused briefly to bow to Gloria, Umi, and Princess Rowen, their gestures respectful and measured, before ascending the stage to stand beside Father Mike.

A collective murmur of adoration swept the room as two young ring bearers emerged, a boy and a girl dressed in miniature finery. The boy's chest puffed out with pride while the girl's radiant smile lit up the aisle. They carried the rings with the gravity of seasoned knights, earning chuckles and applause as they reached the stage and stood solemnly near Brian and Aaron.

The soft chords of the harp transitioned into the familiar strains of "Here Comes the Bride." A hush fell over the crowd as Stephanie appeared, framed by the glowing backdrop of the open tent. Her gown was a masterpiece of white lace and satin, and tiny flowers adorned her intricately braided hair. She exuded a radiant joy, her eyes shining with emotion. Behind her, Amber followed in a matching gown, holding the train with delicate care.

Stephanie's gaze locked with Brian's as she approached the stage. His expression was one of awe, his deep blue eyes filled with love and wonder. The moment she reached him, he extended a hand, which she took with a smile that spoke volumes. Together, they turned to face the crowd, the room brimming with anticipation for what was to follow.

Princess Rowen stepped forward, her regal bearing complemented by a kindness in her eyes that drew everyone into the moment. Her voice rang clear and strong, imbued with the significance of the occasion.

"Dear friends and beloved family, today we gather to witness a moment of profound beauty and unity. This day marks not one, but *two* sacred bonds, a testament to the strength of love and the shared commitment of this extraordinary family."

Her gaze moved warmly over the gathered crowd before settling on Brian and Stephanie. "Brian and Stephanie, you are the first to stand here today, ready to declare your promises and unite your lives through the ancient ritual of handfasting. Your love, as steadfast and true as the vows you are about to speak, is an inspiration to all who know you."

She extended her hands toward them, her tone gentle yet commanding. "As you prepare to exchange your promises, remember that this ceremony is not only a declaration of your present love but a foundation for all that lies ahead. And know that as you take these sacred steps together, you are part of something greater, a celebration of love that will continue as the bonds of family deepen and grow."

Princess Rowen's eyes sparkled with emotion as she looked between them. "Brian and Stephanie, this is your moment. Speak now the words that bind your hearts and souls, the promises you make freely and joyfully to one another."

She stepped back slightly, her presence still steady and grounding, giving them the space to face each other and speak their vows.

Brian took Stephanie's hands, his voice steady as he began.

"Stephanie," Brian began, his voice steady but filled with emotion, "I've known you for as long as I can remember, since we were kids racing through backyards, sharing scraped knees, and dreaming about what the future might hold. Back then, I didn't truly understand what love meant. But now, standing here, I realize it's something that grew with us, moment by moment, step by step."

He paused, his gaze locking with hers. "You've always had this quiet strength, a way of grounding those around you, especially me. Through the years, whether it was tackling school projects, gathering for family dinners and game nights, or those countless late-night talks, you became my anchor before I even realized I needed one. You've seen me at my best and my worst, and you've loved me through it all."

Taking a deep breath, Brian continued, his voice soft yet resolute. "Today, I stand here not just as the boy who grew up beside you, but as the man who is honored to walk beside you for the rest of our lives. I promise to cherish the journey that has brought us to this moment, to celebrate our past, hold dear our present, and build a future that shines even brighter."

His voice caught slightly, filled with quiet determination. "I vow to be your partner in every way, to share in your joys, to lighten your burdens, and to never stop learning from you. Stephanie, you are not just the love of my life; you *are* my life. And I promise to stand beside you, always, through all the adventures that await us."

Stephanie's eyes glistened as she responded, her voice soft but resolute.

"Brian," Stephanie began, her voice soft but steady, "we've grown up together in every sense of the word. You've been by my side for every scraped knee, every milestone, and every dream I was too scared to chase on my own. You've been my constant, the steady presence I didn't always know I needed, but now I can't imagine life without."

She paused, her eyes shining as she continued. "What I've always admired most about you is your heart. You have this quiet strength, this unwavering capacity to care so deeply, not just for me, but for everyone fortunate enough to know you. You've shown me what it truly means to feel safe, to be loved for exactly who I am, without condition or expectation."

Stephanie's voice caught slightly, but she steadied herself with a deep breath. "Today, as I stand here with you, I know I've found my home. I promise to honor the life we've shared and the life we'll continue to build together. I vow to see the best in you, even when life feels heavy, and to stand by your side through every challenge, just as you've stood by mine."

Her voice softened, her emotions clear in every word. "Brian, you are my best friend, my greatest blessing, and the one who makes me feel like the best version of myself. I promise to love you with my whole heart for all the days of my life."

Steadily, Brian slipped the ring onto Stephanie's finger. Stephanie's fingers trembled slightly as she slipped her ring onto Brian's finger.

Princess Rowen stepped forward, her hands resting lightly over Brian and Stephanie's bound ones, her gaze warm and filled with reverence. Her voice carried a melodic strength, resonating through the tent.

"Brian and Stephanie, your hands are now bound together, a symbol of the promises you have made this day, promises of love, trust, and unwavering partnership. These ribbons, entwined around your hands, are more than fabric; they are the threads of your shared life, woven with the strength of your devotion and the depth of your commitment."

She paused, allowing the weight of her words to settle over the gathered crowd. "With these promises spoken, and these hands joined, I proclaim your handfasting complete. From this day forward, you are bound by your promises, a testament to the love and life you have chosen to share."

Princess Rowen gently removed the ribbons, holding them aloft for the audience to see. "These ties will remind you, as you walk together through the journey of life, of this sacred moment and the bond you created here today."

Her smile deepened, radiant with pride and joy. "Go forth as partners, as companions, and as the truest of friends, bound not only by these ribbons but by the love that shines so brightly between you."

She stepped back, her hands gracefully motioning toward the couple. "May all who have witnessed this moment celebrate with you and honor the beauty of what you have created together."

Father Mike stepped forward, his robes gently swaying as he joined the newly handfasted couple at the center of the stage. His eyes shone with warmth and reverence as he addressed Brian and Stephanie.

"Brian and Stephanie, you have made your promises before this gathering of loved ones and under the watchful gaze of the divine. Your hands are now bound, a testament to your shared commitment and a symbol of your unity as you walk forward together in life."

He extended his hands over theirs, palms upward in a gesture of blessing. "May this bond you have created today bring you strength in times of challenge and joy in times of celebration. May you always find in each other a source of comfort, encouragement, and inspiration. Let the love you share be a light that guides you, not only today but in every day to come."

The priest's voice softened, carrying an almost melodic cadence. "May your partnership flourish, built on trust, respect, and kindness. May you walk side by side through life, always supporting, always understanding, and always cherishing the sacred connection you have forged here today."

Drawing his hands together in a prayerful gesture, he concluded with a serene smile. "Go forward, bound in the beauty of love and unity, and may you be a blessing to each other and to all whose lives you touch."

He stepped back, his words leaving a profound stillness in the air as the audience absorbed the sacred moment.

The tent filled with applause and cheers as Brian and Stephanie shared their first kiss as a handfasted couple. The bubble machines flanking the arch released a gentle stream of bubbles, catching the light as the newlyweds walked down the aisle together, radiant and joyous.

After a brief interlude, the guests returned to their seats, the tent's ambiance shifting slightly to reflect the unique tone of Brittney's ceremony. The lights seemed warmer, the music softer and more playful.

The herald stepped forward once more, his voice ringing with the same commanding authority. "Lords and Ladies and honored guests! It is with great joy that we now witness the handfasting of our noble Prince Brian and Lady Brittney. I ask you to rise once more and prepare to celebrate this union."

The soft strains of a harp filled the tent, its melody shifting to a cheerful and hopeful tune as Brian and Aaron appeared at the far end of the aisle. Brian's princely attire, unchanged but no less striking, caught the light as he walked with steady assurance. Aaron, ever the loyal companion, walked beside him, his posture proud and his presence strong. The crowd greeted them with warm applause as they made their way forward.

As they approached the stage, the two men paused briefly, bowing to Princess Rowen before taking their places to the left of the stage, their expressions calm and resolute.

The harpist's melody grew softer, almost playful, as two young ring bearers emerged, their youthful exuberance lighting up the aisle. The boy, holding the rings on a delicate pillow, walked with a purposeful stride, his chin lifted with pride. The girl, her basket of flower petals swinging lightly at her side, scattered her petals with grace and a wide, infectious smile. The audience clapped softly, charmed by the duo as they reached the stage and stood beside Brian and Aaron, their roles fulfilled with the gravity of true knights.

Then, the harpist shifted to a new melody, soft and melodic, signaling the arrival of Brittney and her attendant, Taylor. Brittney appeared radiant in a gown of shimmering gold that seemed to capture the glow of the setting sun. Her hair, styled elegantly, was adorned with tiny pearl pins that sparkled as she moved. By her side was Taylor, dressed in a gown of soft lavender, her presence a perfect complement to Brittney's brilliance. The two walked arm in arm, their steps synchronized, and their expressions a mix of joy and calm determination.

The crowd clapped warmly as Brittney and Taylor made their way down the aisle, the white tones of Brittney's dress catching the light and illuminating her as if touched by the sun itself. Reaching the stage, they paused briefly, bowing with quiet dignity to Princess Rowen before Brittney turned to join Brian at the center. Taylor moved to stand beside Aaron, her proud smile evident as she observed the couple she was there to support.

Brian and Brittney stood side by side, their joined hands glowing with a shared warmth as they faced Princess Rowen. The harpist's final notes faded into a reverent silence, the air in the tent filled with anticipation for the sacred promises to follow.

Princess Rowen stepped forward once again, her gaze warm and thoughtful as it fell on Brian and Brittney. She paused, allowing the moment to settle, her presence grounding the significance of what was about to unfold.

"Dear friends and beloved family, we gather again to witness a union that is as unique as it is meaningful. This is not simply another ceremony, but a celebration of love that binds not just two hearts, but *three* as a family, in an extraordinary way."

Her voice softened as she addressed Brian and Brittney directly, her words carrying the weight of both wisdom and joy. "Brian and Brittney, your journey is unlike any other. What you share is a bond forged not only by love but by a profound understanding of what it means to support one another through life's trials and triumphs. Today, you stand before us, ready to commit to a partnership that honors this deep connection."

She extended her hands toward them, her expression serene. "As we prepare to bind your hands, reflect on the strength and trust that has brought you here. This ceremony is a symbol of your shared promise to walk through life not as two individuals, but as partners, each uplifting and supporting the other. This union is a reminder that love takes many forms, and it grows stronger when it is nurtured with respect, care, and honesty."

Princess Rowen paused, her gaze sweeping the audience before returning to Brian and Brittney. "This day is a celebration of love's vast and varied nature, a recognition of the ways it unites us and the ways it strengthens the bonds of family. Brian and Brittney, this is your moment. Speak now the promises that come from your hearts, freely and joyfully given."

She stepped back, her hands resting lightly at her sides, leaving Brian and Brittney to share their promises as the audience watched with rapt attention.

Brian began, his voice steady but warm.

"Brittney," Brian began, his voice steady but carrying a warmth that brought a soft smile to her face, "from the moment we met, which, let's be honest, was before either of us had a choice, you've been a force of light and energy in my life. Growing up with you meant endless laughter, wild adventures, and more than a few moments of mischief that only *you* could convince me were brilliant ideas."

He paused, a playful twinkle in his eye as he continued. "You have this incredible gift, Brittney, the way you see the world, turning the ordinary into something extraordinary. Your creativity, your wonder, your boundless imagination — they inspire everyone around you, but especially me. You've shown me what it means to dream bigger, to laugh louder, and to embrace life with all its chaos and beauty. Watching you has taught me bravery, to face my fears and trust in the unknown."

Brian's tone softened, the weight of his words anchoring the moment. "Today, I promise to be your constant, your anchor in the storm, and your biggest cheerleader. I vow to cherish the way you make the world brighter, to encourage you to chase your dreams fearlessly and to stand by your side through every twist, turn, triumph, and trial."

He took a deep breath, his gaze locked on hers. "Brittney, you are my joy, my muse, and my heart. I promise to love you for everything you are—your magic, your laughter, your passion, and for the way you bring life into every moment we share. With you, every day is an adventure waiting to unfold, and I can't wait to see what we'll create together."

"Brian," Brittney began, her voice soft but carrying a brightness that lit up the space, "you've been part of my life for as long as I can remember, and honestly, I can't imagine it without you. From the days when we were just kids, causing trouble and laughing until our sides hurt, to the times when you've been my calm in the storm, you've always been there. You've seen me at my best, my worst, and my most ridiculous, and somehow, you've loved me through it all, even in the moments when I forgot how to love myself."

Her voice caught slightly, her eyes glistening with unshed tears. She took a steadying breath, a soft smile gracing her lips as she pressed on. "What I love most about you is the way you make life feel bigger, brighter, and more magical just by being in it. You see me, the *real* me, and you never ask me to be anything but that. With you, I can be as creative, messy, and whimsical as I want, and I know you'll be right there beside me, cheering me on with that quiet strength of yours."

Brittney's gaze never wavered as she continued, her voice filled with emotion. "Today, I promise to bring laughter into our lives, to remind you to dream as boldly as you inspire me to, and to make every ordinary day feel like an extraordinary adventure. I vow to love you with all the passion and fierceness of my heart, to protect the magic we create together, and to stand by your side through every twist and turn life throws our way."

Her smile deepened, her love for Brian radiating in her every word. "Brian, you are not just my love; you are my partner, my muse, and my very best friend. With you, I've found the kind of love I used to dream about, a love that inspires me to be braver and better every day. I can't wait to see what our future holds because, with you, every possibility feels like a promise waiting to unfold."

A soft sniffle echoed from the crowd, a sound that brought a small laugh from Brittney as she finished, her hand gripping Brian's just a little tighter.

Princess Rowen stepped forward, her regal presence radiating warmth and pride. She placed her hands lightly over Brian and Brittney's bound ones, her gaze tender as it swept across the couple.

"Brian and Brittney, your hands are now bound together, a testament to the promises you have spoken here today. These ribbons are not merely symbols; they are the threads of your shared journey, woven with the love, laughter, and creativity that define your bond."

With a steady hand, Brian slipped the ring onto Brittney's finger. Brittney fumbled and almost dropped her ring. She paused, looking into Brian's eyes as she regained herself and slowly slipped the ring onto his finger.

Princess Rowen's voice softened, her words imbued with quiet reverence. "This handfasting is not just a ceremony but a celebration of the life you have chosen to build together, a life where joy is shared, dreams are encouraged, and love flows freely. The ties that unite you today are unbreakable, forged in trust, respect, and the unshakable belief in one another."

Princess Rowen gently lifted the ribbons from their hands, holding them aloft for all to see. "With these promises spoken and these ties bound, I proclaim your handfasting complete. From this day forward, you are bound by your words and your hearts, a union of love, creativity, and unwavering partnership."

Her smile deepened as she addressed the gathering. "Let us honor this bond and celebrate the unique and extraordinary connection we have witnessed today. Brian and Brittney, go forward together as partners in life and in all the adventures yet to come."

She stepped back, her hands clasped before her, as the audience erupted in applause, their cheers ringing out to celebrate the couple's sacred union.

Father Mike stepped forward, his presence calm and reassuring as he joined Brian and Brittney at the center of the stage. His kind gaze rested on their joined hands, still faintly marked by the impression of the ribbons.

"Brian and Brittney," he began, his voice carrying a serene strength, "today, you have spoken promises that reflect the unique beauty of your bond. You have chosen to walk through life together, embracing the adventure, creativity, and love that define your connection."

He extended his hands over theirs, palms upward, as though lifting their union toward the heavens. "May your journey together be filled with the courage to dream boldly and the wisdom to find joy in life's smallest moments. May you always lift each other up, celebrating the brightness that you both bring to the world."

His voice softened, carrying a quiet reverence. "May this bond you've created remind you of the strength in partnership and the power of shared laughter. As you face life's challenges, may your creativity and love continue to be a beacon that lights the way, guiding you through all that is to come."

Drawing his hands together in a gesture of blessing, he smiled warmly. "Go forth, bound not just by these promises but by the spirit of joy and mutual respect that has brought you to this moment. May your union inspire not only each other but all who are fortunate enough to witness your love."

He stepped back, his words leaving a peaceful stillness in the air, as if the blessing itself lingered, wrapping the couple in its embrace.

The bubble machines whirred to life again, and the newlyweds made their way down the aisle, waving to the cheering guests as the sun dipped below the horizon, casting the tent in a golden glow.

As the guests rose to congratulate the couples, the sun set fully over the lake, marking the end of the ceremonies and the beginning of the celebration to come. The tent buzzed with energy and joy, a testament to the love and care that had gone into the day.

Umi leaned into Gloria's ear. "We were wrong; Brian didn't tear up once. But, Brittney, well, she kept it together, right?"

Gloria smiled. "Your girls were beautiful and awesome brides. Brittney's tears only solidify what we know; she sees her tomorrow as bright. You want to know what *else* changes?"

Umi looked at her. "Now what?"

Gloria smiled brightly. "Now, Umi, we really *are* a family," her voice soft and gentle.

CHAPTER 36

The first soft notes of "Better Together" by Jack Johnson filled the tent, and the bubble machines whirred softly to life. A cascade of shimmering bubbles floated across the dance floor, catching the flickering fairy lights above. The bubbles sparkled like tiny stars, creating an ethereal glow that seemed to wrap around Brittney and Brian as they stepped into the center of the floor.

The DJ's voice was warm and inviting as he announced, "Ladies and gentlemen, it is my honor to present to you for the first time tonight, Mr. and Mrs. Brian Cole!" The crowd erupted into cheers and applause, their excitement filling the air as Brittney and Brian began to sway to the music.

Hand in hand, they moved with an easy grace, their smiles glowing brighter than the lights around them. Guests clapped softly, enchanted by the scene that felt as though it had been pulled straight from a fairytale. As the final notes of the song faded, the bubble machines slowed, leaving the couple framed in a perfect silhouette as the audience applauded with joyful fervor. Brittney hugged Brian tightly before heading to sit beside Umi, her radiant smile mirrored by the cheering crowd.

The DJ gave a soft nod to Gloria, then stepped forward again. "And now, please welcome Mr. and Mrs. Brian Cole back to the dance floor—this time with Stephanie Cole! Their first dance together as a couple will be to 'Thinking Out Loud' by Ed Sheeran."

The first few notes of the song rang out, and the bubble machines resumed, releasing another soft stream of bubbles that floated delicately around Brian and Stephanie. The bubbles shimmered with the flickering fairy lights, casting a dreamy glow as the couple began their dance.

They moved with tender grace, their connection visible in every step, every glance. The room seemed to hold its breath, captivated by the heartfelt emotions on display. The guests watched in quiet awe, some wiping away tears as the couple shared this intimate moment. As the song concluded, the bubble machines once again ceased, leaving the final embrace framed against the warm, glowing backdrop. The applause that followed was thunderous, a tribute to the love and joy the couple shared.

The DJ's voice rang out once more, a smile evident in his tone. "And now, in a moment of true family magic, we invite Brian, Brittney, and Stephanie to share the dance floor together. Let's celebrate their bond with 'What a Wonderful World' by Louis Armstrong."

As the song began, the bubble machines activated again, creating a sparkling cascade that enveloped the trio as they formed a small circle. They swayed together, their hands linked, laughter and quiet words passing between them. The bubbles, catching the fairy lights, added an enchanting shimmer to the already heartwarming scene.

Midway through the song, the DJ spoke, his voice filled with warmth and reverence:

"Ladies and gentlemen, this is a storybook moment, if ever there was one, a true celebration of love, family, and connection. Tonight, we witness the start of a beautiful 'happily ever after.' Let's join them in making this a celebration to remember!"

With perfect timing, the DJ transitioned to "I Wanna Dance with Somebody" by Whitney Houston. The mood shifted, laughter bubbled up from the crowd, and the DJ called out, "Everyone, let's fill the dance floor and celebrate this incredible happily ever after together!"

The guests flooded the dance floor, their energy contagious as the newly handfasted couples were surrounded by loved ones. The bubble machines remained on a low setting, releasing just enough to add a playful sparkle to the lively scene. Meanwhile, the DJ adjusted the lighting to vibrant patterns that matched the tempo of the music, signaling that the evening had transitioned into full celebration mode.

Laughter, cheers, and joyful dancing filled the tent, the bubbles mingling with twinkling lights as the party unfolded. The couples remained at the heart of it all, their love and happiness shining brighter than any fairy tale's magic.

*****

Hours later, inside the bride's yurt, it was quiet and warm, golden light creating a sanctuary from the lively reception just outside. Soft pillows were scattered across the floor, and the faint scent of lavender and cedar lingered in the air. Stephanie and Brittney sat side by side, their bridal gowns slightly wrinkled from hours of celebration. Their postures were tense, their hands fidgeting with nervous energy.

The flap of the yurt door rustled, and Umi and Gloria stepped inside, their laughter fading as they noticed the atmosphere.

"Well, there you are!" Gloria said brightly, brushing a loose strand of hair from her face. "We wondered where the two brides had run off to. The party isn't over, you know."

Stephanie glanced up, her cheeks flushing pink. Brittney didn't lift her gaze, her fingers twisting a thread on her dress.

"What's wrong?" Umi asked softly, sitting beside Brittney and placing a gentle hand on her shoulder. "You both seem… preoccupied."

Stephanie glanced at her sister as if asking permission before speaking. "We were… talking. About the honeymoon."

"And other stuff," Brittney added quietly, still not meeting their eyes.

Gloria's expression softened as she lowered herself beside Stephanie. "Other stuff, hmm? You can tell us."

There was a long pause before Stephanie's words tumbled out. "We're nervous, okay? Neither of us knows what we're doing. And I don't want to… mess it up."

Umi exchanged a knowing look with Gloria, a gentle smile curving her lips. "Ah. That's perfectly normal, my Angels."

Gloria reached for Stephanie's hand. "Absolutely. It's completely natural to feel unsure about something so new and intimate. And let me tell you about those moments; they're worth everything."

Stephanie's voice dropped to a whisper. "But what if I freeze? Or I don't know what to do?"

Umi took Stephanie's hands in hers, her gaze steady. "Sweetheart, there's no script for these moments. They're about love, trust, and being present with each other. That's all."

Gloria nodded. "And Brian? He's the gentlest soul I've ever known. If you're nervous, just tell him. He'll be patient and kind. He loves you both so deeply; he'll meet you wherever you are. I honestly believed Brian when he told you about what making love is all about."

Stephanie bit her lip but smiled faintly. "He *is* gentle. I know that."

Brittney shifted uneasily beside her. "What if it's… uncomfortable? Or… I can't?" Her voice wavered, and she finally looked up, her eyes glistening.

Umi turned her attention to Brittney, her expression soft and steady. "Oh, Brittney. It's okay to feel this way. Healing takes time, and trust isn't something you give all at once. It's built slowly, with someone who respects your boundaries and earns your trust, exactly who Brian is."

Gloria added gently, "Brian isn't just patient; he's understanding. He knows you're both different, and he loves you for exactly who you are. And if you're not ready for anything, that's okay. We know Brian will wait. His love for you both is boundless."

Brittney's voice cracked. "But… What if I never feel normal again? What if I can't trust myself or him?"

Umi wrapped an arm around her daughter's shoulders. "Sweetheart, what you've been through doesn't define you. You're so much more than that. The fact that you're even asking these questions shows how strong you are. When you're ready, you'll know."

Gloria smiled warmly. "And Brian will still be there. He's the kind of man who will love you through every step of this journey."

Umi hesitated before speaking, her voice tinged with nostalgia. "You know, when I married Kaito, I remember feeling so nervous about getting everything right. But I learned something quickly: intimacy isn't about being perfect. It's about being real, sharing your heart, and trusting your partner to cherish it."

Gloria chuckled softly. "She's right. When I married Tom, I thought I had to know everything. But it's not about that. It's about learning together. And when you have love and trust, even the awkward moments are beautiful."

Stephanie and Brittney exchanged small smiles, the tension easing slightly.

Stephanie shifted closer to Gloria. "But… what if I'm not ready tonight?"

Gloria squeezed her hand. "Then you tell him. He loves you, sweetheart. He'll understand, just like he's always understood you."

Brittney spoke hesitantly. "And… what if it hurts?"

Umi brushed a strand of hair from her daughter's face. "It might, especially at first. But that's okay. Your body and heart are both learning something new. If it doesn't feel right, you can stop. Communicating is key."

Gloria nodded. "And those moments when you feel vulnerable? They're the moments that make your bond stronger. Love is about showing up, even when you're scared."

Both girls seemed to relax, their shoulders easing as their mothers' words sank in. Stephanie leaned into Gloria's side while Brittney rested her head against Umi's shoulder.

"Thank you," Stephanie murmured. "I feel... better now."

"Me too," Brittney added, her voice soft but sincere.

Gloria pressed a kiss to Stephanie's forehead. "We'll always be here for you, no matter what."

Umi hugged Brittney close. "And remember, love isn't about being perfect. It's about being yourself. Brian loves you both for exactly who you are."

As the girls smiled faintly, the sound of laughter and music drifted in from outside.

"Well," Gloria said, standing and smoothing her dress, "shall we get back to the reception? I think people might start wondering where the brides have disappeared to."

Umi stood, holding out a hand to Brittney. "Come on, my angels. Let's celebrate the start of this next chapter."

With renewed confidence, the girls took their mothers' hands and stepped back into the festivities, bolstered by the warmth of love and support.

*****

Several hours later, in the back of the dimly lit limousine, Brittney and Stephanie sat on either side of Brian, the three of them replaying moments from their shared wedding ceremony. Their hearts were full, yet a quiet tension hummed in the air.

Brian ran a hand through his shaggy, trimmed hair, trying to think of a way to ease the uneasiness he could feel building between them. The sound of the limousine seemed to amplify his own nervousness.

Brittney watched him, her lips curving into a faint smile. "When you do that, I know you're nervous about something, so spill it, Mr. Groom."

Brian chuckled softly, looking at her. "You can read me that well?"

Stephanie leaned closer, her voice playful but warm. "Yup, now spill it," she said, her eyes filled with love.

Brian sighed, his voice low but steady. "I know we've talked about this, and we've all agreed, but… I just want to make sure you're both comfortable with this, all of it."

Stephanie looked around Brian to Brittney, seeing the slight blush on her sister's cheeks. She felt her own face flush with color.

Brittney spoke first, her voice soft and unsure. "I'll admit I'm nervous. I don't know what to do or how it'll work."

Stephanie nodded. "Me too. I mean, I know we love each other, but this is a first for us."

Brian's cheeks turned pink. "Umm… my loves, it's a first for me too."

Stephanie blinked in surprise. "Wait, you're serious?"

Brittney tilted her head, her curiosity piqued. "But the way you explained making love… I thought you'd…" Her voice trailed off.

Brian chuckled nervously. "Nope. I was close once, last year, but Mom came home early, and… well, it didn't happen."

Brittney's eyes widened in realization. "That's why you were so sure you weren't the baby's father."

517

Stephanie added softly, "Brian and I made a promise early on. It was important to us. We wanted to wait."

Brittney's eyes grew wet, her voice trembling. "Oh my God..."

Brian took her hand firmly, his voice gentle but strong. "Don't go there, my love. That's all in the past, and it's done, gone, over, and forgotten. Tonight is about us, the three of us, and all the 'tomorrows' we're going to share."

Brittney closed her eyes, taking a deep breath. "That's hard, but I understand."

Stephanie nodded. "I'm with Britt on this. I'm nervous about the 'how.'"

Brian smiled softly, his tone patient. "Honestly, I'm nervous too. I know you're both different and what works for one of you might not for the other. But remember what I said, 'Every kiss, every touch, is meant to show you that you're loved and treasured and that you're the most important thing in my life.' That's what this is about. If something feels awkward, we'll figure it out together."

Brittney's face softened, her voice dreamy. "I almost can't wait to find out what happens after that kiss."

Stephanie cuddled closer to Brian, her voice light but filled with affection. "My heart races just thinking about it."

Brian looked at both of them, his own voice dropping to a whisper. "I get excited just imagining touching you both."

Stephanie giggled nervously. "Are you perving on us, Mr. Groom?"

Brittney's breath caught as she waited for his reply.

Brian blushed deeply. "Oh no, Mrs. Bride, not at all. It's just... well... after all these years of not... um... touching, and the teasing you've done in your swimsuits... I, well, you know, maybe a little."

Brittney's expression shifted, becoming more serious. "And my... umm... marks?" Her voice was barely above a whisper, filled with doubt.

Brian turned to her, looking deeply into her eyes. "My love, your marks don't matter to me. It's who you *are* that I love. If you'd let me, I'd kiss each and every one of them to show you how much you mean to me."

Tears glistened in Brittney's eyes as she smiled, her fears melting away. "I love you, my charming husband," she whispered.

Brian leaned down, pressing a tender kiss to her forehead. "And I love you, my adorning wife."

Stephanie squeezed his hand, drawing his attention. Brian smiled at his beautiful wives, his cheeks still pink. "I have just one rule," he said with a playful grin. "Whatever happens in the bedroom stays there. If you need to talk with the moms or each other, just... don't tell me about it. I'd die of embarrassment if either mom brought it up."

The girls exchanged a mischievous look before Stephanie replied. "So we can compare notes, but we just can't tell you?"

Brian groaned playfully. "Yeah, that's about it."

As the girls giggled, Brittney reached into her purse and pulled out her cell and taped on her mom's name.

Moments later, Umi's happy voice answered the phone. "Really? Again?"

Brittney smiled as she put the call on speaker. "I just wanted to check in with you and Tommy. How's my baby doing?" she asked, a slight giggle still in her voice.

Umi answered, giggling. "He's doing fine. Gloria and I are spoiling him rotten. I'm surprised you can't smell him there."

Everyone could hear Gloria in the background. "And we're having tons of fun doing it!"

Brittney laughed. "Just as long as you clean it up, I'm good with that."

Umi's voice took a more serious tone. "Is everything ok?"

Stephanie spoke with a hint of laughter. "Everything's ok here. You know little Miss Worrywart here."

Brian and the twins could hear Umi exhale. "Good. Okay, anything you need before I kick you off the phone to go and spoil your baby and make you go and enjoy your honeymoon?"

The twins smiled, giggling when they answered in unison, "Good night, Moms!"

Before Brittney ended the call, Brian shouted, "Good night, Moms," having missed when the twins said it.

While Brittney put her phone away, the lights in the limo brightened, signaling their arrival at the hotel.

Moments later, there was a slight knock on the door, a pause, and it opened. The chauffeur, an older man, stood there, holding the door, offering his hand to Stephanie. "Good evening, ma'am," he said respectfully.

Stephanie took his hand and stepped out onto the sidewalk, taking in the sight of the grand entrance to the hotel. Looking up, she read the sign. "Brian, The Plaza? Really?"

Brittney stepped out, looking up. "Wow."

Stephanie giggled. "I've never been inside a place like this."

Stephanie's contagious giggle seeped into Brittney. "Neither have I," she added.

Brian went to the back of the limousine, expecting to grab the girls' bags. The chauffeur added gently, "I'll get you the ladies' handbags, sir. I'll take care of the rest."

Brian looked at the man. "Umm, thank you, sir." He paused for a moment. "Umm, do you accept tips? I… I don't want to offend you or anything like that," Brian asked in earnest.

"Not necessary, sir," the man replied with a smile. "I really enjoy doing what I do. Did you enjoy your ride?"

Brian smiled. "Yes, we did. Thank you for everything," reaching his hand out.

The driver shook his hand. "You're very welcome, and thank you, sir. Please enjoy your stay in the city, and I'll see you in a week."

"Great, see you then. Thank you again," he said as he took the girls' handbags and walked over between them.

He looked at their gowns; both were similar in style, white and flowing, but with subtle differences. Brian smiled as he placed a hand on each of their lower backs. "You like?"

Brittney looked at him. "I love it, but, really, The Plaza?"

As they entered the building, Brian replied with a nonchalant gesture. "Nothing but the best for my wives."

*****THE END*****

EPILOGUE

Three years later, Stephanie and Brittney were walking home from Brian's house. They were both laughing and giggling as Brittney waved a newspaper in her hand. "You know, Steph, this marks the day when all my dreams and fantasies have come true. Can you believe it? I've got everything I've ever dreamed of. A family that loves me, my son Tommy, and a husband who actually puts up with me. I mean, pinch me! Is this real?"

"Oh, I get it, Britt. It feels surreal, doesn't it? Like, after everything, we're finally... happy," Stephanie replied, suppressing a big smile.

Stephanie reached over and took Brittney's hand. "You deserve every bit of this, Britt. Watching you chase your dreams makes me feel like I can conquer anything, too."

The twins opened the front door to see Umi and Gloria at the kitchen table.

"Hi, Moms," they both said in unison.

"Hi, Angels," Umi said, followed by Gloria's, "Hi, kiddos."

Brittney's smile stretched from ear to ear. "How was my son today? Did he run you both ragged?" she asked.

"Tommy was perfect as usual, taking a nap. You know us grandmas, we had to spoil him some, well, maybe a lot," Gloria replied with a big smile.

Stephanie smiled right back. "As if we expected anything else. Brittney has some news to share; want to sit in the living room?"

Brittney smiled big. "Moms, you both are going to love this."

Everyone moved to the living room. Brittney was almost jumping while she waited for them to sit down.

"Okay, angel, what's got you so excited today?" Umi asked.

"I got a call from Ashley today," she started and immediately saw Gloria's question. "Ashley Diaz," she clarified.

Umi looked up. "What about?" she asked, somewhat seriously.

Brittney gently unfolded the newspaper, pointing at the front page. "Recognize this, right?"

Both Umi and Gloria nodded.

Brittney opened the paper to an earmarked page. "Look at this," she said, handing them the paper. Her smile couldn't get any bigger.

Gloria gasped as her eyes found what Brittney was talking about.

"Brittney, is that really your comic?" Umi asked.

Brittney nodded. "Yup. Notice how my comic is near the top? I'm told it's getting a lot of attention."

Gloria stood up, rushed over, and hugged Brittney. "Oh my God, Brittney! That's awesome!"

Umi wasn't far behind her. "Congratulations, Angel!" hugging her just as tight.

Brittney wiggled to free her hands and hugged them both. "It's a dream come true. A year ago, I never thought something I'd drawn would be in color inside one of the largest newspapers in print."

Gloria and Umi let her go. Umi looked at her oldest girl. "I'm so proud of you, my angel," her eyes bright.

Gloria smiled. "See, we told you all that hard work would pay off, right?"

Everyone sat down as Brittney told her story of how her comic strip made it into *The New York Times* newspaper.

Brittney smiled. "Some of my best jokes or satire comes straight from our lives. Little Tommy is definitely my muse," she giggled, "and so is Brian. I've called them the dynamic duo in several of my strips," she admitted.

"One of the most commented strips is where Tommy is helping Daddy fix the car. That came from the morning when Brian was making breakfast for our birthday this year," Brittney commented.

Brittney looked up, reflecting on the past four years. "I started drawing during some of my darkest days. I'd never thought I'd share them with anyone; I never imagined seeing them in print. Everyone here believed in me, even when I didn't. Thank you, all of you. I was just telling Stephanie that all my dreams and fantasies have come true. And it's because of all of you, Stephanie and Brian," she admitted.

"Brittney, you did all the work," Stephanie explained while squeezing Brittney's hand.

"Maybe, but if you and Brian hadn't helped me when I needed it most, I would have never made it as far as I did," Brittney told her, her eyes getting big.

"Oh no, Brittney, don't you go crying again," Stephanie said, gently bumping into her.

"I'm just so happy, that's all," she said softly.

The conversation turned to her new job, how she didn't have to go to New York, and how she could do everything from home, making it easy to take care of Tommy.

Stephanie laid back on the plush couch, her hands moving to the top and front of her stomach. At a small break in the conversation, Stephanie asked, "Moms, does Tommy wear you guys down?" Her voice was soft.

Gloria smiled. "Oh no, dear. I think he's helping to keep us young, right, Umi?"

Umi smiled right back. "You bet. It's fun playing with him, winding him all up, and then sending him home to his mamas," she said with a little giggle.

Gloria raised an eyebrow. "That's a strange question. Why do you ask?"

Stephanie glanced at Brittney, who had settled into the chair beside her, still glowing from her own news. Taking a deep breath, she rubbed her hand on her stomach and said softly, "Oh, nothing yet, but you and Mom Gloria have about seven months to start planning."

The room went still as everyone processed her words.

Brittney jumped up from her chair, pointing at Stephanie, her voice nearly a shout. "You're expecting, aren't you, Steph?"

Stephanie nodded, her smile widening. "Yes," she said softly, looking at her moms. "You both get to be Obaasan to either Kaito Brian Cole or Gloria Brittney Cole, depending on how things go."

Gloria and Umi both stood at once, exclaiming together, "You're expecting!"

Stephanie laughed and nodded again. "And I haven't told Brian yet."

Gloria looked at Umi, squeezing her hand, looking at the twins. "You three, you've built something beautiful. It might not be what people expect, but it's perfect because it's full of love, and that's all that matters."

Brittney looked at Gloria. "I know we've had our challenges and, in each love, won. I know some people look at us like we're crazy, but it works, and I wouldn't trade it for anything."

Umi nodded, her gaze warm and loving. "It's incredible to see how much love this family has. Watching all of you grow, it's everything and more than I could have hoped for. And we're adding another little one? I can't wait."

Brittney looked at her sister. "I was nervous at first," Brittney admitted, "but watching Brian and how he's always there when we need him, the perfect daddy, you, and our moms raising Tommy together, we've got this, Steph. And now, another little one? This is going to be amazing."

The conversation dissolved into details of a soon-to-be-pending baby shower. About thirty minutes later, the front door opened, and Brian walked into the house. "Hi, everyone. I went home and found an empty house. What's going on?"

Stephanie walked over to him, hugged him tightly, and whispered into his ear, her voice trembling with excitement. "My perfect husband, our family is growing. We're going to have a little one."

Moments later, he asked, "Really?"

Stephanie nodded. "Really."

Brian started smiling. "You're not teasing me?" he asked, still holding her tightly.

Brittney walked over and hugged Brian, saying, "You're going to be a Daddy again, my perfect husband," as she placed a small kiss on his cheek.

Brian pulled Brittney into a tight embrace with Stephanie, looking into Stephanie's eyes, locked into the very soul of his wife as only a husband can do. "My perfect wife, Stephanie Ann Cole, I love you."

Stephanie kissed him on the lips. "I love you, Brian Richard Cole."

Brian turned his eyes onto Brittney with the same intensity. "My perfect wife, Brittney Rose Cole, I love you."

Brittney kissed him on the lips. "And I love you, Brian Richard Cole."

All three hugged tightly. Brian looked at his moms. "You both are the start and end of my world, and in between, we are three."

A moment later, with a big grin, he added, "Wait a minute, I'm going to be a Daddy again? Seriously? Someone could have clued me in!"

A moment later, he added, "This just keeps getting better and better, and I love it! I am the luckiest man alive."

Everyone broke into laughter. Brittney shared her news, and just like Umi and Gloria, he congratulated her.

Brian looked at his mother and honorary mother, Umi. "I guess you both are going to be busy spoiling another grandson."

Both nodded yes. "And then some," Umi added.

"We may have to add a new room or two to the house. I'm thinking of a playroom and a study or guest room," Brian suggested.

"You know," Brittney added, "We could add a big rec room, too. Space for everyone to gather in."

As the discussion about new rooms continued, Umi and Gloria stood up. Their eyes met, the soft glow of the setting sun adding a golden light to their expressions. Gloria took a deep breath, her voice steady and filled with emotion. Gloria reached over and took Umi's hand.

"Do you remember when we thought we'd never laugh like this again? After Kaito and Tom died, it felt like my world had ended. But you held me together. You and your daughters helped me see the light of a tomorrow that I couldn't—gave me hope when I didn't have any."

Gloria's eyes filled with tears as she continued, "Watching our kids like this, happy, strong, and full of love, reminds me of just how lucky I am to have you by my side. You are my rock, Umi Welch. Words can't express how much you mean to me."

The teens' conversation faded into silence as they looked up and listened to their moms.

Brittney wiped a tear from her cheek, her voice soft with wonder. "They've always been more than just our moms, haven't they?"

Stephanie nodded, her hand squeezing Brian's. "It's because of them that we are who we are. They've always been a team in every way that matters."

Umi's eyes shimmered as she squeezed Gloria's hand tightly. "And you are my island, Gloria Cole. You helped me up when I fell, you held me up when I wanted to quit. You and your son have been an inspiration to live by. I can't imagine living without you being here with me."

In that moment, time stood still; the room felt warmer, the air filled with unspoken promises and love, the two held each other in a tight embrace, a quiet and sentimental statement to their deep friendship.

The story doesn't end here—the journey continues.
Download quote cards, journal prompts, discussion guides,
and exclusive extras!

https://www.fredkerber.com

Or scan the QR code or visit the site to get started!

www.ingramcontent.com/pod-product-compliance
Lightning Source LLC
Chambersburg PA
CBHW021601120626
46545CB00001B/19